LF

LATIN AMERICA: A Guide to Illustrations

A. Curtis Wilgus

The Scarecrow Press, Inc.
Metuchen, N.J., & London
1981

Library of Congress Cataloging in Publication Data

Wilgus, A. Curtis (Alva Curtis), 1897-1981.
    Latin America, a guide to illustrations.

    Includes indexes.
    1. Latin America--History--Pictorial works--Catalogs.
2. Latin America--Biography--Portraits--Catalogs.
I. Title.
F1408.W667   980   81-9070
ISBN 0-8108-1459-5   AACR2

TABLE OF CONTENTS

To all Latin Americanists--scholarly or other--trying to grasp the look of the diversities of the southern Americas, and especially to the reference librarians to whom they turn for help in the quest, this is the final contribution of a dedicated Latin Americanist, historian, scholar and educator, A. Curtis Wilgus, 1897-1981.

INTRODUCTION

This volume fills a gap in publications in English relating to Latin America by providing an aid for the better understanding of the rise and development of these countries. Surprisingly no one has ever prepared such a Guide although they exist for other parts of the world. Several years ago when I compiled my Maps Relating to Latin America in Books and Periodicals (Washington, The Pan American Union, 1933, 103p.) I planned a guide to Latin American pictures. Meanwhile many tasks have occupied my attention and I am only now attempting what I had hoped someone else might have accomplished. By referring to available illustrations in encyclopedias, books, and periodicals, this Guide makes available a new dimension of supplementary information about Latin America for teachers, students, librarians, and the general reader. It should be particularly helpful as a supplement to the 23 volumes in the series of Historical Dictionaries of Latin America (Scarecrow Press, 1967-1981). The Guide furthermore provides a useful background of knowledge and information which should help to clarify and make more intelligent much of the daily news reported by the press, radio, and particularly television about each of the countries.

The United States Bicentennial Year clearly showed the importance of visual concepts in history and culture. Every day television emphasizes the importance of visual impressions and helps to prove, as is often said, that one picture may be worth a thousand words. Eye-mindedness and visual memory of many people make a Guide of this nature of great importance to them. The popular desire to visit museums and art galleries continually encourages pleasurable learning. Books with illustrations are generally more interesting than those without. Certainly the "visual aid" method in teaching in our schools promotes an increasing use of illustrated materials.

I.

Before using this volume it should be understood that it is not in any sense a comprehensive classified picture index of things Latin American. It is not intended to have the characteristics of a gazetteer, a dictionary, or an encyclopedia. Its contents cannot be all-inclusive in scope because the references to illustrations are of necessity limited to those pictures which can be found in comparatively recent--and hence readily available--books and periodicals in English. To have added references to foreign books and to those printed in other languages would have made the work impracticable and even frustrating for effective use because many of these volumes are not easy to find. By providing references to visual impressions of Latin American development since early times, this Guide might well be considered a form of picture archive or repository but with references to illustrations instead of the pictures themselves.

In order to see at a glance the nature and scope of the Guide an "Analytical Outline of Topics" has been prepared, divided into five sections:

1. Pre-Colonial; 2. Discovery and Conquest; 3. Colonial Development; 4. Independence Achieved; 5. National Period. The Index of Persons, an alphabetical list of some 2500 individuals (with related personal facts, who have been or still are active participants in Latin American affairs, is of equal value. It gives a vital and necessary corrective to the historical approach of the first five sections.

To facilitate the location of the thousands of pictures illustrating the subjects in the Guide, I have prepared a Reference-Key Index consisting of 2-, 3-, or 4-letter symbols which identify the sources where the pictures can be found. These symbols are listed alphabetically for ready reference. This index gives sufficient bibliographical information for effective identification of the more than 500 publications to which they refer. Take as a whole this list provides a good working bibliography for anyone interested in a cross-section of books on Latin America covering several centuries.

II.

The selection of pictures for this Guide, each of which I have examined, has been limited by my own judgment and by their availability. This has necessitated a critical exercise in organization and classification. Gaps in subject matter are inevitable because illustrations, especially for the colonial period, cannot be found for everyone and everything. For many topics there are no illustrations at all no matter how desirable they might be. All of Latin America is covered geographically, including the Caribbean and related parts of the United States. The character of the pictures, whether in color or black and white, varies considerably since they may be photographs, sketches, paintings or imaginative concepts. I have generally excluded cartoons and caricatures, but pictures of places, things, and events, action pictures and pictures of individuals are all included. Some illustrations, unfortunately, are not always clear but they give acceptable impressions. Many persons are shown at different times and in different situations. For many topics there are multiple references, thus offering a choice of pictures. Often connected with illustrations are descriptive texts which enhance their importance. Some illustrations are dated, at least approximately, but for those that are not the date of publication of the references in many instances--except in the case of reprints--often indicates an approximate one.

Few illustrations are listed more than once, and cross-references are used sparingly. However, although some illustrations embrace many subjects, I have tried to list each under the topical classification where it logically belongs. But the twilight zone between some subjects suggests that an illustration might be listed under more than one topic. Therefore, in some cases an examination of several subject classifications, and especially the Index of Persons, is desirable and often necessary. This is generally true when several subjects, events, and people appear in the same illustration, or when similar or common activities occur in more than one location.

The question arises: Are the picture captions accurate and reliable? The answer can be perplexing, frustrating, or amusing. In a high school history textbook I remember seeing a picture showing a low river bank with a log fort over which an American flag was flying. It was labled "Columbus landing in America." Generally there are few mislabled pictures although some are misdated. In the sixteenth century, especially, one sees the same face with different clothing or posture each with a different personal name. There are more than 40 portraits of Columbus, but none was made by anyone who saw him.

III.

It must be realized that this Guide, although it contains a mine of environmental, descriptive, historical, and cultural information in pictures, is not complete and never will be.   Even as I type this Introduction, pictures are being published which might be included here.   It is my sincere hope that my efforts may be of help to those who need the information provided.   In the fifteenth century an astronomer, Ulug Beg, wrote: "Mosques fall, Palaces crumble into dust, but knowledge remains."   We are fortunate that so much of this knowledge remains in pictures.   Fiat Lux.

A. Curtis Wilgus

Prepared under the auspices of the Inter-American Bibliographical and Library Association.

LIST OF ABBREVIATIONS

bc.	back cover
c.	about
cent.	century
fc.	front cover
fig.	figure
ff.	following pages
fr.	frontispiece
ibc.	inside back cover
ifc.	inside front cover
illus.	illustration
L. A.	Latin America(n)
no.	number
p.	page
pass.	here and there; scattered
pic.	picture; portrait
wk.	work(s); handiwork

Note: reference dates are indicated as follows: the 20th century has only the final two digits (78 means 1978); the full year is given for earlier centuries.

ANALYTICAL OUTLINE OF TOPICS

Part II.   Discovery and Conquest

A.   EUROPEAN BACKGROUND

B.   THE CONQUEST

Part III.   Colonial Development

A.   DESCRIPTIONS

B.   GOVERNMENT

D.   CARIBBEAN AND THE WEST INDIES

Part I

PRE-COLONIAL LATIN AMERICA

A.   ARCHAEOLOGICAL BACKGROUND

I.   <u>Caribbean</u>

1.   General
Art, ESB, 261-5
Boat, PDS, 6 (dugout), 1 (substitute)
Hammock, PDS, 212; BCC, 127
Images, WIA, II, 377-92 pass.
Pottery, WIA, II, 373-87 pass.

2.   Greater Antilles

General
    Pottery, JCA, 250, 252
    Stone implements, JCA, 230, 236 (axes), 212 (pestles), 242 (heads)
    Wooden bird, JCA, 218 (idol)
    Wooden seat, JCA, 222
Puerto Rico
    Art, JCA, 186-91 pass. , 223-46 pass.
    Pottery, DIA, plates 160, 163
Dominican Republic
    Art, JCA, 186-220 pass. , 248-50 pass.
    Pottery, DIA, plates 158-59, 161
Haiti
    Art, CAH, 96 ff.
    Pottery, DIA, plate 166
    Stone ax, NG (11/75), 593
Jamaica: Art, JCA, 182, 234-49 pass.
Trinidad: Art, JCA, 252

3.   Lesser Antilles: Art, JCA, 254

4.   Guianas: Artifacts, DIA, plates 203-06, 209, 224

II.   <u>Meso-America--General</u>

1.   Time Periods
a.   Pre-Classic (before A.D. 300)
    Architecture
        Central Plateau, WPM, 262-63
        Gulf Coast, WPM, 266-67
        Maya Region, WPM, 268-69
    Art, Artifacts, Culture, WIA, I, 93-108 pass.; WPC, 29-59, 83-151;
        ESB 52-70, 121-41
    Ceramics
        Central Plateau, WPM, 202-03
        West Mexico, WPM, 204-05

3

III.   Mayas

1.   Sites

Ruins, HGA, 218-19, CCC, 136-37
Kabah
    Architecture, KMA, plate 34; IMC, 149-52
    General view, FRM, 106-11
    Plan, AMC, fig. 230; CCC, 90
    Pyramid, IMC, 153
    Ruins, AMC, figs. 231-47; CCC, 89-95; RSM, plates 54, 55;
        SLA, 118-23; MAM, 212; HMC, 108-12; HIA, 110-11, 257-60
Kaminaljuyú: Ruins, HGA, 191-92; CCC, 23; WCK, 63-385 pass.
Labna
    Architecture, SSM, plates 4, 9, 19, 15; KMA, plate 32; IMC, 159-65 pass.
    General view, FRM, 124-32
    Plan, AMC, fig. 248; CCC, 98
    Ruins, CCC, 97-105 pass.; HGA, 110-11, 168-74; AMC, figs. 249-61
Mayapán
    Plan, AMC, figs. 311, 312, HPC, 262
    Ruins, IMC, 120; AMC, figs. 313-22, CCC, 127
Mixco Viejo
    Plan, HGA, 207
    Ruins, HGA, 209-12
Naranjo
    Altar, GCM, 102
    Plan, GEC, 6-7
    Stairway, GCM, 107-10
    Stele, SSM, plate 23; MAM, 341; GEC, plates 1-24; GCM, plates 25-40
Oxkintok
    Plan, AMC, fig. 181
    Ruins, AMC, figs. 82-90
Palenque
    Cross, BMC, 547-54 pass.
    General view, FRM, 15, 26-63; ART, 64
    Palace, ALM, 45-50
    Plan, HGA, 128-29; AMC, figs. 79-104; CCC, 56; SLA, 45-46; MFA, 124
    Pyramids, WPM, 298-306
    Ruins, HGA, 132-157 pass.; AMC, 80-104; CCC, 54-65 pass.; RSM,
        plates 41-48; CHL, 45; FSW, 114-15; MAM, 292; HPC, 232; MT,
        68-69; HGA, 110-11; SLA, 13-44 pass.; DCS, 360; SIT, II, 309,
        336-38
    Temples, HMC, 94-97; KMA, plates 26, 27, 79, 81; IMC, 60-77 pass.
    Temple plan, KAA, 132-33; IMC, 63-75 pass.; HGA, 147
    Temple of Inscriptions, LF (4/27/53), 70-74; ART, 241; MAM, 181;
        HMC, 136; AML, 53, 55
    Temple of Sun (cutaway), VAC, 29
    Tombs, MAM, 412-13; MC, fr.; DCS, 365; BGK, 65
Piedras Negras
    Excavations (1930), NG (11/35), 538-70
    Morley expedition (1921), MSM, 103-06
    Plan, HPC, 93
    Stele, MAM, 338
    Temple, KAA, 137; AMC, figs. 55, 56; MAM, 303, 305
Quiriguá
    Plan, HGA, 113
    Ruins, MAM, 272; AMC, figs. 146-57; HGA, 118, 123; RSM, plates
        28, 29; NG, (12/75), 757
    Stele, SSM, plate 23; IMC, 44, 45, 48; MAM, 305; MT, 127 (A.D. 766)
    Temple, IMC, 46; KAA, 131; AMC, figs. 144, 145
Sabacche: Architecture, SSM, plates 6, 15
Salinas de los Nueve Cerros
    Plan, DSN, 67, 70

General view, FRM, 120-21
Ruins, HGA, 266-67
Xultún: Stele, MAM, 346
Yaxchilán
 Plan, HGA, 160-61; AMC, fig. 57
 Ruins, HGA, 110-111, 163, 165, 167; AMC, figs. 58-67; RSM, plates 30-38
 Temple plan, KAA, 135, 136; IMC, 56-59
Xunantunich
 Altar, GCM, 127
 Stele, GCM, 121-25
Zaculeu
 Plan, HGA, 195; AMC, 343
 Ruins, HGA, 197, 199; AMC, figs. 344-50

2. Culture
 a. Art, LTA, 95-127 pass; WPC, 297-335 pass.; ESB, 207-35; SSM, 222-28
    Hachas, WIA, I, 144
    Masks, SSM, 119-24; BLM, 251-57 (Chichén Itzá); BOW, 183 (Uaxactún)
    Painting, VAC, 49-62
    Stone yokes, WIA, I, 143
 b. Astronomy, Calendar
    Astronomical glyphs, BMW, 186-98 pass.; HMN, 167-77
    Astronomical observatory (Chichén Itzá), MAM, 289; ART, 177
    Calendar, DAA, 178 (Uaxactún); ART, 211 (Copán); KIM, 28-48 pass.
    Computing time, FRM, 12; MFA, 109-10
    Counting system, GMR, 75; ARM, 11, MAM, 239, 241
    Oldest dated monument (31 B.C.), RCH, 2
    Zodiac signs, MAM, 253
       Days, MIS, 28, 29; WIA, I, 133; MAM, 232; GMR, 64
       Months, MJS, 49, 50, 153; WIA, I, 134; MAM, 233, 238; GMR, 68
       Other signs, MIS, 68-83 pass.
 c. Economy
    Lime-kiln, SLA, 133
    Quarrying, SLA, 133
    Stone chisels, MAM, 331
 d. Figurines, Sculpture, etc.
    Aquatic symbols, TCA, 32
    Figurines, GMR, 7-192 pass.; MAM, 261-64; SSM, plate 17; WPM, 90-160 pass.; KMA, plates, 96-98, 125-42 pass.
    Heads, HGA, 25-36 pass.; MAM, 406-11
    Human forms, SSM, 21-30 pass.; BNC, 600; CMA, 177-210 pass.
    Serpent, SSM, 34-37, 59-63
    Tortoise, BMC, 424-28
    Sculpture
       Acanceh, MAM, 361
       Chichén Itzá, IMC, 98-103; SSM, plates 5-15 pass.; KMA, plates 28-42, 92, 93; CE, 84; MAM, 355-56, 409; BLM, 222-45 pass.
       Comalcalco, MAM, 360
       Copán, KMA, plates 83-90 pass.; IMC, 29-31; ART, 149, 151; SSM, plate 36; RCH, 48-52, 144-45, plates 69-70; BOW, 182; WPM, 132, 133; VAC, 40, 41
       Kabah, SSM, plates 8, 16; MAM, 357
       Palenque, KMA, plate 305; IMC, 73; MAM, 274, 350-59, 411; CE, 84; HMC, 98, 100; LOR, 131, 156-57; NG (12/75), 730-31
       Piedras Negras, KMA, plates 72-74, 78
       Quiriguá, SSM, plates 1, 2; IMC, 47; MAM, 354, 358
       Seibal, IMC, 53-55

Art styles
Chiriquí, EST, 106, 110
Coclé, EST, 90-99; LP, 1-108 pass.; AM (2/66), 21-25
Diquís, EST, 104-09 pass.
Veragua, EST, 103-11 pass.
Artifacts, WAP (Carib. vol.), 209-10
Beadwork, DIA, 473
Figurines, WIA, II, 327-33 pass.
Jewelry (gold), NCE, X, 940; JCA, 124, 146; KMA, plates 221-25
Pottery, NG (3/49), 376; WIA, II, 329-38 pass.; JCA, fr.; DIA,
149-57 pass.
Tapestry, DIA, 474-76

VI. Incas, Pre-Incas (Peru, Bolivia, Ecuador)

1. Sites
Cajamarca: Irrigation system, MHI, 68
Cajamarquilla: General view, HPC, 349
Callo: House of Inca, DCS, 9
Chan-Chan
Citadel, HPC, 371-75
General view, HPC, 360-63; DAA, frontispiece; WIA, II, 165
Plan, HPC, 367
Restoration, NG (3/73), 326-27
Ruins, KMA, plate 43; NG (1/33), 91; NG (3/73), 318-45 pass.; LAO,
plates 13, 14, p. 50-53; MHI, 35; MAC, 186
Chavín
Monoliths, LAO, 31-33
Ruins, WIA, I, 119
Style, LTA, 157-63
Chichacara: Ruins, EAW, 191
Chimú
Ruins, LAO, plates 13, 14; HHI, 35; MAC, 88-89, 186
Temple, KAA, 267-74 pass.
Chuquimancu: Fortress, MAC, 191
Chuquitana
Plan, WIA, II, 98
Ruins, WIA, II, 98
Colca: General view, MFE, 44
Cuzco
Huaca, MHI, 134
Plan, MAC, 241, 321; KAA, 313; HPC, 349; NG (12/73), 774-75
(c.1887)
Ruins, LAO, plates 8, 9, 88-95, 98-102; MHS, 147; MAC, 241, 299,
316-17
Sacsahuamán fort, KAA, plate 164
Stone work, HPC, 449
Temple of the Sun, HNM (vol. 7), 16
Throne, MHI, 83
El Paraíso: General view, EAW, 102
Huánuco Viejo: Plan, HPC, 478-79
Huari: Plan, HPC, 338
Incahuasi
Plan, HPC, 466
Palace, HPC, 469
Storehouse, MHI, 59
Ingapirca: General view, AM (1/75), 23-24
Kenko: Amphitheater, WAP (Br. vol.), 181

Chicama, LAO, plates 57-85 pass.
Chimbote, LAO, plates 59-87 pass.
Icá, LAO, plates 103-04, 106
Moche, MHI, 26; LPC, figs. 346-59
Mochica, BMP, 23-104 pass.
Nazca, LAO, plates 20-44, 97
Pachacamac, LAO, plates 46-49
Recuay-Vicus, LAO, plates 53-56
Tiahuanaco, LAO, plates 15-19; KAA, plate 55
Sculpture
Chan-Chan, CHL, 86
Chavín, MAC, 139; LAO, 34-35; MHI, 22; WIA, II, 120-21
Huari, LPC, figs. 582-84
Mochica (heads), KMA, plates 159-61
Pucará, WIA, II, 153
Taino, AM (Nov.-Dec., 1976), 33-38
Tiahuanaco, MAC, 107; CHL, 82-83
Artifacts, NG (12/73), 966-70; DIS, plates 43-75, 208-25 pass.; LAE,
25, 53-62; DIA, plates 177-79, 227-47 pass.; WIA, II, 92-183 pass.;
KMA, plates 275-77; LF (4/12/54), 100-05; EBR, (vol. 1), 689-90
Chavín, CHL, 70, 73
Paracas, CHL, 71-72; AM (10/78), 36-44
e. Jewelry
Ornaments, KMA, plates 209-12; WIA, II, 303; KMA, plates 193-209
pass.; HNM (vol. 10), 634
Beads, NPH, 452
Gold cups, KMA, plates 200-01
Silver work, MOC, 45
Styles
Chimú, CHL, 88; LPC, figs. 163-51 pass.
Huari, LPC, figs. 564-67
Moche, LAO, 25, 30; CHL, 80
Mochica, BMP, 107-110
Nazca, LAO, 25, 30; CHL, 80
Pachacamac, LAO, plate ix
f. Music
Instruments, HLA, 11, 15; BMP, 110-14 (Moche); MOC, 97; HNM
(vol. 110), 635; KMA, plates 294-95
Pan pipes, AM (5/49), 32; MHT, 129
Gourd flute, NCE, VIII, 479
Dances, HLA, 36
Harvest festival, LNW, 75
g. Pottery
General, MPS, plates 45-64; WIA, II, 265-306 pass.; MPS, plates 1-
25; MPS, 24-44, 181-90, 482, 490; DIA, plates 195-306; LPC, figs.
668-718 pass.; MDC, 12-110 pass.; HNM (vol. 107), 78-85; WIA,
II, 102-183 pass.; LAE, 18-37 pass.
Portraits, OIA, plates 1-8; BNL, 136-37
Whistling jars, NCE, VI, 595; OIA, plates 2, 4
Types
Chancoy, LAO, 58-60; MAC, 187; CHL, 89
Chavín, LPC, figs. 1-139 pass.; KAA, plates 125-32; WIA, II, 124-
28
Chicama, LAO, 22-55 pass.
Chimú, WIA, II, 167-68, 178; MAC, 73-87, 103, 180-83; LPC, figs.
597-656 pass.
Cienega, WIA, II, 219-20
Cuzco, LAO, 27-29

El Mole, WIA, II, 216-18
Huari, LPC, figs. 530-81 pass.
Icá, LAO, 15
Jijón, MAC, 156-61 pass.
＼ Moche, WIA, II, 139-43; BDA, 106-39 pass.; CHL, 76, 77; LPC, figs. 236-345 pass.
Mochica, BAP, 19-153 pass.; KMA, plates 152-58; NCE, xi, 187
Nazca, KAA, plate 150; WIA, II, 146-49; LAO, plates v-vii; MAC, 90-102, 196-97; CHL, 79; LPC, figs. 466-529 pass.
Pachacamac, LAO, 12, 57; MAC, 476
Paracas, KAA, plates 144-48; LPC, 140-60, 188-222 pass.
Pucará, WIA, II, 154
Recuay-Vicus, LAO, 59; LPC, figs. 409-65 pass.
Tiahuanaco, LAO, 20, 21; MAC, 138-39; CHL, 84, 85; KMA, plates 166, 167; WIA, II, 157-62
Tembladura, AM (10/77), 1bc.
h. Science: Trephining skulls: MOC, 108; WNC, I, 244
i. Society
Inca life: NG (12/73), 747-53
People types: NG (2/38), 229-36; MOC, 74; OIA, plates 13-29 pass.
Costumes: ruler, CE, xii, 605; people, AM (9/58), 812
Utensils: HNM (vol. 110), 636, 639
Scales: EAW, 192
Knives: LPC, figs. 698-99
Tools: MOC, 27, 44
j. Textiles, Tapestry, Weaving, etc.
Tapestry, DIA, plates 196, 213-40 pass., 491-93; KMA, plates 174-91; WIA, II, 92-183 pass.
Weaving, AM (12/63), 30-33; DIA, plate 489; LPC, figs. 658-708 pass.; DTA, 7-66 pass.; MOC, 19-94 pass.; MAC, 465-519 pass.
Embroidery, DTA, 119-30 pass.
Braiding, DTA, 73-98 pass.
Nets, DTA, 101-14 pass.
Trimmings, DTA, 132-205
Feather work, KMA, plates 289, 290
Styles
Chancoy, LAO, plates 126, 127
Chimú, LPC, figs. 607, 622, 648, 653
Huari, LPC, figs. 538-96 pass.
Icá, LAO, plates 113-16
Mochica, KAA, 147-64, plates 131-38 pass.
Nazca, LAO, plates i-xii pass., pages 110-14; LPA 518-26
Pachacamac, LAO plate viii, pages 117-25
Paracas, KAA, 294-97; BDA, 153-59; MAC, 106; LPC 161-87, 196-208, 226
Tiahuanaco, MAC, 477; KAA, plate 149
k. Religion
Ceremonial gold gloves: NG (12/73) 786 (Mochica)
Gold idols: MHI, 122
Llama sacrifice: PWL, 62
Tombs:
Cajamarca, HMI, 72
Pachacamac, NG (1/33), 92
Paracas, KAA, 285
Titicaca Lake, JIV, 142-43
Mummies, WNC, I, 276-77; NPH, 293, 429-32 pass.; KAW, 73, 87; NG (2/38), 239 (excavations); AM (1/50), 7-10, 41; DCS, 55-64 pass.; MHI, 132; HNM (vol. 7), 29; MOC, 89; FLC, 29; LF

        (4/5/54), 25-27 (child)
  l. Writing: Quipus, WNC, I, 243; NPH, 457; WIA, II, 183; DCS, 105;
        MHI, 109; KMA, plate 299; GHS, 31; MOC, 104-05; MAC, 328; MHP,
        126-27
  m. Miscellaneous
        Ruins explored, AM (3/75), 3-11
        Weapons, WIA, II, 52-60 pass., 204-05; MOC, 65
        One-man boat, BMP, 72

VII. <u>Pre-Colonial Venezuela, Colombia</u>

1. Sites (Chibcha)
    Colima, EDG, 68-82
    Muisca, EDG, 104-13
    Nariño, EDG, 62-65
    Quimbaya, EDG, 84-93
    San Agustín, NG (5/40), 628-47
    Sinú, EDG, 116-23
    Tairona, EDG, 126-39
    Tolima, EDG, 96-101

2. Culture
  a. Art, LTA, 146-51 pass.; CHL, 62-66 pass.
    Styles
        Chibcha, EST, 84-88
        Colima, EST, 60-65
        Darién, EST, 76-78
        Quimbaya, EST, 70-73
        Sinú, EST, 79-80
        Tairona, EST, 81-82
        Tolima, EST, 66-68
  b. Jewelry: Ornaments (gold), EOG, 62-139 pass.; KMA, plates 213-20;
    DIA, plates 171, 179, 180; LPC, 830-34
  c. Pottery, WIA, II, 309-12; DSA, plates 191-92; DIA, 167-78
  d. Sculpture, figurines, artifacts
    Sculpture
        Heads, AM (June-July, 1972), 25-30, ibc.
        Images, WIA, II, 322-24
        Monuments, WIA, II, 314
    Figurines: Chibcha gold, NCE, III, 558; WIA, II, 325; AM (4/54), 24-
      28; LPC, figs. 804-59 pass.; KAA, 114-19
    Artifacts, WAP (Ven. vol.), 112-23 pass., 150-55; DIS, plates 1-24,
      201-02, 207; AM (4/54), 24-28 (in Gold Museum, Bogotá)
  e. Society; natives Orinoco valley, AM (1/52), 17
  f. Textiles, tapestry, weaving, DSA, plate 478; DIA, 477; TCA, 182-86
  g. Miscellaneous; Warao Indian concept of universe, BDA, 164-185 pass.

VIII. <u>Pre-Colonial Chile</u>

1. Sites
    Easter Island, BGK, 199 (inscriptions)
    San Pedro de Atacama, AM (11/59), 18-20 (discoveries)

2. Culture
    Art, CHI, 31 (Araucanian silver); LPC, 871-93 pass. (masks)
    Artifacts, DIS, plates 180-92, 240-45
    Figures, LPC, figs. 884-88

Jewelry, DIA, plate 494
Pottery, DIA, plates 242-43; WIA, II, 232-47 pass.; LPC, figs. 860-89
  pass.
Tapestry, DIA, 495

IX.   Pre-Colonial La Plata (Argentina, Paraguay)

1.   Sites
Patagonia: Ruins, NG (3/76), 290-332

2.   Culture
Patagonia
     Artifacts, DIS, plates 193-200, 149, 250
     Pottery, DIA, 244-45; WIA, II, 456-57, 465-73
     Stone engravings, AM (4/70), 32-37
     Stone implements, NPH, 27, 55
     Weapons, WIA, II, 463, 475-77
Paraguay: Artifacts, DIS, plates 226-35 pass.

X.   Pre-Colonial Brazil

1.   Sites
Lagoa Santo (excavations), AM (7/57), 7-10
Marajó, CHL, 67; WSH, 82
Paraiba (inscriptions--500 B.C.?), GRH, 73-85

2.   Culture
Artifacts, DIS, plates 76-88, 215-222, 234
Cave paintings, AM (1/63), 12-15, 27
Figurines, WIA, II, 407, 414-16
Pottery, LPC, figs. 895-910; DIA, plates, 193-94, 483-85; WIA, II, 419-
  20, 448-51; CHL, 67; WSH, 82
Stone tools and weapons, WIA, II, 444-45
Tapestry, DIA, plate 488
Tomb, WIA, II, 447

Part II

DISCOVERY AND CONQUEST

A. EUROPEAN BACKGROUND

I. Early Discoveries

1. Phoenician (?)
   Ships, HM, 66; GRH, 62-63
   Inscriptions (Paraiba, Brazil), HM, 211; GRH, 73-85
2. Buddhists (?): Central America, HNM (vol. 103), 251-58
3. Vikings
   Ships, WNC, I, 62; JCH, 3; ARM, 39; GMV, 18-104 pass.; AM (9/67),
      21; AS, 34-43 pass.; GRH, 63; HM, 231
   Ruins, HM, 265, 328, 360; GMV, 46-110 pass.; HNM (vol. 65), 515-25;
      LF (9/15/67), 53-56; HND, 74-288 pass.
   Greenland, WNC, I, 86
   Vinland, NG (11/64), 709-33
   Markland, GMV, 103
   New England
      Sacrificial stone (New Hampshire), DIC, 120-21
      Spirit Pond (Maine), GRH, 38-39, 132-42
      Stone tower (Newport), GMV, 141
      Dighton Rock, WNC, I, 101
   Kensingston Stone (Minnesota), HND, 102-311 pass.; GMV, 145; GRH, 31,
      109-17 pass.; HM, 222-23; DLC, 120-21
   Carvings, GMV, 41
   Weapons, WNC, I, 65; HM, 329
   Compass, GMV, 55
   Burials, GMV, 82
4. Others
   Celts, FAB, 6-151
   St. Brendan (6th century), STB, 1-247 pass.
   Semitic (?)
   Bat Creek (Tennessee), DLC, 120-1; GRH, 146
   Unknown, TSL, 82-83, 192-93
   Prayer Rock (South Dakota), DIC, 120-21

II. Navigation Problems

1. Sea Creatures
   Sea of Darkness, WNC, I, 74
   Marine Life, CMF, 158-59
   Monsters, AM (9/76), s-4; CMF, 158-59; WWE, 64, 72; HE, 20-21
2. Ships
   Fifteenth century, WNC, I, 73, II, 7-10; CMF, 22-26; AS, 57-115; NRM,
      66-67
   Sixteenth century, BMM, I, 322-23; LSA, 69-70; HE, 48-51, 86-87
   Columbus' three ships--Santa María, Niña, Pinta: NRM, 82-83
3. Sailing instruments, NRM, 77, 132-33; RMP, 45-48; HAE, 90-93; HE,
      93-96

Compass, HAE, 81; WNC, II, 94; WWE, 15, 22
Astrolabe, WNC, II, 96-97; WHS, 114; HAE, 72, 91; PDS, 158; WWE, 29
Quadrant, HAE, 78
Hourglass, CMF, 141
"Nocturnal" clock, CMF, 152

III. Spain (15th and 16th centuries)

Cádiz, BCC, 178-79
Palos, IF (10/10/55), 118-19
Sevilla, BCC, 166; MED, 28-29; HE, 126-27 (c.1570)

IV. Portugal (15th and 16th centuries)

Lisbon, NG (10/32), 704; BCC, 156; PDS, 172; HE, 18-19
Seamen, HM, 424
Ships, PDS, 154

V. Italy (15th century): Genoa, HE, 54 (c.1481)

B. THE CONQUEST

I. Mysterious beliefs

Cannibals, PDS, 223
Fountain of Youth, MED, 504
Gran Quivira, AM (9/76), 11
Strange animals, LNW, 123-34
Strange people, HAE, 33

II. Mexico

Aztec-Spanish relations, AM (10/50), 24-27
Spanish invasion
  Indians massacred at Cholula, HNM, (vol. 12), 16
  Spaniards see Aztec capital, HNM, (vol. 12), 17
  Aztec idols destroyed, HNM (vol. 12), 12
  Montezuma killed, HNM (vol. 12), 21
  Guatemozín captured, HNM, (vol. 12), 24
  Battle of Causeway, HNM, (vol. 12), 22
  La Noche Triste, ALA, 36
  Fleeing Indians, SSH, 136

III. Peru

Atahualpa seized, MHI, 13
Cuzco captured, MHI, 14

Part III

COLONIAL DEVELOPMENT

A. DESCRIPTIONS

I. Cities, towns, villages

Acapulco, Mexico, WNC, VIII, 197 (harbor, c.1620); WPA, (Mex. vol.),
   119 (17th century)

Alamo, Texas (founded 1718), AM (9/76), 12

Antigua, Guatemala, KHG, 10 (16th century); OLA, 73; ACL, 57; NG
   (10/36), 454, (10/47), 531; AM (8/56), 24, (Nov.-Dec. 1973), 24-25

Bahia, Brazil, LSH, 87 (1635); SSH, 154

Buenos Aires, Argentina, AM (4/60), 34-35 (1794), (3/61), 30 (1812),
   (5/67), 30 (c.1580); LUL, 320 (1700); CRH, 34-35 (c.1800)

Callao, Peru, WNC, VIII, 298-99 (c.1620); WWE, 126

Caracas, Venezuela, AM (2/77), S-5 (1569)

Carolina, Puerto Rico, INW, 97 (17th century)

Cartagena, Colombia, ACS, 163 (1544); WNC, II, 192 (17th century); AM
   (6/69), 21-29, (2/77), S-8

   City wall, AM (6/69), 26

   Fort San Fernando de Bocachica, AM (6/69), 27

Cartago, Costa Rica (ruins), CR, 20

Cuzco, Peru, AM (9/76), S-1 (17th century), (2/77), S-1

   City plan, WNC, II, 554

Darién, Panama, AM (7/69), 23-30

Guanajuato, Mexico, HAC, 157

Havana, Cuba

   Harbor, WNC, II, 202 (16th century), VIII, 273 (1720); TPC, 546-47 (1762)

   The Market place (late 18th century), TPC, 546-47

   Colonial Captains-General (portraits), TPC, 546-47 (19th century)

Lima, Peru, WNC, VIII, 312 (c.1766); AM (9/76), S-7 (18th century),
   (2/77), S-8

Mexico City, Mexico, ISH, 214 (c.1500); LBT, xiii (1628), xvii (c.1650);
   LNW, 99 (c.1670); AM (5/59), 7 (c.1800), (2/77), S-4 (17th century)

   Aqueduct, NG (12/34), 755 (18th century)

   House of Tiles, BOL, 62 (18th century)

   Palaces, AM (9/71), 2-9; SSH, 151

   Plaza Mayor, AHC, 44-45 (17th century)

   Waterworks (Salta de Agua), HNW (vol. 94), 509 (1620); NG (12/34), 572

Monterey, California, DSW, 69 (c.1800); NMW, 102 (1846)

Nombre de Diós, Panama, SSH, 144

Pensacola, Florida (Fort San Carlos), AM (9/76), 10 (1797)

Pernambuco, Brazil, AM (3/49), 24

Porto Bello, Panama, WNC, VIII, 207 (c.1720)

   Ruins, PBK, 172-73

Potosí, Bolivia (and Silver Mountain Mine), ISH, 167; MHS, 111; LNW, 81;
   HHL, I, 262; PMN, 13 (1553), 44 (1584)

Quito, Ecuador, AM, (2/77), S-7

Rio de Janeiro, Brazil, WNC, VIII, 403 (bay)

San Antonio, Texas, DSW, 14-15 (market, c.1820)

Santiago, Chile, WNC, VIII, 321 (street plan c.1777)

Santo Domingo, Hispaniola, ACL, 49 (16th century); AM (2/77), S-10; LNW,

C.   ECONOMY

I.   Coinage, FCL, 65-100 pass.; GCW, 339-42, Illus. 790-92

1.   Portugal, PBK, 172-73 (17th century)
2.   Spain, PMK, 172-73 (17th century); WWE, 138 (Philip II)
3.   Spanish colonies, BCA, 9-29; FCL, 259
4.   Mexico, FCL, 8-17 pass.; NCF, i-xiii (1536-72); VSC, 15-44
     First mint, NFC, 10
     Copper coins (1536-72), NCF, 127-34
     Silver coins (1536-72), NCF, 53-113 pass.
5.   Peru, AM (9/76), S-10
6.   Brazil, BCA, 62-65; FCL, 232, 241, 302-03
7.   West Indies
     British, BCA, 77-90
     French, BCA, 71-74
     Dutch, BCA, 66

II.   Industry

1.   Mining, MHI, 8-9; WNC, VIII, 192-93 (silver, 16th century)
     Brazil, PMN, 12 (gold, 1556), 29, 60 (diamond, 1812)
     Peru, WAP (Brazil vol.), 155
     Potosí, Bolivia, PMN, 44-45 (1602)
     Zacatecas, Mexico, PMN, 28 (silver, 1812)
2.   Fishing
     Fish hooks (California), CCM, 16
     Pearls (Venezuela, 16th century), PDS, 226; BCC, 246
3.   Manufacturing
     Metal working
         Peru, DCS, 40
         New Mexico, DSW, 127
     Ship building, PDS, 249 (16th century)
     Sugar
         Sixteenth century, BMC, 82; AM (5/72), 24-25
         Seventeenth century (Antilles), BCI, 383-84
         Eighteenth century, AM (10/65), 5 (c.1760); WHM, 71
     Wood work, MHI, 45 (beaker)
4.   Agriculture
     Planting, JCH, 64 (by Indians); AHC, 43 (cactus, 1630)
     Harvesting, WAM, 275 (cochineal, Mexico)
     Fruits and vegetables, LNW, 135-46; HAE, 132-33
     Tobacco, SSH, 158
     Wood plow, DSW, 54; WAM, 270
     Water lift, WAM, 271
     Cart, WAM, 290 (two wheels)
     Cattle corral, DSW, 8-9 (California, c.1820)
     Haciendas, LUL, 78; DSW, 100-01 (Texas c.1800)
5.   Transportation; communication
     Travel methods, MFE, 186; ART, 198 (Indian back)
     Roads, NG (2/29), 163
     Mission road (south west United States), PEC, 98
     Santa Fe Trail (c.1830), DSW, 138-39
     Bridges
         Peru, HAE, 108; NG (6/30), 772; MHI, 116
         Ecuador, NG (1/29), 51

Gold mining, LNW, 105, 115 (16th century); JCH, 36, 38
Gold smelting, JCH, 38 (16th century)
Hunting, JCH, 33
Making beads, BCC, 223 (c.1570)
Playing games, JCH, 66
Smoking, BCC, 130
Committing suicide, BCC, 221

III. Negroes

1. Slave trade
    Slave ships, NG (12/77), 730-31; MNS, plate 1; CSI, 199 (middle passage)
    Landing at Hispaniola, BCC, 201
    Landing at Rio de Janeiro, MNS, plate 2
    Slave sale, MNS, plates 3, 4
2. Slave treatment
    Branding, MNS, plate 5
    Cruelties, MNS, plate 13
    Whipping, MNS, plate 14
    Pacification, AJ, 19 (18th century)
3. Labor
    Farm, MNS, plates 6-8
    Refining mill, MNS, plate 9
4. Negro-Indian mixture, MNS, plate 10

IV. Spanish-Indian Relations

1. Fighting, LF (3/22/48), 86-87; WAP (Carib. vol.), 74 (Arawaks); LNW,
    88; BCC, 208
2. Indian treatment of Spaniards
    Offering treasure, ELA, 57
    Feeding Spaniards gold, BCC, 220
    Torturing Spaniards, HHL, I, 2
    Eating Spaniards, INW, 105; SSH, 139; BCC, II, 158, 190; CFF, II, 100
3. Spanish treatment of Indians
    Use of dogs, AM (6/66), 21
    Punishment, WNC, VIII, 194, 195; SSH, 136, 137, 140-41; HAE, 176-77;
        DAH, 239; MFI, 88; ELA, 89; KCH, 71
    Torture, NG (8/49), 13-15; CFI, I, fig. 27
    "Justice," MHI, 152, 165

V. Amusements

Bear and bull fight, DHA, 132
Dancing, MNS, plates 11, 12; HLA, 48; IDS, 82-83 (bolero); AM (9/76),
    S-10 (pole dance); DSW, 90-91 (Texas, fandango, c.1800)
Fiestas, SSH, 148-49 (Mexico, c.1650)
Games, CCM, 34 (California, 1816)
Hunting bear, DHA, 131
"Snatching rooster," DHA, 136

E.   CULTURE

I.   Architecture

1. Baroque
    Bolivia, CHL, 173-75
    Brazil, CHL, 183-95
    Central America, CHL, 138-47
    Ecuador, CHL, 153-57
    Mexico, CHL, 118-35 pass.
    Peru, CHL, 165-71; MFE, 168
2. Plateresque
    Mexico, CHL, 106-110
    Peru, CHL, 111
    Santo Domingo, CHL, 103-04
3. Homes, ELA, 79; CFI, I, 424 (Hispaniola, 1557)
4. New Mexico, BPS, 3-77, pass.
5. Aqueducts, CCS, 27

II. Music

1. Instruments, IEM, 159-92 pass. (16th to 18th centuries)
    Flutes, SM, 56 (Peru), 89 (Central America)
    Drums, SM, 121 (Brazil)
    Harp, SM, 57 (Ecuador)
    Human bones, SM, 121 (Mexico)
    Marimba, SM, 89 (Guatemala)
    Musical bow, SM, 89 (Patagonia)
    Pan Pipes, SM, 56 (Bolivia), 57 (Ecuador)
    Rattles, SM, 120 (Mexico)
    Trumpet, SM, 120 (Brazil)
    Whistle, SM, 120 (Mexico)
2. Music book, NCE, I, 406 (18th century)

III. Plastic Arts

1. Paintings, drawings
    Bolivia, NCE, VIII, 430-34: AM (9/76), S-5 (17th cent.)
    Brazil, WIA, II, 439 (Indian, 16th cent.)
    Ecuador, AM (6/68), 3-9
    New Mexico
      Folk art, DSW, 132-35 (18th cent.)   /
      Graphics, BPS, 82-117
      Metals, BPS, 269-301
      Painting on hides, BPS, 119-41
      Panels, BPS, 145-68
      Religious (Santero), BPS, 333-439
      Woodwork, BPS, 247-62
    Paraguay, AM (Nov.-Dec. 1976), A-1, 12-14 (mission)
    Peru, NCE, VIII, 430-34
      Cuzco, AM (7/65), 4-11
      Lima, AM (9/76), S-5 (18th cent.)
    Indian art, AM (5/58), 26-31
    Religious decorations, PM, 69
    Sunken treasure art, NG (12/77), 724-26
2. Tapestry, weaving, textiles
    Tapestry, KMA, plate 192
    Textiles, BPS, 170-241 pass.
    Weaving, MHI, 167; CCM, 18; BOL, 63 (dolls)
3. Furniture, MFE, 266, 278; DWS, 20-21 (California, c.1800)

F. RELIGION

I. Churches, missions

1. La Plata
    Jesuit reductions, LUL, 82; AM (10/71), 32-35; WAP (Arg. vol.), 28
    Jesuit churches
      Paraguay, CLP, 234-35
      Argentina, CLP, 98-99
    Jesuit's house, CLP, 98-99
    Jesuit estancia, CLP, 98-99
2. Southwest United States--Missions
    La Purísima Concepción (San Antonio, Texas), NFM, plate 2; CCM, 28-38
      pass., 70-71; NCE, IX, 957; CE, XIV, 748
    Nuestra Señora del Espíritu Santa de Zúñiga (Texas), NCE, IX, 960
    San Antonio de Padua, NFM, plates 6, 7; CCM, 28-77 pass.; CE, III, 182;
      NCE, IX, 958 (interior)
    San Antonio de Valero (The Alamo), GE, XIII, 625
    San Buenaventura, NFM, plates 57-58; CCM, 13, 31, 64-65
    San Carlos (Carmel), NFM, plates 11-14; CCM, 10, 80-81; CE, III, 182;
      NCE, IX, 1084
    San Carlos de Monterey, NFM, plate 10 (1792); NCE, I, 405
    San Diego de Alcalá, CCM, 54-55; NCE, IX, 957, XII, 1021
    San Esteban de Acoma (New Mexico), NCE, IX, 960
    San Fernando Rey, NFM, plates 62-63 (1797); CCM, 18, 46, 62, 63; NCE,
      IX, 96
    San Francisco (Dolores), NFM, plate 66; AM (9/76), 15; CCM, 90-91;
      NCE, XII, 1024
    San Francisco de Estado, CE, XIV, 545 (1730)
    San Francisco Solano, CCM, 94-95; NCE, XII, 1067
    San Gabriel, NFM, plate 42; CCM, 40-60 pass.; CE, III, 181-82; NCE,
      VIII, 1001
    San Gerónimo (Taos), NG (9/78), 430
    San José (San Antonio, Texas), CE, XIV, 547; NCE, XII, 1019; CCM, 20,
      88-89
    San Juan Bautista, NFM, plates 4, 5; CCM, 82-83
    San Juan Capistrano, NFM, plates 18-22; CCM, 58-59; CE, III, 182
    San Luis Obispo, CCM, 23, 24, 72-73
    San Luis Rey, NFM, plates 47-51, 73; CCM, 28, 56-57; CE, III, 182
    San Miguel (Santa Fe), NG (9/78), 433
    San Miguel Arcángel, NFM, plate 3; CCM, 9-36 pass., 74-75
    San Rafael, CCM, 92-93
    San Xavier del Bac (Tucson, 1700), NFM, plates 8-9; NCE, IX, 963; AM
      (9/76), 14; DSW, 128-29
    Santa Bárbara (1786), NFM, plates 31-34; CCM, 7-67 pass.; CE, III, 182;
      NCE, IX, 636-690; AM (9/76), 15
    Santa Clara, NFM, plate 74; CCM, 36-37
    Santa Cruz, CCM, 84-85
    Santa Inés, CCM, 28-33, 68-69; NCE, IX, 959
    Soledad, CCM, 46, 78-79
3. Baja California, DSW, 78-79
4. Florida, NCE, IX, 862

II. Ceremonies

    Conversion of Indians, BCC, 180 (17th century)

Baptism, NCE, V, 459, VIII, 152, IX, 945 (16th century)
Confession, MHI, 172
Marrying, MHS, 56-57; NCE, IV, 138 (18th century)
Cremation, CCM, 16 (California)
Fiestas, processions, etc.
  Celebration (California), CCM, 15
  Corpus Christi procession, NCE, II, 191 (c.1660)
  Cuzco procession, KCH, 71 (c.1660)
  Santa Bárbara fiestas, DSW, 178-79
Religious life, NCE, XI, 189 (17th century)

III. Inquisition

Spain, MFI, 119, 120-21 (16th century); CS, 90 (1609)
Peru, NCE, VIII, 463; MNC, VIII, 310

IV. Miscellaneous

Twelve Franciscan missionaries in Mexico, NCE, IX, 945
Religious images
  French monument worship (16th century Florida), JFC, 64
  "La Conquistadora" (New Mexico, 1625), NCE, XII, 1062
  "Passion Cross" (Azacoalca, Mexico, 17th century), NCE, IC, 775
  "Virgin of Christopher Columbus" (16th century), KCH, 61
First Christian pulpit (Tlaxcala, Mexico), CCS, 58
Catafalque (Mexico), AM (4/68), 27-33
Picture writing catechism (Mexico), NCE, III, 233

G. FOREIGN RELATIONS

I. French in Florida (16th cent.)

French land, INW, 85-87
Relations with Indians, ADN, 17-59
Fort San Marcos, NG (1/66), 220-23
Fort Caroline, LEF, 186; NG (1/66), 214-15
Spanish ships attack French ships, NG (1/66), 206-07
Spanish march on Ft. Caroline, NG (1/66), 213
Ribault massacre, NG (1/66), 216-17; LEF, 186-87
St. Augustine on fire (1702), NG (1/66), 224-25

II. Dutch in Brazil (16th cent.)

Invade Pernambuco (1648), AM, (8/51), 6
Dutch forts
  Olinda, AM, (5/66), 34
  Pedras Grandes (1640), AM, (5/66), 33
Governor's palace, Recife, AM (Nov.-Dec., 1975), 16, 17

III. British attacks

Morgan captures Panama (1671), HNM (vol. 19), 435

Part IV

INDEPENDENCE ACHIEVED

A. CAMPAIGNS, BATTLES

I.   Battle of Angostura (Aug. 7, 1819), AM (5/69), 2

II. Battle of Ayacucho (Dec. 9, 1824), AM (Nov.-Dec., 1974), 15

III. Battle of Boyacá (Aug. 7, 1819), AM (4/51), 24

IV. Battle of Carabobo (June 24, 1821), AM (1/78), 29; (monument) WHV, 67-68

V.   Battle of Cerrito (Dec. 3, 1812), AM (6/51), 25

VI. Battle of Chacabuco (Feb. 12, 1817), AM (3/53), 11, (9/65), 8, (4/72), 34-35, (3/75), 34-35

VII. Battle of Maipó (Apr. 5, 1818), GHS, 356; AM (9/65), 21, (3/75), 24-25

VIII. Battle of Montevideo (Feb. 3, 1806), AM (6/51), 25

IX. Battle of Tucumán (Aug. 6, 1824), AM (9/75), 34 (battlefield)

B. INDEPENDENCE DECLARED

I. Argentina

Tucumán (house where Independence was declared), AM (11/66), 1
Tucumán (Independence declared, July 9, 1816), AM (11/66), 1, (Aug.-
   Sept., 1973), 5, (3/75), 24-25, (2/78), 5
Congress of Tucumán, AM (2/78), 5

II. Ecuador

Quito, Independence declared, Aug. 10, 1809, SEP, 35

III. Venezuela

Caracas, Independence declared, July 5, 1811, WAP (Ven. vol.), 51; LF
   (7/14/61), 83; RLM, II, 124; AM (4/67), 22, (1/78), 29
Congress of Angostura (Mar. 12, 1819), AM (4/67), 17, (5/69), 4

C. MISCELLANEOUS

French in Spain and Portugal (1808-14), RW, 96-97

Spanish Cortes members (Cádiz, 1810), RW, 97

Part V

NATIONAL PERIOD

A. LATIN AMERICA--GENERAL

I. Environment

Flora, SEN, 400-58 pass.

Fauna, SEN, 414-50 pass.

Scenes, AM (Nov.-Dec. 1977), 21-48

II. Politics

Political activity, CSM, 170-85 pass.

American chiefs of state, AM (6/67), 1-6

Symbols
    Flags, NG (6/49), 647-56 pass.; EEN, fr.
    Stamps, AM (3/73), 10-12, bc.
        Showing fruits, AM (5/50), 40
        Showing maps, AM (4/50), 40
        Showing musical instruments, AM (9/76), 19-20
        Showing airplanes, AM (June-July, 1978), ibc

III. Society

1. People types, AM (4/76), 16-17, (Nov.-Dec. 1977), 17-19
    At work, AM (4/49), 4-7, (4/77), 13-18, (8/77), 2-6
    City life, CSM, 52-73 pass., 100-09
    Poor people, CSM, 8-50 pass.
    "New Peasants," CSM, 110-67 pass.
    Youths, AM (1/74), 24-25, (11/57), 3-7
    Women, AM (12/67), 26-29, (4/74), 24-25

2. Amusements
    Baseball, AM (6/57), 9-11, 40-41
    Bull fights, AM (10/50), 10-13
    Bicycling, AM (9/50), 28-30
    Games
        Colombian Indians, GGW, 156-57
        International (Caribbean, Central American), AM, (2/74), 38-39
        Maya Indians, GGW, 200-01
        Mexican Indians, GGW, 231-36

1. Geographical features

    a. Mountains
        Iztaccihuatl, LUL, 117; AM (5/62), 8; MEX, 4; CCS, 20; HNM (vol. 94),
            515; NG (10/61), 508-09
        Orizaba, FM, 103; RM, 10-11; OTM, 219
        Paricutín, WAP (Mex. vol.), 17
        Popocatépetl, NG (9/40), 365, 374, (12/51), 815; HNM (vol. 94), 755;
            FEW, 351; BAR, 67; BNL, 136-37; OTM, 392; FM, 102; AM (5/62),
            8, 20-22; BOL, 14; CMC, 9; BFF, 113; HMP, 22-23
        Sierra Madre Occidental, NG (8/68), 160-61, (5/76), 704-05; JMS, 1-12,
            305-63 pass.; FEW, 350; PMA, 12
        Sierra Madre Oriental, WAM, 27
        Sierra de Minas Viegas, FEW, 355
        Tarahumara, NG (8/68), 154-55
    b. Highlands
        Amecameca, WAM, 25
        Forests (Chiapas), CFE, 26-27
        Land erosion (Oaxaca), WAM, 310
        Mesa del Sur (Oaxaca), WAM, 29
    c. Valleys
        Central, OTM, fr.
        Oaxaca, WZP, 17 (air)
        Tula (1885), OTM, 431, 474
    d. Volcanos
        Colima, BWS, plate 43 (1909)
        Jorullo, OTM, 372
        Paricutín, LUC, 118; NG (2/44), 130-54 pass., (10/52), 534-35; FWS,
            7 (1970); LF (3/17/52), 58-60
    e. Canyons
        Huasteca, FEW, 358
        Sumidero, FEW, 356
    f. Lakes
        Chapala, NG (3/34), 339, (3/67), 430-31; EA (vol. 18), 762; WHM, 80
        Pátzcuaro, ESS, 88, 122; WAP, 32-33, 67; BMCA, 64; FM, 106-07; AM
            (2/50), 3, (5/78), 35-41
        Xochimilco, EA (vol. 18), 762, 770; HMP, 29, 73
    g. Rivers
        Balsas, NG (8/46), 255-70
        Casas Grandes, JSM, 140
        Grijalva, WAM, 30
        Usumacinta, NG (11/35), 564
    h. Falls
        Guanacatlán, NG (3/34), 340
        Tzaráracua, NG (5/37), 634
    i. Deserts
        Samalayuca, NG (8/68), 173
        Sonora, RM, 17; JSM, 145-47
    j. Coastal areas
        Acapulco Bay, LF (2/28/44), 84
        Guaymas, CMC, 17
        Mazatlán, CMC, 28
        Raza Island (Gulf of California), NG (2/51), 241-48
    k. Miscellaneous
        Cloud forest, (Chiapas), AM (4/53), 20-23
        Grass pasture lands (Durango), WAM, 54
        National Park (Atzimba, Michoacán), RM, 6-7
        Rainfall, AM (1/75), 6-12

2. Flora, Fauna

Flora, BTP, plates 10-286 pass.; ABT, 101-94 pass.; JSM, 68-83, 105-77
        pass.
    Desert shrubs (Coahuila), WAM, 55
    Tropical trees, HTT, 1-64
Fauna, VAM, 36, plates 7-9, 20; JSM, 89-100 pass.; NG (2/45), 193-208
        (Veracruz and Tabasco); TMW, 32-109 pass.
    Birds, PCF, plates 1-48; SBW, 3, 22; SPM, 2-101; DFG, plates 1-48;
        DPT, 9-145; TND, 534, 789; AGG, 23-94; EFG, plates 1-24; SBM,
        xiv-176 pass.
    Fish, MGA, 151-56, 223, 409, 417, 439
    Insects (cochineal), SSH, 152
    Mammals, RPG, 24-267 pass.; JAA, 38-180 pass.
    Snakes, SSW, 46-135 pass.

3. Scenes, BWS, plates 163-68 (1930); AM (5/75), 19-29, (3/77), S-2 to S-
    12; FM, 100-08; LAP, 194-235 pass.; WAP (Mex. vol.), 7-45 pass.; LF
    (4/24/47), 93-101, (1/9/50), 54-65, (9/15/52), 116-21, (7/12/68), 32-44;
    HMP, 21-31, 47-73; ENB (vol. 15), 336-37; LK (9/3/68), 28-44

    1850, HNM (vol. 17), 171-85
    1870, HNM (vol. 49), 1-14, 168-80, 324-34
    1890, HNM (vol. 88), 72-80, 350-58, 515-27
    1896, HNM (vol. 94), 365-82, 498-517, 743-58
    1915, HNM (vol. 134), 97-100
    1930, BWS, plates 163-8 pass.

4. Disasters

    Earthquakes, LF (8/12/57), 29-30; AAY, 388 (Puebla, Aug. 28, 1974)
    Volcanic eruptions, LF (10/25/43), 35, (4/17/44), 86-93 (Paracutín)

II. Political

1. Divisions
    Baja California
        Scenes, PBC, 14-38 pass.; AM (7/54), 6-8, 43-45; NG (10/72), 542,
            567; HOB, 30-146 pass.
        People types, NG (10/72), 542-67; NDI, 53, 83-117
        Flora, NDI, 31-33 (plants); NDI, 63 (fruit)
        Fauna, NDI, 55-61 (animals); NDI, 65-81 (birds); NDI, 121 (fish)
        Beaches, HOB, 22-38, 114, 117
        San Felipe Bay, NG (8/42), 262
        Desert islands, NG (9/41), 342-65 pass.
        Roads, HOB, 12-123 pass.
        Architecture, NDI, 35-49
    Michoacán, AM (1/51), 10-12
    Nayarit, AM (10/50), 32-34
    Sonora, NG (2/55), 2, 8-41
    Yucatán, HNM (vol. 70), 372-85 (1880); HNM (vol. 128), 759-65 (1912)

2. Symbols
    Coat of arms, EA (vol. 18), 740; SFF, 258
    National emblem (1821-), LOR, 136

Flags, EFW, 44-45; SFT, 258
National coins, AJG, 274-411 pass.; GCW, 342-47; COW, illus. 793-94;
    FCL, 162-85 pass.; VSC, 46-138
State coins, FCL, 191-211
Paper money, VSC, 173-256
Stamps, MDS, plate 93
Medals, SSC, 139-72
Evolution of Mexican Eagle, FCL, 140-43

3. Activities
    a. Revolution, rebellion
        Independence heroes (1810-11), AM (Nov.-Dec., 1976), 17-19
        Revolution (1910-14), AM (Nov.-Dec., 1978), 17-19
            Women soldiers, LF (1/12/48), 14
            Rebels hanged, LF (1/12/48), 14
            Zapatistas, LF (1/12/48), 14-15
        Revolutionaries (Ciudad Juárez, 1911), MBB, 128-29
        Battle of Juárez (1911), BIG, 112-13
        Anti-Díaz revolutionaries, MFG, 1
        Revolutionary destruction (Mexico City, c.1840), CIM, 418-19
        Cristeros rebellion (1926-29), MCR, 155-58
        "Massacre" of Mexican students (Oct. 2, 1968), LF (10/2/68), 173-98
    b. Demonstrations
        Independence Day celebration (Sept. 16, 1910), BWS, plates 54-55;
            (Sept. 16, 1942); BWS, plate 181
        Communists May Day parade (1915), AHC, 179
        Demonstration (Zócolo, Mar. 20, 1976), HMI, 118-19
        Political parade (1970), RM, 56
        Student violence (July, 1968), BBY (vol. 1969), 519
    c. Officials
        Provisional government officials (Apr. 30, 1911), BIG, 112-13
        Constitutional committee (1917), BWS, plate 113; NRG, 178-79
        Oath taking (Jan. 31, 1917), NRG, 198
        Presidential election campaign, (1940), LF (7/1/40), 19-23
        Twenty congressmen in jail (1948), LF (1/12/48), 14-15
        Members of Congress (c.1970), RM, 55
        Banquet for Governor of Oaxaca (1844), AHC, 78
    d. Miscellaneous
        American escapes from Santa María Acatitla prison (Aug. 18, 1971),
            AHT, 116-117
        Election cartoon (1932), CRH, 107
        Relations with U.S. Border Patrol, PBP, x-xii, 14-120 pass.
        Visit of USSR Anastas Mikoyan (Jan. 1958), LF (12/7/59), 51-52

4. Military
    Edifices
        Acapulco fort (1894), HNM (vol. 90), 397
        Chapultepec Military College, GFF, 185
        Fort Loreto (French defeated, May 5, 1862), PAN, 64
        Mexico City Artillery School, NG (2/44), 135
        Mexico City La Merced Barracks (1896), HNM (vol. 94), 506
        Veracruz, Fort San Juan de Ulloa (c.1840), CLM, 52, 258-59; NMW,
            6-7; MVT, 36
    Weapons
        Guns (1865-1900), HMA, 2-31; (1902-1954), HMA, 32-49
        Machine guns (1867-1896), HMA, 91-99; (1910-1950), HMA, 100-117
        Pistols, revolvers (1871-1893), HMA, 56-76; (1902-1938), HMA, 77-85

Personal
    Army drum corps, HNM (vol. 79), 817 (1888)
    Army lancers, CIM, 569
    Army of "Three Guarantees" (1821), RWP, 138-39; AHC, 70
    Rurales under Díaz, BWS, plate 8; SFF, 571
    Soldiers, BWS, plates 89-95; GFF, 571; NG (5/78), 618-19 (Zapatistas)
    Soldiers punished, LF (8/7/44), 33-36
    Women revolutionaries as soldiers, HMI, 118-19

III.   Cities--Towns--Villages

Acapulco
    Scenes, SST, 94 (night); MEX, 11; AM (1/55), 37; NG (10/61), 530-33,
       (11/73), 670-71, 696-97; HMP, 26; MVT, 33-39 pass.; NBK (vol. 12), 246
    Bay, FBM, 178-79, 586-87; NG (11/73), 694-95
    Harbor, NG (12/34), 780
    Beach, LUL, 107; FWS, 148; NG (3/78), 645 (night)
    La Quebrada cliffs (diving), MIM, 31; ASS, 22
    Plaza, HNM (vol. 90), 398 (1894)
    Hotels, NG (11/73), 696-97
Aguacatenango (Chiapas): Scenes, CFE, 164-65
Aguacalientes: National palace, GFF, 143
Alamos: Scenes, SST, 54 (air); SFB, 75; NG (2/55), 216-17 (air)
Amatenango (Chiapas): Scenes, CFE, 74-75 (air)
Amecameca: Scenes, NG (9/40), 350
Atlixco: Scenes, CLM, 578-79 (c. 1840)
Campeche: Scenes, NG (11/36), 637 (air)
Cancún: Scenes, MVT, 57
Cedros (Baja California), HOB, 36; Scenes, HOB, 36
Chamula: Scenes, NG (11/42), 652
Chiapas: National Indian Institute building, CFE, 189
Chihuahua
    Scenes, FBM, 586-87 (air); HNM (vol. 94), 369, 370 (1895)
    Guadalupe street, GFF, 129
Cholula: Scenes, HNM (vol. 49), 14 (1870); RM, 12 (air); NG (9/40), 357
Ciudad Juárez
    Scenes, MBB, 128-29 (1896)
    American consulate (1950s), MBB, 128-29
    Avenida Juárez (1935), MBB, 128-29
    Customshouse (1909), MBB, 128-29
    Highway bridge to El Paso (1920), MBB, 128-29
    Race track (1909), MBB, 128-29
    Railroad bridge to El Paso, MBB, 128-29
    Shopping center, MBB, 128-29
    Slums, MBB, 128-29
Cuernavaca
    Scenes, CMC, 73; WAP (Mex. vol.), 39
    Cortés palace, ESS, 74; HMP, 12
    Jewish rest home, LMJ, 47-48
Durango: Scenes, GFF, 549 (air); HNM (vol. 7), 175 (1850)
El Catorce (Monterrey): Scene, SST, 127, 131
Ensenada: Scene, NG (8/42), 260
Guadalajara
    Scenes, NG (3/34), 333, (3/67), 428-29 (air); MAP (Mex. vol.), 26, 30
    People types, NG (3/34), 335-56 pass., (3/67), 412-40 pass.
    Alcalde Park, NG (3/67), 424-25
    Avenida Juárez, NG (3/67), 417 (night)
    Degallado Theater, SST, 67

Central Plaza, LAP, V, 230 (air)
Governor's palace, ESS, 154
Minerva Fountain, MVT, 65
Guanajuato
    Scenes, SST, 81-82; FBM, 586-87 (air); RM, 14-15; OTM, 437 (1885);
        HAC, 157 (c.1820); ESS, 104 (air); WAM, 285 (air); HNM (vol. 94),
        379 (1895); MEX, 16; NG (3/53), 327-42 pass., (3/57), 332-33 (air),
        (5/78), 630-31
    People types, NG (3/53), 329-50 pass.
    Drinking-water pump, PLA, 164
Guaymas
    Scenes, OTM, 651 (1885); AM (9/57), 28-31
    Plaza, MIM, 48-49
    Port, RM, 156-57
    San Carlos Bay, MIM, 46
Hermosillo: Library, AM (2/52), 4
Jalapa: Scenes, CLM, 71, 73, 258-59 (c.1840)
Jonotla: Scenes, RST, 16-215 pass.
La Paz (Baja California): Scenes, FWS, 9 (air); NG (10/72), 552-55 (air)
Las Hadas: Scenes, NG (11/73), 692-93
Manzanillo: Scenes, AM (2/50), 4 (air); MVT, 73
Matamoros: Scenes (c.1840), NMW, 62
Mazatlán
    Scenes, NG (8/68), 166-67 (air, night), (11/73), 682-83 (air); MVT, 77
    Beach, EA (vol. 18), 762
Mérida
    Scenes, HNM (vol. 70), 373, 375 (1880); WAP (Mex. vol.), 31
    Casa Municipal, OTM, 33; AM (3/72), 24-25
    Horse drawn taxis, AHC, 212
    Museum of Archaeology, MIM, 48-49; MVT, 78
Mexicali: Scenes, NG (8/42), 256
Mexcaltitán: Scenes, NG (6/68), 876
Mexico City
    Scenes, CLM, 258-59 (c.1840); HNM (vol. 69), 748 (1884); NG (7/30),
        46 (air); HNM (vol. 112), 879-87 (c.1905); WAM, 357 (air); OTM,
        245; MEX, 9; WAP (Mex. vol.), 8-27 pass.; LF (2/22/37), 12 (air);
        AM (4/49), 21 (air); NG (12/34), 745 (air), (9/40), 373 (air), (12/51),
        386-824 pass., (10/52), 518-46 pass., (10/61), 249-538 pass.; HMP,
        13-63 pass.; MVT, 41-51 pass.
    People types, OTM, 275-511 pass.; NG (5/73), 638-39 pass.
    Zócalo, VAC, 9 (c.1930); FWS, 84; CLM, 258-59; GFF, 159; IM, 390
        (early views); FM, 98-99; MEX, 7; NG (6/37), 728, (12/51), 790-91;
        WBE (vol. 13), 374 (night)
    Alameda, OTM, 361; WHM, 42; LMJ, 235
    Xochimilco Gardens, WHM, 72; ESS, 108; FBM, 178; TPM, 115; NG
        (12/34), 747, (10/61), 202-03
    Chapultepec, BTM, 234-35 (1848); HNM (vol. 49), 169-70 (c.1870); (vol.
        95), 749-57 pass.; CCS, 6 (1885); BOL, 88; BWS, plate 30; CIM,
        115; SST, 111, 119; IMJ, 252, 304; NG (7/30), 50, 52 (air), (12/34),
        741, 743; (5/73), 664-65 (air)
    Museum of Anthropology, HMC, 170-71; KML, 156-59; HNM (vol. 164),
        209-25 (1880); FWS, 123 (interior); BOL, 142; ESS, 14, 19; NG
        (10/68), 492-521 pass.; EBR (vol. 1), 1098
    Public facilities
        Bank of Mexico, BWS, plates 125-26
        Communications building, BOL, 141; EA (vol. 18), 838
        Fire Department, NG (2/44), 142
        Inquisition building (entrance), CCS, 4

Penitentiary, NG (7/30), 55
Museum, WNC, I, 181 (c. 1880)
National Auditorium, AM (4/59), 23
National Conservatory of Music, HNM (vol. 94), 507
National Library (1896), HNM (vol. 94), 508
National Lottery building, LMJ, 322
National Palace, SMT, 180-81 (1860); GFF, 451; CLM, 107; CCS,
    29 (c. 1885); HNM (vol. 94), 500 (1898); NG (6/37), 728
Post Office, BWS, plate 51
Social Security building, AM (11/51), 7
Tribunal de Minería building, HHL, II, 246 (c. 1843)
Streets, plazas
    Paseo Bucareli, CLM, 165-66
    Columbus Circle, FBM, 586-87
    Plaza de la Constitución, MIM, 48-49 (night)
    Plaza de Liberación, MIM, 42; SST, 65
    Paseo de la Reforma, CLI, 150 (1810); FWS, 126; RM, 88-89 (night)
    Plaza of the Three Cultures, FWS, 1; WAA, 149 (c. 1960); PLA, 17;
        LAT, 139; MIM, 48-49; AM (1/73), 33 (air); NG (8/68), 190-91
Monuments
    Independence monument, WHM, frontispiece; SST, 106; NG (7/30), 84
    Monument of the Race, NG (5/78), 622-63
    Monument of the Revolution, LMJ, 316; AM (9/66), 42 (night)
    Noche Triste Tree, OTM, 269 (1885); NG (7/30), 80
    Towers, Satelite subdivision, KML, 145
    Ancient cyprus tree, NG (7/30), 58
Hotels
    Camino Real, KML, 141
    Iturbide, OTM, 255
    Plaza Vista Hermosa, COE (vol. 16), 83
Amusement centers
    Bull Ring, SST, 120
    Country Club, BWS, plate 130; NG (9/40), 363
    Iturbide theater, NRG, 178-79
    Jewish sports center, LMJ, 19-20 (1950)
    Race track (Hipódromo de las Américas), LMG, 191
    Stadium, FSW, 135; CMC, 92; LF (3/2/55), 28-29; NG (5/73), 657
Medical centers
    Hospital de Jesús, NCE, VIII, 509 (courtyard); HNM (vol. 94), 499
        (1898)
    San Hipólito hospital, AM (3/63), 2
    Institute of Cardiology, AM (9/59), 8, (1/61), 32; EA (vol. 18), 771
Miscellaneous
    First printing office (1536), HNM (vol. 94), 502
    German Consulate, BWS, 173
    Keys to City of Mexico, NG (5/28), 533
    U.S. cemetery (1870), HNM (vol. 49), 178
    U.S. Embassy, HNM (vol. 49), 178 (1870)
Monterrey
    Modern hotel, SST, 126
    Scenes, EA (vol. 18), 763; OTM, 556 (c. 1845); CMC, 95; HNM (vol. 69),
        748-57 (1884); AM (6/60), 3-8; WAP (Mex. vol.), 18 (air)
    Zaragoza Plaza, SST, 126; HNM (vol. 79), 752 (1884)
Morelia: Scenes, MIM, 61
Naranja
    Scenes, FAR, 16, 129
    Plaza, FAR, 122
Nogales: Celebration, AM (7/59), 24-26

Nuevo Loredo: International bridge, WHM, 8
Oaxaca
    Scenes, WHM, 2-3; NG (2/29), 191
    Governor's palace, OTM, 521 (1885)
    Municipal building, NG (10/32), 488
    Public Secretary office, ELA, 173
Orizaba: Scenes, HNW (vol. 49), 9, 10 (c.1870); NG (9/40), 356
Pachuca: Scenes, OTM, 449 (1885)
Palenque: Palace Hotel, SIT, II, 313
Paso del Norte: Scenes, OTM, 589 (1885)
Pátzcuaro
    Scenes, CLM, 578-79 (c.1840); NG (5/37), 636-48 pass., (10/61), 524-
        25; AM (1/73), 32
    Plaza, LAT, 138
Progresso (Yucatán): Customs house, OTM, 26
Puebla
    Scenes, CLM, 82, 407 (c.1840); HNM (vol. 19), 12-13 (c.1870); AM
        (8/52), 12-15; WAP (Mex. vol.), 40; GFF, 452; OTM, 499 (1885);
        NMW, 176-77 (1847)
    Casa de Maternidad, GFF, 444
    Theater (oldest in America), HMP, 19
Puerto Vallarta
    Scenes, NG (8/68), 168-69 (night, air), (11/73), 688-89; RM, 168
    Beach, BVT, 89
Querétaro
    Scenes, OTM, 479 (1885)
    Aqueduct, SST, 87 (18th cent.); BNL, 424-25
    Avenida Libertad Oriente, SST, 88
    Plaza de la Independencia, SST, 88
Saltillo
    Calle Real, GFF, 36
    University, SST, 125
San Andrés: Scenes, CMS, 22
San Cristóbal Las Casas: Scenes, HAC, 272; CFE, 11, 168-69 (air)
San Felipe: Scene, AM (7/54), fc.
San José: Salta de Agua, CLM, 499 (c.1840)
San Juan Purua: Scenes, ESS, 120
San Luis Potosí: Scenes, WAP (Mex. vol.), 19
San Miguel de Allende: Scenes, SST, 84; ESS, 124 (air); NG (5/53), 322;
    AM (1/48), fr., (10/56), 10-15, (3/63), 23-26; LAP, V, 230; MVT, 95
San Miguel de Saldado: Scenes, CLM, 258-59 (c.1840)
Santo Tomás (old and new): Scenes, AM (4/56), 3-7
Sultepec: Scenes, WAM, 290
Tacubaya: Scenes, CLM, 418-19 (c.1840)
Tehuantepec
    Scenes, CMS, plate 43 (1852), plate 43 (1967); NG (9/41), 312-16
    Town Hall, CMS, plate 51 (1882)
Tampico: Scenes, CLM 529 (c.1840); WAM, 346 (air)
Taxco: Scenes, SST, 91, 92; RM, 86-87; BMCA, 32-33; CMC, 166 (air);
    ESS, 76, 92; ELA, 23; TPM, 58; LAP, V, 229 (air); HMP, 21, 41
Tepec: Scenes, WAM, 260 (air)
Tepotzotlán: Aqueduct, CE, X, 258
Tijuana
    Avenida Revolución, PTU, 88-89
    Hot springs, PTU, 88
    U.S. border entry, PTU, 88-89
Toluca: Capitol, MVT, 98
Torreón: Scenes, WAP (Mex. vol.), 41

Tzintzuntzán: Scenes, AM (5/78), 35-41
Veracruz
   Scenes, WAP (Mex. vol.), 31; FBN, 178-79 (night); OTM, 183; CIM,
      52, 55, 64 (c.1840); CMC, 126; HNM (vol. 49), 3 (c.1870); LAP, V,
      211
   People types, HNM (vol. 49), 3-13 pass., 176, 326-32 pass. (1870)
   City Hall and plaza, RM, 82-83; FWS, 83; ESS, 52
   City wall, OTM, 175; CLM, 258, 610 (c.1840)
   Governor's palace, SST, 138; HNM (vol. 49), 2 (c.1870)
   Harbor, WHM, 12; HNM (vol. 64), 221 (1880); NG (9/40), 132; PMA, 14
   Zócalo, CMS, 3
Zacatecas
   Scenes, GFF, 140 (air)
   Aqueduct, HNM (vol. 49), 376 (1895)
   People types, HNM (vol. 49), 367 (1895)
Zempoala: Aqueduct, CLM, 419 (c.1840)

IV. Society

1. People types, CLM, 578-79 (c.1840); WAM, 281, 367; CCS, 3-55 pass.;
    RM, 64-81 pass.; NMP, 98, 99; POE, IV, 16-100 pass.; WAP (Mex.
    vol.), 20-23, 32-103 pass.; LF (1/9/50), 54-65, (7/12/68), 32-42; AM
    (5/50), 29; NG (7/30), 59-75 pass., (5/37), 639-49, (11/42), 637-61
    pass., (2/44), 137-64, (2/47), 145-72 pass., (12/51), 793-824 pass.,
    (10/52), 518-46 pass., (10/61), 493-538 pass., (8/68), 145-192 pass.,
    (5/78), 612-44 pass.; PMA, 104-27 pass.; HMP, 32-63 pass.
   In Chapingo, HAC, 186 (1825)
   In Mexico City, OTM, 275-511 pass.
   In Tehuantepec, CMS, plates 49-83
   In Yucatán, HNM (vol. 70), 377-85 pass. (1880); NG (11/36), 592-644 pass.
   Women, CLM, 418-19 (c.1840); CMS, 248-62 pass. (clothing)
      Head dress, FM, 78-80
      Washing clothes, CHL, 471
   Men
      Caballeros, CCS, 3, 8
      Charros, ESS, 42
      Rancheros, HAC, 187 (c.1850)
   Daily life, FM, 125-78 pass.
      Kitchen utensils, CMS, 277-80
   Peons, HNM (vol. 106), 34, 41, (vol. 135), 273-80
   Braceros, LF (2/15/54), 26-29; AM (3/49), 14-16

2. Indians
   Types, HNM (vol. 17), 182-85 (1850); AM (3/54), 19-21, (2/64), 9-14
   Tribes, groups
      Aztec
         Men (1529), CFI, I, fig. 9
         Women (1553), CFI, I, fig. 14
         Noblemen (1529), CFI, I, fig. 8
      Chamula, POE, IV, 94-101
      Coapenola, NG (12/34), 774
      Cora, NG (6/71), 780-95
      Huichol, POE, IV, 60-67; NG (6/77), 833-53
      Jicaque, VAM, plate 10
      Lacadón, CL, xiv, ff.; AM (1/60), 31-35; POE, IV, 84-93; OLA, 107;
        RSG, 15-18

Maya, MAM, 25-30, 152-53
Mayo, ECC, 61, 75, 103, 107
Mixe, BEW, 143-63 (1933)
Otomí, AM (6/49), 16-21, (12/59), 13-17
San Blas, LAP, V, 201
Seri, POE, IV, 44-51
Tarahumara, NG (5/76), 702-18; JSM, 156-59 (1890); POE, IV, 52-59
Tarascan, POE, IV, 76-83; BCT, 16-45 pass., plates 1-7; FAR, 28-30
Toluca, WAM, 227; WHM, 31, fr.
Tzintzuntzán, KMT, 16-211 pass.
Yaqui, ECC, 63, 74
Zapotec, CIZ, 6-75 pass.; WZP, 227-45 pass.; HAC, 226 (19th century)

3. Amusements
Festivals, NG (3/67), 420-21 (October festival); HLA, 58-59
Aguascalientes, CMC, 60
Chamula, NG (10/61), 519
Chiapas, TPM, 286
Guadalajara, NG (3/24), 330
Guadalupe, RM, 122-23
Juchitán, TPM, 194-95
Mazatlán, MEX, 27
Mexico City, AM (12/50), 24-25; TPM, 118
Puebla (May Day), AAY (vol. 1972), 460
Tehuantepec, CMS, 83-93
Zapotec, CIZ, 69-72
Sports, AM (3/50), 33-35 (participants)
Automobile races, AM (7/50), 23, (8/58), 10-13; LF (12/7/53), 32-37
   (Fourth Pan American); NG (10/72), 569-75 (Mexican 1000)
Ball team (Monterrey boys), LF (9/9/57), 116-22
Bull fights, CCS, 45-46; FWS, 112; NMP, 34-35
Bull ring, LAP, V, 214; CLM, 258-59 (c.1840)
Cock fight, OTM, 373 (1885)
Elk hunt, LF (12/25/39), 56-58
Jumping bean contest, LF (4/3/44), 117-20
Pan American games, LF (5/28/55), 26-29 (March 1955); BBY (vol.
   1976), 508 (Oct. 1976)
Snake and bird fight, LK (5/24/38), 58-59
Voladores, CM, 123; LF (10/6/47), 119

4. Miscellaneous
Amusements for rich visitors, LF (2/28/44), 78-85
Conjugal jail visits, LF (10/27/41), 49-50
Criminal executed, LF (12/27/37), 58-59
Paulette Goddard visit to Mexico, LK (7/16/40), 38-45, (7/30), 40, 42-45
Resort, Cozumel Island, LF (3/5/65), 117-126

V. Culture

1. Architecture

Architecture types, WHM, 40-44
Church architecture (contemporary), NCE, III, 841
Haciendas, HNM (vol. 17), 174 (1850), PNM, 45 (Proaño, Zacatecas)

Home examples, (3/17), 419, (5/38), 637; IFF, 219-29 (1885)
House of Tiles (Mexico City), CCS, 9; CLM, 298; RM, 95
Housing development, KML, 154-55; AM (12/58), 5-8, (5/73), 24-25; WHM,
    65 (Tlatelolco); NG (5/73), 658-59 (Cerro de la Estrella); LAP, V, 235;
    CPM, 44-46; CCS, 31
Indian houses, CMS, 248-52, plate 48 (three types); WAM, 228, 362-63,
    370; ART, 80; MAM, 213; ECC, 61-64
New architecture, AM (5/66), 26-29; LF (2/24/47), 98-99
Sinking buildings, NG (5/73), 659; LF (11/17/52), 59-64
Slums, WAM, 357 (Villa Madero, Mexico City); HMI, 118-19; GPM, 33,
    40-43; WHM, 40-44
Tropical architecture
    Mexico City, FDT, illus. 68-70, 109
    Acapulco, FDT, illus. 55, 66
Urban center (President Juárez), FDT, illus. 87
Vacation homes (Acapulco), LF (5/6/66), 116-21

2. Art

General examples, AM (2/79), 31-38
Regional arts
    Chiapas state, TPM, 197-207
    Guanajuato state, TPM, 169
    Guerrero state, TPM, 58-79
    Hidalgo state, TPM, 165, 168
    Jalisco state, TPM, 80-88
    Mexico state, TPM, 122-49
    Mexico City, TPM, 99-121
    Michoacán state, TPM, 85-98
    Nayarit state, TPM, 43-57
    Oaxaca state, TPM, 174-96
    Puebla state, TPM, 150-64, 166-67
Exhibits
    Art markets, TOM, 112-15
    Artists' fair, (Mexico City), BOL, 89
    Childrens' paintings, AM (6/49), 36-37
    Fiesta art, SCM, 132-39; PMF, 111-166 pass.
    Huichol Indian art, SCM, 76-91
    Outdoor, (Mexico City), AM (11/66), 29-32
Six women artists, AM (8/62), 25-29
Religious art (18th century), AM (9/78), 20-21; PMF, 65-78 pass.
Toys, PMF, 13-56 pass.; SCM, 109-19; AM (3/70), 36-41
    Piñata, SCL, 140-43; FWS, 106; GFF, 265 (1885); RM, 126
    Wheeled toy dog, HM, 264; BGK, 49

3. Crafts

Clay, HCM, 140-77
Folk, SCM, 120-31; NG (5/78), 649-69
Glass, JAC, 51
Lacquer, SCM, 60-75; TMP, 84-87
Leather, TMP, 79
Masks, TMP, 88-90; TPM, 59
Metal, JAC, 34-37; TMP, 74-78, 103-33
Paper, HCM, 221-38; BOL, 149-50
Stone rubbings, AM, (9/70), 30-35

Tin, SCM, 28-33
Wood, JAC, 40-45; HCM, 187-214

4. Education

Air Pilot Training School, AM (3/64), 29-31
Colegio de las Vizcaínas, CLM, 258-59 (c.1840)
Guanajuato Teacher Training School, RM, 106-07
Instituto Mexicano de Investigaciones Tecnológica, AM (8/66), 6-7
Mexico City College, AM (5/53), 21-22
Monterrey Technological Institute, AM (3/55), 16-19, (1/60), 4, (4/66),
    19; MEX, 18; LAP, V, 219
Morelia College of San Nicolás, GFF, 309, 313
National Library, BOL, 100; BNL, 424-45; FWS, 93; NCE, IX, 782, 784
    Library Directors, AM (3/53), 22-27, 41
National School of Fine Arts, AM (2/75), 26 (1/63), 14 (c.1870)
National Teacher's College, IMJ, 222
National University, LMJ, 247-49; LAR, 57; KML, 138-39; AM (9/57), 6;
    SLA, 4-7 (1964)
  College of Science, BOL, 101; WAP (Mex. vol.), 200-01
  Cosmic ray laboratory, SBL, 66; AM (11/61), 5
  School of Engineering, EA (vol. 18), 763
  School of Medicine, ESS, 136; AM (11/51), 22
  School of Mines, AM (2/75), 27
Pátzcuaro University, NCE, V, 151 (entrance)
Primary, secondary schools
  Oaxaca children's school, BNL, 424-25
  Open air school (Chapultepec), AM (2/70), 9-11
  Primary boarding school, AM (2/60), 18-21
  Public schools, AM (12/61), 17-19
  Rural schools, FWS, 71
Saltillo University, SST, 125
San Miguel de Allende Institute, SST, 130

5. Jewelry, SCM, 19-26; AM (7/60), 21-23

Manufacturing, AM (7/60), 21-23
Silver, WHM, 26; NG (9/49), 26-27

6. Landscaping

Atreas (courtyards)
  Altacomulco (Mexico state), KML, 94
  Amecameca (Mexico state), KML, 97
  Atlatláuhcan, KML, 83
  Coalcalco (Mexico state), KML, 95
  Cuautinchán (Puebla), KML, 96
  Huejotzingo (Puebla), KML, 96
  Huexalta (Mexico state), KML, 90
  Santa Cruz Atoyec (Federal District), KML, 71
  Tepoztlán (Morelos), KML, 85
  Tlalpujahua (Michoacán), KML, 89
Gardens
  Iztapalapa (of Montezuma), KML, 78
  Los Clubes, Las Arboledas, KML, 152-53

        Taxco Theater, BOL, 73
    c. Musicians, LEM, 478; NMP, 34-35
        Mariachi band, FWS, 130
        "Mariachi Vargas," AM (1/68), 36
        Strolling musicians, AM (11/66), 34-37
    d. Instruments
        Drums, CM, 114-22, 129; HDA, 128, 135
        Guitars, EGM, 212-13
        Violins, LEM, 477
    e. Theater and actors, AM (7/53), 6-7, 41-43, (4/58), 12-17
    f. New Movie films, AM (5/78), 3-8

8. Painting, AM (8/74), 17-25

    Retablos
        Ex-voto, GMF, 121-39
        Folk, GMF, 21-59
        Saints, GMF, 64-116

9. Pottery, DFM, 9-21; JAC, 4-18; TMP, 57-72; SCM, 92-108; NG (9/40),
    351; WM, 1-47 pass.

10. Textiles, SCM, 48-55; DFM, 23-37, 45

    Costumes, HNM (vol. 17), 171 (1850); AM (5/76), 5-13; LF (6/25/45), 96-
        99 (sarong)
    Embroidery, GEM, 7-75 pass.; SCM, 56-59; TMP, 47-55
    Weaving, SCM, 34-45; JAC, 22-29; TMP, 24-39 (cotton), 41-44 (reed);
        HCM, 7-94 pass.; CMS, 28-62 pass., 255-56, plate 36

11. Miscellaneous

    Building a school, NG (10/61), 515
    Five young writers, AM (6/12), 29-31
    Hand gesture communication, GFF, 211-13 (1885)
    Movie making, NG (9/72), 8-15, (4/74), 15-201; LF (10/4/63), 39
    Public letter writer, AHC, 176; NG (7/30), 56, (3/34), 334

VI. Religion

1. Edifices
    Acatlán: Church, BMCA, 64-65
    Acólman
        Church, RM, 115
        Convent, HHL, I, 164
        Monastery of San Agustín (1550), NCE, XII, 302; RSC, plate 4; WAP
            (Mex. vol.), 172; CHL, 105
    Actopán (Hidalgo): Church of San Agustín, RSC, plates 2, 7; CHL, 106
    Aguascalientes: Church of Our Lady of Guadalupe, CE, X, 259
    Alamos: Church, NG (2/55), 230
    Amecameca
        Church of Sacre Monti, GFF, 577
        Dominican cloister, RSC, plate 16

College of Santa Cruz, NCE, XIV, 183
Tlamanalco
    Chapel, RSC, plate 14 (open air)
    Cloister, RSC, plate 8
Tlaxcala: Church, SST, 6
Tohmec: Church (Franciscan), EI (vol. 12), 20
Tonantzintla: (Church) Santa María, CHL, 131
Tula (Hidalgo): Convent, Franciscan, RSC, plate 3
Tumacacori: (Church) San José (1691), NG (1/64), 20-21
Tupátaro: (Church) Santiago, AM (June-July, 1973), 2-11, ibc.
Tzintzuntzán: La Solidad church, AM (5/78), 39, ibc.
Veracruz (Churches)
    Chapel, WAA, 148
    Cathedral, CLM, 61
Vista Hermosa: Church, ASM, 59
Yanhuitlán: Convent, CSM, plate 39 (1550)
Yepapixtla (Morales): Convent, Agustinian, RSC, plate 5
Yuriria (Guanajuato): (Church) Augustinian, RSC, plate 5 (interior)
Zacatecas
    Cathedral, AM (4/62), ibc. (1761)
    Monastery of Guadalupe, CHL, 135
Miscellaneous
    Synagogues, LMJ, 82, 84
    First Protestant church in Mexico, CCS, 57
    Examples of churches, NG (2/76), 2-11

2. Ceremonies, practices, activities
    Religious ceremonial center, Zinacantán, Chiapas, CFE, 152-53
    Processions, San Miguel de Allende, SST, 86
    Ceremonies
        Chiapas, SST, 145
        San Juan Chamula, SST, 134
    Practices, POE, IV, 36-43
        All Souls Day, FWS, 105
        Corpus Cristi, AM (6/70), 40-43
        Day of the Dead, CIM, 578-91; NG (8/68), 146-47; Pátzcuaro, NCE, IX,
            779
        Easter, OLA, 198 (Michoacán)
        Feast of the Assumption, NG (8/68), 182-85
        "Fiesta for God," ECC, 107-10
        Fire purification, NG (12/75), 734-35
        Holy Week, AHC, 60-61; RWP, 42-43
        Palm Sunday, HNM (vol. 135), 878: San Luis Potosí, NMP, 34-35
        Witchcraft, LK (1/17/39), 16-17
    Worship
        Our Lady of Tonantzín, FWS, 72
        Virgin of Guadalupe, NCE, IX, 778; LA (1/10/38), 48; FM, 83-84; FWS,
            102; CE, VII, 44; SFT, 74 (her standard)
        Virgin of Zapópan, NG (3/67), 425; WHM, 74 (Guadalajara)
        Pilgrims, FM, 71-77
    Activities
        Blessing of the animals, NG (12/51), 820-21, (10/61), 479
        Baptism of medals, FCL, 212-15
        Marriage
            Tarascan, BCT, 184
            Zapotec, CIZ, 58
        Death
            Cemeteries, LF (1/9/50), 60; CE, VII, 42

Plows, BCT, 22; CCS, 2
Slash burning, WAM, 316
Farmer's strike, NG (5/78), 617
Products
Cattle, RCS, 166-279 pass.
Cotton, FWS, 14; ELA, 166
Garlic, WAM, 359
Grapes, RM, 131
Henequén, LUL, 115; SST, 156
Maize, WAM, 362; WHM, 38
Organ cactus, NG (7/30), 77 (fences); PMA, 17
Peyote, BIM, 120-21
Pineapples, NG (5/78), 632-33
Soybeans, NG (11/73), 684-85
Sugar, CLM, 578-79 (c.1840); BAR, 42; WAN, 325
Vanilla, AM (8/59), 13-16
Storage
Corn, NG (12/51), 798; AM (10/50), ibc.
Government, FBM, 586-87
Indian, WAM, 236

3. Business
"Bank on wheels," AM (7/56), 23-25
Bird sellers, FRM, 586-87
Bread delivery, SST, 105
Country store, GFF, 105 (1885)
Grass seller, OTM, 87 (Yucatán, 1885)
Pawnshop, AM (10/54), 12-15
Pottery venders, GFF, 418 (1885)
Supermarkets, AM (1/59), 32-33, (5/62), 34-37 (on wheels)
Wine carriers, AM (9/52), 26 (1860)

4. Markets, fairs
General, HAC, 179 (c.1850); GFF, 91 (c.1885); RM, 2-3, 84; NMP, 164-
65; AHC, 90; FBM, 178-79; SCM, 7-9; HNM (vol. 70), 383 (fair); WM,
48-64 (pottery); HMP, 42
Regional
Acaxochitlán (Hidalgo), TPM, 168
Chiapas, OLA, 231
Copala, TPM, 180 (outdoors)
Guadalajara, MIM, 41; LAP, V, 210; NG (10/61), 535, (3/71), 426, 434-35
Mexico City, NG (8/68), 174-75; LMG, 357; CCS, 50; WAA, 163; FWS,
78; HNM (vol. 49), 174 (c.1870)
Flea market, AHC, 200
Flower, NG (7/30), 47
Merced, WHM, 200
Stores, shops, CCS, 6
Supermarket, NBK (vol. 12), 252
Thieves, NG (7/30), 49
Oaxaca, OTM, 526 (1885); ESS, 98; NG (10/32), 491; AM (1/56), 11
San Cristóbal Las Casas, TPM, 197 (outdoor)
Tlapehuala, NG (8/40), 258-59
Toluca, BAR, 68; TPM, 148; NBK (vol. 12), 245
Zapotec, CIZ, 17, 37 (outdoor)

5. Dams
Aguascalientes, AM (12/52), 5
Amistad (Río Grande), RM, 142-43

Calles, BWS, 129
Culiacán, AM (7/61), ibc.
La Angostura, AM (4/49), 24
Malpaso, BOL, 145
Obregón (Yaqui river), WAM, 320
Sinaloa, AM (3/78), 38

6. Miscellaneous
Conservation, AM (4/50), 25-27, 46
Ejidos, CFE, 162-63, 166
Water pipeline (Guerrero), WHM, 35
Wind mills (Yucatán), NG (11/36), 638

VIII. Transportation, Communication

1. Highways
Scenes, AM (4/67), 33
Baja California, SST, 29
Camping sites (parks), CMC, 57-130 pass.
Chiapas, CFE, 24
Durango, AM (4/63), 23
Mexico--Cuernavaca, AM (1/58), 2
Mexico--Veracruz, AM (9/75), 15; NMW, 7-8 (c.1840)
Signs, CMC, 33-34
Sierra Madre, RM, 152

2. Bridges
Early bridge (c.1880), WNC, I, 185
Encarnación railroad bridge, GFF, 145 (1895)
Nuevo Laredo international bridge, WHM, 8
Puente Nacional (Antigua, River), CLM, 258-59 (c.1840)
Veracruz national bridge, OTM, 187

3. Railroads, BWS, plates 22, 23 (c.1910)
Chihuahua--Pacific, FWS, 141; SST, 20-21
Guadalupe, AM (9/75), 12-13 (c.1850); AHC, 94-95 (station)

4. Boats
La Paz, Baja California Ferry, SST, 38
Lighthouse, SST, 38
Papaloápan River, CMS, plate 26
Tehuantepec proposed canal (1884), CMS, plate 42; AM (7/59), 14-16

5. Air: Acapulco airport, FDT, illus. 84

6. Land
Carriages (c.1885), OTM, 56, 113
Mule packtrain, BNL, 424-25
Street car tokens, FCL, 216
Subway (Mexico City), AM (7/70), 30-35, (4/71), 13-19

IX. Miscellaneous

People
Handicapped workers, AM (11/60), 31-34
Strikers, BWS, plate 42

United States Embassy staff (1911), HNM (vol. 135), 519
"Wetbacks," NG (5/78), 635
Halley's Comet watching (1910), BWS, plates 44-45
United States astronauts in Mexico (1966), FWS, 3
Satellite tracking station, PLA, 170 (c. 1970)
United States Bicentennial exhibit, Mexico City, PAM, 148
Santa Clara colony of 300 Spanish War refugees, LF (7/2/40), 24-27

C. CENTRAL AMERICA

I. General

1. Flora, BTP, plates 66, 111, 183, 274
    Jungles, MCA, 91-115 pass.
    Tropical trees, HTT, 1-64 pass.

2. Fauna
    Animals, JAA, 38-134 pass.
       Monkeys, MCA, 103-15
    Birds, DFG, plates 1-48; DPT, 9-145 pass.; TND, 153, 321, 445, 534,
       671, 704-899 pass.; AGG, 21-94 pass.
    Butterflies, FFW, 7a-65a pass.
    Snakes, SSW, 46-135 pass.

3. Scenes, (c. 1895), HNM (vol. 91), 490-504, 731-38

4. Miscellaneous
    Highway building, LUL, 129
    Products, AM (4/52), 38-39
    United Fruit Company, MAA, 52-53 (the Board), 180-81 (officials)
    United Fruit Company women workers, JTG, 123

II. Costa Rica

1. Environment
    Geographical features
       Cartago basin, WAM, 450
       Central Plateau, SCR, 5, 10; LAP, vi, 185
       Cocos Island, AM (5/60), 31-34
       Gulf of Nicoya, HNM (vol. 20), 20-23 (c. 1855)
       Ojo de Agua, SCR, 46
       Pacuar River, WAM, 457
       Piñar del Río, EA (vol. 8), 297
       Puntarenas coast, SCR, 7
       Talamanca Mountain range, WAM, 52
       Talamanca River, NG (5/97), 150
       Tortuguero Island, MCA, 135-37
       Volcanos
          Arenal, OLA, 9; BBY (vol. 1969), 236 (eruption, July 1969)
          Poás, MCA, 64-73 pass.; AM (9/70), bc.
          San Pedro, HNM (vol. 20), 31 (1855)
          Turrialba, SPC, 10
          Irazú, CR, 13; OLA, 8; MCA, 62-63; SCR, 11, 63; NG (10/46), 427,
             440, (7/65), 123-37 pass.; AM (4/64), 23-27; EA (vol. 8), 50; LF
             (4/5/63), 32-33

Flora, fauna
   Flora, ARF, 116-408 pass.; NG (10/46), 454-56; SCR, 12-14; MCA,
      140-49; SPC, 1-21
   Fauna, NG (10/46), 454-55; MCA, 139, 146-47
      Birds, TND, 55, 789, 899; NG (10/46), 23-66 pass.; DPT, 29, 99-
         127 pass.; SBW, 174
      Snakes, SSW, 47
   Scenes, CCS, 197-217 (1885); HNM (vol. 20), 18-37 (c.1855), (vol. 75),
      668-86 pass.; NG (7/65), 122-51; AM (4/50), 20-21, (Aug.-Sept. 1973),
      32-33; LAP, iv, 183-93 pass.; WAP (Carib. vol.), 185-90

2.   Political
   Activities (1948), AM (3/49), 2-8, 42
      Women voters, AM (6/55), 306
   The military, AM (3/49), 2-8, 42
      Soldiers, LF (8/25/47), 36
   Coat of arms, EA (vol. 8), 50; SFT, 224
   Independence plaque, SCR, 20
   Flags, EFW, 47; SFT, 224 (adopted Oct. 21, 1964)
   Coins, FCL, 341; GCW, 86; CCW, illus. 801; AJG, 160-66
   Stamps, MDS, plate 94

3.   Cities, towns, villages
   Golfito
      Scenes, SCR, 19
      Port, Golfo Dulce, WAM, 460
   Puerto Limón
      Scenes, NG (5/1897), 144; SCR, 19
      Harbor, SCR, 47; CR, 15
   Puntarenas: Beach, NG (7/65), 150-51
   San José
      Scenes, SCR, 2-17 pass.; NG (5/1897), 147, (7/65), 126-27 (air); AM
         (8/59), 8-12, (Aug.-Sept. 1973), 32-33; WAP (Carib. vol.), 185; WBE
         (vol. 4), 860
      Capitol building, EA (vol. 8), 52
      Central American Institute of Public Administration, SCR, 62
      Durán Sanitarium, CR, 29
      Edificio Rex, CR, 9
      National Museum, WAP (Carib. vol.), 199
      National Theater, CR, 8; SCR, 39; NG (7/65), 128 (interior); AM
         (10/60), 3, (5/71), 3; IAP, vi, 192
      Post office, SCR, 29 (1930); CR, 7; AM (7/50), 31
      Union Club, SCR, 17

4.   Society
   People types, CCS, 203-15 pass. (1885); NG (10/46), 410-53 pass.; (7/65),
      127-49 pass.; AM (4/70), 30-31; WAP (Carib. vol.), 191-93
      Chinese (settlers), OLM, 136
      Indians, AM (1/53), 9-11
      Italians (colonists), AM (6/63), 38-41
      Quakers (colony), AM (3/10), 24-26
   Amusements (bullring), SCR, 35

5.   Culture
   Architecture, AM (10/76), 12-15
   Education
      University City, AM (11/59), 14-17
      National University, SCR, 32, 41; CR, 25; AM (2/62), 15; Chemistry

(vol. 75), 671 (1885); AM (6/56), 18-21
Ox carts, LUL, 154; SCR, 37-38
Railroad, Puerto Limón (begun 1880s), SCR, 57

III. El Salvador

1. Environment
    Geographical features
        Mountain: San Salvador peak, WAP (Carib. vol.), 165
        Volcanos
            Ilopango, WAM, 33; ELS, 7; HHE, 9; AM (1/73), 34
            Izalco, HHE, 8, 9; ELS, 4; ACL, 8; CCS, 191 (1885); AM (2/73),
                24-25; NG (5/28), 555; (11/44), 578-600 pass.; EBR (vol. 6), 731
            "Lighthouse," LUL, 146
            San Miguel, HHE, 8; WES, 144-45
            San Vicente, WAM, 424; ELS, 8; WES, 144-45; LAP, vi, 210; AM
                (2/72), 19
        Rivers
            Lempa (1853), SNC, 308
            Jíboa (valley), SNC, 313 (1853); AM (4/62), 10
        Lake: Coatepeque, HHE, 10; ELS, 12; EA (vol. 10), 262; AM (2/50),
            2, (2/73), 24-25
    Scenes: LUL, 148; CCS, 175-94 pass. (1885); LAP, vi, 210-19 pass.;
        QAP (Carib. vol.), 163-65; AM (7/49), 24-25, (5/59), 26-28, (2/72),
        19-24, (2/73), 24-25
    Disasters: Earthquake (1951), AM (7/51), 7-8

2. Political
    Revolutionaries (1811), AM (3/65), 10
    "Soccer War" victory celebration (1969), HHE, 16
    Officers Club, Military Polytechnical School, San Salvador, WES, 144
    Shield, national arms, SFT, 231
    Flag (adopted Sept. 27, 1972), EFW, 46; SFT, 231
    Coins, CCW, 399, illus. 800; AJG, 477-82
    Stamps, MDS, plate 95

3. Cities, Towns, Villages
    Chalatenango, LAP, iv, 211
    La Libertad, HHE, 7
    La Unión, SNC, 303 (port, 1853)
    San Salvador, LAT, 141; WES, 144-45 (1910, 1960); HHE, 13; WAP (Carib.
        vol.), 168; AM (7/49), 23 (air); (4/50), 30-31; (7/53), 17-19
        Independence Monument, WAP (Carib. vol.), 169; NBK, (vol. 5), 182
        Inter-Continental Hotel, ELS, 34
        Olympic stadium, NG (11/44), 583
        Parks, AM (1/68), 6-10
            Amapulapa, ELS, 10
            Atecozol, ELS, 14; HHE, 5
            Balboa, HHE, 12
            Libertad, ELS, 16; WES, 144-45; LAP, iv, 38; AM (2/73), 24-25
        Presidential palace, WES, 144-45; HHE, 25; EA (vol. 10), 260; AM
            (7/49), 24, (6/50), ibc., (2/73), 24-25; NBK (vol. 5), 184
        National Library, NBK (vol. 5), 180
        National theater, LAP, 16
    Santa Ana, AM (10/52), 6-8, 27-28; Government buildings, NNE, 21
    Sonsonate, AM (2/73), 24-25

8. Transportation, Communication
    Airport (Llapanga), EIS, 15
    Boats, CCS, 172 ("La Libertad," 1885)
    Bridges, NG (11/44), 602 (Lempa-Cuseatlán)
    Pan American Highway, HHE, 60; AM (4/63), 23
    Road building, NG (11/44), 614

9. Miscellaneous
    Boy's Town, AM (8/63), 12-15
    Honduras war refugees (July 1969), WES, 144-45

IV. Guatemala

1. Environment
    Geographical features
      Lakes
        Atitlán, NCE (vol. 19), 183 (c.1850); FEW, 306; LAT, 53; ACL, V,
          12; PMG, 132; GUA, 13; HPG, 4; BGL, 132, 156; KHG, 103; NG
          (7/45), 90, (10/47), 536-37; AM (1/50), 49, (2/50), 5, (Nov.-Dec.,
          1972), 24-25; EA (vol. 13), 544; WAP (Carib. vol.), 130
        Petén, MAM, 10; NG (11/74), 683 (Flores Island; air)
      Mountains
        Cuehumatanes, MAM, 6
      Rivers
        Cahabón, AM (7/60), 3104
        Chacón, BGL, 55 (Dragon rocks, c.1887), 324 (forest)
        Dulce, BGL, 41 (c.1887); SIT, 11, 50 (c.1840)
        Usumacinta, MAM, 8
      Valleys
        Chixoy, BGL, 114
        Esquintla, SIT, ii, 290 (c.1840)
        Totonicapán, BGL, 138
        Zunil, PMG, 126
      Volcanos
        Agua, MAM, 6; KHG, 97; SIT, ii, 267 (c.1840); BGL, 159 (c.1887);
          AM (6/53), 44
        Atitlán, MCA, 54-55; WAM, 404
        Coseguina, BGL, 399
        Fuego, BOL, 392 (c.1887); NG (10/47), 528
        Moyuta, BBY (vol. 1978), 417
        Pacaya, MCA, 36-37, 61
        Santa María, NG (10/36), 448, (11/74), 672
        Tolimán, WAM, 404; NG (10/36), 438
      Miscellaneous
        Central Savanna, MAM, 10
        Sulphur spring, BGL, 63 (c.1887)
    Flora, Fauna
      Flora, MCA, 27-45, 167-79 pass.; BTP, plates, 185-59
        Flowers, CFG, plates 1-50 pass.
        Rain forest, MAM, 13
      Fauna, MCA, 159-60
        Birds, SBW, 28, 33
          Quetzal, HNW (vol. 104), 156; BOL, 97; NG (1/69), 140-50
        Fish, WGA, 153, 402
        Iguanas, BOL, 47
        Snakes, SSW, 63, 83
    Scenes, AM (3/49), 18-21, (4/50), 28-31; POE, IV, 106-13; WAP (Carib.

vol.), 127-31; NG (11/74), 662-88 pass.; ENB (vol. 10), 987-93
Disasters
 Earthquake (1885), CCS, 64-85 pass.
 Earthquake (Feb. 4, 1976), NG (6/76), 810-28; AM (4/76), 17-18, 24,
  (10/76), 2-8; VEH, 160-62

2. Political
 Activities
  Alcaldes (4 officers), BGL, 146 (c.1887)
  Communists, LF (10/12/53), 169-77; KHG (1951), 58
  Guerrilla leaders (1916), BBY (vol. 1967), 382
  Presidential election (Jan. 1958), LF (1/3/58), 22-23
  Student demonstrations, BBY (vol. 1963), 423
 Insignia
  Coat of arms, EA (vol. 13), 544; SFT, 236
  Flag (adopted Sept. 15, 1968), SFT, 236
  Coins, FCL, 338; GCW, 232-34; CCW, illus. 795-96; AJG, 208-20;
   CTC, 8-28
  Stamps, MDS, plate 94
 Military
  Army, BHG, 29
  Forts
   San Felipe (Lake Isabal), KHG, 102
   San José, HNM (vol. 71), 896 (c.1885)
  Military academy (founded, 1873, Guatemala City), KHG, 67

3. Cities, Towns, Villages
 Antigua: Scenes, KHG, 51; NG (7/45), 101; AM (8/65), 10-19, (Nov.-Dec.,
  1972), 24-25, (5/74), 23-25
 Chicamón: Scenes, BGL, 109 (c.1887)
 Chichicastenango: Scenes, ACL, 94-95; WAP, (Carib. vol.), 129
 Cobán: Cabildo, BGL, 93 (c.1887)
 Esquipulas: Scenes, SIT, ii, 166 (c.1840)
 Guatemala City
  Scenes, CCS, 62-101 pass. (1885); HNM (vol. 71), 887-900 (1885); BGL,
   176-78 (c.1887); KHG, 88, 108; WAN, 407 (air); ACL, 90-91; LAP,
   VI, 229-37 pass.; NG (10/36), 435, (10/47), 536-64, (11/74), 674-75
   (air); AM (Nov.-Dec. 1972), 24-25
  Public buildings
   Bank of Guatemala, GUA, 8; EA (vol. 13), 550
   City Hall, EA (vol. 13), 550
   Civic Center, KHG, 107; LAP, VI, 229
   Congress, KHG, 64
   Grand Plaza (c.1840), AM (8/77), 9
   Hotels
    Alemán, BGL, 91 (c.1887)
    Nicolás de Ovando, AM (8/77), 22-28
   National Palace, LUL, 136; KHG, 65; GUA, 22; COE (vol. 11), 590
   Parque Central, NG (10/47), 530
   Social Security, GUA, 8, 32; EA (vol. 13), 550
   Supreme Court, NG (11/74), 675
   Theater, KHG, 93
 Isabal
  Scenes, BOL, 225 (c.1887)
  Castle San Felipe, AM (5/63), ibc.
 Livingston: Scenes, BGL, 27-28, 59 (c.1887)
 Matías de Galvés: Scenes, KHG, 112 (port)
 Panajachel

Scenes, HPG, 5-29 pass.
New hotel, HPG, 174
Puerto Barrios: Scenes, BGL, 61 (c. 1887); GUA, 44 (port)
Quetzaltenango
    Scenes, SIT, II, 204 (c. 1840)
    Central American Park, GUA, 15
San Antonio (in Lake Atitlán): Scenes, HPG, 4
San Cristóbal Totonicapán: Scenes, PMG, 22 (air)
San José: Port, CCS, 87 (1885); HNM (vol. 71), 887
Santa María Cauqué: Scenes, MCS, 10-204 pass.
Todos Santos: Scenes, PMG, 211

4. Society
People types, CCS, 103 (1885); KHG, 21-122 pass.; JTG, 12-35 pass.;
    HPG, 2-29 pass.; GUA, 11-35 pass.; PMG, 89, 139, 233; NG (10/36),
    430-53 pass.; (7/45), 89-104 pass.; (10/47), 526-64 pass.; (3/60), 406-
    16; AM (3/49), 18-21, (4/50), 28-31; (1/79), 27-31
Amusements
    Indian fiesta, LAP, VI, 231
    Cock fight, POE, IV, 108
    Kite flying, AM (10/76), 16-18
Children, BMCA, 112-13 (Atitlán)
Food (tortillas), BGL, 31 (c. 1887)
Indians, BGL, 275 (c. 1887); AM (3/54), 4-7; NG (7/45), 103
    Carib, BGL, 272-74 (women, children)
    Cobán, BGL, 99 (c. 1887)
Inoculation field unit, ALA, 63

5. Culture
Architecture, AM (8/69), 30-39
    Housing, KHG, 70-71; HPG, 26 (Panajachel)
    Homes of Indians, BGL, 30 (c. 1887); WIA, I, 122
    Slums (La Limonada, Guatemala City), JTG, 106-07
Crafts
    Fiber, OIC, 275-76
    Gourds, OIC, 328-29
    Masks, NG (3/60), 413
Education
    San Carlos University (Antigua), KHG, 5, 17, 122 (1930); NCE, V, 153;
        BMD, 186; AM (8/71), 24-25; CHL, 140
    Esquola de Cristo (Antigua), NG (5/28), 550
    Nutrition Institute, AM (2/60), 4
    Central American Institute of Industrial Research and Technology (Guate-
        mala City), AM (5/60), 21-23
Music, dance
    Dance of Conquistadores (Sololá), BNL, 136-37; AM (1/56), 31-35
    Marimbas, BGL, 123 (c. 1887); GUA, 50; NG (5/49), 31
Pottery, LUL, 137; WAM, 240; OIC, 313-14; PMG, 41; NG (5/28), 551
Textiles, HPG, 46
    Costumes
        Women, OIC, 93-267 pass.; PMG, 19-263 pass.
        Men, OIC, 155-265 pass.; PMG, 145-231 pass.
        Children, DMG, 109
    Embroidery, GEM, 6-73 pass.
    Huipiles, MAM, 173; AM (1/74), 2-6
    Weaving, SBL, 58; WAM, 404; BGL, 36 (c. 1887); MAM, 382; OIC, 26-
        92 pass.; AM (12/51), 20-22

6. Religion
    Edifices
        Antigua
            Cathedral San José, ESS, 118; KHG, 47; BGL, 161 (c. 1887); HNM
                (vol. 71), 899 (1885); HUA, 10; CEN, 85; AM (5/50), ibc., (4/71),
                23-25
            Convent Santa Clara, CGU, 11; CHL, 138
            El Calvario church, AM (4/71), 24-25
            La Merced church, NG (10/36), 444, 459, (10/47), 549, (2/50), 7
            San Francisco church, CHL, 140
        Chichicastenago: Santo Tomás church, ESS, 48; LUL, 138; BNL, 424-
            25; NG (7/45), 89, 91, (10/47), 553
        Cobán: Church, BGL, 94-95 (c. 1887)
        Esquipulas: Santo Cristo church, KHG, 26; BGL, 202 (c. 1887); NCE,
            IV, 829; GUA, 19 (Black Christ); AM (1/79), 26 (Basilica)
        San Mateo: Ixtatán church, NG (11/74), 686-87
        Guatemala City: Metropolitan Cathedral, NCE, IV, 829; GHU, 8; LAP,
            VI, 21; NG (10/45), 559, AM (Nov.-Dec., 1972), 24-25
        Quezaltenango: Church, BGL, 143 (c. 1887)
    Ceremonies
        Burial services, NCE, III, 235 (Huchuetenango)
        Copal use, NG (12/75), 754
        Easter, AM (3/55), 24-26
        Good Friday, NG (4/60), 408-09; AM (4/69), fc. (Antigua), (11/74),
            668-69
        Holyweek, GUA, 11 (Antigua)
        Palm Sunday, PMG, 116
        Processions, NG (7/45), 94-51; ACL, 78
    Miscellaneous
        Maryknoll activity, NCE, VIII, 470
        Saints, AM (5/71), 10-15
        Religious elders, NG (12/75), 178

7. Economy
    Industry
        Brick making, LUL, 134 (adobe)
        Shirt factory, JTG, 140
        Weaving (foot loom), PMG, 113
        Workers, BGL, 24, 198, 279 (c. 1887); Demonstrations, BIA, 144-45
    Agriculture
        Farming, NG (11/74), 662-63
            Irrigation, NG (12/75), 744-45
            Terrace, WAM, 403
            Truck, HPC, 11
        Plough (Indian), BGL, 356 (c. 1887)
        Products
            Bananas, NG (11/74), 677; United Fruit Tequisate plantation, LF
                (10/12/53), 172-73
            Cassava, BGL, 32 (c. 1887)
            Cattle, RCS, 176, 269, 272
            Chicle, LUL, 134
            Coffee, WCB, 4-389 pass.; GUA, 39; NG (11/74), 676; LAP, VI, 20
                (tasting); WBE (vol. 8), 405; NBK (vol. 7), 394
            Corn, NG (11/74), 680-81, (12/75), 728
            Forests, BGL, 50 (cutting, c. 1887)
            Rice, BGL, 356 (c. 1887)
            Sugar, BGL, 344 (mill, c. 1887)
        Markets, NG (2/29), 188, (7/45), 92-93, 102, (12/75), 752-53; PMG,

41-181 pass.
Antigua, LUL, 135; HAC, 289
Atitlán, AM (5/70), fc.; WAM, 239
Chichicastenago, LAP, IV, 232; EA (vol. 13), 546; AM (1/54), 41;
    BNL, 424-25; WBE, (vol. 8), 404
Guatemala City, AM (5/70), 6
Panajachel, HPG, 68
Sololá, NG (3/60), 441

8. Transportation, communication
Airport, "La Aurora," (Guatemala City), NG (5/28), 548
Bridges, BGL, 107 (rope, 1887); NG (2/29), 190; AM (1/61), ibc.
"Going to market," JTG, 19, 32, 36
Highway to Guatemala City, CCS, 92 (1885); HNM (vol. 71), 891 (1885)
Railroads, NG (5/28), 552 (construction)
Riding on Indian-back (silla), SIT, II, 274 (c.1840)

V. Honduras

1. Environment
Geographical features
    Bay of Fonseca, SNC, 96 (1853)
    Bay Islands, AM (6/54), 16-19, 43-45, (5/79), 8-16 (under water)
    Comayagua volcano, HNM (vol. 12), 724 (1850)
    Río Lindo, CBS, 15
Flora, BTP, plate 199
Fauna
    Birds, DPT, 6-51 pass.
    Fish, MGA, 153, 410
Scenes, CCS, 115-34 pass. (1885); HNM (vol. 9), 202-19 (c.1885); CNE,
    50-72 pass.; WP, 4-26 pass.; AM (6/49), 26-28; NG (3/42), 361-68;
    LAP, VI, 242-49 pass.; WAP (Carib. vol.), 150-53
Disasters
    Earthquake (1850), HNM (vol. 14), 164-73
    Floods (Sept., 1974), AM (3/75), fc.
    Hurricane (Sept. 14, 1974), AM (3/75), 20-24; AAY (vol. 1975), 173

2. Political
Coat of arms, EA (vol. 14), 336; SFT, 241
National flag (adopted 1/18/49), SFT, 241; EFW, 46
Coins, FCL, 136, 339; GCW, 236; CCW, illus. 798; AJG, 259-69
Stamps, plate 94

3. Cities, Towns, Villages
Amapala: Scenes, CBE, 70, 79 (port. 1915)
Comayagua
    Scenes, SNB, 122 (1853); SLR, 207 (1881)
    Independence monument, HNM (vol. 19), 604
Comayagüela: Scenes, CBE, 20
Guanaja: Scenes, CBE, 14 (air)
Intibucat: Scenes, SNC, 132 (1853)
Puerto Caballos: Scenes, SNC, 241 (1853)
Puerto Cortés: Scenes, CBE, 87 (air); HON, 10
San Antonio de Oriente: Scenes, CNE, 12, 52; WAM, 431; AM (12/52),
    9-11
San Pedro Sula
    Scenes, WP, 13, 26, 40

EA (vol. 14), 337; WP, 45-48; CEF (vol. 10), 213
Farming, EA (vol. 14), 339
Cattle, WP, 52, 54; RCS, 177-280, pass.
Corn, HNM (vol. 12), 723 (mill, 1850)
Timber, LAP, VI, 248; WP, 51-55; ACL, 100-01; ES (vol. 14), 343
  Mahogany, SNC, 172 (1853)
Markets, EA (vol. 12), 342; WP, 23 (San Pedro Sula)

8. Transportation, communication
Airports
  San Pedro Sula, WP, 57-58
  Tegucigalpa (La Ceiba), HON, 35
Highways, CBE, 68
  Pan American Highway (Río Goascorán), HON, 34; SLR, 164
Transportation, WP, 17-22, 55-60 pass.

VI. Nicaragua

1. Environment
Geographical features
  Volcanos, CCS, 162-64; AM (13/52), 21-23, 45-46
    Chonco, HNP, 8
    Concepción, AM (9/77), bc.; WAP (Carib. vol.), 178
    Consequina, NG (5/28), 559, (7/44), 176
    Momotombo, NIC, 5; AM (Nov.-Dec., 1970), bc., 24-25, (9/72),
      36; NG (5/28), 558, (5/32), 615, (7/44), 168, 180; LAP, VI, 250
    Mombracho, NBK (vol. 13), 248
  Rivers
    Escondido, WAM, 446
    Rama, WAM, 446
  Lakes
    Asososca, NG (5/32), 622
    Managua, NG (3/30), 318; WAP (Carib. vol.), 175, 177
    Nejapa, HNP, 5
    Nicaragua, LUL, 150; HNP, 6, 7; AM (9/72), 34-35; NG (3/30),
      314; WAP, (Carib. vol.), 178
Island: Zapatera, NG (5/32), 623
Scenes, CCS, 129-67 pass. (1885); NIC, 4, 25-27; AM (9/72), 34-37,
  (8/76), 16-17; LAP, VI, 250-57 pass.; WAP (Carib. vol.), 175-78
Disasters
  Earthquake (Dec. 23, 1972), AM (9/77), 13-18; HNP, 10; VEH, 99,
    172-73, 182
  Volcanic eruptions
    Cerro Negro (1968), WAM, 35; AM (2/73), 25-26
    Masaya (1850), MCA, 49; HNM (vol. 11), 749

2. Political
Insignia
  Coat of arms (shield), EA (vol. 20), 312; SFT, 265
  National flag (adopted 8/27/71), SFT, 265; EFW, 47
  Stamps, MDS, plate 95; WPB "volcano stamp," 299
  Coins, FCL, 340; GCW, 360; CCW, illus. 799; AJG, 413-14; SAC 7-
    57 pass. (paper money)

3. Cities, Towns, Villages
Corinto: Scenes, CCS, 140, 143 (harbor, 1885); HNP, 61 (port); NG
  (5/28), 559 (air)

El Castillo Viejo: Scenes, HNM (vol. 10), 60 (1853)
León: Scenes, HNM (vol. 11), 754-56 (1850); AM (8/76), 16-17 (air)
Managua
   Scenes, HNP, 8 (air, 1921); LUL, 151; NIC, 6 (air), 20-21; AM (8/76),
      16-17; NG (5/32), 603, (7/44), 175; EA (vol. 20), 313; LAP, VI, 225
      (air)
   Public buildings
      Capitol, HNP, 15
      Casino Militar, NIC, 16
      Central Park, AM (2/50), 3, (12/56), 29-32
      City Hall, EA (vol. 20), 316; EI (vol. 13), 162
      Inter-Continental Hotel, HAC, 300
      National Bank, HNP, 56
      Presidential Palace, HNP, 111; NIC, 16; WAP (Carib. vol.), 174
      F. D. Roosevelt monument, COE (vol. 17), 521
      Soldier's Monument, HNP, 28; NIC, 13
      Theater, Rubén Darío, LAP, VI, 256
      United States consulate (1885), CCS, 154
Nueva Segovia: Scenes, SNC, 354
Rama: Scenes, WAM, 446 (air)
Realejo: Scenes, HNM (vol. 11), 761-62 (port, 1850)
San Carlos: Scenes, NIC, 9
San Juan del Norte (Greytown): Scenes, HNM (vol. 10), 52 (1849), 54-57
   (1853)
San Juan del Sur: Scenes, NG (3/30), 313 (air)

4. Society
  People types, CCS, 145, 150 (1885); HNP, 35-60 pass.; NG (7/44), 162-89
     pass.; WAP (Carib. vol.), 179
  Indians (Mosquito), CCS, 145
  Negroes (Amerind village), OLA, 119

5. Culture
  Architecture: Hacienda, HNM (vol. 11), 745 (c.1850)
  Arts and artists, AM (2/54), 18-19
  Education
    Activities, HNP, 42-47
    Puerto Cabezas school (and children), HAC, 317
  Theater (Rubén Darío), LAP, VI, 256

6. Religion
  Edifices
    Granada
      Cathedral, AM (8/76), ibc.; EA (vol. 20), 317; LAP, VI, 257
      La Merced church, WAP (Carib. vol.), 182 (dome)
      María Auxiliadora chapel, NG (5/32), 605
      San Francisco church, AM (9/72), 37, (9/76), 16-17; NG (5/32), 606
    León
      Cathedral, CCS, 154; HNP, 12; NIC, 11; AM (9/72), 37, (8/76), 16-
        17; WAP (Carib. vol.), 181
      La Recolección church, LAT, 140
    Managua: Cathedral, NCE, IX, 141; HNP, 18; NIC, 7
  Ceremonies
    Holy Week procession, HNM (vol. 11), 758 (1850)
    Religious processions, NG (4/32), 608

7. Economy
  Industry

Brooms, EA (vol. 20), 319a
Cement, HNP, 58
Fishing, HNP, 14 (shrimp); AM (11/51), 12-15, 42-43
Gold mining, HNP, 55; EI (vol. 13), 160
Metal, AM (9/76), 5
Shoes, HNP, 58
Agriculture
Bananas, HNP, 14, 54, 60
Cattle, RCS, 174, 278
Cotton, HNP, 57 (factory); LAP, VI, 254; WBE (vol. 14), 316
Indigo, HNM (vol. 11), 746 (c.1850)
Mahogany, HNP, 10
Sugar cane, HNP, 51; ENB (vol. 16), 475
Markets, HNP, 3, 39
Managua, ELA, 234; LAP, VI, 251

8. Transportation, communication
Airport (Bonanza mine), BSA, 184
Customs house (Nicaragua-Honduras), LAT, 141
Highways
Building, HNP, 13, 571; AM (8/76), 16-17
Pan American, NG (7/44), 174; AM (4/63), 2
Ox cart, CCS, 141 (1885)

9. Miscellaneous
Battle scene (1848), ACL, 63
Canal route mapping, U.S. engineers, NG (5/32), 592-626 pass.
Satellite station, AM (1/79), 49
E. G. Squier expedition (1853), HNM (vol. 11), 745-62

VII. Panama

1. Environment
Geographical features
Almirante Bay, NG (11/75), 623
Barro Colorado, AM (7/53), 13-15
Chagres River, MPB, 90 (c.1880); AM (10/64), 16-19, 30-31
Gulf of Panama, WAP (Carib. vol.), 204
Darién Gap, AM (8/57), 22-26
Río Indio valley, NG (8/53), 287
San Blas islands (Pidertupo island), LAT, 53
Tobago island, EPC, 10, 11
Flora: Jungle plants, ABT, 48, 84
Fauna, MCA, 179; ABT, 69
Birds, TND, 55, 688, 789, 899; AGG, 23-63 pass.; DPT, 29-145 pass.
"Golden frog," LF (9/22/52), 123
Snakes, SSW, 47
Scenes, HNM (vol. 19), 433-53 pass. (c.1850); AM (10/49), 24-28, (1/51),
24-27, 47 (c.1850), (4/52), 9-11, 41-42, (10/53), 6-8, 30-31, 41-43; LAP,
VI, 261-71 pass.; WAP (Carib. vol.), 201-05; NG (3/49), 374-98, (8/53),
272-87, (3/61), 368-89, (3/70), 402-40; ENB (vol. 17), 201-03

2. Political
Coat of Arms, EA (vol. 21), 227; SFT, 271
Flag (adopted 6/4/1904), SFT, 271; EFW, 47
Coins, FCL, 342; CCW, illus. 803; AJG, 415
Stamps, MDS, plate 96

Founders of Republic (1903), MPB, 301
Forts
    Porto Bello, NG (11/41), 628; AM (June-July, 1971), 19
    San Lorenzo, AM (2/70), 2-7
Panama Embassy, Washington, D.C., AM (6/49), 5

3. Cities, Towns, Villages
Balboa: Scenes, EPC, 27 (harbor)
Bella Vista: Scenes, LAP, 262
Colón
    Scenes, EPC, 23 (air); PAN, 9 (air); NG (5/28), 572; AM (Nov.-Dec.,
       1971), 24-25 (air)
    Front street, MPB, 9 (c.1880)
    Municipal park, EPC, 20
Cristóbal: Scenes, EPC, 64 (harbor); WAP (Carib. vol.), 203
Old Panama: Scenes, EPC, 3, 19, 29 (tower); PAN, 4; NG (5/28), 571
    (air), (11/41), 595; AM (7/56), 3 (c.1826); LAP, VI, 261; WAP (Carib.
    vol.), 213
Panama City
    Scenes, AM (7/56), 4, 19-22 (air), (1/60), 36-39, (Nov.-Dec. 1970), 24-
       25, (June-July, 1971), 10 (1855), 18, (Nov.-Dec., 1971), 24-25; WAP
       (Carib. vol.), 205; AE (vol. 21), 228; EPC, 2, 9 (air); PAN, 7, 17;
       LUL, 169; HNM (vol. 90), 399; NG (5/28), 689 (air), (11/41), 602
       (air), (3/61), 370-71; EI (vol. 14), 31
    Public buildings
        Cabildo, NHM (vol. 19), 441 (c.1850)
        Legislative palace, APC, 42; PAN, 17; AM (7/65), 16
        Palace of Justice, APC, 17, 40
        Presidential palace, EPC, 41, 44; NG (3/30), 306
    Streets
        Balboa boulevard, EPC, 19
        Central Avenue, EPC, 20; LAP, VI, 266
    Plazas
        Cathedral MPB, 91 (c.1880)
        France, NG (11/41), 606
    Hotels
        El Continental, APC, 18
        El Panamá, AM (7/56), 22
        Hilton, EPC, 22; LF (1/7/52), 50-57
    Monument to Justice, WAP (Carib. vol.), 208
Porto Bello: Scenes, WAP (Carib. vol.), 202; NG (5/28), 570; AM (12/51),
    13, (8/76), 20-30 (ruins)

4. Society
People types: WAP (Carib. vol.), 206-07; APC, 46-60 pass.; NG (3/49),
    374-92, (11/41), 592-623 pass., (2/50), 228-46 pass., (8/53), 272-89
    pass., (3/61), 374-89; AM (10/49), 24-28, (1/51), 24-27, 47 (c.1850),
    (4/53), 9-11, 41-42, (10/53), 6-8, 30-31, 41-43, (1/60), 36-39
Indians
    Choco, NG (3/61), 374-87 pass.
    Cuna (San Blas), POE, IV, 114-21; PMF, frontispiece, 8-189 pass.;
       LAP, VI, 23; CEN, 146; BNL, 136-37; JSA, 101; EPC, 45; EA (vol.
       21), 233; NG (5/28), 567, (2/41), 194-219 pass., (3/70), 432-37; AM
       (10/49), 26, (3/70), 23, (7/70), 18-20; CEF (vol. 12), 135; EBR
       (vol. 3), 1108
    Quaymí, AM (2/53), 24-26
Amusements
    Carnival, NG (3/70), 418-19; AM (Nov.-Dec., 1971), ifc

Dancing (Indian), AM (11/49), 31-33 (Colón); HDA, 120 (drums)
Horse racing (race track, Panama City), EPC, 62
National lottery, NG (11/41), 597
Health
Leprosarium, AM (June-July, 1971), 16
Santo Tomás hospital, AM (10/53), 5

5. Culture
Architecture, WAM, 465 (Indian house)
Arts
Painting, SSH, 146-47
Weaving (appliqué), PMF, 38-240 pass. (Cuna Indians); KAF, 18-41
(Mola)
Dolls, PMF, 177
Education
University City, AM (2/52), 4
University of Panama, EPC, 52; AM (Nov.-Dec., 1971), 24-25; EA
(vol. 21), 231; WAP (Carib. vol.), 214; PAN, 24 (School of Agricul-
ture)

6. Religion
Edifices
David church, APC, 4
Natá church (1520), COE (vol. 18), 384
Panama City
Cathedral, HNM (vol. 19), 440 (c.1850), (vol. 131), 271 (c.1810);
WAP (Carib. vol.), 214; CHL, 141
Our Lady of Mount Carmen church, NCE, X, 942
Porto Bello church, AM (8/70), ifc
San José church, EPC, 51 (altar); MG (3/30), 308 (altar)
Ceremonies
Black Christ procession, AM (12/51), 39
Holy Week, EPC, 50
Idols for worship, PMT, 183

7. Economy
Industry: Plastics, AM (9/76), 5
Agriculture
Coffee, WCB, 129
Grain (elevators), PAN, 30
Dams
Bayano, BBY (vol. 1977), 549
Madden (Chagres River), EPC, 10

8. Transportation, communications
Highways, NG (3/61), 375-86 pass.
Pan American, WBE (vol. 15), 97
Trans-Isthmian, NG (11/41), 627 (construction)
Railroads
Panama Railroad, EPV, 31; JNM (vol. 18), 145-67; AM (2/65), 11-17
Stations
Gatún, HNM (vol. 18), 158 (c.1858)
Mamee, HNM (vol. 18), 164 (c.1858)
Paraíso, HNM (vol. 18), 168 (c.1858)
San Pablo, HNM (vol. 18), 164 (c.1858)
Bridges
Chagres River, HNM (vol. 18), 163 (Barbacoa)
San Pablo River, PAN, 13

9. Miscellaneous
    Canal Treaties signed (Sept. 7, 1977), RPC, 162-63
    Puerto de las Americas (opened 1962), AM (Nov.-Dec., 1971), 24-25

VIII. Panama Canal Zone

1. French period
    Scenes, MPB, 94-100
    Construction, NG (2/1896), 62
    Machinery, MPB, 93-100 pass.; ACS, 403
    Hospital, MPB, 94
    Graves, NG (2/78), 290
    Culebra Cut (1854), AM (Nov.-Dec., 1971), 24-25

2. United States Zone
    Scenes, AM (1/51), 30, (8/53), 24-27; ELA, 237; EA (vol. 21), 230
    People, NG (3/70), 402-11, 422-23; NG (2/78), 278-93 pass.
    Construction, NG (10/58), 579 (1906), MPB, 434-37, 326 (c.1910); LF
        (1/24/64), 37; ENB (vol. 17), 211
        Machinery
            Steam shovel, LF (1/24/64), 37
            Dredging (Gamboa), EPC, 38
    Locks, NG (2/78), 278-87 (machinery)
        Gatún, MPB, 525-26 (construction); AM (7/53), 13-15; EPC, 25; ACL,
            144-45; BNL, 424-25; EA (vol. 21), 236; MPB, 528 (official opening,
            1914)
        Method of use, LUL, 158; LF (2/30/39), 22-23 (U.S. Fleet passage)
        Miraflores, EPC, 7 (night), 26, 39; WAM, 469 (air); NG (3/61), 368-69;
            LAP, VI, 271; WAP (Carib. vol.), 215; CEF (vol. 16), 95
        Pedro Miguel, EPC, 36 (1910); EA (vol. 21), 235
    Cuts
        Culebra, NG (2/78), 286-87 (c.1908); AM (5/72), 20; MCA, 82-83 (con-
            struction); MPB, 327, 521 (slides), 528 (official opening, Aug. 15,
            1914)
        Gaillard, EPC, 27, 34-35
    Gatún Dam, EPC, 24
    Thatcher Bridge (opened 1962), APC, 63; EA (vol. 21), 237; NBK (vol. 15),
        49
    "Bridge of the Americas," BBY (vol. 1963), 631
    Laborers
        Labor types, MPB, 422-23 (c.1910)
        West Indian, MPB, 518-19 (c.1910)
    Administration
        Administration building, EPC, 37
        Canal Governor's residence (Balboa Heights), EPC, 43
        Post Captain's office, EA (vol. 21), 237
        Canal defense (Second World War), LF (11/6/39), 77-98
        United States air base, LF (3/17/41), 36-37
        United States sailors, LF (2/6/39), 62-65
        Zone housing (c.1910), MPB, 514
        Zone recreation (c.1910), MPB, 515, 519
        Gorgona school, EPC, 56 (1904)
        Gorgas hospital, AM (June-July, 1971), 17; APC, 56
        Zone official seal, EPC, 43
        Zone stamp, MDS, plate 96
        Yellow fever control, MPB, 428-29
    Miscellaneous

Flag riot, LF (1/24/64), 22-31
United States flag replaced by Panama flag (June 1978), BBY (vol. 1978),
575

D. CARIBBEAN AND WEST INDIES

I. General

1. Environment
Geographical features
   Leeward Islands, NG (10/66), 488-537 pass.
   Vacation spots, LF (2/11/57), 24-33
Flora, BTP, plates 71, 119, 135-99 pass., 241, 251
   Trees, HTT, 1-61 pass.; HCR, 26-76 pass.; PFT, 3-115 pass.
Fauna
   Coral types, HCR, 25-112 pass.
   Birds, TND, 225, 829, 858, 899; AGG, 25-90 pass.
   Fish, MGA, 148, 472
   Green turtles, NG (6/67), 876-90
   Sea shells, WAC, 231-317 pass.
   Seashore life, VSL, 19-152 pass.
Scenes, AM (June-July, 1977), 21-32, (June-July, 1978), 37-43 (buildings)

2. Miscellaneous
Cruising, LF (1/3/49), 28-44; NG (1/48), 1-56 pass.
Leeward Islands stamps, MDS, plates 106-07
Windward Islands stamps, MDS, plate 108

II. <u>Cuba</u>

1. Environment
Geographical features
   Coast (waterfront), LF (12/30/46), 36
   Isle of Pines, WIT, fr., 215
   Sierra de Escambray, WAP (Carib. vol.), 10-11
   Sierra Maestra, WIT, fr., 215
   Viñales valley, NG (1/47), 10, (1/77), 62-63
Flora, BTD, plates, 170, 199, 239
Fauna
   Birds, TND, 304; AGG, 26-67 pass.; DPT, 85
   Fish, MGA, 308
   Snakes, SSW, 50
Scenes, LAP, V, 155-64 pass.; LF (3/21/49), 108-13, (2/14/69), 620-28;
   ACL, 82-83; MKF, 118-19; HNM (vol. 43), 350-64 (1870); NG (1/47),
   2-56 pass.; WAP (Carib. vol.), 10-19; AM (June-July, 1978), 17-23;
   HCP, 5-63 pass.; BBY (vol. 1963), 302
Disasters: Hurricane "Flora," LF (10/18/63), 34-43, (11/1/63), 36b-36c

2. Political
Symbols
   Coat of Arms, EA (vol. 8), 294; SFT, 225
   Flags, EFW, 38
   National flag (adopted 5/20/1902), SFT, 225
   Presidential flag, SFT, 225
   Coins, AJG, 167-69

Palacio Gallego, WAP (Carib. vol.), 31
Pantheon of Basque organization, DAB, 146-47
Presidential Palace, NG (9/33), 363
Parks, streets
  Central Park, NG (1/47), 17
  Paseo de Isabel II, AM (10/73), 5
  Plaza de Armas, CLM, 269 (c.1840); AM (June-July, 1972), 2 (4/76), 12
  San Francisco Plaza, AM (9/53), 24 (c.1840)
Hotels
  La Rampa (once Hilton), BCI, 383-84
  Nacional, TCP, 1090-91
Monuments
  Bacchantes fountain, NG (1/47), 17
  Maine Memorial, LUL, 170; LA (5/19/61), 44-47 (removed)
Varadaro beach, NG (1/47), 44
Malacón, WIT, 162
El Vedado section, EBR (vol. 8), 669
Las Pozas: Scenes, HNM (vol. 6), 174 (1850)
Matanzas: Scenes, AM (June-July, 1978), 18 (1848)
Santiago: Scenes, NG (1/31), 13 (harbor), (9/33), 377 (harbor), BCI, 383-84
Trinidad: Scenes, AM (4/59), 12-17

4. Society
People types, HNM (vol. 43), 350-64 (1870); NG (1/47), 11-53, (1/77), 32-68 pass.; MKF, 118-19; POE, V, 16-27; WAP (Carib. vol.), 23; AM (1/52), 6-8, 43 (19th century), (4/59), 12-17; (June-July, 1978), 19-23; WIT, 19-293 pass.
Women, LF (5/5/58), 64-71
Workers, HNM (vol. 6), 169 (1850)
Life under Castro, LF (2/8/63), 40-40b, (3/15/63), 28-44
"High Society," LF (2/6/50), 114-19
Havana honeymoon of U.S. couple, LK (8/31/48), 28-33
Amusements
  Carnivals, BNL, 424-25
  Dancing (Afro-Cuban), AM (9/77), 30-32
  Folk Festivals, WAP (Carib. vol.), 36
  May Day celebrations, NG (1/77), 32-33; CEF (vol. 12), 146
  Sports, NG (1/77), 46-47
    Bull fight, AM (2/75), 29 (c.1850)
    Cockfight, WAP (Carib. vol.), 23
    Duck hunt, LF (12/4/39), 102-05
    Gambling, LF (3/10/58), 32-36
    Jai-alai, NG (9/33), 355 (court)

5. Culture
Architecture
  Housing, WIT, 37-38, 43-44, 174-75
    New, NG (1/77), 44-45
    Low cost, FDT, illus. 170-74 pass.
    Luxury, WAA, 157
    Slum (Havana), CEN, 52
    Farm, HNM (vol. 6), 164 (1850)
    Varadaro area, EA (vol. 8), 296
    Quinta Palantino house, FDT, illus. 168, 199
Education, CCT, 120-21; NG (1/77), 49, 51; WIT, 79, 96-114 pass.
  Cuba-Harvard teacher exchange, AM (3/51), 3-5, 43

9. Miscellaneous
    Americans leave Cuba, LF (1/13/61), 26-27
    Batista's planes load munitions (Guantanamo, 1958), LUR, 244
    Cuban refugees in Miami, LF (12/10/71), 36-41; AM (2/79), 13-15
    Cuban refugees go to United States, LF (11/5/65), 38-39
    "Model prison," Isle of Pines, WIT, 265
    Plane hijacking to Cuba, LF (4/18/69), 22d-29
    Revolutionaries (c. 1880), AM (1/73), 12
    A. H. Robins Company employees visit Cuba, LA (12/16/57), 125-26
    U.S. Senators in Cuba, AAY (vol. 1975), 200

III. Dominican Republic

1. Environment
    Geographical features
        Constanza valley, BCI, 383-84
        Jabaracoa national forest, HHD, 57
        Ozanco river, NG (1/31), 100
        Samaná Bay, AM (6/52), 17
    Scenes, AM (6/57), 16-20, (9/71), 24-25; HHD, 3-63 pass.; LAP, VI,
        165-71 pass.; ZCV, 32-33; NBK (vol. 4), 281
    Disasters
        Hurricane destruction (1930), NG (1/31), 109

2. Political
    Symbols
        Coat of arms, EA (vol. 9), 268; SFT, 276
        Coat of arms for City of Santo Domingo (1508), AM (10/76), ifc
        Flag (adopted, Nov. 6, 1844 and Sept. 14, 1863); SFT, 275
        Coins, FCL, 395-96; GCW, 400; AJG, 190-92, 485-95
        Stamps, MDS, plate 104
    Activities
        Civilian Junta members, LF (10/18/63), 50
        Civil war (1965)
            Revolt, LF (5/14/65), 30-38d
            Rebel parade, SBL, 29
            United States forces activities, LF (5/7/65), 85-88
            Inter-American Peace Force, AM (7/65), 1-3, (8/65), 41; BBY (vol.
                1966), 257

3. Cities, Towns, Villages
    Hato Mayor: Scene, BCI, 383-84
    Puerto del Conde: Scene, NG (1/31), 100
    Puerto Plata: Scenes, AM (6/52), 17, 18 (c. 1870); NG (1/31), 108 (air)
    Santo Domingo (Ciudad Trujillo)
        Scenes, AM (10/76), 18, 19 (late 18th century), (2/50), 37; EA (vol. 9),
            268 (air); WAP (Carib. vol.), 57-59; NG (1/31), 90, (10/77), 554-55
        Public buildings
            Capitol building, AM (6/51), 18
            Columbus palace, WAP (Carib. vol.), 58
            Palace of Fine Arts, AM (9/72), 24-25; HHD, 18
            Presidential Palace, AM (9/71), 24-25; HHD, 36
        Hotels
            El Embajador, HHD, 14
            Jaragua, AM (6/51), 17, (1/54), 4; NG (2/44), 216
        Avenida George Washington, HHD, 12; COE (vol. 8), 334
        "Monumental Zone," AM (10/76), bc
        Fountain of Lights, LF (2/11/57), 30

Santiago: City Hall, HHD, 29

4. Society
    People types, AM (6/57), 16-20; NG (2/44), 209-23 pass., (10/77), 529-65
        pass.; HHD, 3-63; WAP (Carib. vol.), 60-63
    Women's costumes, NG (1/31), 84-85
    Amusements
        Baseball, NG (10/77), 552-53; HHD, 42 (stadium)
        Golf course, NG (10/77), 562
        National lottery, NG (2/44), 199
    Health, AM (9/77), 7-12

5. Culture
    Architecture
        Homes
            Bohíos (native), AM (June-July, 1977), 10
            Middle class, NG (10/77), 543
            Workers', AM (6/51), 19
        Arts, AM (10/76), S-1--S-12
        Colonial, AM (5/51), 24-26
        Contemporary, AM (1/69), 32-37
        Casas Reales museum, AM (10/76), fc. (interior)
    Education
        University, HHD, 45; EA (vol. 9), 273; LAP, VI, 171

6. Religion
    Edifices
        Higüey, Our Lady of Altagracia church, WAP (Carib. vol.), 68
        Santo Domingo
            Cathedral, CE, V, 111 (façade); AM (6/51), 20 (June-July, 1977), 10;
                HHD, fr.; WAP (Carib. vol.), 65-67
            Our Lady of Mercy church, WAP (Carib. vol.), 69 (façade)
            Santa María La Menor church, NCE, XII, 1077; AM (June-July, 1967),
                9, (9/71), 24-25; NG (10/77), 554
        Santa Clara Shrine, NG (2/44), 210

7. Economy
    Industry
        Bauxite mining, ACL, 104
        Cigars, NG (10/77), 564-65
        Fishing, NG (10/77), 547, 551
        Salt mining, AM (3/56), 19-21; NG (4/44), 201
    Agriculture
        Bananas, EI (vol. 6), 79, 234
        Cattle, NG (10/77), 560-61 (roundup); RCS, 198-201, 266, ibc.
        Rice, EA (vol. 9), 270
        Sugar, WAM, 82 (central); ACL, 126; AM (4/52), 17-18 (mill), (9/71),
            24-25 (colonial); NG (1/31), 92-93, (2/44), 204, (10/77), 548-49; EI
            (vol. 6), 80
    Markets, LUL, 178; NG (2/44), 220; EI (vol. 6), 79

8. Transportation, communication
    Airport (Santo Domingo), AM (9/71), 24-25

9. Miscellaneous
    Industrial Fair (Ciudad Trujillo), AM (8/56), 32-34
    Miss Universe Beauty Contest (1977), AM (10/77), 23-24

IV. Haiti

1. Environment
   Geographical features
      Tiburón peninsula, WAP (Carib. vol.), 40
   Scenes, AM (12/49), 2-8, 13, (11/53), 28-29, (1/57), 7-10, (2/75), 2-9;
      NG (2/61), 226-52 pass., (1/76), 70-97 pass.; LAP, V, 176-86 pass.;
      WAP (Carib. vol.), 39-42; WH, 5-14 pass.
   Disasters
      Hurricane "Hazel," LF (10/25/54), 30-31

2. Political
   Symbols
      Coat of arms, SFT, 238
      Flags, EFW, 38
         National flag (adopted 6/21/64), SFT, 238
      Coins, FCL, 293-94, 407, 432, 434; GCW, 235-36; CCW, illus. 321,
         322; AJG, 221-58 pass.
      Stamps, MDS, plate 104
   United States Marines in Haiti (1929-1934), LF (7/14/61), 85
   Revolutionaries, AM (6/50), 10-11
   Revolution (May, 1957), LF (6/3/57), 40-41, (6/10/57), 41-44

3. Cities, Towns, Villages   •
   Cap-Hatïen
      Scenes, AM (3/72), 24-25 (19th century); NG (10/34), 475 (air), (3/38),
         304
      Independence monument, BNL, 424-25
   Jacmel: Scenes, WAM, 8; AM (2/75), 8
   Pétionville: Cabane Choucoune night club, WH, 62
   Port-au-Prince
      Scenes, LUL, 182; AM (12/49), 3-13 pass., (3/72), 24-25; NG (5/28),
         594, 596 (air), (1/31), 16, (10/34), 434-59 pass., (2/61), 228-37
         pass., (1/76), 78 (air, night); WH, 58 (harbor); NBK (vol. 8), 11
      Public buildings
         Chamber of Commerce, WH, 57
         City Hall, WH, 57
         Hotel Castelhaiti, WH, 63
         Legislative Palace, WAP (Carib. vol.), 42; WH, 27
         Palace of Justice, NG (1/31), 15
         Presidential Palace, NG (5/28), 595, (10/34), 437, (2/61), 237;
            WAP (Carib. vol.), 50
         Théâtre de Verdure, WH, 42

4. Society
   People types, LF (3/13/50), 98-104; POE, V, 56-63; WH, 28-62 pass.;
      WAP (Carib. vol.), 34-40, bc.; AM (11/53), 28-29, (2/56), 26-29
      (peasants), (1/57), 7-10, (12/54), 3-8, (2/78), 34-40, bc.; NG (1/31),
      10-19, (10/34), 446-49, 471-86 pass., (9/44), 309-27 pass., (2/61),
      226-59 pass., (1/76), 28-62 pass.; WAM, 172 (peasant women)
   Life under Duvalier (1957-71), LF (3/8/63), 26-35
   Amusements, WH, 43-45
      Mardi Gras, CEN, 87
      Night club (Pétionville), WH, 62
   Health
      Disease prevention, AM (5/55), 3-6

5. Culture

8.   Transportation, communication
     Travel, WH, 3, 58-60
        Bus, NG (10/34), 438
        Cart, NG (1/76), 80
     Roads, WA, 158
     Palace of Tourism (Port-au-Prince), AM (2/50), 5

9.   Miscellaneous
     Americans in Haiti (1915-16), HGD, 150-51
     U.S. Senatorial Commission, Port-au-Prince (1923), GMB, 101

V.   United States Caribbean

1.   Puerto Rico
     Environment
        Geographical features
           Phosphorescent Bay, NG (7/60), 120-29, (7/71), 51
           Rain forest, NG (12/62), 764-65
        Flora: Ferns, (Luquillo forest), KCF, 6-11, 23-119 pass.
        Scenes, BCI, 383-84; LAP, V, 243-55 pass.; WAP (Carib. vol.), 75-
           79; LF (3/8/43), 23-31, (1/24/49), 19-35; SWC, 1-87 pass.; AM
           (6/50), 2-5, 41, (5/52), 3-5, 41-43, (6/53), 10-12, (1/78), 10-16;
           NG (12/39), 698-738, (4/51), 420-60 pass.; WHP, 7-162 pass.; ZCV,
           9; PPR, 110-37 pass.
     Political
        Symbols
           Flag, EFW, 42
           Coins, AJG, 476 (colonial)
        Military
           El Morro, HWI, 38; LAP, V, 243; NG (1/31), 23, (4/51), 420; SHL,
              201
           Fort San Gerónimo, WPR, 64-65; WAP (Carib. vol.), 82
           La Fortaleza (Governor's palace), WPR, 64-65
        Government officials (1897), WPR, 64-65
        Members, constitutional convention, AM (5/52), 5
     Cities, Towns, Villages
        Arecibo: Radio receiver antenna, LF (11/8/63), 119-21
        Barranquitos: Scenes, LAP, V, 253 (air)
        Comerio: Scenes, AM (10/56), 2-4, ibc.
        Mayagüez
           Scenes, WHP, 60 (plaza)
           Hospital, FDT, 309, 310
        Ponce: Hospital, WHP, 122
        San Juan
           Scenes, WPR, 64-65 (17th century); LUL, 190; ACL, 163; NCE, XI,
              1018; WHP, 12 (air), 92 (harbor, 1625); BCI, 383-84 (air); NG
              (1/31), 24, 26, (12/62), 756-61
           Capitol, NG (4/31), 422
           Hotel Caribe Hilton, WHP, 115
           Old City, NG (4/51), 428
     Society
        People types, AM (6/50), 2-5, 41; SWA, 271 pass.; WHP, 7-162 pass.;
           WAP (Carib. vol.), 80-81; NG (12/39), 698-738 pass., (4/51),
           425-60 pass., (12/62), 758-93 pass.; PPR, 16-154 pass.
        Important people (1925), NFP, 92-93
        Jíbaros, AM (8/50), 20-21, 45
        Health

The islands
    <u>St. Thomas</u>, BCI, 383-84
        Charlotte Amalie, EBP, 59 (carnival)
        Bay, ECP, 63; HWI, 199
    <u>St. Croix</u>
        Christiansted, BCI, 383-84
        Old mill, ZCV, 76
    <u>St. John</u>
        Scenes, ZCV, 9
        Trunk Bay, HWI, 200
    Early Danish coins, AJG, 171-87 pass.

VI.   <u>British Caribbean</u>

1.   General
    Scenes, WAP (Carib. vol.), 88-92
    Stamps, MDS, plate 105
    Coins, AJG, 188-89, 207, 270-72, 433-508 pass.

2.   Anguilla
    Bay, HWI, 18

3.   Antigua, NG (1/70), 499-503
    Nelson's dock, HWI, 110
    United States base, LF (4/7/41), 82-83

4.   Bahamas
    Scenes, people, WAP (Carib. vol.), 108-12; ASB, 44-282 pass.; LF
       (2/3/67), 58-74; NG (2/58), 146-203 pass., (2/67), 218-67
    <u>Nassau</u>
        Scenes, EVP, 44-58
        Changing of the Guard, WAM, 3
        Government House, LSP, V, 49
        Harbor, LAP, V, 50
        Rawson Square, ZCV, 14
    <u>Bimini Island</u>
        Underwater archaeological discoveries, ZSA, 20-64, 146-65 pass.
    <u>San Salvador Island</u>, BCC, 123
        Lighthouse, ECP, 45
    General
       "Blue Holes" discovered by Cousteau, CTA, 152-256 pass.; NG (9/70),
         346-63 pass.
       Visit of Duke and Duchess of Windsor, LK (10/8/70), 18-21, (4/8/41),
         10-13
       Stamps, MDS, plate 110

5.   Barbados
    Scenes, AM (5/77), 30-31, (3/79), 23-29; MCJ, 63, 73 (c.1850); NG
       (3/52), 364-92 pass.; LBI, 1-24; ECP, 23-43
    Bridgetown
       Codrington College, LAP, V, 152; ECP, 42
       General hospital, ECP, 43
       Harbor, LAP, V, 53; HWI, 182; ECP, 23, 39; AM (3/79), 22-23
       Nelson's Dock Yard ruins, ECP, 27
    English Harbor, ECP, 29
    Industry

Solar energy, AM (10/77), 8
Stone quarry, WAM, 96
Agriculture: Sugar cane, WAM, 83
Miscellaneous
"Ra II" from Morocco, NG (1/71), 44-71
Stamps, MDS, 109

6. Belize
Scenes, NG (5/28), 553-54, (1/72), 124-26; WAP, 146-49; LAP, VI, 143-46
Belize City, WAP, 147 (air)
Legislative Assembly, WAP, 123
Coins, AJG, 121-22

7. Bermuda
Scenes, WAP (Carib. vol.), 113-14; NG (7/71), 96-121 pass.; ZCV, 9-10,
    17-18
Hamilton Harbor, IAP, V, 57
Tourists, LF (5/12/58), 117-22; LK (12/11/45), 40-42
Sunken ships
    British (Tempest, 1609), LF (3/23/59), 59-62
    Spanish, LF (1/9/56), 38-46
United States military station, LF (8/18/41), 61-68
Stamps, MDS, plate 110
Vincent Astor ranch, LF (1/29/40), 76-78

8. Dominica
People types, POE, V, 42-48
Water fall, HWI, 74

9. Grenada
Scenes, LF (1/11/54), 78-81; AM (9/77), 33-40, (8/78), 35-37, (1/79), 12-
    16; ZCV, 41
Peasant homesteads, WAM, 88
St. George
    Fort, EPC, 35-36
    Harbor, LAP, V, 144; St. George's Port, EPC, 35-36
    Market, HWI, 164

10. Guyana (Guiana)
Scenes, LAP, VI, 238-40; WAP (Ven. vol.), 161-66; NG (3/55), 330-41,
    (6/57), 852-74 pass.; LA (7/18/38), 31 (Kukenaam falls); EBR (vol. 8),
    508 (King George falls)
People types, GGP, 5-83 pass.
Flora, PTP, 66, 103, 119, 163; NG (10/32), 618-48 pass., (1/62), 134-39
Fauna, NG (10/32), 618-42, (1/62), 134-39 pass.
    Fish, MGA, 145-436 pass.
    Hoatzin bird, NG (9/62), 390-401 pass.
Products
    Cattle, RCA, 264-65, ibc.
    Bauxite, WAA, 195
Symbols
    Coins, AJG, 119-20
    Stamps, MDS, plate 101
Political violence, LF (7/19/63), 31, ifc., ibc.
Georgetown: Scenes, LUL, 427; WAA, 195

11. Jamaica
Scenes, LF (12/30/46), 40-41, (1/19/53), 89-97; LAP, V, 186-89; WAP

(Carib. vol.), 70-74; NG (3/53), 335-62 pass., (12/67), 842-73 pass.;
     AJ, 55-159 pass.; AM (10/69), 2-13, (4/78), 23; BCI, 383-84
People types, BJB, 1-96; AM (10/69), 2-13; POE, VI, 34-41
     Negroes
          Free Black elite, CSI, 340
          Free Black peasants, CSI, 355 (1890)
          Overseer, CSI, 254
          Owner, CSI, 258
          Punishment, CSI, 244, 248-49 (c.1837)
          Rebellion, CSI, 252 (1831)
          Slaves, CSI, frontispiece, 50, 136-241 pass.
     Kingston
          Harbor, WNC, VIII, 278 (1774)
          University of West Indies, AM (7/58), 8, (5/72), 3; FDT, illus. 281-315
               pass.
     Port Royal, NG (2/60), 152-83 pass.; NCE, XI, 598 (17th century); AJ, 37
          (1825); AM (7/54), 20-23, (12/62), 22-31
     Industry
          Bauxite, BCI, 383-84; WAM, 181; BAR, 136; BCI, 383-84
          Cement, PLA, 89
          Rum, CSG, 230 (c.1850)
     Agriculture
          Bananas, SB, 112-353 pass., 465
          Cane cutters, 274 (1890), 368-69 (c.1920)
          Sugar, CSI, 4-5, 134-70 pass.
     Markets, CSI, 284-85 (c.1840); BAR, 137
     Flora, BTP, plates 99, 168, 189, 271
     Fauna
          Birds, TND, 662; AGG, 67-72 pass.
          Fish, MGA, 147; LF (12/30/46), 42
     Miscellaneous
          Blue Mountains, LAP, V, 187
          Hurricane (August, 1951), LF (9/3/51), 34-37
          Independence ceremonies with Princess Margaret (1962), LUL, 186
          Mass baptism (1842), AJ, 37
          Visitors, LF, (3/14/38), 82-85
          Youth Corps, AM (4/63), 13-15

12. Nevis
     Scenes, AM (Nov.-Dec. 1978), 45-49, ibc.
     Old bath house, HWI, 128

13. St. Kitts
     Scenes, NG (1/70), 512-15; AM (Nov.-Dec., 1978), 45-48
     Basse-Terre, HWI, 109
     Sugar cane (c.1800), CSI, 52

14. St. Lucia
     Scenes, LAP, 139; LF (1/11/54), 83; ESL, 2-151 pass.
     Bananas, WAM, 87
     The Pitons peaks, FEW, 443, 663; BCI, 383-84
     Soufrière volcano, HWI, 145

15. St. Vincent
     Scenes, MCJ, 159-93 pass. (c.1850); LF (1/11/54), 82
     Kingston church, HWI, 163

16. Virgins, NG (10/66), 526-37 pass.
     Long Bay, WHI, 56

17. Trinidad-Tobago
  Scenes, WAP (Carib. vol.), 101-03; LAP, V, 260-65; BCI, 383-84 (air);
    NG (1/53), 37-75 pass., (1/57), 192-216 pass., (9/58), 429-40 pass.,
    (11/71), 690-701 pass., LF (1/11/54), 76-77; MTT, 6-79 pass.; BPP,
    17-104 pass.; ECP, 7-22
  People types, POE, V, 28-33; AM (3/63), 8-13, (4/63), 7-12
    East Indian Hindus, LF (12/30/46), 37; WAM, 2, 190
  Port of Spain, MTT, 40, 56
    Episcopalian church, WAM, 190
    General hospital, ECP, 18
    Hindu Mosque, BCI, 384
    Hyde Park, ECP, 7
    Kennedy Library, MTT, 72 (university)
    Parliament, MTT, 75
    Queen's Royal College, ECP, 19
    "Red House," ECP, 8
    Victorian House, LF (12/30/46), 37
    Whitehall (Prime minister's office), MTT, 33
  St. Augustine
    University of the West Indies, BBP, 72
  Scarborough, Tobago: Scenes, LAP, V, 260; ZCV, 72
  Pitch Lake, NG (1/31), 35
  Baiolet Bay, Tobago, HWI, 73
  Amusements
    Calypso steel bands, LF (2/11/57), 32-33; AM (2/77), 20; BPP, 88, 90-
      91; MTT, 6, 11; LAP, V, 151, 262
    Carnival, AM (2/77), 19-24, (4/79), 41-44, bc.
    Musicians, LF (3/19/56), 193-94
  Housing, BPP, 38-39
  Freeways, BPP, 44
  Industry
    Bananas, SB, 25-352 pass.
    Oil refinery, PPB, 1023
    Solar energy, AM (10/77), 8
  Flora, BTP, plate 29
  Fauna
    Birds, TND, 257
    Fish, MGA, 232-97 pass.
  Stamps, MDS, plate 109
  Miscellaneous
    U.S. military base, LF (4/7/41), 77-81
    Visit of Princess Margaret, LF (2/21/55), 27-35

VII. Dutch Caribbean

1. General
  Scenes, WAP (Carib. vol.), 184-87; NG (1/70), 115-46 pass.; HNA, 17-96
    pass.
  Symbols
    Stamps, MDS, plate 111
    Coins, AJG, 170, 193, 484

2. Surinam (Dutch Guiana)
  Scenes, JSA, 124; AM (10/51), 13-16, (4/79), 5-7; LAP, VI, 308-13; WAP
    (Ven. vol.), 167
  Paramaribo
    Scenes, BHS, 193

Kersten Hotel, LAT, 43
Geographical features
Bonito Peak, FEW, 488
Corantijn River, FEW, 489
Bush negroes, AM (10/54), 6-8, 40-43; ESA, 148
Bauxite, LUL, 428-29; TFS, 102 (Aluminum Company); ESA, 130
Market (vegetables), AWW, 196

3. Islands
Aruba: Scenes, NG (1/70), 126-33 pass.
Bonaire: Scenes, NG (1/70), 135
Curaçao
    Scenes, JSA, 121-23; LAP, V, 145; HWI, 17; NG (1/70), 114-21
    Willemstad, BCI, 383-84; WAM, 9, 208 (harbor; air); ZCV, 57
Saba: Scenes, LF (1/11/54), 88; AM (10/35), 21-25; NG (1/70), 140-45,
    518-21
St. Eustatius
    Scenes, NG (1/70), 138-39
    Quill volcano, RCI, 383-84
Sint Maarten (St. Martin): Scenes, NG (10/66), 522, (1/70), 134-36

VIII. French Caribbean

1. General
Scenes, WAP (Carib. vol.), 93-100
Stamps, MDS, plate 111
Coins, AJG, 205-06, 273, 496

2. Guyane (Guiana)
Scenes, LAP, VI, 222-24; WAP (Ven. vol.), 168
Rain forest, ABT, 15-52 pass., 183
Devil's Island, NG (2/49), 259 (air); JIV, 29; LA (6/12/39), 65-71

3. Islands
Guadalupe: Scenes, LA (1/11/54), 86-87; POE, V, 70; NG (1/70), 493-97;
    ZCV, 36
Pointe-à-Pitre
    Harbor, BCI, 383-84
    Landholdings, BCI, 383-84
    Scenes, WAM, 121 (air); NG (10/66), 494-97 (air)
Martinique
    Scenes, ABT, 42; POE, V, 70; NG (5/58), 41, (2/59), 256-82 pass.,
    (1/75), 124-49
    Fort-de-France
        Scenes, HWI, 91
    Shore, BCC, 148
St. Barthélemy: Scenes, NG (10/66), 522
St. Martin: Scenes, NG (10/66), 522

E. SOUTH AMERICA

I. General (see also individual countries)

1. Geographical features
    a. Mountains

Andes, LF (8/2/48), 46-58; BNL, 136-37; NG (10/72), 445; BAR, 320; WAP (Arg. vol.), 42-43

Huascarán, LAP, VI, 57
Roraima, NG (11/30), 599-60
Torre Egger, NG (12/76), 812-23 (climbing)
Uspalleta Pass, NG (5/31), 602, 605

b. Volcanos
Lanvín, LAP, VI, 11
Sangay, NG (10/72), 448

c. Lakes
Andes lakes, LUL, 29-307, pass.
Lake of the Inca, AM (1/73), 39
Titicaca, HNM (vol. 36), 565, (vol. 37), 17-28 pass.; AM (2/67), 27; EA, IV, 165; WAP (Br. vol.), 190; NG (2/71), 274-91 pass., (12/73), 730-71 pass.; POE, VII, 80-86; BGK, 86 (reed boats); EBR (vol. 17), 85

d. Rivers
La Plata, BAR, 369 (estuary)
Paraná and Paraguay, MED, 549 (air)

e. Falls
Iguazú (Iguassú), JSA, 113; BHS, 162; FFS, 497; LAT, 11, 147; EA, II, 260; CLA, 14; BNL, 136-37; MED, 572 (air); CEN, 246; NG (4/33), 286, (3/58), 298-99, (9/62), 342-43, (3/75), 303 (air), 304-05; AM (11/49), 19, (5/63), 6, (3/68), 3-7, (Nov.-Dec., 1977), 49 (night); EBR, (vol. 17), 99
Guairá (on Paraná), AM (2/75), 24-25

f. Strait of Magellan, LAP, VI, 165; NG (10/32), 69, (6/76), 730-31; AM (2/64), 42; MED, 482-84; HNM (vol. 82), 442-60 (1890); (vol. 149), 587; JSA, 51; CHF, 130-31
Seal Island, NG (1/67), 84-85

g. Tierra del Fuego
Scenes, WAA, 139; CMF, 142; EA, II, 259; NG (12/37), 752-77 pass., (3/58), 350-51, (2/64), 35-42; AM (12/55), 13-16, (10/57), 14-18; ERB (vol. 17), 82
Beagle Channel, (10/69), 454-55, (10/75), 324; WAP (Arg. vol.), 61
Marinelli glacier, LF (6/1/59), 72-73

2. Flora, Fauna
a. Flora
Pollen, spores, MPF, 2-10, plates 1/43
Tierra del Fuego plants, LF (6/1/59), 74-78
Tropical trees, NTT, 1-54 pass.

b. Fauna, JAA, 38-174 pass.; LF (2/26/59), 46-57; ABT, 64
Alpaca, PWL, frontispiece, 82-83
Birds, MGB, plates 1-50 pass.; TND, 57-899 pass.; AGG, 13-94 pass.
Butterflies, FFW, 7a-60c pass.
Chulengos, PWL, 24
Condor, NG (5/71), 686-709 pass.
Guanaco, PWL, 8-38 pass., 86
Insects, LIW, 57, 188-146 pass., 219, 309, 351
Llama, PWL, 9-85 pass.; AM (7/58), 32-34
Mosquito (malarial), LIW, 365
Rhea (ostrich), GHS, 516
Snakes, SSW, 46-139 pass.
Vicuña, NG (1/73), 76-91; AM (3/69), 2-7; PWL, 44-95 pass.

II. Argentina

1. Environment

a. Geographical features
    Mountains
        Aconcagua, HNM (vol. 100), 112-30 (c.1895), (vol. 118), 175-85
            (1906); NG (2/29), 108, (5/31), 6-616, pass., (1/67), 96-97,
            (10/72), 445, (3/75), 300-01; AM (4/75), 9; HNM (vol. 75), 571;
            WAP (Arg. vol.), 43; LAP, VI, 79; CCS, 506 (1885); BCP, 6
        Cerro Boneto, ARG, 4
        Cerro Fitz Roy, WAP (Arg. vol.), 48-49
        Córdoba mountains, AM (1/50), 27
        Maimara Hills, NG (3/75), 326-27
        Sarmiento, HNM (vol. 82), 442 (1890), (vol. 100), 223-28 (c.1895);
            AM (6/62), 18 (1838)
        Uspallata Pass, HNM (vol. 17), 89 (1850)
        Vallecitos, AM (6/75), ibc.
    Glaciers
        Moreno, NG (1/67), 82-83
        Patagonia, CHI, 7
    Lakes
        Andes lakes, JSA, 14
        Huechulafquen, ESA, 30
        Mascardi, ARG, 4
        Nahuel Huapí, NG (3/75), 318-19; LAP, VI, 81; LAT, 61
        San Roque, WAP (Arg. vol.), 69
    Rivers
        Grande de Jujuy, WAP (Arg. vol.), 46
        Limay, WAP (Arg. vol.), 26
        Río del Pluma, LEL, 160-61
        Río de la Plata, AM (3/56), 27-29, (6/59), 8-12
    Pampa, LUL, 18, 332-33; ARG, 26; LA (11/30/36), 54
    Desert, Norte Chico, TFS, 255
    National Parks
        Nahuel Huapí, WAP (Arg. vol.), 37, 144; NG (1/67), 92-93
        Torres del Paine, NG (1/67), 74-75
    Puente del Inca, LEL, 160-61
    Point Pirámides (Patagonia), NG (10/69), 471-72
    Strait of Magellan
        Point Famine, CCS, 526 (1885)
        Cape Forward, CCS, 517 (1885)
    Falkland Islands
        Scenes, NG (3/56), 387-416; WAP, 214-16
        Harbor, NG (1/48), 134
b. Flora
    Trees, ENI, 208-47
c. Fauna
    Birds, TND, 175, 304, 698-718 pass.; AGG, 301; DPT, 11-137 pass.
    Fish, MGA, 226, 238, 302
    Locusts, LEL, 160-61; LF (10/13/47), 42-43 (plague)
    Pampa fauna, LEL, 160-61
    Patagonia fauna, NG (3/76), 290-332 pass.
    "Right Whales," NG (10/72), 576-87
    Snakes, SSW, 46
d. Scenes, NG (11/67), 662-95 pass., (3/75), 296-333; WAP (Arg. vol.),
        36-77 pass.; LAP, VI, 64-94 pass.; AM (1/64), 36-38; ENB (vol. 2),
        358-71 pass.
    Córdoba province, AM (7/55), 28-31
    Patagonia, WAP (Arg. vol.), 44-45; LAP, VI, 80; HNM (vol. 118), 336-
        47 (c.1908), (vol. 119), 127-36 (1908), (vol. 121), 53-61, (vol.
        122), 813-37 (c.1910)
        Prison, NG (12/37), 768

2. Political
  a. Symbols
      Coat of Arms, SA, II, 255; SFT, 211
      State Seal, CET, 703 (c.1907)
      National flag (adopted 7/25/1816), SFT, 211
      Presidential flag, SFT, 211
      Coins, AJG, 12-54; GCW, 26-29; CCW, 812;
        Buenos Aires, FCL, 313-14
        River Plate Provinces, FCL, 224
        Mendoza (1823), FCL, 227-28
      Stamps, MDS, plate 97, 112
  b. Activities
      Anti-Perón, LF (9/12/55), 35-43, (7/4/55), 14-15
      Government Junta, (1977), AAY (vol. 1977), 99
      Independence celebration, NG (11/67), 682-83
      Peronistas, LF (1/5/59), 26-27
      Political rally for Pres. Héctor Cámpora, NG (3/75), 332-33
  c. Military
      Forts
        Buenos Aires (1820), AM (4/60), 33
        Cabo Alarcón, AM (June-July, 1973), 14
        Pampa (1850), HNM (vol. 17), 773
      Soldiers (in Spanish Civil War), LF (11/30/36), 57

3. Cities, Towns, Villages
  Alta Gracia: Scenes, AM (3/73), 24-25
  Bahia Blanca: Scenes, AM (6/61), 15; WAP (Arg. vol.), 126
  Buenos Aires
    Scenes, AM (9/53), 9-11, (3/55), 30 (air), (6/55), 12-16, (4/59), 7-11,
      (Nov.-Dec. 1970), 24-25, (2/72), 31 (1930), (8/72), 2-8, (9/72), 19,
      (5/73), 22 (1943, air); LAP, VI, 84-87; WAP (Arg. vol.), 38-105
      pass.; ARG, 10 (air); ELA, 190 (night); NHM (vol. 75), 895-902
      pass. (c.1875); BAR, 311; CRH, 34-35 (c.1800); CCS, 544 (1885);
      LF (11/30/36), 50-51; NG (1/31), 76, (5/31), 597-98 (air), (11/39),
      562-600 pass., (11/67), 666-67, 678-79 (air), (3/75), 298-99 (air)
    Public Buildings
      Cabildo, AM (10/49), bc., (3/75), 15; ARG, 23; BNL, 24-25
      Capitol, BNL, 424-25; GHS, 488; NG (2/29), 136, (3/30), 265, (11/39),
        598; LAP, VI, 14; AM (7/65), 13; JSA, 35; EA, II, 71; EBR (vol.
        3), 448
      Colón Theater, WAP (Arg. vol.), 142; LAP, VI, 85
      Jockey Club, LF (5/3/48), 130-36
      Museum of Decorative Arts, AM (5/66), 22
      Presidential Palace, CCS, 570 (1885); WAP (Arg. vol.), 116-17
      Soccer stadium, LAP, 86
    Other buildings
      Cavanagh, AM (3/53), 31; NG (11/39), 554; WAP (Arg. vol.), 119
      La Prensa, AM (3/75), 15
    Streets
      Corrientes, AM (7/59), 10
      Florida, LAP, VI, 44; JSA, 34; LUL, 322; PLA, 163
      Mayo, AM (3/75), 12 (avenue)
      9th of July, FFS, 496-97; ESA, 26; LUL, 323; ELA, 243
    Parks
      Lezama, LEL, 160-61
      Palermo, NG (11/39), 593-97, (1/67), 98 (air), (11/67), 684
      Plaza de Mayo, AM (3/75), 16 (1875), ibc.; BHS, 146; ESA, 16;
        ELA, 216; NG (11/39), 582; CEN, 5

Plaza San Martín, HNM (vol. 82), 499 (1890)
Zoological Gardens, LEL, 160-61; WAP (Arg. vol.), 91
Monuments
    Chacabuco Battle, WAP (Arg. vol.), 112-13
    Gaucho, WAP (Arg. vol.), 87
    Independence, NG (1/31), 78
    Obelisk, AM (7/50), fc.
Book stalls, AM (5/62), 27
La Boca, WAP (Arg. vol.), 92-97 pass.
La Recoleta cemetery, POE, VI, 68
Plan of city, LUL, 321
Subway, NG (11/39), 287
Underground garages, NG (11/39), 586
Comodoro Rivadavia: Scenes, WAP (Arg. vol.), 59 (air)
Córdoba
    Scenes, AM (1/50), 24-27; ARG, 18; WAP (Arg. vol.), 58
    Cabildo, AM (11/59), 10, (4/60), 36
    Palace of Justice, AM (1/50), 39
    Riviera Indarte theater, WAP (Arg. vol.), 137
    Viceroy's palace, AM (11/59), 10 (interior)
Corrientes
    Scenes, NG (3/75), 306-07
    Cabildo (1890), HNM (vol. 83), 41
El Turbio: Scene, WAP (Arg. vol.), 51
Jujuy: Scene, WAP (Arg. vol.), 50
La Plata
    Plaza Moreno, LAP, VI, 89
    Basque gateway, LEL, 160-61
Las Palmas: Scene, LEL, 160-61
Mar del Plata: Scenes, AM (6/70), ifc.; ESA, 38; EA, II, 257; NG
    (3/75), 312-13; POE, VI, 64-65; LAP, VI, 90; ESA, 34 (fishing boats);
    ARG, 12; NBK (vol. 1), 395
Mendoza
    Scenes, AM (4/75), 8, 14-16; NG (5/31), 630 (air); WAP (Arg. vol.), 53
    Army of Andes monument, AM (9/65), 19
    San Martín park, ES (vol. 17), 30
Paraná
    Asociación Español, RPS, 168-69
    City hall, RPS, 168-69
    La Playa Central, RPS, 168-69 (air)
    Public library, RPS, 168-69
    Russian-German people, RPS, 168-69
Port Desire: Scenes, MED, 367
Puerto San Julián: Scenes, MED, 370
Punta Arenas: Scenes, HNM (vol. 82), 458 (1890)
Río Grande: Scenes, WAP (Arg. vol.), 62
Rosario: Scenes, WAP (Arg. vol.), 52
San Carlos de Bariloche (resort)
    Scenes, AM (3/74), 34, (5/74), 10-15; ESA, 36, 40; WAP (Arg. vol.),
        57; AM (9/78), 36, 37; NBK (vol. 1), 392
    Ski shelter, ARG, 19
Santa Isabel: Scenes, LEL, 160-61 (1883, 1888)
Tucumán
    Scenes, AM (5/57), 12-17; WAP (Arg. vol.), 64
    House where independence was declared (1816), AM (11/66), 1
Ushuaía: Scenes, AM (10/59), 15-19; LAP, VI, 65; WAP (Arg. vol.), 60

4. Society

Folk art, AM (5/69), 35-41
Film festival (Mar del Plata), AM (6/70), 18
Museums
    Decorative art (Buenos Aires), AM (5/66), 22
    La Plata museum, LEL, 160-61
Recent developments, AM (12/61), 24-27
  c. Educational Institutions
Buenos Aires
    Basque school and orphanage, DAB, 146-47
    Colegio Nacional (late 19th century), AM (7/66), 13
    Petronila Rodríguez (1890), HNM (vol. 82), 505
    School of Law and Social Sciences, ARG, 28
Córdoba
    Monserrat National High School, AM (1/69), 16
    University of San Carlos, AM (4/70), 16
Cuyo: University, AM (4/75), 12
Paraná: Normal school, AM (4/73), 11-13
  d. Music, drama
Actors, AM (2/56), 22-23, (1/58), 12-17, (11/62), 32-51; NG (11/67),
    691 (street actors)
Musicians
    "Camerata Bariloche," AM (7/66), 39
    "Los Chalcholeros," AM (7/66), 39
    Louis Armstrong's band (Buenos Aires), LF (11/25/57), 169-70
Singers
    "Little Singers," AM (3/66), 41 (Córdoba)
    Opera, AM (10/64), 35-38 (Buenos Aires)
Theaters
    Buenos Aires: Colón Theater, HNM (vol. 75), 895 (1875); CCS, 554;
      NG (2/29), 137-38, (10/32), 727, (11/67), 692-93 (interior); EA,
      II, 269 (interior); BHS, 138 (interior); SBL, 61 (interior); WAP
      (Arg. vol.), 142; LAP, VI, 85; AM (1/71), 17-19
    Córdoba: Riviera Indarte Theater, WAP (Arg. vol.), 137
    Corrientes: Repertory Theater, AM (1/62), 23-25 (visit of U.S. ac-
      tors)

6. Religion
  a. Edifices
Buenos Aires
    Cathedral, CCS, 567 (1885); CE, II, 35; HNM (vol. 75), 902
    San Francisco Basilica, NCE, I, 782
Córdoba
    Candonga church, AM (1/50), 25
    Cathedral, LUL, 338; CHL, 180 (tower)
    Corazón de María church, AM (1/50), 26
    Jesuit church, AM (4/70), 16
Jujuy: Cathedral, LAP, VI, 94
La Plata: Cathedral, NCE, VIII, 383
Luján: Cathedral, NCE, I, 783
Paraná: Cathedral, RPS, 168-69
Salta
    Cathedral, WAP (Arg. vol.), 123
    San Bernardo convent, ARP, 14 (entrance)
  b. Religious festival, Paraná, RPS, 168-69

7. Economy
  a. Industry
General, WAP (Arg. vol.), 75; AM (11/59), 10-13 (Córdoba)

(1/12/53), 11-15
La Prensa newspaper closed by Perón, LF (3/12/51), 24-25
Observation of eclipse (May 20, 1947), NG (9/47), 280-324 pass.
Rescue of Swedish Antarctic expedition (1903), AM (8/76), 7-15

III. Bolivia

1. Environment
    a. Geographical features
        Mountains
            Andes, HNM (vol. 36), 545-65 (c.1860), (vol. 37), 16-32; EBR (vol.
                17), 80
            Cerro Rico Potosí, NG (3/43), 320, (1/66), 189, (7/66), 2
            Huayna Potosí, NG (10/50), 482
        Volcanos
            Huayna, AM (5/73), 9
            Illimani, AM (5/73), 9; NG (1/66), 172-73
        Lakes
            Green Lake (Laguna Verde), NG (12/73), 743
            Red Lake (Laguna Colorada), NG (12/73), 742-43
            Salt Lake (Salar de Uyuni), AM (10/54), 24-26
            Titicaca, NG (10/50), 483-96 pass., (11/66), 668; BBP, 10-11; LUL,
                16; CCS, 424 (1885); AM (10/50), 22 (air), (5/78), ifc., 13
                Strait of Tequina, LAT, 144
        Rivers
            Mamoré, ENB (vol. 3), 876
            Pastanza, LF (8/2/48), 48
        Altiplano, NG (3/43), 334, (10/50), 484; JSA, 83; BWG, 233; AM
            (9/53), 21-23, (2/69), 1-9; LAP, V, 98-107 pass.
        "Moon Valley," AM (10/73), 24-25
        Guano islands, CCS, 432-35 (1885)
    b. Fauna
        Birds, APT, 9-137 pass.
    c. Scenes, WAP (Br. vol.), 189-97; NG (10/50), 481-96 pass., (9/64),
        314-21 (air), (1/66), 153-95; AM (10/73), 24-25, (5/78), 11-16; CCS,
        417-51 pass. (1885); ENB (vol. 3), 878-86

2. Political
    a. Symbols
        Coat of arms, EA, IV, 163; SFT, 216
        Flag (adopted 7/14/88), SFT, 216; EFW, 50
        War ensign, SFT, 216
        Coins, FCL, 310-11; GCW, 53-55; CCW, illus. 810; AJG, 56-76 pass.
        Stamps, MDS, plate 98
    b. Activities: Chamber of Deputies session, NG (3/43), 331
    c. Military
        Soldiers (1885), CCS, 447
        Guerrillas, NG (10/72), 470

3. Cities, Towns, Villages
    Charcas: Scenes, AM (3/76), 6-7
    Copacabana: Scenes, AM (6/61), 38; NG (10/50), 494 (air)
    La Paz
        Scenes, NG (3/42), 312, (10/50), 485-92 pass., (1/66), 154-64 pass.;
            AM (7/44), 4 (air), (10/50), 22, (3/52), 49, (6/61), 35, (7/65), 14,
            (10/73), 24-25, (8/74), 6 (1863); LAT, 144; ESA, 52 (air); HBP, 5,
            13-17; LUL, 268; GHS, 482 (c.1910, air); CCS, 442 (1885); CE, II,

627 (1905); HNM (vol. 111), 23 (c.1900); EA, IV, 169; LF (8/2/48), 46-47 (air); LAP, VI, 102; WAP (Br. vol.), 189, 2-4 (air); CEF (vol. 3), 236 (air); AI (vol. 3), 113

Public buildings
  Health clinic, BBP, 32
  Legislative palace, BBP, 30; EA, IV, 171
  Municipal library, BBP, 31
Avenue 16th of July, BBP, 14
Potosí
  Scenes, MED, 544; NG (1/66), 187-89; WAP (Br. vol.), 197; AM (7/66), 1-5, (3/70), 4-5, (1/73), 24-25, (9/76), bc.
  Royal mint, PMN, 76; NG (9/33), 254
Puno: Scenes, NG (6/30), 159
Santa Cruz
  Scenes, BBP, 20; AM (3/78), 11-15
  Plaza, BBP, 19
Sorata: Scenes, AM (1/63), 39
Sucre: Scenes, AM (10/71), 10; AM (9/76), 21
Tarija: Scenes, AM (10/60), 52-55

4. Society
  a. People types, NG (3/43), 311-27 pass., (10/50), 481-96 pass., (1/66), 153-95 pass.; AM (9/53), 21-23, (4/63), 33-37; ELA, 100-08, 245; BBP, 6-60 pass.; CCS, 437-47 pass. (1885); HNM (vol. 36), 558-62 pass. (c.1865), (vol. 111), 22, 25 (c.1900); EA, IV, 165; WAP (Br. vol.), 212-16
     Peasants, LF (6/30/61), 70-73
  b. Indians, NG (2/29), 149-57 pass., (1/66), 172-73; AM (3/54), 112-15; LAP, VI, 66 (village)
     Aymará, PWL, 56-81 pass.
     Chipaya, POE, VII, 98-103; AM (8/10), 19-22
     Tocoalla, NG (9/64), 316-17 (village)
  c. Amusements
     Carnival, NG (10/50), 489 (La Paz)
     Festival (Copacabana), CTA, 126-27
     Fiestas, LAP, VI, 107; BBP, 41; NG (10/50), 493
     Skiing, LAT, 45 (Chacaltaya lodge)
     Soccer, NG (10/50), 490

5. Culture
  a. Architecture
     Housing
       Rural, AM (12-57), 16-18
       Miners, LUL, 273, 277
  b. Art
     Folk art, AM (1/51), 20-23
     Handcrafts, AM (6/63), 29-32
  c. Education
     Universities
       La Paz, BBP, 16
       San Andrés, NG (1/66), 162
       Sucre (San Francisco Xavier), WAP (Br. vol.), 215; AM (10/73), 24-25, (9/76), 23
     Activities, BBP, 44-47; AM (10/49), 12-14, (8/55), 26-29
       Girl's school (La Paz), LAP, VI, 41
       Farmer education (Altiplano), PLA, 110
       Industrial education, AM (5/57), 21-25
       Physics teaching, AM (11/56), 306

                  Radio Aymará language school, AM (7/58), 26-29
   d. Music, dance
      Musical instruments, CM, 133, 134
         Conch shell, LEM, 42
         Drums, HDA, 125
      Dances, CM, 135-37; HLA, 49, 63; LAP, VI, 47; AM (1/54), 24-27

6. Religion
   Edifices
      Copacabana: Cathedral, BBP, 26; CE, II, 629; NCE, II, 645 (sanctuary),
         IX, 954; AM (10/73), 24-25 (sanctuary); JAS, 84; HNM (vol. 36), 16
         (shrine)
      Chiantle: Church altar, BBP, 42
      Loja: Church, LF (8/2/48), 52
      La Paz
         Cathedral, ESA, 54; CCS, 443 (1885)
         María Auxiliadora Church, BBP, 17
         San Francisco church (facade), NCE, IX, 382
         Santo Domingo church, JSA, 85
      Potosí
         Cathedral, BBP, 20; AM (3/70), ifc.
         Jesuit church of Belén, NCE, II, 646, IX, 953
         San Lorenzo, CHL, 173
      Santa Cruz: Cathedral, BBP, 19; AM (10/73), 24-25
      Sucre
         Cathedral, NCE, II, 645; AM (9/68), 28 (interior)
         La Merced church, AM (9/68), 26
         Las Monicas church, AM (9/68), 25
         Recoleta Monastery, AM (5/78), 16
         San Felipe Neri church, AM (3/70), 7
   Images, CHL, 174-75
   Processions, NG (1/66), 170-71
   Cemeteries, AM (9/57), ibc.
   Novitiate of Salesian Fathers, NCE, IX, 955

7. Economy
   a. Industry
      Guano, CCS, 432, 435 (1885)
      Oil, BBP, 62 (storage); COE (vol. 4), 337 (refinery)
      Silver, LAP, VI, 98
      Solar energy, AM (10/77), 8
      Thermoelectric power, AM (10/77), ifc., 11
      Tin (mines, miners), LAF (6/30/61), 66-67; POE, VII, 104-08; NHS,
         123; BBP, 3, 48-50; AM (4/60), 24-29, (5/72), 124-25, (9/76),
         24 (1914); OIA, plate 15 (1910); EA, IV, 167; NG (9/33), 26, (10/40),
         600-08, (3/43), 330 (Llalagua), (1/66), 180-81; EI (vol. 3), 111
   b. Agriculture
      Cattle, RCS, 110-17, 258, 276
      Dairying, BBP, 57
      Potatoes, CEF (vol. 3), 238
      Rubber, GLT, 246
      Sheep, EA, IV, 166
      Sugar, COE (vol. 4), 337
      Experiment station (Altiplano), BNL, 424-25
      Farms, farming, BMD, 431; TFS, 28
         Tractors vs. Oxen plowing, AM (8/62), 38
   c. Markets, ESA, 46, 50; BBO, 15, 34 (outdoors)
      Copacabana, NG (9/64), 318; LAP, VI, 104

Coroico, BHS, 116
La Paz, NG (10/50), 488

8. Transportation, communication
Balsa boats (Lake Titicaca), WAA, 179; BHS, 118; NG (1/66), 168-69
Bridges
    La Paz (1885), CCS, 445
    Pilcomayo River, NG (1/66), 186
Highways, BBP, 60; BSA, 178; LUL, 247 (road to La Paz); NG (1/66),
    167; CEN, 237
Llama pack train, OIA, plate 23 (1950)
Ox carts, GLT, 303 (1930)

9. Miscellaneous
Cousteau expedition, Lake Titicaca, CTA, 98-149 pass.
Observatory (Chacaltaya), WM (10/73), 25-27
Miners' rebellion (Sept. 1965), BBY (vol. 1966), 153
Peace Corps activities, AM (10/63), 13-18; NG (9/64), 298
Riot, Siglo Veinte tin mine, LF (1/64), 62-68

IV. Brazil

1. Environment
a. Geographical features
    Mountains
        Canê (iron mountain), NG (1/44), 54
        Dedo de Deus, GR, 76
        Morro de Mina, NG (1/44), 54
        Orgão mountains, AJB, 486, 490
    Rivers
        Amazon, JSV, 78-79; SBP, 259; LUL, 16, 18 (air); HNM (vol. 58),
            365-78 (c.1875); AJB, 258; HAE, 114-15; HRM, 100-01; NG (9/28),
            277, 283 (delta), (2/49), 243-45, (11/70), 718-19 (delta); AM
            (2/61), 7-12, (10/72), 20-24; SBP, 417 (air); BHS, 43
        Jara, AM (10/78), 15
        Mauches, AJB, 304
        Rio Negro, NG (11/33), 603, (9/62), 330-35, (10/71), 452; HNM
            (vol. 123), 763-70, 942-43 (c.1910)
        "River of Doubt," AM (10/70), 15-23
        Tapajós, NG (10/72), 453
        Taquarí, WAP (Br. vol.), 17
        Vermelho, MED, 573 (air)
        Xingú, SMG, 46
    Falls
        Cachoeira, WAP, 12, 32
        Gramado, RBT, 64-65
        Paulo Afonso, BRA, 17; NG (1/31), 67; WAP (Br. vol.), 18
    Lakes: Pantanal country, NG (11/77), 694-95
    Islands
        Itamaracá, AM (4/58), 30-33
        Marajó, NG (11/38), 636-70 pass.; HNM (vol. 58), 365-71 (c.1875)
    Coasts
        Costa Verde, NG (2/78), 258-59
        São Salvador vicinity, MED, 586
    Campos Cerrados region, AM (7/63), 11-13
b. Flora, BTP, plates 1-292 pass.; BNR, 22, 34, 63, 149, 248, 267,
    348; ED, 16-17; HAC, 112-13; LA (11/3/59); ABT, 55-185 pass.

Militia, LF (11/23/36), 43
President's motorcycle guard, NG (12/37), 292
Troops in World War II, KPA, 182-97 pass.; AM (7/69), 9-15; DCB, 266-67
Officers
    Headquarters club, KPA, 157
    Military club (Rio de Janeiro), KPA, 156
Forts
    Cabo Frio, GR, 236
    São Marcelo, WAP (Br. vol.), 79

3. Cities, Towns, Villages
Acaraby: Scenes, LF (11/23/36), 43
Amapá: Scenes, AM (5/56), 3-7
Aparecido do Norte: Scenes, AM (2/58), 30-33
Aracajú: Public library, AM (1/54), 43
Bahía (Salvador)
    Scenes, BHA, 41; RBT, 64-65; GR, 84; HNM (vol. 39), 502-04; NG (12/30), 761, (1/31), 63 (air), (10/42), 504, (9/62), 320, (10/69), 464-65; AM (11/54), 3-11, (1/75), 33-34; WAP (Br. vol.), 28-29
    Archbishop's residence, AM (4/71), 24-25
    Lighthouse, NG (9/28), 264
    Monastery museum of art, AM (4/63), 8-11
    Pelourinho Plaza, AM (9/69), 2-3
    Port, BHS, 174; LUL, 411; LAP, VI, 136; EI (vol. 3), 244; NBK (vol. 2), 381
Belém
    Scenes, BRA, 15; NCE, II, 767; NG (2/49), 251 (air), (10/72), 454-55 (air, night); LAP, VI, 17, 55
    Harbor, LAT, 55; LUL, 414
    Intercontinental Hotel, ESA, 72
Belo Horizonte
    Scenes, BHB, 58; ELA, 248; NG (10/42), 510, (1/44), 67, (10/48), 491-504 pass., (9/62), 321; AM (5/49), 4, (1/51), 7-8, 42-44; LAP, VI, 34 (air)
    Hospital, Fundação Benjamín Guimaraes, NG (1/44), 70
    Jewel museum, NG (1/44), 65
    Pampulha casino, NG (1/44), 66; FDT, illus. 162
    Yacht club, FDT, illus. 225
Boa Vista: Scenes, (10/72), 480 (air)
Bom Jesus da Lapa: Scenes, SBP, 525
Brasília
    Scenes, BRA, 5 (air); BHB, 22; RBT, 64-65; BHS, 183; FFS, 177, 209; LAT, 32, 52; BAR, 422 (air), 433; NG, (5/60), 704-24, (9/62), 340-41, (11/77), 690; AM (8/58), 2-8, (8/63), 13-17, (10/72), 24-25; ETB, plates 122-39 pass.
    Business center, ETB, plates 199-211
    City plan, NG (5/60), 720-21
    Government buildings, ETB, plates 213-37
        Congress, EBP, 112; ELA, 159; BNL, 424-25; AM (6/62), 35; ENB (vol. 4), 126
        Esplanade of Ministeries, EBP, 112
        President's residence, BHB, 26; LUL, 394; DEL, 33; EBP, 112-13
Campina Grande: Scenes, WCF, 77 (air)
Curitiba
    Scenes, BHB, 13; NG (2/78), 264-65 (air)
    University, WAP (Br. vol.), 100
Farinha: Scenes, WCF, 130 (1942), 131-32 (1959)

Fortaleza: Scenes, BHB, 48
Goiana: Scenes, WCF, 108 (1942), 109-10 (1859)
João Pessoa: Scenes, WCF, 106 (1942), 107 (1959)
Joazeirnho: Scenes, WCF, 126 (1942), 127 (1959)
Livramento: Scenes, AM (2/59), 24-27
Londrina: Scenes, BHA, 74-75
Manáus
    Scenes, NG (11/33), 593 (air), 599, (2/49), 249-54
    Governor's Palace, NG (9/28), 278
    Harbor, LUL, 419; AM (4/50), bc.; LAP, VI, 123; NG (10/73), 474-75
    Opera House, RBT, 64-65, JSA, 30; ELA, 133; NG (11/33), 595,
        (10/42), 506, (9/62), 326 (interior); LAP, VI, 122
Maranhão
    Scenes, NG (1/31), 59
    Harbor, NG (1/31), 31
Obidos: Scenes, AM (7/59), 28-30
Ouro Preto
    Scenes, WB, 148-49; BRA, 8 (air); ESA, 76; JSA, 32; BNL, 424-25;
        BAR, 399; NG (10/48), 492; AM (5/49), 6, (12/59), 18-21, (3/62),
        17-21, (4/71), 24-25, (1/73), 24-25, (2/74), 7; EA, VI, 469; LAP,
        VI, 137; EB, 27
    Town hall, WAP (Br. vol.), 83
Pará: Scenes, HNM (vol. 39), 493-95 (1865), (vol. 58), 372-78 (1875);
    NG (11/23), 587 (air), (12/30), 576 (water front); GLT, 427 ff.
Pernambuco (see Recife)
Petropolis
    President's residence, HAT, 291; WAP (Br. vol.), 84
    Quintandinha Hotel, EB, 42
Pôrto Alegre
    Scenes, BRA, 14 (air); NG (9/62), 321; AM (1/52), 6-8, (12/56), 28
    Military college, DCB, 266-67
Recife (Pernambuco): Scenes, NG (1/31), 61 (seawall), (10/32), 725,
    (10/42), 509, (9/62), 320; WB, 148-49; BHB, 45; HNM (vol. 39), 489-
    501 pass. (1865); AM (1/57), 12-15 pass.; LAP, VI, 119; EB, 15 (air);
    LUL, 11 (water front); GJV, 97 (c.1822); LPB, 102
Rio de Janeiro
    Scenes, GJV, 163-70 pass., 220, 246, 307 (c.1822); AE, IV, 465; LAP,
        VI, 15 (air); WB, 148-49 (1821); BRA, 10 (air); HAT, 304 (air, 1940);
        ETB, plates 2-22 pass., 338 (air); CTC, plates 10-80 pass.; GR, 8,
        40, 160; BGH, 170; ESA, 8, 66; LSA, 19 (air); WAA, 193 (air); CCS,
        662-72 pass. (1885); BAR, 406; NCE, XII, 508; HNM (vol. 39), 625-
        39 pass. (1885); NG (9/28), 265 (air), (12/30), 734-50 pass., (8/39),
        284-324 pass., (10/42), 528-36, (3/55), 290-328 pass., (9/62), 300-
        53 pass., (10/69), 467-70 (night), (6/76), 24-25 (air, night); AM
        (7/49), 17-18 (c.1822), (3/65), 4 (early 19th century), (4/65), 5-8
        (air), (4/72), 36, (10/72), 29 (1940), (8/74), 5 (1916, 1956), (Nov.-
        Dec., 1975), 16-17, (1/77), S-10 (1800), 5-7 (c.1820); BRJ, 10-49
        pass.; EBR (vol. 17), 58 (air)
    Public buildings
        Congress Building, AM (7/65), 15
        Foreign Office library, GR, 16
        Guanabara Palace, ETP, plate 86
        Itamaratí Palace, GR, 124 (dining room)
        Maracañá stadium, NG (2/78), 251
        Marshal Deodoro building, KPA, 156 (1930s)
        Mercy hospital, CE, II, 746 (c.1907)
        Ministry of Education, ETB, plates 105-08; FDT, illus. 161; WAP
            (Br. vol.), 95

Martinelli building, NG (5/39), 684
Ministry of Education, AM (3/60), 10
Municipal Library, AM (1/51), 43, (2/52), 4
Municipal Stadium, NG (1/44), 62
Museums
    Art, AM (10/54), 20-23, (12/63), 18 (interior)
    Sacred art, AM (4/73), 20
    State Forestry Department, NG (5/39), 681
    Ipiranga, NG (12/32), 766, (5/39), 665
Palace of Nations, WAP (Br. vol.), 85
City features
    Anhangabohú park, NG (5/39), 665
    Bandeirantes monument, BRA, 19; WAP (Br. vol.), 81
    Coffee monument, WAP (Br. vol.), 23
    Ipiranga avenue, AM (1/62), 39
    Plaza of the Republic, AM (9/70), 43
    São João Avenue, ESA, 80
    Subway, AM (8/78), 6
Miscellaneous
    Automat, NG (5/39), 680
    Butantán Institute (snake farm), LUL, 403; NG (1/30), 773-74, (5/39),
       673-74; AM (2/50), 12-14, (5/52), 24-27; LAP, VI, 127
    First electric streetcar (1900), SHL, 584
    Traffic policeman, NG (5/30), 682
São Vicente: Scenes, JSA, 27
Soledade: Scenes, WCF, 128 (1942), 129 (1959)
Ubatuba: Scenes, AM (2/56), 7-10
Vitoria: Scenes, NG (12/30), 755, (1/31), 64 (air); GLT, 427 ff.

4. Society
  a. People types, AM (5/49), 2-7, 44-45, (1/77), S2-S12 (c.1825), ifc.,
     ibc., bc.; EB, 30-35; WAP (Br. vol.), 40-75 pass.; SBP, 13-20
     pass., 61, 181, 216; CCS, 676-703 pass.; NG (12/30), 475-78, 590-
     97, (10/48), 480-508 pass., (5/59), 642-49 pass., (9/62), 302-500
     pass., (2/78), 246-76 pass.; BRJ, 7-147 pass.
    Brasilia squatters, EPB, 113
    Gaúchos (Rio Grande do Sul), BHB, 82
    Laborers, HNM (vol. 10), 727-32 (c.1850)
    Lepers, AM (5/52), 16-19, 28
    Mato Grosso people, SMG, 37-280 pass.; NG (11/52), 697-98, 702-07
    Negroes, AJB, 83-84
    Rio de Janeiro citizens, LF (11/1/54), 103-11
    Vaqueiros, POE, VI, 88-97
    Women (styles), AM (11/52), 16-17; LF (3/7/60), 67-77
  b. Indians
    Types, AM (5/53), 3-5, 30-31, (3/54), 16-18, (8/55), 22-25; NG (7/61), 64-
     89 (blue eyes)
      Amazon, LAP, VI, 11 (village); NG (11/30), 590-97, (5/59), 642-69
       pass., (10/72), 456-95 pass., (11/77), 684-706 pass.; HGS, 88-89,
       168-69; TPM, 23; HNM (vol. 40), 344-58 pass. (c.1890); AJB,
       245, 314; AM (9/71), 19-24
      Mato Grosso, NG (5/64), 336-57; AM (5/49), 29; EA, IV, 456
    Tribes
      Camayura, LF (9/20/48), 88-91 ("stone age" natives)
      Cinta Largas, NG (9/71), 421-44 ("stone age" natives)
      Gayapo, SRA, 86-87, 150-51
      Kalapolo, LF (12/22/67), 40-46
      Kamayurá, NG (10/73), 488
      Krabo, NG (10/72), 481

Baroque, AM (June-July, 1974), 24-25
Good and bad housing, EB, 34-35; AM (3/60), 10-16; EA, IV, 458
Plantation homes, WB, 148-49; CCS, 669 (1885); AJB, 203 (1866)
Bahía: Housing, BHB, 30
Belém: Slums, BNL, 424-25
Brasilia
  Apartments, ETB, plates, 112-13, 170-85; NG (5/60), 708-09
  Houses, ETB, plates 112-13, 186-95 pass.; SBL, 67; ETB, plates
    163-95
  New Housing, ETB, plates 163-68
  Slums, BHB, 20; ETB, plates 156-62
Minas Gerais
  Fazenda (c.1860), SHL, 471
  Housing, AM (10/52), 16-19, 44-45
Rio de Janeiro, ETB, plates 42-52, 115-20 pass.
  Apartments, FDT, illus. 151
  Banks, office buildings, FDT, illus. 219-23
  Favelas, slums, POE, VI, 122-29; LAP, VI, 112; ETB, plates 34-
    41; ELA, 191; AM (9/60), 12; COE (vol. 14), 343; BRJ, 52-65
  Neighborhood housing units, FDT, plates 185-99
  New housing, AM (12/64), 32-33
  Private residences, ETB, plates 84-102
São Paulo, FDT, illus. 71-75
  Apartments, FDT, illus. 166
  Collapsed building, LF (2/24/58), 38
  Residence gardens, FDT, illus. 164-65
  Slums, AM (5/61), 6-9
b. Art
São Paulo Biennial exhibits
  1951: AM (8/52), 20-23
  1953: AM (3/54), 29-44, (5/54), 38; LF (5/31/54), 78-84
  1957: AM (1/58), 30-33
  1961: AM (1/62), 3-9
  1963: AM (1/63), 18-21
  1965: AM (1/66), 31-35
Ceramics (Caruarú, Pernambuco), AM (10/59), 29-31
Paintings and painters, AM (5/67), 2108
Skull decorating (Minas Gerais), FFS, 209
c. Education
Activities
  Brazilian teachers at Pan American Union, AM (2/51), 40
  Students, AM (2/77), 7-8; EB, 41
  Training agricultural workers, BHB, 106
Institutions
  Brasilia University, AM (6/63), 9-11
  Brazilian Indian Foundation, AM (10/74), 17-23
  Curitiba University, WAP (Br. vol.), 100
  Instituto Agronômico, LF (5/22/39), 64
  National Institute of Technology, EB, 3 (library), 22
  Recife University law school, AM (1/62), 14, (8/71), 24-25; LPB, 104
  Rio Branco Institute, AM (3/58), 3-7
  São Paulo
    Catholic University, NCE, XII, 108 (administration building); NCE,
      V, 161
    Itú Jesuit College, CE, II, 746 (c.1907)
    Law school, CE, II, 346 (c.1907)
    Mackenzie University, AM (2/55), 18-23
    University, AM (Nov.-Dec., 1975), 16-17

University City, AM (1/64), 11
University of Brazil, AM (9/59), 8
  Pediatric clinic, FDT, illus. 163
Other schools
  Boy's school (Caio Martins), AM (3/51), 21-23
  Brasilia schools, ETB, plates 196-98; BHB, plate 34
  Dance school, AM (2/61), 13-16
  Nursing schools
    São Paulo, AM (12/49), 28-30
    Rio de Janeiro, AM (5/51), 35
d. Music, Drama
  Activities
    Band, São Paulo city employees, NG (5/39), 675
    Childrens' theater, Rio de Janeiro, AM (2/57), 7-10
    Dances
      Folk dances, AM (3/52), 28-29, 35
      Mask dances (Tucuna Indians), BNR, 379 (c.1850)
      Students from Brazil in United States, AM (2/52), 18-21
    Movies and actors, AM (6/53), 13-16
    Rural troubadours, AM (6/50), 29-31
    Samba musicians, AM (4/76), 17-21
    String quartet, University of Brazil, AM (6/65), 47
    Theater plays and players, AM (6/49), 122-23
  Institute of Players, São Paulo, AM (4/72), 24-25
  Manáus opera house, RBT, 64-65; JSA, 30; ELA, 133; LAP, VI, 122;
    NG (11/33), 595, (10/42), 506, (9/62), 326 (interior)
  Municipal Theater, Rio de Janeiro, NG (12/30), 741
  Musical instruments, CM, 144-71 pass.
    Flutes (Kamaiurá Indians), LEM, 42
    Drums, HDA, 122, 123

6. Religion
  a. Edifices
    Bahía, BHB, 43; ESA, 68; NCE, II, 767
      Bomfim church, CE, II, 747 (c.1907)
      Cathedral, CHL, 186; NCE, II, 437
      Nossa Senhora da Conceição da Praía church, CHL, 184
      Nossa Senhora do Rosario, AM (9/69), 4, 5
      Residence, Archbishop, AM (4/71), 24-25
      Third Order of St. Francis church, EB, 37 (interior); CHL, 135;
        NCE, VIII, 436; WAP (Br. vol.), 80; AM (1/75), 3
    Belém, NCE, II, 767
      Third Order of St. Francis church, AM (9/69), 8
    Belo Horizonte
      Pampulha church, LAT, 65; NCE, II, 771
      St. Francis Chapel church, AM (8/50), fc.
    Brasilia
      Cathedral (lighted cross), DEL, 43
      Lady of Fátima chapel, BRA, 28
    Canide: Shrine of St. Francis, NCE, V, 1032
    Congonhas do Campo: Bom Jesus de Matozinhos church, PMN, 60-61;
      MPA, 12, 37, 56, 59; RBT, 64-65
    Manáus: Cathedral, BHB, 87; NCE, IX, 143
    Minas Gerais state, NCE, VIII, 437
      Nossa Senhora de Expectação do Parto church, CHL, 188
      Nossa Senhora do Rosario do Barro church, CHL, 189
    Olinda: Church, AM (4/43), ibc.
    Ouro Prêto

Igreja do Carmo church, MPA, 15-16
Rosario church, AM (5/66), 24
Third Order of St. Francis church, BHB, 52; ELA, 127-30; HHL, I,
    414; EA, IV, 471; MPA, 19-25; CHL, 195; AM (5/71), 24-25
Pernambuco: Saints Côsme and Damião churches, NCE, IX, 966
Recife
    Jaqueira Chapel, NCE, IX, 967
    São Antônio church, AM (12/50), 29, (5/68), 40
    São Pedro dos Cléricos, NCE, X, 681; CHL, 183
Rio de Janeiro
    Candalaria church, ETP, plate 70; GR, 64; CE, II, 747 (c.1907);
        AM (Nov.-Dec., 1970), 24-4
    Cathedral, GR, 72; NCE, XII, 509; AM (6/62), 15 (plaza, 1838)
    "Church of the Rock," NG (12/30), 743
    Nossa Senhora da Gloria de Oteiro church, GR, 56
    Santa Anna church, NCE, X, 726 (1850)
    Santa Rita church, NCE, X, 723-24 (1850)
    São Benito church, GR, 60, 120 (interior)
    Silvestre Chapel, AM (5/54), ibc.
Sabará: Igreija do Carmo church, MPA, 26-29
Others
    São João d'el Rey church, AM (1/61), 27
    São João d'el Rey, Lady of Mt. Carmel church, AM (1/61), 28
b. Ceremonies, activities, etc.
Festivals
    Bahía, WAP (Br. vol.), 62-63
    Congonhas, WAP (Br. vol.), 59
    Day of the Dead feast, POE, VI, 70-71
    Procession, Minas Gerais, BHB, 6; NG (10/48), 497
    St. Benedict, AM (7/51), 11-15, (5/61), 14-16
    Whitsuntide, AM (6/57), 24-26
Ceremonies
    Funeral, HNM, X, 733
    Macumba, POE, VI, 76-83; SBP, 543; AM (6/65), 16-19, (June-July,
        1975), 6-13; BRJ, 134-61
    Passion play, AM (4/61), 11-13
Saints, CCS, 691 (1885)
English cemetery (c.1822), AJV, 307

7. Economy
a. Industry
Economic projects, AM (5/53), 3-5
Fishing, BNR, 297 (turtles, c.1850); SBP, 23 (rafts); NG (1/31), 33
    (traps); AM (9/52), 9-11, 45, (5/72), 24-25; POE, VI, 98-104; WB,
    148-49; WAA, 192
Manufacturing
    Automobiles, LAA, 60; AM (6/59), 3-7; BHB, 71; BRA, 39 (trucks);
        CEF, (vol. 12), 144
    Chemicals, FDT, illus. 207-12 (São Paulo)
    Corn flour, SBP, 239
    Electric power, AM (5/59), 9-17, (8/59), 30-31 (Itacurú), (3/71), 39
        (Paraíba), BHB, 92 (Minas Gerais); LF (4/14/67), 46-47
    Heavy machinery, AM (9/76), 4
    Nuclear energy (Angra dos Reis), NG (2/78), 261
    Rubber, BHA, 2; WAA, 190; NG (10/73), 468 (smoked); AM (10/78), 14
    Solar energy, AM (10/77), 8
    Steel, WAP (Br. vol.), 31; BRA, 38; LUL, 410; AM (7/57), 5 (Volta

                     Redonda)
             Sugar mill, NAB, 238-39 (Minas, c.1870); SHL, 268 (19th century)
             Wax, BHB, 50
             Wood products, BHB, 11 (sawmill)
         Mining
             Diamonds, WAP (Br. vol.), 37
             Gold, AM (1/77), S-12 (c.1820)
             Iron, LUL, 42; EA, VI, 461; LAP, VI, 126; COE (vol. 4), 495
             Oil, NG (12/37), 788
             Mica, NG (1/44), 46, 76
             Manganese, AM (3/67), 20-27
             Quartz, NG (1/44), 55-56, (10/48), 486-88
         Shipping, AM (3/58), 15-19 (Amazon)
         Waterworks (Belém), AM (4/69), 16
         Dams
             Cedros, Ceará, AM (9/61), 8
             Paraná, AM (Nov.-Dec., 1978), 24-25
     b. Agriculture, EB, 7-9, 51-60; LAP, VI, 18 (trench farming, São Paulo)
         Products
             Cattle, CEF (vol. 3), 307
             Coffee, EA, IV, 463; EB, 51-52; BRA, 36 (drying); SBP, 180, 240;
                 LUL, 404-05; PLA, 52; GHS, 520; WCB, 106, 176, 289-369
                 pass.; AM (12/30), 763-69, (5/39), 668, (9/62), 322; AM
                 (1/50), 2-5, (9/53), 25 (c.1835), (3/61), 29, (10/62), 4
             Destroyed, LF (8/2/37), 49-50; NG (12/37), 793; AM (3/61), 28
             Surplus storage, LF (2/8/43), 35-36
             Tasters, LF (5/22/39), 63; LUL, 399
             Beef, NG (10/42), 519 (drying)
             Brazil nuts, NG (12/30), 765 (warehouse)
             Forests, SMG, 223-25 (burning)
             Grains, BHB, 94; BHS, 30 (grinding)
             Jute, COE (vol. 14), 349
             Mandioca, SBP, 235 (pressing)
             Rubber, LF (5/24/43), 19-25; NG (12/37), 789, (10/42), 511-13; CEF
                 (vol. 3), 306
             Ford plantation, NG (10/37), 789; NG (10/42), 511
             Water buffalo, AM (5/70), 35-39
         Disasters
             Drought, LA (4/27/53), 53-56, (4/21/58), 47
             Foot and Mouth disease, AM (9/59), 35-36 (São Paulo)
             Thunder storm destruction (Rio de Janeiro), LF (9/27/54), 37
     c. Markets
         Bahía, ELA, 12; WAP (Br. vol.), 73
         Belém, JVI, 78-79
         Belo Horizonte, BHB, 59; EB, 14
         Campinas, TFS, 181
         Rio de Janeiro, GR, 108-12; NG (8/39), 324; AM (1/77), ifc. (1822)

8. Transportation, communication, EB, 8-63 pass.; SBP, 373-84 pass.; AM
     (9/53), 26 (1827)
     a. Highways
         Amazon highway, NG (10/72), 483, (11/77), 688, 702-03; LAT, 157;
             SMG, 51, 267; AM (11/62), 1-6, (2/72), 4-11
         Bahía highway, BHB, 8
         Building, São Paulo, NG (1/44), 78
         Rio de Janeiro to Petropolis, CCS, 683
         Saõ Paulo to Santos, BRA, 43; LAT, 154; NBK (vol. 2), 377
     b. Railroads, BSA, 92

BLP, 8-147, 152 pass.; GJR, 262 (1922); MCL, 4, 160, 242, 312;
AM (4/49), 14-19, (4/50), 2-8; NG (2/29), 100-113 pass., (7/41),
97-104 pass., (10/44), 478-500 pass., (2/60), 184-235 pass.; WAP
(Arg. vol.), 181-91; BCP, 24-63 pass.; LF (3/3/52), 50-58
Germans, LF (6/30/41), 76-80
Cowboys, HNM (vol. 81), 771 (1890); LAP, VI, 154
  b. Indians
Araucanians, LAP, VI, 153; GHS, 124-44 pass.; HNM (vol. 81), 776-82
pass. (1890)
Mapuche, SLH, 39-153 pass.
  c. Amusements
Ojos del Salado park, AM (5/57), ibc.
Racing, Viña del Mar, NG (2/29), 222, (3/30), 269 (track)
Rodeo, AM (3/57), 30-33
Skiing
    Farrellones resort, LAP, VI, 162
    Portillo resort, LF (8/2/48), 57
Soccer, BCP, 44 (stadium)

5. Culture
  a. Architecture
Housing
    Anglo-Lautaro Nitrate Corporation housing, CHI, 28; AM (6/69), 19
    Rural, HNM (vol. 81), 767 (c.1890); BCR, 62-63
      Haciendas, LUL, 304; MCL, 5, 51, 160, 358-59; NG (10/73), 470-
        71
      Farm tenant home, BCR, 62-63 (c.1860)
    Urban, MCL, 5, 50, 252-53, 302-67 pass.; ELA, 25; AM (8/58), 14-
        17
      Shanty (Santiago), HSC, 97
  b. Art
Carvings, MEI, 29, 131, 146 (Easter Island)
Geometric art, AM (1/68), 6-11
Handcrafts, AM (4/70), 21-26
  c. Education
Antofagasta: University of the North, BLP, 120; AM (11/67), 20
Concepción: University, BLP, 93; AM (9/60), 4; NG (2/60), 219; CHI,
    29 (entrance)
La Serna: University Center, AM (11/67), 18
Santa Marta: Technical University, BLP, 82
Santiago
    University of Chile, EA, VI, 484; LAP, 161; BOP, 42-43; AM (9/59),
        5, (5/74), 26
    Catholic University, LUL, 302
    Abraham Lincoln School, BLP, 144
Valparaíso: Federico Santa María Technical University, AM (1/62), 15
  d. Music, Drama
"Ancient Music Group," AM (2/70), 46
Dancing
    Ballet, AM (2/61), 30-33
    Dancing art form, AM (12/63), 12-16
    National dance, "Cueca," BHS, 126
Municipal theater (Santiago), AM (3/77), 25; WAP (Arg. vol.), 207
Public bandstand (Chuquicamata), BCP, 50
Radio broadcasting, AM (10/55), 6-9
Tertulias (19th century), AM (June-July, 1976), 16-17

6. Religion

   a.   Edifices
        Achao (Chiloé): Church, RTA, 113
        Arica: San Marcos church, ELA, 200
        Antofagasta: Roadside shrine, BLP, 136
        Chillán: Cathedral, EA, VI, 481
        Pucón: Church, ESA, 78
        Santiago
           Cathedral, HNM (vol. 81), 902 (c. 1890); CE, III, 661 (1907); NEC,
              XII, 1072; LEL, 160-61; CLI, 164 (c. 1910); AM (3/67), 24-25;
              NG (2/29), 224; POE, VII, 25; BCP, 40 (interior)
           San Francisco church, WAP (Arg. vol.), 201; NEC, III, 585, XII,
              1070
        Valparaíso: Matriz church, GIR, 116 (1822)
        Viña del Mar: San José church, BCP, 28
   b.   Ceremonies
        Lamenting the dead, CM, 172-73
        Processions, PLB, 138
           Corpus Cristi, HNM (vol. 81), 909 (c. 1890)
           Virgin Mary, NG (2/60), 235

7.   Economy
   a.   Industry
        Copper, EA, VI, 479; WAP (Arg. vol.), 176-77; CHI, 21; NG (3/60),
              273, (2/60), 226-29; COE (vol. 4), 286
           Mining, LF (8/2/48), 32; LAP, IV, 166; COE (vol. 6), 250, 258
              Braden mine, NG (2/59), 235
              Chuquicamata mine, BAR, 290; WAA, 180 (smelting)
              El Salvador mine, BCP, 8; AM (2/61), ibc.
              El Teniente mine, AAY, 191
           Refining, PMN, 76-77; NG (10/73), 456
           Transportation train, BLP, 150; COE (vol. 14), 347 (loading)
        Hydroelectric, LUL, 311; CHI, 24; AM (5/72), 19; NG (2/29), 242;
              BBY (vol. 1978), 247 (Coya); WBC (vol. 3), 370 (Los Moles)
        Nitrates, LUL, 295-96; AM (1/56), 25-81 pass.; NG (2/29), 233, (12/37),
              801-02; EA, VI, 478; BCP, 54-57; CEF (vol. 4), 285; COE (vol. 6),
              259
        Paper, BCP, 62
        Petroleum, BCP, 58
        Rugs, AM (9/76), 5
        Steel Mills
           Concepción, BLP, 94
           Huachipato, AM (5/53), 9-12, 46
        Whaling, AM (10/52), 16-18
        Worker demonstration, HSC, 96-97
   b.   Agriculture
        Products
           Cattle, WAP (Arg. vol.), 172, 187; BCP, 60
           Grain, BCR, 62-63 (c. 1830); WAP (Arg. vol.), 129
           Grapes, MCL, 54; AM (2/55), 9-12; NG (2/29), 241; LAP, VI, 156;
              BCP, 60
           Sheep, LUL, 308; LAP, VI, 167; WAP (Arg. vol.), 174-86 pass.;
              EI (vol. 4), 323
        Irrigation
           Atacama Desert, LAP, VI, 158
           Central valley, WAA, 182
        Farms, LUL, 292 (Central Valley); GIR, 24 (Salinas)
   c.   Markets, LEL, 100-01 (outdoor, Santiago)

8.   Transportation, communication

National flag (adopted Nov. 28, 1861), SFT, 223; EFW, 48
State flags (4), SFT, 223
Coins, AJG, 141-59; FCL, 298-300; GCW, 81-84; CCW, illus. 803-05
Stamps, MDS, plate 100
c. Military
Fort San Felipe Barajas (Cartagena), BNL, 424-25; LCS, 230 (1885);
  ESA, 96; COL, 4; ELA, 76; AM (6/69), 25-31; WAP (Ven. vol.),
  107; EA, VII, 275, XIII, 37
Fort San Fernando (near Bogotá), AM (3/79), 18
Guerrillas (1960s), SHL, 766
Hospital (Bogotá), COL, 37
Soldiers, NG (10/40), 527; CCS, 233
Troops in Korean war, AM (12/51), 9-10

3. Cities, Towns, Villages
Barranquilla
   Scenes, CCS, 226 (1885); SCP, 17; WAP (Ven. vol.), 81
   Port, BSA, 187
Bogotá
   Scenes, CCS, 342-45 (1885); HNM (vol. 71), 47-52 (c.1885); BAR, 213;
     WAA, 173; LUL, 239; JSA, 90; BHS, 17; SCP, 13-21; COL, 26; SCP,
     49; NG (10/40), 820, (5/47), 620 (air), (8/70), 242-43 (air); AM
     (6/52), 39 (air), (11/63), 29, (June-July, 1971), 29-30 (air), (10/73),
     38; LAP, VI, 177 (night); EI (vol. 5), 17 (air); COE (vol. 6), 734
   Public buildings
      Capitol, COL, 23; NG (10/40), 522
      Colonial Museum, ESA, 92; AM (9/49), ifc.
      Country Club, SCP, 42
      Bank of the Republic, AM (1/60), 24-28
      Gold Museum, AM (3/70), 13-17
      Luis Angel Arango library, SCP, 44; AM (7/66), 15 (interior)
      San Carlos hospital, AM (3/49), 25, 47
      San Carlos Palace (president's residence), SCP, 23
   Other buildings
      Basque Social Club, DAB, 146-47
      Book store, BHS, 84
      Tequendama hotel, COL, 7
   Parks
      Plaza Bolívar, EA, VII, 267
      Plaza of Martyrs, CCS, 346 (1885)
   Monument, Los Martires, HNM (vol. 71), 55
Buenaventura: Bay, NG (3/30), 304
Cali
   Scenes, COL, 11 (air); ESA, 10 (air); AM (10/59), 4; WAP (Ven. vol.),
     71
   Country club, SCP, 43
Cáqueza: Scenes (Palm Sunday), LAP, VI, 170
Cartagena
   Scenes, CCS, 227 (1885); HNM (vol. 127), 4-16 (c.1910), (vol. 150),
     521-29 (c.1910); LAT, 57; SCP, 19; ESA, 98; AM (5/53), 13-16,
     (8/67), 41, (1/72), 37, (June-July, 1972), 24-25; NG (10/40), 510,
     (8/70), 262-63 (air); LAP, VI, 26; WAP (Ven. vol.), 67 (air); WBE
     (vol. 4), 624 (air)
   City wall, JSA, 94
   Clock tower, SCP, 19
   Fort, CEF (vol. 5), 441
   Harbor, LAP, VI, 179; COL, 17
   Plaza Colón, AM (11/49), ibc.

Public buildings
    Palace of Inquisition, SCP, 32; AM (8/67), 40
Guatavita: Scenes, AM (1/75), 2-5, bc.; LF (2/14/67), 52-53
Manizales: Scenes, AM (2/52), 6-8
Medellín: Scenes, COL, 8 (air); LUL, 235; AM (1/50), 16, (5/60), 27-30,
    (Nov.-Dec., 1970), 24-25 (air), (June-July, 1972), 24-25; NG (10/40),
    518, 529, (5/47), 650 (air); LF (9/29/47), 110-111
Pacatramu: Scenes, EAW, 179 (air)
Pamplona: Scenes, AM (4/56), 8-12
Popayán: Scenes, AM (4/71), 25-30
Porto Bello: Scenes, HNM (vol. 131), 272 (c.1910)
Santa Marta
    Scenes, GHS, 536 (c.1910); SCP, 5, 8
    Beach, LAP, VI, 178
Valdivia: Scenes, LAP, VI, 171 (Indians)
Viam ("Model Town" of Unesco): Scenes, AM (8/49), 16-19
Villa de la Va: Scenes, AM (1/74), 8-12
Villavicencio: Scenes, AM (9/49), 8-11, 30; NG (8/48), 258

4. Society
    a. People types, LF (9/29/47), 112-16, (10/5/53), 30-31; POE, VII, 14-
        23; WAP, (Ven. vol.), 89-103 pass.; CCS, 249-50 (1885); MG (10/40),
        507-35 pass., (5/47), 619-60 pass., (8/48), 522-73 pass., (9/52), 375-
        86 pass., (5/66), 682-93 pass., (8/70), 234-71; LK (3/24/42), 18-21
    b. Indians
        Types, SCP, 44-48, 50-63 pass.
            Kogi, POE, VII, 44-49
            Northwest Amazon, RSJ, 24-25, 42-43, 96-97, 156-57, 174-75
            Pigmies, AM (5/62), 12-16
            Tukano, RAC, 168-69
    c. Amusements
        Bull ring, Bogotá, LAP, VI, 47; JSA, 92; SCP, 42
        Coffee Queen contest, Manizales, LF (3/16/59), 124-26
        Festival, Cartagena, AM (7/59), 17-20
        Fiestas, AM (4/61), 25-29
        Playgrounds, Bogotá, BNL, 424-25
        Skiing, Santa Marta, ESA, 102 (sand)

5. Culture
    a. Architecture
        Buildings (Bogotá), AM (June-July, 1971), 25-30
        Church, NCE, III, 841 (contemporary)
        Peasants homes, EAW, 270-71 (Andes)
        Slums
            Bogotá, AM (9/60), 12
            Cali, AM (5/58), 20-22, (6/69), 14
        Stilt houses, WAP (Ven. vol.), 70
    b. Art
        Art collection (Medellín), AM (Nov.-Dec., 1972), 2-8
        Flower festival (Medellín), JSA, 98
        Guasam mission art, AM (12/62), 15-21
        International art fairs (Bogotá), AM (2/56), 5, (5/70), 45
        International Fall Festival (Manizales), JSA, 145
    c. Education
        Baranquilla: Atlantic School of Fine Arts, AM (1/62), 15
        Bogotá
            Caro y Cuervo Institute, AM (1/64), 4-9 (languages)
            University, LAP, VI, 40 (classroom)

Gold, LUL, 243
Phosphate, AM (3/72), 25-30
Salt, POE, VII, 18-19; NG (8/70), 270-71; WBE (vol. 4), 625
Petroleum, AM (10/61), ibc.; WAP (Ven. vol.), 88
Steel, AM (5/54), 9-11, 44-45
Textile workers visit the U.S., AM (6/58), 23-25
b. Agriculture
Cattle, RCS, 138-63 pass., 241-75 pass., ibc.
c. Markets
Bogotá, SCP, 37; WAP (Ven. vol.), 82; NG (5/28), 577, (2/29), 177
Medellín, LAP, VI, 42 (supermarket)
Pasto, AM (1/50), 177

8. Transportation, communication
a. Highways, CCS, 341 (1885)
Construction, PLA, 70; AM (6/54), 20-23
Cali to Buenaventura, AM (1/54), 4
Pan American, EA, VII, 266 (bridge); AM (4/63), 22 (in desert); WAP
(Ven. vol.), 68-69
Modes of travel, MCP, 116 (1840)
Ox cart, HNM (vol. 17), 579 (1950)
Carriage, BLP, 68 (c.1810); GJR, fr. (c.1822); HNM (vol. 17), 577
(1850)
Pack train, NG (2/29), 181, (5/47), 649
b. River
Stern wheeler (Magdalena), BNL, 424-25
River bridge (Cali), ESA, 110
c. Air
El Dorado airport, SCP, 61; AM (June-July, 1971), 24-25
Scadta plane (c.1928), BSA, 14
d. Cablecar (Monserrat), SCP, 15

9. Miscellaneous
Five Year Plan, AM (7/51), 4-5, 41-43
Mountain Nevada de Hulla expedition, AM (1/70), 121-26
Peace Corps activity, LF (1/5/62), 18-25
Prison island (Gorgona), JIV, 142-43
Satellite station (Choconta), AM (1/79), ifc.

VII. Ecuador

1. Environment
a. Geographical features
Mountains
Antisana, WTA, 110
Capa Urcu, NG (2/68), 280-81
Cayambe, NG (2/68), 274-75; WTA, 128
Chimborazo, AM (7/49), 28 (c.1800), (5/59), 4; NG (1/29), 50,
(3/30), 301, (3/46), 355; SCP, 7; WTA, 13-37 pass., 174, 192;
WAP (Ven. vol.), 13
Iliniza, NG (3/30), 303
Pichincha, AM (4/47), fr.
Sincholagua, WTA, 105
Sumaco, NG (1/29), 79
Volcanos
Cotacachi, NG (2/68), 268-69
Cotopaxi, SCU, 13; SEP, 8; WTA, 71-87 pass., 175; AM (1/50),
124-25, (Nov.-Dec., 1971), 30, (3/79), 13, 19; EBR (vol. 17), 78

Sangay, FEW, 268; NG (1/29), 57-60, (1/50), 119, 127; AM (3/79), 21
    Tungurahua, SCU, 11; NG (1/29), 66-67, (2/34), 134
Lakes
    Laguna de Cuicocha, SEP, 9
    San Pablo, NG (1/29), 74
River: Napo, NG (2/68), 294
Falls
    Agoyán, NG (1/29), 62
    La Merced, NG (2/34), 172
Islands (Galapagos)
    Scenes, CGS, 20-21, 53; JSA, 66-72; NG (5/59), 608-703 pass.,
        (10/69), 488-49; SEP, 28-29; CTA, 14-96 pass.; AM (12/58), 19-
        21 (7/67), 9 (c.1834), (3/69), 21-29; LAP, VI, 225-28
    Flora, Fauna, LA, (9/8/58), 56-76; NG (4/67), 451-85 pass.
        Flora, CGS, 47-49, 96
        Fauna, CGS, 10-89 pass.; NG (9/78), 362-81 pass.
            Tortoises, NG (11/72), 632-49
Guayas basin, WIA, II, 304 (air)
Jungles, AM (8/55), 14-18
Valley of Alao, NG (1/29), 55
b. Flora, ABT, 150-86 pass.; BTP, plate 19; AM (4/69), 33-37
c. Fauna
    Birds, TND, 225, 867; AGG, 23, 66; DPT, 3-145 pass.; SBW, 65, 86,
        145
    Butterflies, FFW, 21a, 21b
    Fish, MGA, 240, 333, 338
d. Scenes, CCS, 299-352 pass. (1885); SEP, 6-16 pass.; BAR, 240; AM
    (4/49), 9-13, (5/50), 6-10, (7/51), 12-15, 46-47, (9/72), 24-25; NG
    (2/68), 258-98 pass.; LAP, VI, 198-209; WAP (Ven. vol.), 131-43 pass.;
    NBK (vol. 5), 52-56; ENB (vol. 7), 948-56 pass.
e. Disasters
    Earthquakes (August 5, 1949 and May, 1950), AM (9/49), 2-3 (Cuzco),
        (7/50), 12-13, (7/53), 2-5, 30 (rebuilding); VEH, 110 (1949), 124
        (1970)

2. Political
    Symbols
        Coat of arms, EA (vol. 9), 516; SFT, 230
        National flag (adopted Nov. 7, 1960), SFT, 48, 230
        Provincial flags (19), SFT, 230
            Guayas (Guayaquil, 1820), SFT, 230
            Galapagos, SFT, 230
        Coins, FCL, 301; GCW, 93; CCW, illus. 807; AJG, 194-204; AMC, 16-
            19
        Stamps, MDS, plate 99
    Government Junta, BBY (vol. 1964), 320; AAY (vol. 1977), 189
    Military Academy, NG (1/29), 72

3. Cities, Towns, Villages
    Ambato: Scenes, AM (2/77), 5-11 (air); LAP, VI, 206
    Baños: Scenes, NG (2/34), 159 (market)
    Cuenca: Scenes, JSA, 80; ECU, 14; NG (2/68), 282-83; LAP, VI, 206
    Esmeraldas: Scenes, SEP, 21
    Guayaquil
        Scenes, ECU, 17, 18; SEP, 16-19; LUL, 251; CCS, 301-11 (1885); AM
            (6/57), 3-8, (5/63), 17-19, (9/72), 24-25 (air); NG (2/68), 286-87
            (air); EA (vol. 9), 618; WAP (Ven. vol.), 134
        City hall, SEP, 17

El Centenario bank, SEP, 17
Harbor, NG (2/34), 135
Malacón, SEP, 18
Monument, Bolívar-San Martín meeting, BNL, 424-25; COE (vol. 11),
    493
Municipal police, SEO, 39
Social Security building, SEP, 64
Water tower, SEP, 33
Ibarra: Scenes, SEP, 28
Loja: Scenes, HLV, 6
Otavalo: Scenes, SEP, 26; AM (9/72), 24-25; EA (vol. 9), 615, 620; POE,
    VIII, 60-67; EI (vol. 6), 233
Quito
    Scenes, LAP, VI, 205; ECU, 1, 7 (air); WAP (Ven. vol.), 140; SEP,
        10, 20-40; HS, 554; CCS, 309-24 pass.; HNM (vol. 40), 348-49; NG
        (1/29), 70 (air), (2/49), 238, (1/50), 130 (air), (2/68), 260-61, 270;
        AM (5/58), 14-19, (1/60), 10-13, (6/61), ibc., (2/67), 21 (air),
        (9/72), ibc., 24-25, (2/77), 8-9, (4/77), S-1 (air)
    Public buildings
        Casa de la Cultura Ecuatoriana, AM (4/62), 133
        Congress, ECU, 19, 20; SEP, 37; AM (7/65), 15, (7/67), 31 (air),
            32; EA (vol. 9), 618
        Government buildings, CCS, 335 (1885)
        National Red Cross, ECU, 10
        Presidential Palace, SEP, 38; CCS, 310 (1885)
        Solar Museum, AM (4/60), 14-17
    Plazas
        Independencia, BHS, 92; SEP, 21; AM (10/75), 5, (4/77), S-4; EA
            (vol. 9), 618-22
        San Francisco, AM (4/70), 15
    Hospitals
        Maternity, ACU, 37
        San Lázaro, AM (3/63), 2 (asylum)
    Hotel Quito, ECU, 6

4. Society
    a. People types, CCS, 306-54 pass. (1885); SEP, 40-48, 51-52; EA (vol.
        9), 618; WAP (Ven. vol.), 144-49; CGS, 24, 75; AM (4/49), 9-13,
        (5/50), 1-10, (1/60), 10-13, (4/78), 9-16; NG (2/34), 137-71 pass.,
        (3/46), 345-72 pass., (1/50), 122-37 pass., (2/68), 258-97 pass.;
        ENB (vol. 7), 949
        Old people (Vilcabamba), AM (1/76), 31-36
        "Water Boy," ALA, 106
    b. Indians
        Types, AM (3/54), 12-15, 30-31; WAA, 174; BWG, 84; NG (1/29), 64-93
            Head hunters, LF (7/15/46), 44-46
        Auca (Amazon), WAD, 50-51; LF (5/20/57), 24-33 (11/24/58), 23-29
            (1958)
        Cayapa, POE, VII, 36-43
        Colorado, JSA, 77
        Guayaqui, UHA, 268
        Jívaro, POE, VI, 38-41; DMH, 81-96; BWG, 218
        Sushira, AM (9/56), 4-7
        Vilcabamba, HLV, 7-166 pass.
    c. Amusements
        Bull fights, AM (8/49), 20-21
        Fiestas, AM (4/78), 10-16
        Guante game, AM (2/58), 19-21

5. Culture
    a. Architecture
        Hotels, CCS, 318, 342 (1885)
        Housing, CCS, 304-47 pass.
        Slums, CCS, 318, 343 (1885)
    b. Art
        Activities, AM (7/54), 13-15, 41-42
        Child artists, AM (5/54), 16-18
        Miniature, WTL, 21-54 pass., 58-108 pass.
        Religious, AM (4/77), S-6-12
        Weaving, AM (1/65), 22-26
    c. Education
        Agricultural school, Ambato, NG (1/29), 72
        Catholic University, Guayaquil, SEP, 47
        School children, PLA, 9; AM (6/68), 11
        University City, Quito, ECU, 30, SEP, 24
            Science faculty, WAP (Ven. vol.), 159
    d. Music
        Indian musicians, Cuzco, LEM, 476
        Instruments
            Panpipes, LEM, 478; AM (5/49), 31
            Guitars, EGM, 214

6. Religion
    a. Edifices
        Ambato: Cathedral, AM (9/72), 24-25
        Cuenca: Cathedral, AM (9/72), 24-25; WAP (Ven. vol.), 141
        Guayaquil: Churches, ESA, 106; CCS, 308; HNM (vol. 90), 402
        Machachi: Church, WTA, 63
        Quito
            Cathedral, NCE, V, 93 (interior); AM (4/77), bc.; CHL, 153-54
            Church of the Hospital, NCE, V, 92
            La Compañía, Jesuit church, SEP, 49; MFE, 202; AM (7/51), 15,
                (3/61), ibc., (4/77), fc.; NG (1/29), 73; SHL, 201
            La Merced convent, SEP, 32; AM (7/51), 14
            La Recoleta convent, AM (9/72), 24-25
            Merced church, WAP (Ven. vol.), 156 (cloisters)
            San Francisco church, JSA, 75; SEP, 24; BLA, 24-25; NCE, IX, 951;
                AM (6/61), 10-13, (9/72), 24-25, (4/77), S-2, ibc.; NG (1/29),
                76, (2/68), 272-73 (interior)
            Santo Domingo church, NCE, V, 93 (portal)
            Santo Domingo monastery, SEP, 20; AM (5/60), 1
            St. Augustine convent, NCE, V, 90 (interior); AM (9/68), 27, (9/72),
                24-25
    b. Ceremonies
        Marriage (couples and children), AHC, 56-57
        St. John's Day, AM (4/78), fc.

7. Economy
    a. Industry, SEP, 58-62
        Bread making, AM (Nov.-Dec., 1968), 11-13
        Fishing, NG (2/68), 290-291 (shrimp)
        Oil, BBY (vol. 1977), 294 (pipe line)
        Panama hats, JSA, 81; NG (2/68), 288; LAP, VI, 200
        Quinine, NG (3/46), 342-63 pass.
        Textiles, AM (5/52), 6-8, (2/56), 18-21
    b. Agriculture
        Activities, SEP, 54-58; EA (vol. 9), 616

    Cultivation in Andes, ABT, 186
    Terraces, NG (1/29), 50
    Farmers, WAP (Ven. vol.), 138, 142
  Products
    Cacao, EA (vol. 9), 618; LAP, VI, 208; BHS, 100 (drying)
    Cattle, RCS, 104-06
    Coffee, EA (vol. 9), 619; LAP, VI, 208; BHS, 100 (drying)
    Bananas, WBC (vol. 6), 45
    Barley, NG (2/68), 290-91 (harvest)
    Pyrethrum, AM (7/59), 3-8
  c. Markets
    Baños, NG (2/34), 159
    Otavalo, AM (7/51), 14; SEP, 25

8. Transportation, communication
  Airports
    Guayaquil, SEP, 63
    Otavalo, LAP, VI, 203
    Shell Oil Co., BSA, 171
  Highways, NG (2/34), 141-55 pass.
    Pan American, ECU, 43; AM (4/63), 26
  Railroad: Quito-Guayaquil, AM (3/77), 14-18
  Rope bridges, AM (9/53), 24 (1820); NG (3/46), 359
  "La Balsa" voyage, Ecuador to Australia (1970), ALB, 64-65, 160-61
  Radio broadcasting, AM (9/61), 27-30

9. Miscellaneous
  Equator monument (zero degree), JSA, 76; ECU, 1; SEP, 24; LUL, 258
  Peace Corps, NG (9/64), 338-45 pass.
  Shrunken heads, LF (7/15/46), 44; MOC, 71; POE, VI, 41

VIII. Paraguay

1. Environment
  a. Geographical features
    Rivers
      Paraguay, GPE, 235, 243; AM (5/67), 42 (1836); PAR, 4
      Paraná, AM (4/66), 4-9 (exploration, 1853-56)
      Tebicuary, WAP (Arg. vol.), 20
    Lake Ypacaraí, HPP, 16; GPE, 233
    Chaco, FEW, 424; LAT, 146 (air); HPP, 8-9, 11; AM (7/50), 10-11,
      41-42
  b. Flora, BTP, plate 62
  c. Fauna
    Ants, GPE, 93-94
    Birds, DPT, 11-89 pass.
    Fish, MGA, 236, 353
      Pirañas, NG (11/70), 714-33
    Snakes, SSW, 51
  d. Scenes, CCS, 627-55 pass. (1885); HNM (vol. 83), 229-41 (1890); HPP,
      6-31 pass.; GPE, 225-75 pass.; AM (8/51), 16-20, 46, (2/60), 31-34,
      (2/75), 24-25; LAP, VI, 272-77; WAP (Arg. vol.), 7-35

2. Political
  a. Symbols
    Coat of arms, EA (vol. 21), 274 ff.; SFT, 272
    Treasury shield, SFT, 272

National flag (adopted 11/27/1842), SFT, 272; EFW, 51
Presidential flag, SFT, 272
Coins, FCL, 314; CCW, illus. 814; AJG, 416-17
Stamps, NDS, plate 102
  b. Military
Parade, HPP, 28; NG (4/33), 388
Flying cadets, HPP, 27 (1929)
Paraguayan War truce meeting, HUP, 24

3. Cities, Towns, Villages
  Asunción
Scenes, HNM (vol. 83), 230-37 (1890); AM (10/58), 34, (4/66), 7 (1853),
(2/67), 2 (air), (2/75), 24-25 (mid-19th century); BHS, 166; HPP,
12; CCS, 225-29 (1885); NG (4/33), 391 (waterfront); PAR, 7 (air);
LAP, VI, 280 (air); CEN, 258 (harbor); WAP (Arg. vol.), 29-35
pass.; CEF (vol. 16), 112 (air); NBK (vol. 15), 6
Public buildings
Capitol, WAP (Arg. vol.), 10; HPP, 30; PAR, 17; AM (7/65), 14;
   NG (10/43), 468; EA (vol. 21), 274 ff.; COE (vol. 18), 428
Constitution Plaza, COE (vol. 18), 428
Customs house, NG (4/33), 389
"El País" Newspaper office, NG (10/43), 463
Government buildings, LUL, 365
Health ministry, HPP, 14
Hotel Guaraní, HPP, 15; GPE, 211
National bank, PAR, 37
National Pantheon, AM (2/75), 24-25; EI (vol. 14), 64
National Palace, HPP, 29
National Telecommunications building, HPP, 14
Supreme Court, HPP, 31
United States Embassy, AM (4/58), 26-28

4. Society
  a. People types, CCS, 634-56 pass. (1885); HNM (vol. 83), 229-47 (1890);
JSA, 128-29; HPP, 32-51; PAR, 28-36; AM (8/51), 16-20, 46, (2/60),
31-34; NG (4/33), 393-415 pass., (10/43), 465-88 pass.; WAP (Arg.
vol.), 21-27
Cavaliers, HNW (vol. 2), 600 (c.1850)
Gauchos, EA (vol. 21), 274 ff.
  b. Indians
Types, AM (4/54), 18-20
Chaco, AM (2/74), 132-37
Guaraní, POE, VI, 106-11
Moro, GPE, 140 (Chaco)
Payaguá, AM (3/63), 31-37

5. Culture
  a. Architecture
Country homes, BLA, 84-85 (c.1890); CCS, 658 (1885)
Estancias, HPP, 61; PAR, 12; CCS, 655 (1885)
Housing, Asunción, HPP, 37 (apartments)
  b. Art: Ñandutí lace, GPE, 233; AM (7/60), 14-15, (4/73), 137; LAP,
VI, 277; AM (9/78), 39-41
  c. Education
Activities, HPP, 47-51
School children, LUL, 361
  d. Handicrafts, AM (4/79), 51-56, ibc.
  e. Music: Instruments, CM, 164-65

6. Religion
    a. Edifices
        Asunción
            Cathedral, CCS, 629, 631, 640 (1885); AM (2/60), 34 (1850), (2/75),
                24-25; HPP, 43
            La Encarnación church, NG (10/43), 475; WAP (Arg. vol.), 31
            La Trinidad church, NCE, I, 994; NG (4/33), 409
            Pantheon of Heroes church, HPP, 17
            San Francisco church, HPP, 18
            San Roque church, NCE, I, 993; NG (4/33), 390
        Atyrá: Church, AM (Nov.-Dec., 1976), ifc.
        Candelaria: Mission, AM (Nov.-Dec., 1976), S-5 (plan)
        Encarnación: Jesuit mission, LAT, 146 (ruin)
        Humaitá: Church, PAR, 10 (ruin)
        San Ignacio
            Mini church, AM (Nov.-Dec., 1976), S-9, 10, 11
            Guazú church, AM (3/61), 21 (interior), (Nov.-Dec., 1976), S-5
        Trinidad: Mission, AM (Nov.-Dec., 1976), S-6, 7, 10
        Yaguarón: San Roque church, PAR, 26; WAP (Arg. vol.), 32
        Jesuit Missions, HPP, 19; GPC, 213, 215 (San Cosme); AM (Nov.-Dec.,
            1976), S-3, 4, 16-17 (Jesús), S-6 (San Juan Bautista); PAR, 14 (Jesús)
    b. Ceremonies
        Funeral (La Recoleta cemetery), HNM (vol. 83), 233 (1890)
        Mennonite wedding, AM (4/54), 39
    c. Huttentes sect, AM (3/52), 10-12, 31

7. Economy
    a. Industry
        Cart wheels, NG (10/43), 479
        Cement, WAP (Arg. vol.), 15
        Electricity (hydroelectric), AM (2/75), 24-25
        Sugar press, OPE, 217, 219
    b. Agriculture
        Farming, HPP, 57-61
            Japanese farmers, HPP, 25
        Products
            Cattle, RCS, 100-01; NG (10/43), 476 (roundup)
            Cotton, LAP, VI, 274; WAP (Arg. vol.), 16
            Tobacco, WAP (Arg. vol.), 12-13
            Sugarcane, WAP (Arg. vol.), 18
            Timber, WAP (Arg. vol.), 15, 17
                Quebracho, ENB (vol. 17), 310; EI (vol. 14), 67; CEF (vol. 16),
                    111
            Wheat, WAP (Arg. vol.), 19
            Yerba Mate, EA (vol. 21), 275 ff.
    c. Markets
        Asunción, CCS, 641 (1885); HNM (vol. 83), 237 (1890); EA (vol. 21),
            274 ff.; WAP (Arg. vol.), 189

8. Transportation, communication
    Bridge (Paraguay-Brazil), HPP, 5
    Car ferry, Paraguay river, PAR, 39
    Paraná river steamer, NG (4/33), 399
    Railroad station, CCS, 633 (1885)
    Stroessner airport (Asunción), PAR, 44

IX. Peru

1. Environment

a. Geographical features
    Mountains
        Andes, LAT, 143; HAE, 106-07; HNW (vol. 36), 545-65 (c.1860),
            (vol. 37), 16-34 (c.1860); AM (2/56), 11-15, (2/61), 24-27; WIA,
            II, 102; WAP (Br. vol.), 118-19
        Ausangate, NG (2/38), 254
        Coropuna, HNM (vol. 124), 489-500 (ascent, 1910)
        Cunurana, NG (2/64), 256-57
        El Misti, FEW, 431; PER, 13; AM (11/66), 29; NG (3/30), 288,
            (1/33), 118 (air), (8/42), 171; LUL, 18; FLC, 85 (crater)
        Huascarón, AM (9/70), 20
        Pass (Guaylillos), GNM (vol. 35), 555
        Ubinas, NG (1/33), 119 (crater)
        Verónica, NG (1/33), 89
        Vilcapampa, MFE, 164
    Lakes
        Glacial, LF (8/2/48), 49
        Lagunillas, WAP (Br. vol.), 110-11
        Llanganuco, AM (9/70), 16
        Parodi, NG (8/64), 282-83
        Titicaca, AM (1/71), 11-16 (islands), (7/52), 20-23; HNM (vol. 7),
            37-38; LUL, 267
    Rivers
        Acayali, NG (2/64), 260-61
        Huallaga, NG (10/72), 451
        Moche, BMP, 21 (valley)
        Perené, PER, 5
        Pisco, AM (6/78), 28
        Santa, WAP, (Br. vol.), 129
        Vilcanota, NG (10/50), 440-41
    Valleys
        Anta, MFE, 68
        Calca, NG (1/34), 110-31
        Cuzco, WOA, II, 79
        Huaylas, AM (9/70), 17-26 pass., (1/73), 37
        Pucará, AM (4/63), 20-23
        Urubamba, HNM (vol. 126), 709; NG (8/42), 196; NG (10/50), 460;
            ENB (vol. 17), 711
        Veru, NG (4/47), 453-82 (exploration)
        Yucay, AM (1/68), 13-17 pass., (9/70), 18, 20
    Deserts, NG (3/30), 298; WIA, II, 80; AM (7/49), 39
        Arequipa, WAP (Br. vol.), 116-17
        Pisco, NG (1/67), 74
    The land, WAP (Br. vol.), 110-29 pass.
    The Coast, WIA, II, 80
    Coastal plain, BAR, 254
    Pampas, IDO, 53
b. Flora, BTP, plates 45-241 pass.; NG (10/50), 464-79; OAS, 83
c. Fauna
    Llamas, NG (5/46), 642-56 pass.
    Birds, TND, 255, 867; AGG, 20, 23, 66; DPT, 7-145 pass.; SBW, 109,
        132, 143
    Fish, MIA, 247, 252, 333, 338
    Snakes, SSW, 133
    Vicuña, AM (4/73), 2-12, bc.; NG (1/67), 114-15
d. Scenes, BAR, 262-67 pass.; CCS, 398-409 pass. (1885); HNM (vol.
        82), 253-70; LAP, 282-303 pass.; AM (1/52), 13-15, (1/60), 13, (9/76),

Scenes, MCP, 116-17 (c.1840); MC, 89-141 pass., 229, 235, fr.; PER,
12; NCE, VIII, 760 (17th century); WAP (Br. vol.), 114-58 pass.;
NG (5/30), 293 (air), (6/30), 750, 762 (air), (2/64), 215-23 pass.;
AM (5/49), 16, (2/50), 15-19, 29, (1/60), 13 (air), (5/62), 28 (air),
(6/70), 28-34 (mid-19th century), (5/71), 24-25, (9/76), 18-19 (18th
century), (2/78), 29-32 (c.1825); MP, 6-7, 37; NBK (vol. 15), 165
(night)
Public buildings
  Archbishop's Palace, SBL, 59; NG (6/30), 770
  Congress, AM (7/65), 12; NG (6/30), 767 (Senate), (8/42), 174
  Institute of Hygiene, NG (6/30), 766
  Military Hospital, MP, 56
  Ministry of Education, PER, fc.; AM (9/58), 16
  Museum of Archaeology and Ethnology, AM (June-July, 1974), 29-37
  National Stadium, PER, 12
  Presidential Palace, NG (6/30), 751; LAP, VI, 302
  Social Security Hospital, PER, 46
  Torre Tagle Palace, PER, 13; HNM (vol. 82), 260 (1890); AM (4/71),
    24-25; NG (6/30), 768-69; GHL, 165
Other buildings
  City Gate, MCP, 116-17 (c.1840)
  Country club, NG (6/30), 751
  Employee's hospital, AM (5/61), 33
  Shopping center (Galería Carmen), NG (6/30), 755
  Society of Engineers building, NG (6/30), 748
  United States Embassy, PER, 11
Plazas, Parks
  Armas, PER, 19; CCS, 362 (1885); AM (2/30), 29; LAP, VI, 294
  La Alameda de los Descalzos, AM (2/50), 17
  Mayor, HNM (vol. 82), 253 (1890); AM (11/60), 10 (colonial)
  San Martín, PER, 18; AM (2/50), 18 (Nov.-Dec., 1976), 24-25
  Washington, AM (5/71), 24-25
Streets
  Avenida Wilson, AM (2/50), 16
  Jirón de la Unión, BHS, 109
Monument: Dos de Mayo, NG (6/30), 746
Mollendo
  Scenes, NG (6/30), 742 (air)
  Harbor, NG (3/30), 285-86, (6/30), 731 (landing)
Pisco: Market, WAP (Br. vol.), 132-43 pass.
Pissac: Scenes, BNL, 136-37
Puno
  Scenes, NG (8/42), 191
  Market, LAP, VI, 24
Sicuani
  Scenes, OAS, 73
  Rotary Club monument, OAS, 170
Talara
  National Petroleum Company, AM (5/51), 39
  Refinery, MP, 43
Teabaya: Scenes, NG (3/30), 284
Tinga María: Scenes, AM (8/71), 15 (air), (8/72), 25-30
Trujillo: Scenes, NG (1/33), 88 (air)
Yanque: Scenes, MFE, 26, 94 (air)

4. Society
  a. People types, HNM (vol. 2), 604 (c.1850), (vol. 36), 558-62 pass.
    (1865), (vol. 54), 357-67; WAP (Br. vol.), 130-50; PER, 34-43 pass.;

MHI, 176-95 pass.; CCS, 370-97 pass. (1885); AM (3/78), 8-10; NG
(6/30), 736-82 pass., (1/33), 106-15 pass., (2/38), 244-63 pass.,
(8/42), 173-96 pass., (10/50), 424-79 pass., (1/55), 136 ff., (2/64),
317-63 pass., (8/64), 292-96, (1/67), 116-17, (12/73), 729-87 pass.;
AM (3/78), 8-10; MP, 10-11, 38-64 pass.; OAS, 41-170 pass.; IDO,
92-186 pass.
Bread seller, AM (9/76), ibc. (1856)
Lima ladies (c.1840), MCP, 116-17; HNW (vol. 2), 603 (c.1850)
Milk seller, CCS, 381 (1885)
Peasants, altiplano, VIP, x
Upper class, LA (7/14/61), 87-90
Women (1838), AM (6/62), 19
  b. Indians
Types, BNL, 136-37; HNM (vol. 2), 603
    Amazon Indians, MWD, 180-81
    Andes Indians, AM (3/54), 12-15, 30-31
    Calca Valley Indians, NG (1/34), 110-31 pass.
    Lake Titicaca Indians, JIV, 142-43; AM (5/51), 21-23
Towns, MFE, 124 (air); AM (10/71), 21; NG (12/73), 762-63
Tribes
    Amahuaca, POE, VI, 32-37
    Aymará, NG (2/71), 272-93 pass.; POE, VII, 88-97
    Campa, POE, VII, 50-59
    Izuchaca, NG (2/64), 227
    Kuyochico, NKC, 29-79 pass.
    Ocucaje, CHM, 64-65, 176
    Quêchua, NG (2/71), 280-93 pass.; POE, VII, 68-78; JIV, 142-43;
      CE, XIII, 604; SRA, 150
    Willka, AM (1/67), 9, 16
  c. Amusements
Festivals
    Cuzco, BHS, 110
    Huancayo, NG (6/30), 161
    Sacsahuamán, SBL, 56
    Zamacueca, AM (9/76), ibc. (1856)
Dances, CM, 138-41; AM (9/76), ibc.; NG (8/42), 184
Cock fighting, ELA, 202 (Choisica)

5. Culture
  a. Architecture
Hacienda (Puna), OAS, 42
Hotels, AM (1/55), 29-30; AM (1/73), 37 (beach club)
Housing, CCS, 358-409 pass. (1885); DAB, 46-47 (Basque); PER, 45
      (modern); AM (6/69), 17 (Callao)
    House designs, AM (2/57), 15-19
  b. Art
Andean art, AM (1/78), 4107
Crafts, AM (Nov.-Dec., 1978), 49-54
Folk art, AM (7/67), 20-25
Indian mantles, AM (9/58), 8-12 (Paracas Indians)
Jungle art, AM (5/79), 2-9
Lenten curtains, AM (3/72), 24-25
Religious dolls, AM (6/69), 7-12 (Cuzco)
  c. Education
Ayacucho: University, AM (12/61), 10-16
Cuzco: University, AM (4/71), 24-25
Lima: San Marcos, AM (9/67), 13; NG (2/64), 221 (students); LAP, VI,
    295; CEF (vol. 12), 141

Pisco, WAP (Br. vol.), 132-43 pass.; NG (8/42), 195; MP, 57
Plantation Indian market, ECC, 181-82
Puno, LAP, VI, 24; OAS, 55, 75
San Jerónimo, VIP, xi
San Pablo, OAS, 41 (barter)

8. Transportation, communication
    Highways
        Andes, BSA, 103
        Coastal, BSA, 177
        Lima-Cerro de Pasco, SBL, 8
        To Machu Picchu, MP, 22
    Railroads
        Andes, BSA, 93; NG (6/30), 779
        Chorifa, WLA, 10
        Oroya, HNM (vol. 82), 289 (1890); EA (vol. 21), 643
        Southern Peruvian, OAS, 148
    Airports
        Lima (Limatambo), AM (4/49), 34; NG (3/30), 29, (1/33), 84, (2/64),
            234-37
        Masisea, BSA, 179
    Hydrofoil, FFS, 460; LA (4/14/67), 42-43 (Lake Titicaca)
    Bridges, NCE, viii, 504 (1610); AM (10/66), fc., (1779); HNM (vol. 36),
        563 (1865); MCP, 116-17 (c.1840); GHS, 34 (c.1910); NG (2/29), 166,
        174 (railroad), (3/30), 295 (railroad), (12/37), 805, (1/73), 782-85
    Modes of travel
        Pack train, NG (12/37), 806, (12/73), 738-39
        Truck, OAS, 150
        Tricycle, OAS, 151

9. Miscellaneous
    Census taking, BWG, 29
    Child born to 5 year old girl, LF (5/29/39), 25
    Conflict with Spain (1866)
        Callao bombarded, AM (5/71), 24-25
        Ruins in Lima, CCS, 274
    "Kon-Tiki" 93 day cruise from Peru (April, 1947), LF (10/20/47), 113-21
    Satellite station (Lurín), AM (1/70), 49

X. Uruguay

1. Environment
    a. Geographical features
        Lobos Island, AM (6/63), 33-37; HUP, 10, 11 (seals)
        National park (Quebrada de los Cuervos), AM (4/61), 32-35
        Piedra del Cucuy, NG (11/33), 623 ("mountain")
        Salta Grande falls, WAP (Ven. vol.), 176
        Uruguay river, WAP (Ven. vol.), 185
            Falls, NG (11/48), 633
    b. Fauna
        Birds, DPT, 89
        Fish, MGA, 238
    c. Scenes, HNM (vol. 75), 907-09 (1885); HUP, 5-14; NG (11/48), 624-54
        pass.; LAP, VI, 315-26 pass.; WAP (Ven. vol.), 175-87 pass.

2. Political
    a. Symbols

Coat of arms, EA (vol. 27), 810; SFT, 295
National flag (adopted 7/11/1830), SFT, 295; EFW, 52
Presidential flag, SFT, 295
Coins, AJG, 499-501; FCL, 271-72, 315; CCW, illus. 813
Stamps, MFS, plate 103
b. Activities
Pro-Castro demonstration (Montevideo), LF (6/2/61), 84-85
Senate in session, HUP, 31
Siege of Montevideo lifted (Aug. 1, 1851), AM (6/51), 26
c. Military
Forts
Montevideo (colonial, 1782), AM (6/51), 24
Santa Teresa, NG (11/48), 628, 642 (c.1750); HUP, 19

3. Cities, Towns, Villages
Montevideo
Scenes, CCS, 591-608 pass. (1885); URU, 4 (air); LAT, 147; ESA, 150;
JSA, 133; HUP, 1 (air), 17 (c.1726); WAP (Ven. vol.), 180, 213
(air); NG (5/30), 262 (beach), (1/31), 71, 73, (1/48), 137 (water-
front), (11/48), 631; AM (7/49), 8, (1/52), 3, 4, (9/59), 30-34,
(7/65), 13, (4/68), 41 (beach); ENB (vol. 22), 808-11; NBK (vol. 19),
235
Harbor, CCS, 593 (1885); BAR, 369; HUP, 13; LUL, 368; AM (11/49),
19; NG (1/31), 74; WAP (Ven. vol.), 129, 210
Public buildings, AM (8/54), 38
Capitol, HNP, 30 (entrance); GHS, 508; ESA, 126; LUL, 368; EA
(vol. 27), 817; WAP (Ven. vol.), 211-12; AM (1/52), 5; WBE
(vol. 20), 179
Ministry of Foreign Affairs, HUP, 34
President's office (Palacio Estévez), HUP, 29
Salvo Palace, AM (10/71), 13; WEB (vol. 20), 178
Stadium, HUP, 27; URU, 44; NG (11/48), 650; EA (vol. 27), 20;
WHV, 131
Yacht Club, NG (11/48), 629
Other buildings
Casino, HUP, 46
Commercial bank, HUP, 18
Hospital de Clínicas, HUP, 53; URU, 24; EA (vol. 27), 818
Parks, Plazas, Streets
Avenida Agraciada, URU, 6
18th of July Avenue, BHS, 157
El Prado Park, HUP, 14
José Batlle y Ordóñez Park, ELA, 261
Plaza Independencia, HUP, 25 (c.1850); AM (7/49), 8, (Nov.-Dec.,
1970), 24-25; EA (vol. 27), 810; LAP, VI, 315; WAP (Ven. vol.),
207
Monuments
La Carreta, ELA, 261; LAT, 47; HUP, 20; LUL, 355; WAP (Ven.
vol.), 196
Obelisk, EA (vol. 27), 820; WAP (Ven. vol.), 200
Subway, AM (8/78), 7-13
Paysandú: Scenes, WAP (Ven. vol.), 209
Pocitos
Scenes, AM (8/50), 13; WAP (Ven. vol.), 192
Beach, PLA, 79; HUP, 47
Punta del Este: Scenes, WAA, 186; ESA, 140 (air); AM (11/49), 17 (air),
(3/79), 19; LF (4/2/51), 120 (air); LAP, VI, 326 (air); WAP (Ven. vol.),
19 (air), 216; BHS, 152 (beach); MED, 363 (harbor); EI (vol. 8), 552;

WBE (vol. 20), 176 (beach)
Solís: Scenes, EA (vol. 27), 813 (beach)

4. Society
    a. People types, HUP, 35-61 pass.; AM (9/59), 30-34; NG (11/48), 624-
        53 pass.; WAP (Ven. vol.), 188-94 pass.; LF (4/2/51), 120-23
        Gauchos, AM (9/49), 14, (4/59), 5-11; EA (vol. 27), 819
        News venders, LAP, VI, 323
    b. Amusements: Gaucho dances, AM (2/53), 16-19

5. Culture
    a. Architecture: New housing, HUP, 53
    b. Education
        University of Montevideo, NG (1/31), 70
            School of Architecture, LUL, 368
            School of Engineering, HUP, 40; URU, 27; AM (6/65), 46
            School of Medicine, HUP, 20
        Labor University, HUP, 40
        University of the Republic, Law School, HUP, 38
        Sayago School of Agriculture, HUP, 39
    c. Music, Drama
        Actors, plays, AM (11/60), 22-25
        Summer theater, HUP, 46; WAP (Ven. vol.), 214 (Montevideo)
        Third International Film Festival, AM (4/54), 32-36
        Musical instruments: Drums, HDA, 126

6. Religion
    Edifice: Jackson Episcopal Church, HUP, 37

7. Economy
    a. Industry
        Electric power, WAP (Ven. vol.), 187
            Dams
                Río Negro, NG (11/48), 646
                Rincón del Bonete, EA (vol. 27), 813
        Fishing, AM (5/79), 13-17
        Meat packing, HUP, 56; URU, 37
        Wool working, AM (10/53), 20
        National refinery, URU, 39
        Textiles, EI (vol. 18), 557
        Water treatment, HUP, 50
    b. Agriculture
        Activities, HUP, 50-54, 60-61
        Cattle, RCS, 98-99; BAR, 367; WAP (Ven. vol.), 182
        Sheep, EA (vol. 27), 814; LAP, VI, 324
    c. Markets
        Montevideo, CEN, 207
        Open air, AM (1/52), 4
        Sheep, NG (11/48), 645

8. Transportation, Communication
    Airports (Carrasco), URU, 43
    Bridges
        Cebollatí River, URU, 41
        Santa Lucía River, LAT, 147; AM (1/73), 41
    Highways, HUP, 42-43

9. Miscellaneous
    "Admiral Graf Spee" sunk (German warship), LF (12/25/39), 16-17

XI. Venezuela

1. Environment
    a. Geographical features
        Mountains
            Andes, WAP (Ven. vol.), 6-17 pass.; BVP, 5, 9
            Avila, NG (1/39), 118
            Cerro Bolívar (iron mountain), WHV, 102; BAR, 205; AM (3/52), 24-
                27, (5/72), 20, (1/78), 35; NG (3/63), 384-85; LAP, VI, 18
            Mirror Peak, BVP, 6
            Pico Bolívar, NG (8/76), 180; BVP, 8; WHV, 70
        Glaciers
            Pico Bolívar, NG (3/63), 368-69
            Timoncito, VEN, 14
        Lakes
            Canaima, WHV, 80; BVP, 11
            Maracaibo, EBR (vol. 17), 91
            Negra, WHV, 20
            Valencia, BVP, 12
        Rivers
            Carrao, NG (8/76), 181; BVP, 11, 15
            Orinoco, LUL, 224; NG (2/96), 55, 57 (delta), (8/56), 192-93; BUP,
                10, 14
            Tocuyo, NG (8/76), 181
        Falls
            Angel, NG (11/49), 658, 682, (3/63), 379-380, (8/76), 208; VEN, 21;
                WHV, 88; JSA, 113; AM (3/53), 13, (1/78), ibc.; BVP, 13; LF
                (5/2/55), 12-13; LAP, VI, 330; CEN, 243; CEF (vol. 21), 276
            Caroní River falls, WAP (Ven. vol.), 14
            Hacha, JSA, 116
            Salta de la Llovizna, BVP, 14
        Guacharo caves, BVP, 20
        Jungles, AM (9/57), 24-27
        Llanos, LUL, 223; HNM (vol. 128), 814-24 (c.1812); NG (8/76), 200
        Los Roques Islands, AM (4/78), 36-42
        Macuta Beach (Caribbean), NBK (vol. 19), 297
        Margarita Island, AM (10/50), 6-8; WAP (Ven. vol.), 53
        Playa Bolívar (beach), AM (3/72), 37
        Sarisariñama plateau "Pit," NIL, 90-91
            "Lost World," NG (3/63), 376-77
        Valley of Caracas, NG (2/1896), 55, 57 (1895)
    b. Flora, BTP, plates 19, 115
    c. Fauna
        Beetles, LF (1/18/43), 6-7
        Birds, TND, 305, 671, 789, 899; SBV, 8-160 pass.; AGG, 23-63 pass.;
            DPT, 3-141 pass.; SBW, 220, 241
            Ibis, NG (5/50), 636-57 pass.
        Fish, MGA, 145-428 pass.
        Snakes, SSW, 76, 133
            Anaconda, NG (1/39), 102
    d. Scenes, LF (9/13/54), 122-31; LAP, VI, 330-45; WAP (Ven. vol.), 6-
        34 pass.; WHV, 23-87 pass.; NG (11/49), 656-90 pass., (3/63), 344-83
        pass.; HNM (vol. 18), 591-99; BVP, 5-24 pass.; ENB (vol. 22), 962
    e. Disasters: Earthquake, Caracas (1967), VEH, 178

2. Political
    a. Division
        State of Lara, AM (7/58), 19-23

  b. Symbols
      Coat of arms, EA (vol. 27), 943; SFT, 296
      National flag (adopted, 2/19/54), SFT, 296; EFW, 48
      Sucre flag, SFT, 296
      Naval flag insignia, RLM, II, 116
      Coins, FCL, 284-98 pass.; GCW, 442-43; CCW, 806; AJG, 502-07
          Leper colony coins, FCL, 296
      Stamps, MDS, plate 103
  c. Military
      Carabobo Battle monument, ESA, 114
      German blockade (1903), LF (7/14/61), 84
      Military Junta (February, 1958), LF (2/3/58), 21
      National guard of honor, NG (4/40), 505

3. Cities, Towns, Villages
    Barquisimeto: Scenes, WAP (Ven. vol.), 18
    Caracas
        Scenes, LF (9/13/54), 122-23 (air, night); LAP, VI, 342; WAP (Ven.
            vol.), 10-62 pass.; BVP, VI, 345; WHV, 6, 40 (air), 44; JSA, 108-
            09; BMP, 479; ESA, 160; LUL, 220-21; BAR, 208; SHS, 562 (c.1910);
            HNM (vol. 17), 187-97 (1850), (vol. 92), 104-110; NG (4/40), 500,
            (2/60), 236, (3/63), 345-59 pass., (8/76), 174-75, 182-83; AM (4/51),
            38-39, (2/54), fc., 7-8, 30, (5/62), 30-33, (5/66), 10 (air), (8/74),
            fc., 17-25 pass.; WBE (vol. 20), 241
        Public buildings
            Congress, HNM (vol. 92), 108 (1895); AM (7/65), 17; NG (1/39),
                120; BVP, 33, 35
            Museum of Science, NG (4/40), 503
            National Library, NG (4/40), 505
            National Pantheon, AM (4/51), 8, (3/67), 30; NG (1/39), 110, (4/40),
                499; WAP (Ven. vol.), 52
            Presidential Palace, NG (1/39), 98; EA (vol. 27), 944
            Simón Bolívar Center, BVP, 17; VSN, 11
        Other buildings
            Country club, NG (1/39), 131, (4/40), 468
            Miranda Bank, WAP (Ven. vol.), 21
            Tamanaco hotel, AM (6/54), 4, 10
            United States Embassy, AM (6/49), 5
        Alamira suburb, VEN, 8
        Cable car to Avila Mountain, BVP, 7
        Independence monument, BNL, 424-25
        Plaza Bolívar (c.1840), CAB, 80
    Ciudad Bolívar: Scenes, NCE, III, 893; BVP, 17
    Ciudad Guayana: Scenes, NG (8/76), 190
    Cumaná: Fort, WHV, 53
    La Guaira
        Scenes, WHV, 5; HNM (vol. 131), 273 (c.1910); NG (2/1896), 53 (1895);
            DAB, 146-47; BVP, 16 (air)
        Harbor, LAP, VI, 342; NG (1/39), 114, (4/40), 484; IE (vol. 19), 36
    Los Nevados, NG (3/36), 372
    Maracaibo: Scenes, LF (9/13/54), 124-25; WAP (Ven. vol.), 25, 29
    Maracay: Scenes, AM (5/68), 2; WAP (Ven. vol.), 28
    Mérida: Scenes, AM (9/52), 20-23; BVP, 34
    Nueva Cádiz: Ruins, AM (7/67), 8-10
    Puerto Caballo
        Scenes, CCS, 296 (1885)
        Waterfront, VEN, 22
    Puerto Hierro: Scenes, VEN, 28 (docks)

Seboruco: Scenes, NG (8/76), 196-97
Valera: Scenes, WAP (Ven. vol.), 18

4. Society
   a. People types, BVP, 37-63 pass.; CCS, 259-94 pass. (1885); HNM (vol.
      17), 189-97, pass. (1850); VEN, 29-40 pass.; AM (11/61), 7-9
      (rural); NG (3/63), 346-86 pass.; WAP (Ven. vol.), 36-49
      Pigmies, AM (3/62), 12-16
      German settlers (Tovar), BVP, 28
   b. Indians, NG (3/63), 363-67
      Guajiras, AM (7/55), 7-12
      Motilones, WHV, 33 (communal house)
      Yanomamos, NG (8/76), 210-23
      Yecuarias, AM (5/74), 2-9
      Yupas, WYF, 61-72
   c. Amusements
      Boxing, NG (4/40), 481
      Bull "flipping," NG (8/76), 198-99; BVP, 37
      Carnival (Maracaibo), JSA, 116
      Horse racing, EA (vol. 21), 948 (Hipódromo)
      Riding (Hípico club), LF (9/13/54), 130
      Soccer, DAB, 146 (Basque team)

5. Culture
   a. Architecture
      Housing, WHV, 8, 14; CCS, 261-89 pass. (1885); FDT, illus. 147 (low
         cost); AM (9/60), 14 (low cost), (8/66), 4 (new); NG (1/39), 106-
         07 (Indian); LF (9/13/54), 126-28
         Caracas, BAR, 198; FDT, illus. 159-60 (apartments); AM (9/49), 15-
            19, (4/51), 40
         Slums, NG (8/76), 185; BAR, 24; AM (4/51), 40; KE, 55-60
         Maracaibo, FDT, illus. 175-84 pass.
         Stilt houses, WAP (Ven. vol.), 22
      La Puerta Gate, WHV, 75
   b. Art
      African (Negro) art styles, AM (8/76), 17-19
      Church decorations (interior), AM (2/73), 33-40
      Indian wall hangings (Guajiro), AM (5/72), 36-38
      Paintings, AM (8/75), 25-32
   c. Dance, AM (7/49), 2-15, (11/49), 20-23 (children), (10/62), 31-34
      (team)
      Devil dance, IEM, 477; AM (8/52), 24-27, (7/61), 38, (June-July, 1973),
         12-13 (San Francisco de Yare)
      Indian dances, CM, 153
   d. Education
      Basque language school, DAB, 146-47
      Central University campus, EI (vol. 19), 35 (air)
      Experimental schools, AM (1/50), 28-30
      Institute of Neurology and Brain Research, AM (8/57), 5
      University of Caracas, AM (6/56), 40; NG (1/39), 113; BVP, 49-51;
         WHV, 50
      University City, SBL, 66; AM (2/54), 4-5, 35 (Caracas)
      University, Mérida, LAP, VI, 332
      Rural Normal school, PLA, 128 (Rubio)
      Teacher training schools, AM (3/56), 14-18
   e. Music, BVP, 44-45
      Festival (Caracas), AM (3/55), 33-38
      Instruments, CM, 151, 155

Road building, AM (7/53), 24-26
b. Railroads, HNM (vol. 92), 105 (1895); WAA, 172 (ore train)
c. Bridges
Liberator's (Venezuela-Colombia boundary), NG (1/39), 129
Lake Maracaibo, WAP (Ven. vol.), 19
Urdaneta, WHV, 99
d. Cable cars
Caracas (Avila mountain), BVP, 7
Mérida, LAP, VI, 337
e. Orinoco River, NG (7/31), 623-44 (journey)

9. Miscellaneous
Protest to Spain (1865), AM (3/71), 24-25
Spanish King and Queen visit Caracas (1978), AAY (vol. 1978), 536

F. DIPLOMATIC AND INTERNATIONAL RELATIONS

I. Wars, Campaigns

1. Mexico-United States war (1846-1848)
a. Battles
Buena Vista (1847), NMW, 81-85; NG (1/65), 103-09; DSW, 208-09;
BTM, 203-04
Cerro Gordo (1847), NMW, 146-47; BTM, 234-35; HNM (vol. 11), 314
Chapultepec (1848), NMW, 209, 212-15
Churubusco (1848), NMW, 190-91, 193; BYM, 234-35; HNM (vol. 11),
318
Contreras (1847), BTM, 234-35
La Mesa (1847), NMW, 124-25
Los Angeles (1847), NMW, 120-21
Mexico City (1848), NMW, 182-83; DSW, 196-97, 221; WBE (vol. 13), 386
(1847)
Scott enters, NMW, 217; HNM (vol. 11), 323
U.S. troops in The Zócolo, DSW, 222-23
Boy Heroes (Niños Héroes), LF (5/17/47), 47
Molina del Rey (1848), MNW, 206-07; HNM (vol. 11), 321
Monterrey (1846), NME, 74-75; DSW, 202-03; BTM, 234-35
Palo Alto (1848), NMW, 24-25
Resaca de la Palma (1846), NMW, 30-31
Sacramento (1846), BTM, 234-35
San Antonio (1847), NMW, 180
Veracruz (1847), NMW, 134-37; BTM, 203-05
b. Scenes, LF (7/23/56), 68-88 pass., (7/30/56), 52-71 pass., (8/6/56),
64-83
c. Mexican troops, NMW, 101
Uniforms, NMW, 50-53
d. United States forces
Soldiers, NMW, 42, 90-95, 224-33
Uniforms, NMW, 44-49
Weapons, NMW, 186-88
Battle flags, NMW, 194-99
Medals, NMW, 218-19
Naval activity, NMW, 152-61
e. Miscellaneous
Cartoons, FCH, 16-25 (1832-56)
Monument to Americans, HNM (vol. 17), 179

III.   Inter-American Organizations

1.   Pan American Union (Organization of American States)
     Headquarters, Washington
          First (before 1910), AM (4/65), 19
          Permanent, PLA, 150; AM (8/50), 48
               Dedicated (April 26, 1910), PLA, 35
               Columbus Memorial Library, AM (6/51), 21-22
               Aztec Fountain, AM (3/50), bc.
     Official flag, SFT, 301

2.   Organization of Central American States
     Headquarters, Cartago, Costa Rica, WES, 145
     Inaugurated (5/08), PDA, 271
     First Peace Conference, Washington (1907), PDA, 271; AM (1/68), 36
          (members)
     Central American Court of Justice (Casa Amarilla), AM (4/52), 39
     Members, AM (10/55), 3-5
     Flag, SFT, 30

3.   Council on Inter-American Relations, LF (4/27/42), 80

IV.   Inter-American Meetings

1.   Political
     a.   Congress of Panama (1826)
          Meeting place, AM (June-July, 1976), 3; BNL, 424-25
          Delegates, AM (7/56), 5
          Commemorative stamp, AM (8/56), 2
     b.   International Conferences of American States
          First (1889-1890) Washington
               Meeting place (Wallach mansion), AM (4/65), 17
               Delegates, AM (3/50), 3, (2/54), 20-23, (3/58), 9, (4/65), 18, (4/70),
                    8-12, (1/71), 24-25
          Second (1901-1902) Mexico City: Delegates, PDA, 270-71
          Third (1906), Rio de Janeiro: Delegates, (United States), PDA, 270-71
          Seventh (1933), Montevideo: Delegates (United States), JMB, 163
          Eighth (1938), Lima: Delegates, LF (12/26/38), 11-13
          Ninth (1840), Bogotá
               Delegates, LF (4/26/48), 28
               Riots, LF (4/26/48), 23-29
          Tenth (1954), Caracas: Delegates, AM (5/54), 3-5, 41-43; BHG, 176-77
     c.   General Assembly meetings, Organization of American States
          First (1970), Washington, AM (9/70), 20-25; PLA, 149
          Second (1972), AM (5/72), 10
          Third (1973), AM (5/73), 10-16
          Fourth (1974), Atlanta, AM (June-July, 1974), 2-7
          Sixth (1976), Santiago, AM (10/76), 35
          Seventh (1977), Grenada, AM (9/77), 3-6
          Eighth (1978), Washington, AM (9/78), 27-32
     d.   Special meetings
          Inter-American Conference for the Maintenance of Peace (1936), Buenos
               Aires, AM (3/50), 3, (4/67), 7
               President Roosevelt attends, ALA, 71
          Declaration of Panamá (10/2/39), LF (10/16/39), 17: Delegates, LF
               (10/16/39), 17-19
          Conference on Hemisphere Security (1940), Havana: Delegates, LF

(8/5/40), 27

Conference of American Foreign Ministers (1942), Rio de Janeiro, LF (2/2/42), 19

Delegates, LF (2/9/42), 25-29

Inter-American Conference on War and Peace (1945), Chapultepec, Mexico: Delegates, LF (4/19/45), 31

Inter-American Defense Conference (1957), Rio de Janeiro, LF (9/1/47), 30-31

Pact of Bogotá (1950), AM (10/50), 40; Ratified (1951), AM (2/52), 40

American Foreign Ministers (1950), Panamá, AM (3/50), 4

Caribbean Fact Finding Commission (1950), AM (3/50), 46

American Foreign Ministers (1951), Washington, AM (4/51), 10-11

American Presidents (1956), Panamá, AM (3/73), 24-25

American Foreign Ministers (1958), Washington, AM (11/58), 2-6

American Foreign Ministers (1960), San José, Costa Rica, AM (10/60), 3-7

American Foreign Ministers (1961), Punte del Este, Uruguay, AM (10/61), 2-7, (5/62), 14

OAS Cuban Missile Crisis (Oct. 23, 1962), AM (12/62), 41, (4/65), 7

American Foreign Ministers (1962), Montevideo, AM (3/62), 2-7, (5/62), 14

First Special Inter-American Conference (1964), AM (2/65), 43

Third Special Inter-American Conference (1967), AM (4/67), 7

American Presidents (1967), Punte del Este, PLA, 30; AM (4/72), 24-25, (3/73), 24-25; HUP, 28; EA (vol. 17), 47

American Foreign Ministers (1969), AM (9/69), 42-45 (Honduras-El Salvador)

Rio Treaty amendment conference (1975), AM (10/75), 18-19

Panamá Canal Treaties signed (9/7/77), AM (Nov.-Dec., 1977), 9-15, fc.; RPC, 162-63

2. Military

Inter-American Defense Board Headquarters, Washington, AM (4/65), 8

Inter-American Defense College, Washington, AM (4/63), 45

Inter-American Defense staff, Washington, AM (3/50), 22

Latin American military officers visit the United States (1940), LF (10/14/40), 36

Latin American naval officers visit the United States (1941), LF (5/19/41), 36-37

United States Navy in the Caribbean

Anti-Castro move, LF (11/28/60), 36-37

United States and South American ship maneuvers, AM (8/63), 35-38

3. Economic

Inter-American Economic and Social Council

Meeting (1953), AM (4/53), 22

Meeting (1954), Petropolis, Brazil, AM (3/55), 12

Meeting (1964), Lima, AM (2/65), 1, (11/65), 2

Inter-American Statistical Institute (1951), AM (5/51), 41

International Coffee Agreement directors, AM (3/61), 27

Labor

Labor and Social Affairs Seminar (1950), Quito, AM (8/50), 14-15, 47

Latin American Ministers of Labor (1963), Bogotá, AM (7/63), 44

International Labor Organization in Latin America, AM (7/69), 16-22

Technical cooperation and development with Latin America, AM (4/60), 4-7

Leaders, AM (10/72), 24-25

4. Cultural

V. Inter-American Cooperative projects

1. Peace Corps

INDEX OF PERSONS

All the persons listed here are in one way or another connected with events in Latin America during the years covered by this guide. Each person has been identified by country and by a brief note regarding interests, occupations, contributions, or significance. When known, vital statistics have also been added. The portraits of some artists have not been found, but examples of their works are indicated.

Abrams, Livio, (Brazil), artist (no pic.): wk. CLA, no. 1

Abularch, Rodolfo, (Guatemala), artist: AM (4/60), 32-34, (1/63), 29; wk. CLA, no. 2 (1969)

Accioly, Hildebrando, (Brazil), statesman (ambassador to U.S.; Chairman OAS): AM (2/52), 40, (9/49), 34, (10/49), 30, (5/50), 41, 47

Acheson, Dean G., 1893-1971, (United States), statesman (U.S. Secretary of State): AM (4/51), 11; LF (2/21/49), 104; MEW, I, 30; EBRF (1), 58

Acuña, Luis Alberto, (Colombia), artist: CLA, 3 (1941): wk. MA (2/79), 52

Acuña, Miguel, 1849-73, (Mexico), writer: WAP (Mex. vol.), 196

Acuña de Chacón, Angela, (Costa Rica), statesman (Ambassador to OAS): AM (4/74), 24-25, (5/75), 30

Adams, John, 1735-1826, (United States), statesman (President, 1797-1801): AM (8/71), 28

Adams, John Quincy, 1767-1848, (United States), statesman (President 1825-29): AM (5/76), 16-17; NMW, 171

Agassiz, Louis, 1807-73, (United States), scientist: AM (2/72), 24-25 (1865); EBR (1), 290 - Birthplace, LLA, 84 - Home, Quincy, Mass., LLA, 84-85 - Wife, AM (2/72), 24-25; LLA, 84-85 (1852) - Brazilian explorations, AM (2/72), 25-32 - At different ages (1833, 1834, 1847, 1855, 1863, 1869, 1872), LLA, 84-85

Agramonte, Roberto, (Cuba), politician (Castro associate): LF (1/19/59), 31

Aguado, Alejandro de, (Argentina), patriot (with San Martín): AM (2/78), 5

Aguilar, Margo, b.1944, (Costa Rica), poet: AM (9/65), 33

Aguirre, José Antonio, (Venezuela), politician (President Basque government in exile): DAB, 146-47

Aguirre, Lope de, c.1508-61, (Spain), Colonial explorer: AM (5/63), 30

Aguirre Cerda, Pedro, 1879-1941, (Chile), Statesman (President, 1938-41): LF (6/30/41), 81 - Funeral, LF (12/15/41), 35

Ahumasa, Miguel, (Mexico), military (general): HNM (vol. 94), 371

Alamán, Lucas, 1782-1853, (Mexico), historian, politician: HHL, II, 108; WNC, VIII, 267; CLM, 422; MEW, I, 83; LF (12/15/52), 34-35

Albán, Laureano, b.1942, (Costa Rica), poet: AM (9/65), 31

Alberdi, Juan Bautista, 1810-85, (Argentina), statesman: NCE, I, 250; MEW, I, 89; WAP (Arg. vol.), 130; AM (6/62), 24, (4/67), 30, (1/71), 24-25, (1/77), 3, 4

Albermarle, George, 1724-72, (Britain), naval officer; Captures Havana (1762): TCP, 546-47

Albizu Campos, Pedro, 1891-1965, (Puerto Rico), revolutionary: LF (3/15/54), 23; WHP, 156; WPR, 64-65

Alcalá, Macedonio, (Mexico), musician: GPM, 82

Aranha, José Pereira da Graça, 1868-1931, (Brazil), writer: AM (12/65),
   2, (3/73), 32
Aranha, Osvaldo, 1894-1960, (Brazil), statesman: MEW, I, 218
Araujo, Arturo, 1878-1968, (El Salvador), statesman (President, 1931): WES,
   144-45
Araujo Sánchez, Francisco, b.1937, (Ecuador), poet: AM (11/64), 31
Araya, Julia, (Costa Rica), singer: AM (2/65), 42
Arbenz Guzmán, Jacobo, b.1914, (Guatemala), statesman (President, 1951-54):
   JTG, 51 (1963); BHG, 176; LF (10/12/53), 176 - In Cuba, LF (8/15/60),
   35 - Wife, LF (10/12/53), 176
Arce, Manuel José, 1783-1847, (El Salvador), statesman (Central American
   Federation President, 1825): AM (4/52), 5, (8/77), 12
Archibald, James F. J., (United States), journalist, (Spanish American War):
   HNM, (vol. 98), 946
Arciniegas, Germán, b.1900, (Colombia), writer; diplomat: AM (3/49), 48,
   (2/67), 48, (4/70), 31, (8/70), 17; LF (10/11/54), 102
Ardévol. José, (Cuba), musician: AM (2/50), 22
Arenal, Luis, (Mexico), artist (no pic.): wk., CLA, no. 6
Arévalo, Juan, b.1904, (Guatemala), statesman (President, 1945-51): AM
   (7/50), 43; BHG, 65; MEW, I, 225
Arévalo Martínez, Rafael, b.1884, (Guatemala), writer: AM (2/65), 9
Argüedas, Alcides, 1879-1946, (Bolivia), writer; historian: CLI, 280; AM
   (2/67), 20
Arias, Arnulfo, b.1902, (Panama), statesman (President, 1940-41; 1949-51): LF
   (5/28/51), 29, (1/17/55), 40 - Wife, LF (5/28/51), 29 - Ousted, LF
   (5/28/51), 28-29
Arias, Hernando, 1886-1962, (Uruguay), military, Statue: HUP, 21
Arias de Avila, Pedro, c.1440-1531, (Panama), colonial official: MEW,
   VIII, 341
Arias de Saavedra, Hernando, 1564-1634, (Paraguay, etc.), colonial explorer:
   AM (5/67), 28
Aridjis, Homero, b.1940, (Mexico), poet: AM (10/63), 11
"Arigo," (Brazil), faith healer: RBT, 64-65
Arista, Mariano, 1802-55, (Mexico), military (General, 1846-48): DSW, 204;
   NMW, 59
Ariza, Gonzalo, (Colombia), painter (no pic.): wk., AM (3/50), 7
Arízago, Carlos Manuel, b.1940, (Ecuador), poet: AM (11/64), 33
Armand, Pierre, (Haiti), politician (colonial): LF (6/11/57), 42
Arnujo, Manuel, (Spain), governor of New Mexico, 1837: DSW, 143
Armstrong, H. E., (United States), journalist (Spanish-American war): HNM
   (vol. 98), 944
Arnarson, Ingolfur, (Northman), colonist (in Iceland), Statue: GMV, 60
Arnoult, Michael, b.1902, (Brazil), architect: BNB, 151
Arosemena, Alcibíades, 1883-1958, (Panama), statesman (President, 1951-52):
   LF (5/28/51), 28
Arosemena, Pablo, 1836-1920, (Panama), statesman (President, 1910-12),
   Monument, Panama City: EPC, 30
Arosemena de Tejeira, Otília, (Panama), stateswoman (chairman, Inter-Amer.
   Commission of Women): AM (Nov.-Dec., 1972), 41
Arosemena Tola, Carlos Julio, 1894-1952, (Ecuador), statesman (President,
   1947-48): AM (10/62), 44
Arosemeno-Gómez, Otto, b.1921 (Ecuador), statesman (President, 1966-68):
   AM (1/68), 45, (3/74), 42; NG (2/68), 262
Arrau, Claudio, b.1903, (Chile), musician (piano): AM (10/49), 16, (1/71),
   21, (3/71), 24-25; LF (8/25/72), 49-52; LEM, 481 - Wife and children,
   AM (6/50), 15, (8/52), 9-11, 28; LF (8/25/72), 49-52
Arteche, Miguel, b.1929, (Chile), poet: AM (5/64), 20
Arthur, Chester Alan, 1830-86, (United States), statesman (President, 1881-

85): MEW, I, 255

Artigas, João Villanova, b.1915, (Brazil), architect: BNB, 151

Artigas, José Gervasio, 1774-1850, (Uruguay), statesman; general: AM
    (8/64), 1, (10/64), 1, 4, (Nov.-Dec., 1970), 24-25, (Nov.-Dec., 1975),
    2; WAP (Ven. vol.), 179; CLI, 89; NCE, I, 926; DEL, 45; BNL, 424-25;
    URU, 18; MEW, I, 256 - Statue (Washington), AM (8/50), 44, (8/66), 44 -
    Statue commemoration (Caracas), AM (5/51), 36 - Monument (Montevideo),
    ESA, 142; WAP (Ven. vol.), 202; AM (8/78), fc. - Image on Uruguay coin,
    (1953), FCL, 46, 274 - Negotiates treaty with English (1806), HUP, 22 -
    Battle of Las Piedras (1811), AM (10/64), 2 - Dictates his "Instructions"
    (4/4/1813), AM (1/51), 25 - Enters Montevideo (1815), HUP, 23 - The
    "Thirty-Three" (1825), AM (4/51), 4, (6/51), 25; HUP, 23

Aspinwall, William H., 1807-75, (United States), merchant; promoter Panama
    Railroad: HNM, XVIII, 147

Astaburnaga, René Amengual, b.1911, (Chile), composer: SM, 217

Asturias, Miguel Angel, 1899-1974, (Guatemala), writer: AM (1/68), 3,
    (4/78), 6; MEW, I, 275; GSL, 170-71

Atahualpa (Inca), c.1502-33, (Peru); WNC, II, 515-16; MEW, I, 276 - Seized
    by Pizarro (Cajamarca), AM (9/72), 24-25 - Funeral, AM (2/74), 22,
    (5/77), 27

Athayde, Roberto, b.1951, (Brazil), dramatist: AM (June-July, 1978), 3

Atl, Gerardo Murillo, b.1877, (Mexico), artist: HMM, 1, 12; wk., HHM, 5,
    8-9

Atúñez, Carmen C. de, (Mexico), sculptor: AM (6/52), 30

Auguste, Toussaint, (Haiti), painter: LF (3/13/50), 101

Austin, Stephen Fuller, 1793-1838, (United States), Texas pioneer: MEW, I,
    304

Austino, Mario F., b.1930, (Brazil), poet: AM (2/64), 33

Avery, John, (England), pirate, 16th century: AM (3/57), 16-18

Avila Camacho, Manuel, 1897-1955, (Mexico), statesman (President, 1940-46):
    BWS, plates 174, 177; MEW, I, 309; HMI, 118-19; LF (7/1/40), 20-21,
    (3/19/15), 31; LK (11/18/41), 24-25 - Inauguration, LF (12/16/40), 17-23 -
    With President Roosevelt, HMI, 218-19 - Home and family, LF (7/1/40),
    96-97, (12/2/40), 96-97 - Wife, LK (11/18/41), 25

Ayala, Daniel, b.1908, (Mexico), musical composer: SM, 249

Ayala, Juan Camilo, (Mexico), painter (no pic.): wk., AM (June-July, 1978),
    32-36, bc.

Ayora, Isidro, (Ecuador), artist: AM (11/59), 21

Ayora, Ruby, (Bolivia), artist: AM (Nov.-Dec., 1968), 56

Azara, Félix de, 1746-1811?, (Spain), naturalist, (colonial): HHG, 365; MEW,
    I, 315

Azevedo, Aluizio de, 1857-1913, (Brazil), writer: NCE, II, 775

Azevedo, Ignatius, (Brazil), churchman (Jesuit martyr): HSA, 245

Backman, John, (Britain), colonial pirate: AM (3/57), 116-18

Baerlein, Ronaldo, b.1934, (Brazil), industrial designer: BNB, 151

Báez, Buenaventura, 1812-84, (Dominican Republic), statesman (President,
    1849-53): MEW, I, 345

Báez, Myrna, (Puerto Rico), artist (no pic.): wk., CLA, no. 7

Baker, L. D., (Jamaica), industrialist: SB, 273

Balaguer, Joaquín, b.1907, (Dominican Republic), statesman (President, 1961-
    62, 1966-78): AM (8/66), 43, (3/74), 41; NG (10/77), 543; MEW, I, 355 -
    Inaugurated (1966), HHD, 35 - With Trujillo, HHD, 33 - With advisors,
    LF (12/1/61), 98 - With King of Spain, AM (10/76), S-7

Balboa, José Antonio, b.1919, (Paraguay), poet: AM (6/67), 33

Balboa, Vasco Núñez de, c.1475-1519, (Spain), conquistador: WNC, II, 195;
    MEW, 357; WHM (vol. 65), 739; GHS, 484 - Statue (Panama), EPC, 28;

NG (11/41), 614; AM (Nov.-Dec., 1971), 24-25; EA (vol. 21), 232 - Scenes in his life (Panama), HNM (vol. 18), 467-84 - March across Isthmus of Panama, HNM (vol. 18), 474 - Receives gold from Indians, HAC, 139 - Use of dogs against Indians, HNM (vol. 18), 480 - Execution, HNM (vol. 18), 484 - Signature, RSD, 10

Baldwin, James L., (United States), engineer (Panama railroad): HNM (vol. 18), 149

Ballivián, José, 1805-52, (Bolivia), statesman (President, 1841-47): MEW, I, 366

Balmaceda, José Manuel, 1840-91, (Chile), statesman (President, 1886-91): HNM (vol. 75), 568; DEL, 59; CLI, 172; MEW, I, 367; AM (12/61), 22

Bancroft, George, 1800-91, (United States), statesman, diplomat, historian: BTM, 203-04

Bancroft, Hubert Howe, 1832-1918, (United States), historian: MEW, I, 372

Bandeira, Antonio, b.1922, (Brazil), painter: BNB, 151

Bandeira, Manuel, b.1886, (Brazil), poet: AM (9/54), 19

Bandelier, Adolph Francis Alphonse, 1840-1914, (United States), historian: FLC, 62 (1878)

Banzer Suárez, Hugo, (Bolivia), statesman (President, 1971-79): AM (3/74), 47; BBY (1972), 152

Baquero-Jiménez, Daniel, (Colombia), guitarist: AM (10/78), 55, (4/79), 38

Baragaño, J. A., (Cuba), poet: FWL, 16

Baratta, María de, b.1894, (El Salvador), musician (composer): SM, 281

Barbacena, Marquês de, (Brazil), statesman (friend of Pedro I): HAT, 198

Barbosa, José Celso, 1857-1921, (Puerto Rico), politician: WHP, 97

Barbosa, Ruy, 1849-1923, (Brazil), statesman: NCE, II, 92; DEL, 67; MEW, I, 383; AM (10/52), 20, (11/62), 28-30

Bardi, Pietro María, (Brazil), Museum director, São Paulo: NG (2/78), 274

Barillas, Manuel Lisandro, 1844-1907, (Guatemala), general, politician: BGL, 145

Barquero, Efraín, b.1931, (Chile), poet: AM (5/64), 18

Barreda, Gabino, 1820-81, (Mexico), statesman: NCE, VIII, 486; CLI, 61

Barreda, Ignacio María, c.1775-1815, (Mexico), painter: NCE, II, 123

Barreto, Tobías, 1839-89, (Brazil), poet: AM (8/71), 24-25

Barrett, John, 1866-1938, (United States), diplomat (Director-General, P.A.U.): AM (4/65), 21

Barrientos, Felipe, (Guatemala), Spanish monk, 18th century: KHG, 48

Barrientos Ortuño, René, 1919-69, (Bolivia), statesman (President, 1966-69): AM (4/67), 48, (3/74), 38; BBY (1969), 174

Barrios, Justo Rufino, 1835-85, (Guatemala), statesman (President, 1873-85): HNM (vol. 71), 900 (c.1885); DEL, 69; BGL, 149; CCS, 75; CRE, 41; MEW, I, 379; AM (Nov.-Dec., 1970), 24-25, (Nov.-Dec., 1972), 24-25 - Bust, AM (3/65), 21 - Monument, AM (10/36), 456 (1935)

Barrira, Juan de la, (Mexico), cadet hero, 1847: DSW, 217

Barros, Eudozia de, (Brazil), musician (piano): AM (7/66), 39

Barros Arana, Diego, 1830-1907, (Chile), statesman, historian: NCE, II, 125; WNC, VIII, 348

Barros Luco, Ramón, 1835-1919, (Chile), politician: GHS, 460

Barros Sierra, Javier, (Mexico), educator (rector National University): PMM, 180 (1968)

Basadre, Jorge, b.1903, (Peru), scholar: AM (3/49), 48, (7/49), 44, (12/49), 36 - Activities, AM (9/58), 13-16 - Wife, AM (2/50), 43, (6/50), 40

Basillat, Maureen, b.1931, (Britain; Brazil), photographer: BNB, 151

Bass, John F., (United States), War correspondent (Spanish American War): HNM (vol. 98), 948

Bastidas, Rodrigo de, c.1460-1526, (Dominican Republic), conquistador (no pic.): Home, Santo Domingo, AM (10/76), 18-19

Batista y Zaldívar, Fulgencio, b.1901, (Cuba), statesman, President, dictator:

MEW, I, 421; ALA, 155 (1933); AM (3/33), 30; LF (1/4/37), 56; TCP,
1090-91 (1936) - Wife and sons, LF (4/21/58), 26-29, (1/12/59), 16 -
Overthrows Prío Socarrás, March 10, 1952, LF (3/24/52), 20-23 - Be-
comes President (1952), TCP, 1090-91, EA, VIII, 303 - As President
(1958), LF (3/10/58), 28-37; WBE (vol. 4), 935 - His troops, LF (1/4/37),
56 - With Grau San Martín (1933), TCP, 546-47 - With Sumner Welles, LF
(4/28/61), 20 - At cock fight, LF (2/15/37), 49 - Anti-Batista revolt, (3/57),
LF (3/25/57), 24-27 - In exile, LF (1/12/59), 16
Batlle y Ordóñez, José, 1856-1829, (Uruguay), statesman (President, 1903-07,
1911-15): DEL, 72; BNL, 424-25; GHS, 512; MEW, I, 423; AM (12/61),
22
Bazile, Castera, (Haiti), artist: ACL, 92; NG (2/61), 241; LF (3/13/50), 101
Beach, Edward L., (United States), military (in Haiti, 1915-16): HGD, 150-51
Beauregard, Pierre Gustave Toutant, 1818-93, (United States), military: HNM,
143 (c.1848)
Beauvoir, Max, (Haiti), Voodoo authority: KV, 104
Becerra, Gustavo, b.1925, (Chile), musical composer: AM (7/64), 26
Behaim, Martin, c.1450-1506, (German), navigator, cosmographer: WHN, II,
104
Belaúnde, Victor Andrés, b.1883, (Peru), statesman, diplomat: AM (3/52),
4; NCE, VIII, 489; LF (3/22/54), 30
Belaúnde Terry, Fernando, b.1912, (Peru), statesman (President, 1963-68):
AM (11/50), 47, (2/65), 2, (3/74), 36; BBY (vol. 1963), 640, (vol. 1966),
604, (vol. 1969), 598 - Returns from exile, BBY (vol. 1977), 552
Belgrano, Manuel, 1770-1820, (Argentina), statesman, patriot: WNC, VIII,
327; MEW, I, 467; AM (4/60), 36, (11/66), 6
Belkin, Arnold, (Mexico), muralist: LMJ, 54-57
Bellegarde, Dantès, 1877-1966, (Haiti), scholar: AM (9/51), 16, (8/78), 18-
21
Bello, Andrés, 1781-1865, (Venezuela), statesman, scholar: WAP (Ven. vol.),
62; NCE, II, 257; MEW, I, 479; AM (10/56), 16, (8/74), 26; CEF (vol.
12), 149 - Birth place (Caracas), AM (10/56), 18, (5/63), 8, (11/64), 1,
3, (2/72), 24-25 - Bust dedication at Pan American Union, AM (2/66), 42 -
Bust, University of Chile (1882), CAB, 81
Beltrán, Enrique, b.1903 (Mexico), conservationist: AM (4/50), 47
Belzú, Manuel Isidoro, 1811-65, (Bolivia), statesman (dictator, 1848-55).
Image on coin (1850): FCL, 52
Benalcázar, Sebastián de, c.1495-c.1555, (Spain; Colombia), conquistador:
AM (9/72), 24-25; MEW, I, 489 - Monument (Cali), SCP, 26
Benavides, Oscar R., 1876-1945, (Peru), statesman (President, 1914-15,
1933-39): AM (3/73), 24-25; LF (12/29/38), 11
Bendersky, Jaime, (Chile), artist (no pic.): AM (3/77), bc.
Benedetti, Mario, b.1920, (Uruguay), poet: AM (9/64), 17
Benedit, Luis Fernando, (Argentina), artist (no pic.): wk., (1974), AM
(1/79), 2
Benítez, Jaime, b.1908, (Puerto Rico), educator: NFP, 92-93; PCI, 913
Bentham, Jeremy, 1748-1832, (Britain), philosopher: AM (8/77), 12
Benton, Thomas Hart, 1782-1858, (United States), statesman; military: BTM,
203-04
Benzoni, Girolano, c.1519-c.1572, (Italy), explorer in America: WNC, II,
347; RSG, 7 - Relations with Indians, ADN, 126-51
Beola, Ignacio, b.1935, (Argentina), poet: AM (10/64), 20
Berckemeyer, Fernando, (Peru), statesman, diplomat: AM (5/50), 41,
(10/50), 9 - Family, AM (5/54), 22 - With wife, AM (7/50), 42
Beresford, William Carr, 1768-1854, (Britain), military; Argentina, 1808:
AM (5/71), 39
Bermúdez, José Francisco, 1782-1831, (Venezuela), patriot: AM (5/69), 5 -
With Bolívar, MBW, 172-73

Bernardes, Artur da Silva, 1875-1955, (Brazil), statesman (President, 1922-26): DAC, 204-05; PBF, 112-13 - Residence, Minas Gerais, DAC, 204-05

Bernardes, Sergio, (Brazil), artist (no pic.): wk., AM (12/60), 24-27

Bernardino, Minerva, (Dominican Republic), chairman, Inter-American Commission of Women: AM (9/49), 34, (5/79), 31

Bernette, Yara, (Brazil), pianist: AM (6/50), 14

Berni, Antonio, b.1905, (Argentina), painter (no pic.): wk., HCL, 251; CLA, no. 8 (1963); AM (10/65), 21-25

Bertrand, María Luisa S. de, (Honduras), Vice Chairman, Inter-American Commission of Women: AM (8/68), 48

Best Maugard, Adolfo, b.1891, (Mexico), painter; writer: HMN, 18

Betancourt, Rómulo, b.1908, (Venezuela), statesman (President, 1945-48, 1959-64); DEL, 77; MEW, I, 549; AM (8/61), 25, (12/64), 4; ENB (vol. 22), 960 - Inauguration (1959), NG (3/63), 357 - Signs Alliance for Progress with President Kennedy, WHV, 138 - With Raúl Leoni, BVP, 36

Betancur, Pedro de San José, 1626-67, (Guatemala), Franciscan priest; patriot: NCE, II, 369

Betancur-Mejía, Gabriel, (Colombia), statesman (Minister of Education): AM (12/66), 44

Betanzos, Domingo de, 1480-1549, (Mexico), Dominican missionary; patriot: NCE, II, 370

Bienville, Jean-Baptiste la Moyne (Sieur de), 1680-1768, (Canada), Founder of New Orleans, 1718: RFW, 100; MEW, I, 565

Bigaud, Wilson, b.1929, (Haiti), painter: LF (12/22/52), 64-65; wk., LF (3/13/50), 101

Bilbao, Francisco, 1823-65, (Chile), writer: AM (5/75), 11

Billinghurst, Guillermo Enrique, 1851-1915, (Peru), statesman (President, 1912-15): GHS, 478

Binder, Theodor, (Peru), doctor in jungle: AM (3/67), 1-7 - Wife, AM (3/67), 1

Bingham, Hiram, 1875-1956, (United States), explorer: AM (8/66), 11 - Search for Vilcabamba, HNW (vol. 125), 697 ff. - Discovery of Machu Picchu, HNM (vol. 126), 709-19

Birrell, Lowell McAfee, (United States), swindler in Brazil: LF (8/10/59), 43-44

Bisbé, Manuel, (Cuba), Castro friend: LUR, 67

Blackbeard (Edward Teach), (Britain), Caribbean pirate, 17th century: ASB, 64

Blaine, James G., 1830-93, (United States), statesman: AM (4/65), 18, (4/70), 11; MEW, II, 9; EBRF (2), 69

Blanco, Teodoro, (Mexico), ceramic artist: WM, 104

Blanco Fombono, Rufino, 1874-1944, (Venezuela), writer: CLI, 264

Blanes, Juan Manuel, 1830-1901, (Uruguay), painter (no pic.): wk., CHL, 214

Blanquet, Aureliano, (Mexico), military: BWS, plate 76

Blest Gana, Alberto, 1830-1920, (Chile), writer: AM (11/61), 43

Bligh, William, 1754-1817, (Britain), Captain of Bounty: AM (Aug.-Sept., 1973), 29

Bliss, Tasker H., 1853-1930, (United States), military (in Mexico, 1914): MFG, 150

Blom, Frans, b.1893, (United States), scholar (Maya): BPA, plate 25 (c.1937), plate 28 (1948)

Blom, Gertrude Duby, (United States), scholar (Maya): BPA, plate 26 (c.1960)

Bo, Lina, b.1914, (Italy; Brazil), architect: BNB, 151

Boas, Franz, 1858-1942, (United States), anthropologist: MEW, II, 30; EBR (2), 1156

Bodega y Cuadra, Juan Francisco de la, b.1740, (Spain), at Nootka Sound: AM (7/70), 4

AM (3/63), 14, (3/74), 75; LF (10/18/63), 49, (5/14/65), 38b; MEW, II, 91 - Takes oath of office, BBY (vol. 1964), 315

Botero, Fernando, (Colombia), artist: AM (1/63), 29; wk., (1972), AM (1/2/79), 6

Boturini Benaducci, Lorenzo, 1680-1740, (Italy), antiquarian; Mexico: WNC, I, 160-61

Bouchard, Hipólito, (France; Argentina), admiral, California: AM (June-July, 1977), 14, 35-37

Bowditch, Charles Pickering, 1842-1921, (United States), archaeologist (Maya): WSH, 73

Bowman, Isaiah, 1878-1950, (United States), geographer: LF (10/22/45), 118

Boyer, Jean Pierre, 1776-1850, (Haiti), statesman, (President-general, 1818-43): AM (6/53), 18; MEW, II, 123

Braden, Spruille, 1894-1978, (United States), statesman; diplomat: BHG, 64-65; LF (3/24/46), 54-62

Braga, Rubem, b.1913, (Brazil), poet: AM (9/54), 19

Braganza, Pedro Gastão d'Orleans, (Portugal), pretender to Brazil throne (1940): HAT, 312-13

Brandy, Carlos, b.1923, (Uruguay), poet: AM (9/64), 17

Brannigan, Sheila, b.1914, (Britain; Brazil), painter: BNB, 152

Brasseur de Bourbourg, Charles Etienne, 1814-1874, (France), churchman; scholar (Mexico): WNC, I, 170

Bravo, Claudio, (Chile), artist (no pic.): wk., (1972), AM (2/79), 3

Bravo, Nicolás, 1787-1854, (Mexico), patriot: WNC, VIII, 226

Brierre, Jean, b.1909, (Haiti), poet: AM (10/74), 35-40

Brinton, Daniel Garrison, 1837-99, (United States), anthropologist: WNC, I, 165

Brión, Pedro Luis, 1782-1821, (Holland; Curaçao), military; with Bolívar: MBW, 172-73

Brito, Raimundo de Farías, (Brazil), writer: AM (12/65), 3, (8/71), 24-25

Brooke, John Rutter, 1838-1926, (United States), military governor, Cuba, 1899: TCP, 546-47

Brown, Clinton, (Jamaica), artist (no pic.): wk., AM (10/78), 32

Brown, Everald, (Jamaica), artist (no pic.): wk., AM (10/78), 32

Brown, William, 1777-1857, (Britain), admiral: AM (3/53), 12; MES, 144

Brum, Baltázar, 1883-1933, (Uruguay), statesman, (President, 1919-23): AM (12/61), 22

Bryan, William Jennings, 1860-1925, (United States), statesman: BWS, plate 83

Bryce, James, 1838-1922, (Britain), historian: MEW, II, 219; EBRF (2), 328

Bucareli y Ursua, Antonio, 1717-79, (Spain), viceroy, (Mexico, 1771-79): CCH, 176; SFB, 33

Buchanan, James, 1701-1868, (United States), statesman, (President, 1857-61); MEW, II, 221; BTM, 203-04; TCP, 546-47 (tries to buy Cuba)

Buchanan, William, 1852-1909 (United States), diplomat; Pan Americanist; PDA, frontispiece - Wife and daughter, PDA, 270-71

Bueno, Maria, (Brazil), tennis champion: LA (9/20/63), 96, (7/17/64), 40

Bueno, Salvador, b.1917, (Cuba), writer: AM (1/52), 2, (12/54), 43

Buneau-Varilla, Philippe, 1859-1940, (France), Panama Canal negotiator: HNM (vol. 131), 171; MPB, 96, 299, 303; MEW, II, 243

Bunker, Ellsworth, b.1894, (United States), diplomat: AM (1/65), 43, (2/65), 4, (7/65), 39; FL (6/9/67), 121-22

Buñuel, Luis, (Mexico), movie director: NMC, 54, 59

Burchard, Pablo, b.1876, (Chile), painter: AM (1/50), 40

Burke, Arleigh, b.1901, (United States), admiral: LF (5/10/63), 81

Burr, Aaron, 1756-1836, (United States), statesman; Vice President, 1801-05: MEW, II, 269

Burreda, Gabino, (Mexico), intellectual: AM (12/61), 21

BWS, plate 131 - In California exile, BWS, plate 155

Camacho, José María, b.1865, (Bolivia), historian: AM (2/67), 20

Camacho Ramírez, Arturo, b.1909, (Argentina), writer: AM (Nov.-Dec., 1970), 21 (1958)

Câmara, Helder, (Brazil), churchman (Recife; Olinda): RBT, 64-65

Câmara Filho, João, b.1944, (Brazil), painter: BNB, 152

Camargo, Iberê, b.1914, (Brazil), painter: BNB, 152

Camnitzer, Luis, (Uruguay), artist (no pic.): wk., CLA, no. 12 (1968); AM (1/79), 8 (1975)

Campbell, John, (United States), army surgeon, Mexican War: NMW, 185

Campeche, José, 1752-1809, (Puerto Rico), artist: WHP, 82

Câmpora, Héctor J., (Argentina), statesman (President, 1973): AAY (1974), 192

Campos, Thereza Leite de Souza, (Brazil), "best dressed woman in Brazil": LF (4/19/54), 136-38

Canales, Antonio, (Mexico), military, Mexican war with the United States: HMW, 67

Candau, M. G., (Brazil), Director, World Health Organization: AM (Nov.-Dec., 1970), 39

Candela, Félix, b.1910, (Mexico), architect (no pic.): wk., CHL, 274; SBL, 66

Cañedo, Juan de Díos, (Mexico), statesman (Foreign Minister, 1840): CLM, 418-19

Canning, George, 1770-1827, (Britain), statesman: MEW, II, 351

Cano, Baldomiro Sanín, c.1861, (Colombia), writer: AM (5/51), 16-19

Cano, Sebastián del, c.1460-1526, (Spain), navigator: CMF, 195; NG (1/76), 752; HE, 159 - Signature, RSD, 35

Cantave, Léon, (Haiti), politician (executive, 1957): LF (6/3/57), 40

Cantín, Federico, b.1908, (Mexico), painter: HMM, 130; wk., HMM, 128-30

Caperton, William Banks, 1855-1941, (United States), admiral (occupied Haiti, 1915): HGD, 150 - Flagship, HGD, 150-51

Cardenal, Ernesto, b.1925, (Nicaragua), poet: AM (10/67), 38

Cárdenas, Lázaro, 1895-1970, (Mexico), statesman (President, 1934-40): BHG, 128-29; AM (11/49), 3, (4/55), 4, (9/57), 4; MEW, II, 364; BWS, plates 147-74 pass. - As boy soldier, BWS, plate 96 - With Lombardo Toledano (1938), AHC, 184 - Divides lands for peasants, BWS, plate 150 - Demonstrations for, HMI, 118-19 - At end of term (1940), LF (12/16/40), 22-23

Cárdenas, Raul, 1885-1979, (Cuba), statesman (Vice-President, 1944-48): LF, (6/26/44), 82-83

Cárdenas, Santiago, (Chile), artist: CLM, no. 13 (1972)

Cárdinas Arroyo, Santiago, (Colombia), artist: CLM, no. 13 (1972)

Cardoza y Aragón, Luis, b.1904, (Guatemala), poet: AM (4/61), 41

Carillo, Alvaro, (Mexico), musician: GPM, 82-83

Carlota, Joaquina, 1775-1830, (Portugal), wife of João VI: HAT, 17 (horseback)

Carnegie, Andrew, 1835-1919, (United States), businessman: MEW, II, 376; EBRF (2), 576 - Lays cornerstone of Pan American Union building (5/11/1908), AM (4/65), 21, (4/70), 12

Caro, José Eusebio, 1817-53, (Colombia), writer: AM (12/65), 2

Caro, Miguel Antonio, 1843-1909, (Colombia), poet, politician: NCE, III, 129 - Statue, NCE, VIII, 487; AM (June-July, 1972), 24-25, (8/74), 24

Carpentier, Alejo, b.1904, (Cuba), writer: FWL, 10, 14; AM (2/50), 46, (7/54), 38, (2/78), 26, (4/78), 8

Carranza, Eduardo, b.1913, (Colombia), writer: AM (Nov.-Dec., 1970), 22

Carranza, Venustiano, 1859-1920, (Mexico), statesman; military (President, 1915-20): BHG, 126; BWS, plates 69-115 pass.; DEL, 110; NRG, 178; MEW, II, 389; MA (11/49), 3, (4/55), 4 - With friends, PZB, 75 - With

constitutional leaders, MFG, 120 (1913) - On horseback, HMI, 118-19
Carrasquilla, Rafael María, 1857-1930, (Colombia), churchman; writer: NCE,
    VIII, 488
Carrasquilla, Tomás, 1858-1940, (Colombia), writer: AM (1/58), 40
Carreño, Mario, b.1913, (Cuba), painter: CHL, 238; LF (3/17/41), 106-07;
    AM (5/77), 8-11
Carreño, Teresa, 1853-1917, (Venezuela), pianist: AM (11/53), 10-12, 44
Carrera, José Miguel, 1785-1821, (Chile), politician: WNC, VIII, 326; MEW,
    II, 391
Carrera, José Rafael, 1814-65, (Guatemala), statesman (President, 1844-48,
    1851-65): DEL, 112; MEW, II, 392 - Image on coin, BGL, 288
Carrera Andrade, Jorge, b.1903, (Ecuador), poet: AM (7/70), 10
Carrillo, Julián, b.1875, (Mexico), musician (violin): SM, 153
Carrillo Flores, Antonio, b.1909, (Mexico), statesman; diplomat: AM (1/66),
    6, (6/70), 12-17
Carrión, Benjamín, b.1898, (Ecuador), novelist: AM (5/64), 32
Carter, Jimmy, b.1924, (United States), statesman (President, 1977-81): AM
    (Nov.-Dec., 1977), 9, 11 - Mrs. Carter, AM (Nov.-Dec., 1977), 11-14;
    BBY, 341 (Ecuador, 1978) - Signs Panama Canal treaties (1977), RPC,
    162-63
Cartier, Jacques, 1494-1557, (France), explorer: CE, III, 329; MGE, 172 -
    Signature, RSD, 28
Casals, Pablo, 1876-1973, (Spain; Puerto Rico), musician: HS, 1-107 pass.;
    AM (3/57), 11 - As young man, HC, 19 - His mother, HC, 53 - His wife
    (Marta Montáñez), HC, 34-49, 53-63 pass. - Signature, RSD, 38
Casanova, Auro Celina, (Venezuela), politician: AM (4/74), 24-25
Casas, Fernando R., (Bolivia), artist (no pic.): wk., (1975), AM (2/79), 5
Casel, Julián, 1863-93, (Cuba), poet: AM (12/64), 18
Caso, Antonio, 1883-1946, (Mexico), philosopher, etc.: NCE, VIII, 486; AM
    (2/51), 82, (10/62), 35-38, (8/71), 24-25
Castalli, Juan José, (Argentina), Independence leader: AM (4/60), 36
Castellanos, Juan de, 1522-1607, (Spain), historian: NCE, II, 583, III, 188
Castellanos, Julio, 1905-47, (Mexico), artist (no pic.): wk., CLA, no. 14;
    BOL, 129
Castello, Pedro de, (Argentina), founder of Mendoza, 1560: AM (4/75), 5
Castello Branco, Humberto, 1900-67, (Brazil), statesman (President, 1964-67):
    AM (12/65), 40; BNL, 424-25; RBT, 64-65; MEW, II, 411; EB, 29; DCB,
    fr. - Life; activities, DCB, 266-67; BBY (1965), 196
Castilho, Edson de, (Brazil), singer: AM (9/53), 28
Castilla, Ramón, 1797-1867, (Peru), statesman (President, 1845-51, 1855-62):
    DEL, 115; MEW, II, 413
Castillo, Canovas del, (Spain), statesman (prime minister, 1898): HNM, (vol.
    98), 457
Castillo, Juan, b.1596, (Argentina), Jesuit in La Plata: HSA, 253
Castillo, Ricardo, b.1891, (Guatemala), musical composer: SM, 281
Castillo, Sergio, (Chile), sculptor: AM (9/67), 43
Castillo, Tito, (Chile), newspaper editor (El Mundo, Antofagasto): AM (10/49),
    30 (with wife)
Castillo Armas, Carlos, 1914-57, (Guatemala), statesman (President, 1954-
    57): JTG, 69, 79; MAA, 52-53; AM (3/74), 26; LF (1/28/54), 15 - Wife
    and mother, LF (8/12/57), 144 - Enters Guatemala (1954), JTG, 52; LF
    (1/28/54), 12-15 - Visits Washington, AM (12/55), 37 - With Vice Presi-
    dent Nixon (1955), JTG, 75, 83 - Assassinated (August, 1957), LF (8/12/57),
    41 - Funeral, LF (8/12/57), 41-43
Castillo Ledón, Amalia, (Mexico), Chairman, Inter-American Commission of
    Women: AM (10/49), 30, (5/79), 31
Castillo Nájara, Francisco, 1886-1954, (Mexico), statesman; diplomat: AM
    (8/49), 9

Castillo de Suro, Piedad Levi, (Ecuador), Chairman Inter-American Commission of Women: AM (8/68), 48
Castillo y Zamora, Cristóbal de, (Peru), churchman; founded University of Ayacucho: AM (10/66), 37
Castre, Bevott, (Haiti), artist: WH, 47
Castro, Dolores, (Mexico), writer: AM (6/60), 41
Castro, Emma, (Cuba), sister of Fidel: LUR, 237
Castro, Héctor David, b.1894, (El Salvador), statesman: AM (1/50), 30, (6/50), 40, (8/51), 40, (10/52), 29
Castro, José María, b.1892, (Argentina), composer; conductor: SM, 185; AM (1/71), 22-23
Castro, Juan José, b.1895, (Argentina), composer: SM, 185
Castro, Juanita, (Cuba), sister of Fidel: LUR, 173; LF (8/28/64), 22
Castro, Ramón, (Cuba), elder brother of Fidel: WIT, 279
Castro, Raúl, (Cuba), brother of Fidel: TCP, 1090-91 - Rebel activities, LF (7/21/58), 29-32 - In Moscow, LF (8/15/60), 35
Castro Alves, Antônio de, 1847-71, (Brazil), poet: MEW, II, 419
Castro Leal, Antonio, b.1896, (Mexico), writer: AM (6/60), 43
Castro Ruz, Fidel, b.1927, (Cuba), statesman; revolutionary: DEL, 117; BNL, 424-25; MEW, II, 416; CCT, 120-21 (1958); NG (1/77), 68-69; LF (8/28/64), 23-26, 33; CEN, 52 (1927); WIT, 258, 274-75 - Life scenes, LF (8/28/64), 27-33 - Cutting cane, TCP, 1090-91 (1965) - Swimming, LF (11/9/62), 1-2 - Snorkling, LF (4/17/70), 40-41 - As a rebel (1957), EA, VIII, 304 - With rebels, TCP, 1090-91; LUR, fr. (1957) - Attacks Moncada barracks, TCP, 1090-91; CCT, 120-21 - In Sierra Maestra Mountains, TCP, 1090-91; LF (3/25/57), 26, (5/27/57), 43, (4/14/58), 36-37; HCP, 33 - March on Havana and celebration, LF (1/19/59), 28-32; WBE (vol. 4), 936 - Takes over government after Batista, LF (1/12/59), 10-19 - First cabinet (1959), TCP, 1090-91 - Signs agrarian reform law (5/17/59), MRC, 254-55 - Signs law to expropriate U.S. property, MRC, 264-65 - Speech, 26th July (1964), LF (8/7/64), 28 - His signature, RSD, 29 - With President Nixon (April 1959), TCP, 1090-91; BHG, 176-77 - In New York City (1959), NHG, 29 - With U.S. ambassador Bonsal (1959), HBG, 176-77 - With Canada Prime Minister Trudeau (1977), AAY (1977), 175 - In Poland (1973), AAY (1977), 213 - With Mikoyan and Guevara, HCP, 36 - With Khrushchev (Sept., 1960), SBL, 35 - At United Nations (1974), AM (3/74), 31; BHG, 177; EA (vol. 8), 306; MRC, 264-65 - In Russia, LF (5/10/63), 82-83, (1/31/64), 34; TCP, 1090-91; HRD, 180-81 - In North Vietnam (1967), TCD, 1090-91 - In Chile with Allende (1971), BMD, 580 - In Panama with Torrijos, RPC, 72 - In Havana with Senator McGovern, WIT, 285
Castrocid, Enrique, (Chile), artist: AM (1/63), 31
Catherine of Aragón, 1485-1536, (Spain), Queen of England: NCE, III, 254; EBRF (2), 642 - Signature, RSD, 39
Catherine de Medici, 1519-89, (Italy), Queen of France: LTV, 57
Catherwood, Frederick, 1799-1854, (Britain), explorer-artist, Central America: VFC, 32-33, 48-49; MT, 124-25
Cato, Luis, (Mexico), painter (no pic.): wk., AHC, 94-95
Cattelani, Raúl, b.1927, (Uruguay), painter (no pic.): wk., AM (8/77), 29-31
Caturla, Alejandro García, 1906-40, (Cuba), composer: SM, 153
Cavalcanti, Carlos de Lima, (Brazil), Pernambuco politician, 1930-37: LPB, 103
Cavalcanti, Emiliano di, b.1897, (Brazil), painter (no pic.): wk., HCL, 252
Cavalcanti, Newton, (Brazil), engraver: BNB, 152
Cavendish, Thomas, c.1555-92, (Britain), navigator; pirate: WNC, III, 83 (c.1580); MED, 710-11; QLV, fr., 11, 13; AM (9/71), 31 - His ship, "Black Pinnace," MED, 721 - Hand-written account of voyage (1591), QLV, 51-135 - Hand-written will, QLV, 137-43 - Signature, QLV, 5

Cazals, Felipe, (Mexico), film director: NMC, 82, 85
Celis, Pérez, (Argentine), artist: AM (12/67), 39
Center, Alexander J., (United States), engineer; Panama railroad: HNM, XVIII, 154
Cervallos, Pedro Fermín, 1812-93, (Ecuador), historian: AM (2/67), 20
Cervantes, Ignacio, 1847-1905, (Cuba), composer: AM (8/74), 12
Cervera y Topete, Pascual, 1839-1909, (Spain), admiral, Spanish American War: HNM (vol. 98), 85; WSA, 28, 107; AM (June-July, 1972), 9
Ceschiatti, Alfredo, (Brazil), painter (no pic.): wk., LF (4/31/54), 82
Céspedes, Carlos Manuel de, 1819-74, (Cuba), revolutionary leader; President, 1869: TCP, 546-57; MEW, II, 452
Chaca y Barba, José Ignacio, 1829-77, (Ecuador), churchman; Archbishop (Quito): NCE, III, 532
Chaffee, Adna Romanza, 1884-1941, (United States), military (Spanish American War): HNM, (vol. 98), 847
Chamie, Mario, b.1933, (Brazil), poet: AM (2/64), 32
Champlain, Samuel de, 1567-1635, (France), explorer: CE, III, 567; WNC, IV, 119; NRM, 115; HHG, 100 - Signature, WNC, IV, 119
Chang, Carlisle F., (Trinidad), painter: AM (5/56), 32-33
Charles II, 1661-1700, (Spain), King, 1665-1700: KCH, 94; LSH, 231; SSH, 216; MEW, II, 513
Charles III, 1716-88, (Spain), King, 1759-88: CFT, 305-06; KCH, 102; MHS, 143; SFB, 48; MEW, II, 514 - Accession to throne (1759), KCH, 101 - Signature, RSD, 36
Charles IV, 1748-1819, (Spain), King, 1788-1808: MEW, 11, 515; SSH, 249; AM (6/63), 26 - With family, CS, 89; CFT, 304-05; DG, fr.; BG, 177, 303; KCH, 112 - Monument (Mexico City), LMJ, 231 - Medallion (with Queen María Luisa), FCL, 82-83
Charles V, 1500-58, (Spain), Emperor; King of Spain, 1516-58: WNC, II, 371, 373; KCH, 64-67; MHS, 102; MEW, II, 499; SSH, 164-65, 169, 171; CE, III, 626; NCE, III, 504 (1521); MED, 334 - Medallion, GKT, 24 - Bust, NCE, VI, 920 - With wife, SSH, 166; MED, 335 - Coat of arms, KCH, 67 - Firearms, LHS, 37, 52 - Helmet, SSA, 162 - As hunter, SSH, 169; CMF, 48 - Handwriting, GKT, 62 - Signature, WNC, II, 289-372; RSD, 42 - Abdication, GKT, 51; SSH, 167 - Death, GKT, 52
Charles, Joseph D., (Haiti), diplomat: AM (4/49), 48, (12/49), 36, (1/50), 31
Charlevoix, Pierre François Xavier de, 1682-1761, (France), Jesuit missionary in America: NCE, III, 511
Charlot, Jean, b.1898, (France; Mexico), painter: AM (7/70), 23-29
Charnay, Claude Joseph Déseré, 1828-1915, (France), archaeologist in America: ART, 194
Chartuni, Maria Helena, b.1943, (Brazil), painter: BNB, 152
Chase, Alfonso, b.1945, (Costa Rica), poet: AM (9/65), 34
Chase, Ann, (Britain), spy for U.S. in Mexican war; With husband, Tampico: NMW, 132
Chauncey, Henry, (United States), with Panama railroad, HMN, XVIII, 147
Chavannes, Etienne, (Haiti), artist (no pic.): wk., AM (10/78), 10-11
Chávez, Carlos, 1899-1978, (Mexico), music composer; conductor: SM, 248; BNL, 424-25; MEW, II, 540; LEM, 482; AM (3/51), 10, (12/53), 18, (7/64), 26, (10/78), 55
Chávez, César, (Mexican-American), labor leader: RM, 179
Chávez, Ignacio, (Mexico), educator; Rector National University resigns (4/26/66): BBY (1967), 542
Chávez, Santos, (Chile), artist (no pic.): wk., CLA, no. 15 (1963)
Chávez y González, Luis, (El Salvador), archbishop: WES, 144-45
Chávez Morado, José, b.1899, (Mexico), artist (no pic.): wk., CLA, no. 16 (1939); BOL, 136-37; HMM, 191; LF (6/3/46), 58

(family), (10/78), 55
Corominas, Enrique V., (Argentina), statesman: AM (10/49), 30
Corona, Ramón, d.1889, (Mexico), military: GFF, 371
Coronado, Francisco Vásquez de, 1510-54, (Spain), conquistador, New Spain:
    WNC, II, 481; DSW, 42 - Signature, WNC, II, 481 - Park (Arizona), AM
    (9/76), 12
Coronado, Juan (José) Vásquez de, c.1525-62, (Spain), conquistador, Guate-
    mala: AM (Aug.-Sept., 1973), 32-33
Corral, Ramón, (Mexico), statesman (Vice President with Díaz): BWS, plate 4
Correal, Edgar, (Bolivia), artist: AM (10/73), 41
Cort, Daniel, 1788-1836, (United States; Peru), painter; merchant (1819-28):
    AM (2/78), 29-32
Cortázar, Julio, b.1914, (Argentina), writer: GSL, 170-71; AM (3/63), 39,
    (2/76), 39, (4/78), 2
Corte Real, Gaspar, born c.1450, (Portugal), explorer, North America: AM
    (June-July, 1973), 31
Corte Real, Miguel, (Portuguese), explorer, North America (no pic.): In-
    scriptions (?) Rhode Island: AM (9/67), 19, (June-July, 1973), 30-35
Cortés, Alfonso, b.1899, (Nicaragua), poet: AM (10/67), 33
Cortés, Hernán, 1485-1547, (Spain), conquistador: WNG, II, 354-89 pass.;
    SSH, 157; LAW, 18; MCE, IV, 183; BNL, 236-37; DEL, 174; CCH, 36;
    MT, 98; ACS, 82; KWW, 81; ELA, 58 (Indian drawing); EBR (5), 194 -
    Coat of arms, WNC, II, 354; JCH, 41 - Armor, WNC, II, 390, 395 -
    His cannon, JCH, 41 - House, HNM (vol. 113), 504-05 - Palace, Cuerna-
    vaca, ESS, 74; BMD, 112 - Church built by, HNM (vol. 49), 324 - Signa-
    ture, WNC, 381; LNW, 18; RSD, 53 - Mistress (Malinche), BMD, 70 -
    Monument, Medellín, Spain, AM (10/77), 39 - Monument, Mexico, NG
    (2/44), 162 - Statue, Cuernavaca, PMA, 55 - CONQUEST OF MEXICO:
    AM (8/66), 23-31; MT, 100-15 pass. - Leaves Cuba, HNM (vol. 12), 4 -
    At Veracruz, HE, 164-65 - Veracruz to Mexico City, NG (9/40), 337-74
    pass. - Enters Tenochtitlán, NCE, IX, 772 - Meets Montezuma, HNM
    (vol. 12), 10, 19; SBL, 63; AHC, 36; WHM, 126; FWS, 39 - Tribute from
    Indians, WIA, I, 159 - Attacks Aztecs, HNM (vol. 12), 7; CE, X, 257 -
    "La Noche Triste," ALA, 36 - Noche Triste Tree, SCS, 41
Cosío Villegas, Daniel, 1900-77, (Mexico), historian: AM (7/53), 27
Costa, Lucio, b.1902, (France; Brazil), architect: NG (2/28), 277
Costa, Sergio Corrêa da, (Brazil), writer; diplomat: AM (7/49), 48
Costa, Zenobio da, (Brazil), military, World War II: KPA, 182 (with troops)
Costa e Silva, Alberto da, b.1931, (Brazil), poet: AM (2/64), 30
Costa e Silva, Arthur da, 1902-69, (Brazil), statesman (President, 1967-69):
    AM (3/67), 44, (7/67), 2
Courvoisier, Bess (Ruth Bessoud), (Brazil), artist (no pic.): wk., CLA, no.
    9 (1967)
Cova, J. A., (Venezuela), historian: AM (4/50), 47
Covarrubias, Miguel, 1904-57, (Mexico), artist: AM (4/57), 7-9; wk., BOL,
    128; HMM, 196; AMS, frontispiece, 50, 98, 246, 262, 310, 366; AM
    (4/57), 7-9, (5/71), 19-24
Crane, Stephen, 1871-1900, (United States), Spanish American War correspon-
    dent: HNM (vol. 98), 947; WSA, 65
Cravo, Mario, (Brazil), artist (no pic.): wk., RBT, 64-65
Crespo, Joaquín, 1845-98, (Venezuela), statesman (President, 1884-86, 1892-
    98): HNM (vol. 92), 106 - Body Guard, HNM (vol. 92), 107
Crespo, Manuel, (Venezuela), diplomat: AM (7/50), 47
Crevenna, Theo., (United States), in Pan American Union: AM (1/67), 44
Croix, Teodoro de, c.1730-91, (Spain), viceroy of Peru, 1784-90: SFB, 78;
    CMP, 105
Crowder, Enoch Herbert, 1859-1932, (United States), military; diplomat in
    Cuba, 1926-27: TCP, 546-47; EBRF (3), 262
Cruz, Oswaldo Gonçalves, 1872-1917, (Brazil), scientist: AM (5/73), 24-25;

MEW, III, 203

Cruz-Díez, Carlos, (Venezuela), artist (no pic.): wk. , CLA, no. 18 (1970)

Cruz Salazar, José Luis, born c.1921, (Guatemala), politician: LF (2/3/58), 22

Cuadra, Pablo Antonio, b.1912, (Nicaragua), poet: AM (10/67), 35

Cuauhtemoc, c.1495-1525, (Mexico), Aztec Emperor: Monument, Mexico City, NG (7/30), 54

Cué, Ana María, (Argentina), pianist: AM (5/77), 40

Cuellar, Migués, (Colombia), chess champion: AM (1/65), 44

Cuevas, José Luis, b.1934, (Mexico), artist: CLA, no. 19 (1971); AM (3/67), 10-16, (Nov. -Dec. , 1978), 2-7, (2/79), 6 (1973)

Cunha, Antônio Flores da, (Brazil), military: KPA, 117 (and sons)

Currea de Aya, María, (Colombia), author: AM (5/79), 30

Currie, Lauchlin, b.1903, (United States), economist: AM (1/50), 46

Curti, Emma, (Argentina), cellist: AM (7/66), 39

Da Costa, Maria Leontina, b.1917, (Brazil), painter: BNB, 153

Dacosta, Milton Rodrigues da Costa, b.1915, (Brazil), painter: BNB, 153

Da Cunha, Euclides Rodrigues Pimenta, 1866-1909, (Brazil), journalist; sociologist; writer: AM (4/78), 33-35; NCE, IV, 534; DEL, 187; MEW, III, 211; AM (10/52), 20

Daen, Lindsay, (United States), artist in Puerto Rico: AM (4/78), 33-35

Da Gama, Domicio, (Brazil), intellectual: AM (3/73), 32

Da Gama, Vasco, c.1460-1524, (Portugal), explorer: MEW, IV, 304; BP, 61 (1498); WCH, II, 42; HAE, 37; NCE, VI, 274; CMF, 17, 53; LF (3/22/48), 75; HE, 90, 100 - Fleet (1497), PDS, 174; NRM, 79 - Reception in Indies, LF (3/22/48), 76-78 - Signature, RSD, 84

Damasio, Virgilio Clímaco, (Brazil), statesman (President, 1889): PBF, 112-13

Dampier, William, 1652-1715, (Britain), freebooter, explorer: NRM, 130; RCV, vii, MEW, III, 258 - Signature, RSD, 57

Daniel, John W. , (United States), United States Senate, 1898: HNM (vol. 98), 508

Daniels, Josephus, 1862-1948, (United States), diplomat; ambassador to Mexico: NWS, plate 161; BHG, 128-29

Daniels, Marietta, (United States), Pan Americanist; librarian: AM (9/54), 28

Darío, Rubén, (Félix Rubén García Sarmiento), 1867-1916, (Nicaragua), writer; poet: NCE, VIII, 515; DEL, 189; AM (2/67), 11, 13, (10/70), 12; MEW, III, 270; WAP (Carib. vol.), 184; CEF (vol. 12), 150; EBRF (30), 379 - Son, HNP, 48 - Monument (Managua), HNP, 49; AM (2/67), 17, (8/76), ifc. - Tomb, León Cathedral, NG (7/44), 181; AM (2/67), 14

Dartiguenave, Philippe Sudré, b.1863, (Haiti), statesman (President, 1915-22): HGD, 150

Darwin, Charles Robert, 1800-82, (Britain), scientist: NCE, IV, 650; NRM, 186; ALL, 84-85 (1854); NG (4/57), 555, (10/69), 451 (young man), 495 (old man); MEW, II, 275; EBR (5), 492 - Scenes in life, NG (10/69), 449-95 pass. - Signature, RSD, 58

Da Silva, (Bolivia), artist (no pic.): wk. , AM (6/61), 28-29

Da Silva, Bento Gonçalves, (Brazil), military: AM (1/61), 13, 21 (c.1845)

Davidovsky, Mario, (Argentina), composer: AM (7/64), 24

Dávila, Carlos Guillermo, 1887-1955, (Chile), diplomat (Secretary-General, OAS): AM (8/49), 46, (7/54), 1 (family), (9/54), 40, (12/55), 3-6 (life scenes), (4/65), 22, (1/71), 24-25

Davis, Acton, (United States), Spanish American war correspondent: HNM (vol. 98), 939

Davis, Cushman Kellogg, 1838-1900, (United States), statesman; Senate, 1898: HNM (vol. 98), 508

Davis, Richard Harding, 1864-1916, (United States), Spanish American war correspondent: WSA, 20, 65; MEW, III, 291

Day, William Rufus, 1849-1923, (United States), statesman; secretary of state, 1898: HNM (vol. 98), 507

Daza, Hilarión Grosale, 1840-94, (Bolivia), politician: Image on coin (1879), FCL, 53

Debravo, Jorge, b.1938, (Costa Rica), poet: AM (9/65), 30

De Bry, Johann Theodore, 1528-98, (Belgium), engraver, artist in America: WNC, I, xxx; PDS, 1, 6, 222; ADN, 6-202 pass.

DeGaulle, Charles, 1890-1970, (France), President, 1958-69: Visit to Mexico, LF (3/27/64), 24-25; BBY (1965), 546

Déjoie, Louis, (Haiti), politician: LF (6/3/57), 41, (6/10/57), 46

Delamónica, Roberto, b.1933, (Brazil), engraver: BNB, 153

Delano Frederick, Jorge ("Coke"), (Chile), artist: AM (11/52), 6-8, 42

De Lesseps, Ferdinand, 1805-94, (France), engineer; canal builder: ACS, 402; MPB, 87; MEW, VI, 454 - Bust, Panama City, EPC, 31 - Wife (second), MPB, 88 - Colleagues, MPB, 92

Delgadillo, Luis A., b.1887, (Nicaragua), musician, composer: SM, 281

Delgado, José Matías, 1767-1832, (El Salvador), churchman; revolutionary (1821): AM (4/52), 5 - With revolutionaries, AM (2/73), 24-25 - Bust, AM (3/65), 21

Delgado Chalbaud, Carlos, 1909-59, (Venezuela), politician; head of military junta: Assassinated (Nov., 1950), LF (11/27/50), 30

Delhez, Victor, (Argentina), artist (no pic.): wk., CLA, no. 20

Del Río, Andrés Manuel, (Mexico), scientist: PMN, 108-09

Del Río, Dolores, b.1905, (Mexico), actress: AM (11/67), 8-16; WLI, 52-53

De Luque, Hernando, d.1352, (Spain), conquistador; priest: With Pizarro and Almagro, Peru, ELA, 63

Del Valle, José Cecilio, 1780-1834, (Guatemala), statesman; patriot: AM (8/65), 9, (1/71), 25 - Bust, AM (8/65), 7, 8

Demicheli, Sofía de, (Uruguay), feminist leader: AM (7/49), 7-10

De Silva, Alfredo, (Bolivia), artist: AM (1/63), 29

Dessalines, Jean Jacques, 1758-1806, (Haiti), patriot; Emperor, 1804-06: WNC, VIII, 287; BNL, 424; RFW, 220; MEW, III, 354; WAP (Carib. vol.), 40; AM (11/53), 9, (3/72), 24-25; WH, 19

d'Eu, Count (Gaston d'Orleans), b.1842, (France; Brazil), military: HAT, 290; WDP, 116

Deus, Waldomiro de, (Brazil), artist: AM (3/78), 45-46

Deustna, Alejandro, 1849-1945, (Peru), scholar: NCE, VIII, 489; AM (8/71), 24-25

De Vries, Erwin, (Surinam), painter: AM (5/56), 32-33

Dewey, George, 1837-1917, (United States), naval commander, Spanish American war: WSA, 24

d'Horta, Arnoldo Pedraso, b.1914, (Brazil), painter: AM (5/53), 28-31; BNB, 157

Dias, Antonio Gonçalves, 1823-64, (Brazil), poet: AM (11/65), 19

Dias, Bartolomeo, c.1599-1627, (Mexico), Franciscan priest: Burned at stake, HSA, 173

Dias, Cícero, b.1907, (Brazil), painter: BNB, 153

Dias de Novais, Bartolomeu, d.1500, (Portugal), explorer: MEW, III, 367

Díaz, Félix, b.1868, (Mexico), revolutionary: BWS, plate 76

Díaz, Juan José Infante, (Mexico), architect: AM (3/71), 16-24

Díaz, Justino, (Puerto Rico), opera singer: NFP, 92-93

Díaz, Manuel, (Chile), violist: AM (4/79), 38

Díaz, Pascual, (Mexico), churchman (archbishop of Mexico): BWS, plate 133

Díaz, Porfirio, 1830-1915, (Mexico), statesman (President, Dictator, 1876-80, 1884-1911): NCE, IV, 854; HNM (vol. 64), 414 (c.1875), (vol. 94), 743 (c.1895), 745 (c.1866), (vol. 71), 763; DEL, 193; GFF, 10; FWS, 62; CCS, 23; CLI, 162; PZB, 77 (c.1900), 76 (c.1910); AM (3/49), 41; BWS,

plate 1; SMT, 180-81; CMS, 224 (1860), 233 (1908); MEW, III, 364; EBRF
(2), 527 - Wife, BWS, plates 29, 56 (1910); HNM (vol. 94), 754; GFF,
frontispiece - Son, HNM (vol. 94), 747; BWS, plate 48 (1910) - Residence
(Oaxaca), HNM (vol. 94), 758 - Audience chamber, National Palace, BWS,
plate 7 - Bodyguard, BWS, plate 49 (1910) - Horse, BWS, plate 48 (1910) -
Automobile, BWS, plate 61 - Bust on coinage, BWS, plate 36 - Political
poster, HMI, 18 - Official reception, WHM, 155 - Enters Puebla, AHC,
115 - With "científicos," BWS, plate 2 - Anti-Díaz revolution (1910), BWS,
plates 57-74 pass.; MFG, 1 - His estates distributed, AHC, 164 - Signa-
ture, RSD, 62
Díaz del Castillo, Bernal, c.1492-1581, (Spain; Mexico), conquistador: WNC,
    I, 154
Díaz y Lanz, Pedro, (Cuba), Castro associate: LF (7/27/59), 28 (and wife) -
    Fugitive from Castro, LF (8/3/59), 20
Díaz de León, Francisco, b.1892, (Mexico), painter (no pic.): wk., HMM,
    188
Díaz de Medina, Federico, (Bolivia), Archaeologist: AM (7/55), 14, 17
Díaz de Medina, Fernando, b.1908, (Bolivia), writer: AM (10/50), 1, (9/53),
    2
Díaz de Medina, Raúl, (Bolivia), diplomat: AM (3/65), 43
Díaz Mirón, Salvador, 1853-1928, (Mexico), poet: HNM (vol. 71), 765 (c.1885)
Díaz Ordaz, Gustavo, 1911-1979, (Mexico), statesman (President, 1964-70):
    HMI, 118-19; FWS, 79; WHM, 214; PMM, 180 (1968); AM (8/69), 7,
    (12/69), 40; BBY (vol. 1971), 510 - With President Johnson, EBR (12), 88
Díaz de Solís, Juan, c.1470-1516, (Spain), conquistador; La Plata: MEW, X,
    123
Di Cavalcanti, Emiliano, b.1897, (Brazil), painter: BNB, 153
Dillon, Augusto, (Ecuador), diplomat: AM (2/50), 43
Dobles Yzaguirre, Julieta, b.1943, (Costa Rica), poet: AM (9/65), 32
Domeyko, Ignacio, 1802-89, (Chile), writer: AM (5/75), 13
Domingo de la Anunciación, 1510-91, (Mexico), churchman (no pic.): Signa-
    ture, CE, I, 591
Domínguez, Lorenzo, (Chile), sculptor: AM (4/71), 35-37
Domínguez Cámpara, Alberto, (Uruguay), diplomat: AM (9/49), 43
Doniphan, Alexander William, 1808-87, (United States), military; Mexican
    War: NMW, 113
Donoso, José, b.1925, (Chile), writer, AM (4/78), 4
Donoso, Ricardo, b.1896, (Chile), historian: AM (2/51), 2
Donnini, Armando, (Argentina), artist (no pic.): wk., (1975), AM (2/79), 5
Donovan, James B., b.1916, (United States), negotiator with Cuba: LF
    (1/4/63), 26
Dorticós Torrado, Osvaldo, b.1919, (Cuba), statesman (President, 1959):
    MRC, 264-65; PCI, 1012; LF (7/27/59), 28 (with Castro); AAY (1974), 192
Dosamantes, Francisco, b.1911, (Mexico), artist (no pic.); wk., CLA, no.
    21 (1940); HMM, 116, 190
Downey, Juan, (Chile), artist (no pic.): wk., CLA, no. 22 (1962)
Drago, Luis María, 1859-1921, (Argentina), diplomat: MEW, III, 431
Drake, Francis, 1545-96, (Britain), military: WNC, III, 81, 84; INW, 22;
    LSA, 18; MA, 141; JCH, 50; ARM, 89; MED, 631; KWW, 97; ACL, 55;
    AM (9/71), 229, (1/74), 36; ACL, 55; HNM (vol. III), 169; GKT, 186;
    ACS, 99; WWE, fr. - "Golden Hind," MED, 639; HNM (vol. 111), 170;
    WWE, 46-47, 180 - His astrolabe, WWE, 210 - Lands he saw, MED,
    640-87 pass. - Attacks Santo Domingo, MHS, 123 - With Caribbean Indians,
    ACS, 162 - With prisoners and booty, HAC, 212 - With California Indians,
    HNM (vol. 111), 175 - Brass plate marker in California, MED, 688; WWE,
    163 - Knighted by Queen Elizabeth, HNM (vol. 111), 173 - Coat of arms,
    WWI, 204 - Signature, WNC, III, 65; LNW, 22; RSD, 65
Dreier, John, b.1906, (United States), diplomat: AM (8/51), 31, (1/52), 29,

(4/52), 37

Dryfus, Bernard, (Nicaragua), artist (no pic.): wk., (1976), AM (1/79), 2

Duarte, Juan Pablo, 1813-76, (Dominican Republic), patriot, revolutionary: AM (9/71), 24-25

Dubart, Emilio, b.1917, (Chile), architect (no pic.): wk., CHL, 283 (1963), (United Nations building, Santiago)

Du Casse, Jean-Baptiste, b.1646, (France), privateer; governor of St. Dominique: RFW, frontispiece

Dufaut, Préfete, (Haiti), painter (no pic.): wk., LF (12/22/52), 64-65

Duggan, Laurence, (United States), scholar: AM (11/49), 32

Dulles, Allen, 1893-1969, (United States), Director CIA: LF (5/10/63), 80

Dulles, John Foster, 1888-1959, (United States), Secretary of State: AM (6/55), 33; LF (6/19/46), 122, (10/4/48), 130, (5/10/54), 29; MEW, III, 470 - At Inter-American Conference, Caracas (March, 1954), BHG, 176-77

Dungan, Ralph A., (United States), diplomat (ambassador to Chile, 1964-67): SOD, 40

Dupuy de Lome, Enrique, (Spain), minister to United States, 1898: HNM (vol. 98), 46

Durán, Nicolás, (Mexico), missionary (California, 1831-38): CCM, 42

Durand, Nicolás, 1510-71, (France; Brazil), military: LTV, 10

Dutra, Eurico Gaspar, 1885-1951, (Brazil), President, 1946-51: AM (5/49), 1; LF (9/15/47), 36-37 (and wife)

Duvalier, François, 1907-71, (Haiti), dictator ("Popa Doc"); BNL, 424-25; AM (3/74), 28; LF (6/3/57), 40, (3/8/63), 28, (7/26/63), 28b; MEW, III, 497; BBY (vol. 1965), 399, (vol. 1968), 387

Duvalier, Jean-Claude, b.1952, (Haiti), dictator ("Baby Doc"): NG (1/76), 78; LF (5/7/71), 34-35

Echeverría, Estéban, 1805-51, (Argentina), statesman; military; writer: AM (4/52), 21-23; MEW, III, 512; WAP (Arg. vol.), 131

Echeverría, Francisco Javier, 1797-1852, (Mexico), official: CLM, 418-19 (1840)

Echeverría Alvarez, Luis, b.1922, (Mexico), statesman (President, 1970-76): AM (5/72), 44, (3/74), 49; GPM, 212 (1970); RM, 54; HMI, 118-19; BBY (vol. 1971), 510 - Addresses United Nations, PMA, 134 - With President Nixon (June, 1973), AAY (1973), 461 - In England with Queen Elizabeth (April, 1974), AAY (1974), 387 - With President Ford (October, 1975), AAY (1975), 379

Egaña, Juan de, 1769-1836, (Chile), statesman; patriot: AM (4/69), 29, (1/71), 24-25

Eisenhower, Dwight David, 1890-1969, (United States), military; statesman (President, 1953-61): LF (8/9/63), 30b-30c

Eisenhower, Milton, (United States), scholar; diplomat: NG (7/69), 1-51 pass. At Brasilia (Feb., 1960), NG (5/60), 723

Elcano, Juan Sebastián, c.1476-1526, (Spain), explorer with Magellan: Ship "Vitoria," MED, 450 (model); OIV, 32; HNM (vol. 149), 477; MED, 459 - Coat of arms, MED, 463

Elhuyar y Zubice, Fausto de, 1755-1833, (Mexico), engineer: PMN, 108

Elizabeth, 1533-1603, (Britain), Queen of England: MGE, 275 - Signature, WNC, III, 106

England, Edward, (Britain), pirate in Caribbean: HDP, 8

Englert, Sebastián, (Chile), churchman, Easter Island (1935-): MEI, 57

Ercilla y Zúñiga, Alonso de, 1533-c.94, (Chile), soldier; poet: CE, XIV, 197; MEW, IV, 11

Ericson, Leif, (Norse), explorer, America: GMV, 105, 120-21

Erik the Red, (Norse), explorer; discovered Greenland 876: LNW, 6

Errázuriz y Valdivieso, Cresente, 1839-1931, (Chile), churchman; historian: NCE, V, 520

Escardó y Amaya, Víctor, (Chile), physician with OAS: AM (8/58), 32-33
Escobar, Marisol, (Venezuela), artist: CLA, no. 47; AM (1/63), 31
Escobedo, Jesús, (Mexico), artist: HMM, 194; LLA, no. 23 (1936)
Escutia, Juan, b.1827, (Mexico), "boy hero," Battle of Chapultepec, Sept.,
    1847: DSW, 217
Espejo, Eugenio, (Ecuador), novelist: AM (5/64), 31
Espinosa, Guillermo, b.1905, (Colombia), musician; conductor: AM (7/60),
    35, (12/65), 38, (2/68), 44, (10/78), 52
Estévez, Antonio, b.1916, (Venezuela), musician; composer: AM (7/64), 27
Estévez, Rafael, (Panama), physician: AM (8/50), 9-13
Estimé, Dumarais, b.1900, (Haiti), statesman (President, 1946-50): AM
    (8/49), 23
Estrada, José, (Mexico), movie director: NMC, 126-35 pass.
Estrada, José María, (Mexico), painter (19th century), (no pic.): wk., CHL,
    217
Estrada Cabrera, Manuel, 1857-1924, (Guatemala), statesman (President-
    dictator, 1898-1920): MEW, IV, 23
Estrada Palma, Tomás, 1835-1908, (Cuba), statesman (President, 1902-06):
    TCP, 546-47; MEW, IV, 24
Etienne, Arnold, (Haiti), artist (no pic.): wk., AM (10/78), 9
Evans, Robley Dunglison, 1846-1912, (United States), Spanish American war
    leader: HNM (vol. 98), 853
Evarts, William Maxwell, 1818-1901, (United States), statesman; Secretary of
    State: MPB, 89
Ezeta, Carlos, 1852-1903, (El Salvador), statesman (President, 1890-94):
    WES, 144-45

Fabregá, Demetrio, b.1932, (Panama), poet: AM (7/64), 19
Facio, Antonio, (Costa Rica), statesman: AM (5/54), 48 (family), (8/54), 29
Facio, Gonzalo, b.1918, (Costa Rica), diplomat: AM (12/56), 30 (family),
    (2/66), 41 (OAS Council member)
Fairbanks, Douglas, b.1909, (United States), actor: LF (6/2/41), 24 - Visits
    South America, LF (6/2/41), 24
Falcón Briceño, Marcos, (Venezuela), writer: AM (12/50), 2
Fall, Albert Bacon, 1861-1944, (United States), statesman; Secretary of State:
    BWS, plate 124
Farquahr, Percival, 1864-1953, (United States), businessman in Latin Ameri-
    ca: GLT, fr., 39, 108 (1931), 275, 427 - Wife, GLT, 427
Faustin, Celéstin, (Haiti), artist (no pic.): wk., AM (10/78), 10
Fawcett, Percy Harrison, (United States), explorer in Brazil: NRM, 191; AM
    (4/75), 18 - Son, AM (4/75), 18
Faz Caimus, Carlos, (Chile), artist (no pic.): wk., CLA, no. 24 (1953)
Feijó, Diogo Antônio, 1784-1843, (Brazil), statesman; Regent, 1835-37: NCE,
    V, 877; MEW, IV, 74
"Felip III," (Ecuador), "King" of Ecuador (1599): SSH, 145
Fenwick, Charles G., b.1880, (United States), jurist: AM (9/63), 26, (2/67),
    47
Ferdinand V of Aragón, 1469-1516 (Spain), King with Isabella: WNC, II, 56,
    85; MED, 37; BCC, 65 - Coat of arms, SFT, 124; MFI, 30 (joint) - Seal
    (1481), MFI, 56 - Sword, MFI, 129 - Signature, WNC, II, 56, 85; FFI,
    132-33; JCH, 9; RSD, 75 - At Prayer, SSH, 126-27 - Statue, MFI, ibc. -
    Images on coin (joint), MFI, 31 - Images on tapestry (joint), KCH, 62 -
    Painting (joint), MFI, 29; BCC, 66 - Tomb, FFI, 132-33; FIC, 338 - [See
    Isabella]
Ferdinand VI, 1712-59, (Spain), King, 1746-59: AM (5/50), 22
Ferdinand VII, 1784-1833, (Spain), King, 1808-33: WNC, VIII, 224; DG, 231;
    KCH, 114-21 pass.; SSH, 255; AM (Aug.-Sept., 1973), 3; MEW, IV, 86;
    RW, 96-97; EBRF (4), 99

Fergusson, Erna, (United States), writer: AM (7/50), 47
Fernandes, Oscar Lorenzo, 1897-1948, (Brazil), musician; composer: SM, 216
Fernández, Agustín, (Cuba), artist (no pic.): wk., CLA, no. 25 (1972)
Fernández, Emilio, (Mexico), movie director: NMC, 13-17 pass.
Fernández, Jorge, b.1912, (Ecuador), writer; diplomat (chairman OAS Council): AM (1/70), 43
Fernández-Dávila, Gabriela Arauibar, (Peru), chairman, Inter-American Commission of Women: AM (4/71), 44
Fernández Ledesma, Gabriel, b.1900, (Mexico), artist (no pic.): wk., HNM, 186; CLA, no. 26 (1935)
Fernández de Lizardi, José Joaquín, 1776-1827, (Mexico), writer: AM (10/65), 7; MEW, IV, 94
Fernández Muro, José Antonio, (Argentina), artist: AM (1/63), 27; ARG, 31
Fernández de Oviedo y Valdés, Gonzalo, 1478-1557, (Spain), historian in America: AM (8/72), 24-25
Ferré, Luis, b.1904, (Puerto Rico), statesman; governor: WHP, 158; WPR, 64-65
Ferreira, Joaquim Leal, (Brazil), statesman; President, 1891-92: PBF, 112-13
Ferreyra, José A., (Argentina), movie director: AM (Nov.-Dec., 1975), 7 (1920)
Ficher, Jacobo, b.1896, (Argentina), musician; composer: SM, 185
Ficker-Hoffman, Lisa, 1879-1962, (Brazil), painter: BNB, 154
Fierro, Pancho, 1803-79, (Peru), painter: AM (5/72), 25-29; CHL, 210
Figari, Pedro, 1861-1938, (Uruguay), painter (no pic.): wk., CHL, 214
Fignolé, Pierre Eustache Daniel, b.1915, (Haiti), statesman (President, 1957): LF (6/3/57), 41, (6/10/57), 41, 44 - Wife, LF (6/10/57), 44
Figueres Ferrer, José, b.1906, (Costa Rica), statesman (President, 1953-58, 1970-74): MEW, IV, 108; DEL, 229; ACR, 27; AM (Nov.-Dec., 1970), 38; LF (1/24/55), 41 - Wife, MAA, 180 - Son, LF (1/24/55), 41 - With President Nixon, MAA, 180
Figueroa, Ana, (Chile), representative at United Nations: AM (5/52), 4
Figueroa, Gabriel, (Mexico), photographer: AM (5/50), 24-28
Finlay, Carlos Juan, 1833-1915, (Cuba), physician; discovered yellow fever: NCE, V, 928; MEW, IV, 111; BNL, 424-25; AM (3/52), 36, (5/68), 31
Flack, Joseph, (United States), diplomat in Bolivia (1943-46): BHG, 64-65
Fleeming, Charles Elphinstone, (Britain). admiral; Venezuela: GJA, 242 - Wife, GJA, 258
Fletcher, Henry, b.1872, (United States), ambassador to Mexico, 1916-20: BHG, 128-29
Flores, Juan José, 1801-64, (Ecuador), statesman (President, 1831-35, 1839-43): DEL, 232; CLI, 87
Flores, Louis, c.1570-1622, (Mexico), churchman: HSA, 165
Flores, Manuel Antonio, 1723-99, (Spain), viceroy, New Granada, Mexico: PPK, 8
Flores, Venancio, 1808-68, (Uruguay), statesman (President, 1852-55, 1865-68): DEL, 233
Flores Magón, Ricardo, 1833-1922, (Mexico), politician: AM (4/62), 43
Florit, Eugenio, b.1903, (Cuba), poet: AM (10/78), 27
Fons, Jorge, (Mexico), movie director: NMC, 116-22 pass.
"Fonseca," (Bolivia), artist: AM (10/73), 42
Fonseca, Hermes Ernesto da, 1855-1923, (Brazil), statesman (President, 1890): PBF, 112-13
Fonseca, Hermes Rodrigues da, (Brazil), statesman (President, 1910-14): PBF, 112-13
Fontecilla, Ernesto, (Chile), artist (no pic.): wk., CLA, no. 27 (1970)
Foraker, Joseph Benson, 1846-1917, (United States), Senator, 1898: HNM

(vol. 98), 508

Forner, Raquel, b.1920, (Argentina), painter: AM (8/68), 7-12, (1961), (9/72), 26-30; CHL, 250

Fox, John Jr., (United States), Spanish American war correspondent: HNM (vol. 98), 942

Francia, José Gaspar Rodríguez de, 1776-1840, (Paraguay), dictator: CCS, 624; HPP, 21; WAP (Arg. vol.), 26; AM (7/50), 46, (Nov.-Dec., 1970), 24-25, (2/75), 24-25

Franco, Francisco, 1892-1975, (Spain), dictator: KWW, 124 (1937) - Signature, RSD, 80

Franco, José, b.1931, (Panama), poet: AM (7/64), 18

François, Jacques A., (Haiti), diplomat: AM (11/53), 41

Frank, Waldo, 1889-1967, (United States), writer: AM (1/52), 37 (c.1950), (9/71), 13, (5/73), 17-18

Frasconi, Antonio, (Uruguay), artist: (5/57), 7-11 (1950); CLA, nos. 28, 29 (1965)

Frei Montalva, Eduardo, b.1911, (Chile), statesman (President, 1964-70): DEL, 239; ALA, 99 (c.1964); AM (9/68), 43, (10/69), 39, (3/74), 38; BLP, 149; SOA, 71; MEW, IV, 227; BBY (vol. 1965), 230, (vol. 1966), 446, (vol. 1967), 198 - Election, LF (9/18/64), 49 - With Allende, SOA, 129

Freire Serrano, Ramón, 1787-1851, (Chile), statesman (dictator, 1823-27): AM (Nov.-Dec., 1968), 10

Fremont, John Charles, 1813-90, (United States), military; in Mexican war: HNM (vol. 8), 577; BTM, 203-04; NMW, 98

Fresnedo Siri, Román, b.1903, (Uruguay), architect; Pan American Health Organization (no pic.): wk., CHL, 285

Freyre, Gilberto, b.1900, (Brazil), sociologist: AM (5/49), 8-10, (2/63), 35; RBT, 64-65; MEW, IV, 238; BNL, 424-25 (at home); LPB, 106

Friedeberg, Pedro, b.1937, (Mexico), painter: AM (3/67), 11

Frobisher, Martin, 1535-94, (Britain), explorer: WNC, III, 87 (c.1575); LSA, 31; MA, 184-85; JCH, 87; AM (9/71), 31; MGE, 279-317 - Signature, RSD, 81

Frondisi, Arturo, b.1908, (Argentina), statesman (President, 1958-62): AM (3/74), 29; WAP (Arg. vol.), 115; LF (9/12/55), 36 - In Washington, AM (3/59), 34-36

Frota, Lelia Coelho, b.1937, (Brazil), poet: AM (2/64), 31

Frye, Alexis Everett, (Cuba), educator: AM (2/74), 13

Frye, William Pierce, 1831-1911, (United States), Senator, 1898: HNM (vol. 98), 508

Fuentes, Carlos, b.1928, (Mexico), writer: MEW, 260; AM (1/78), 52, (4/78), 7

Fugger, Jacob, 1459-1525, (German), banker: HNM (vol. 120), 276 - Palace, Augsburg, HNM (vol. 120), 283 - Correspondence file, HNM (vol. 120), 279

Fulguérez, Manuel, (Mexico), artist: AM (4/79), 45, wk., 46-50

Funes, Gregorio, 1749-1829, (Argentina), churchman; politician: NCE, VI, 227

Gage, Thomas, c.1721-87, (Britain), Dominican, Mexico, Central America: TTG, 76-333 pass.; EBRF (4), 377

Gaillard, Daniel Du Bose, 1859-1913, (United States), military; Panama Canal Commission: MPB, 514 (and wife)

Gainza Paz, Alberto, 1899-1977, (Argentina), publisher of La Prensa: LF (3/12/51), 34, (12/19/55), 45 - La Prensa restored to him, AM (12/19/55), 41-45

Gaitán, Jorge Eliécer, 1898-1948, (Colombia), politician; radical: BCB, 178;

MEW, IV, 284 - On death bed, LF (4/26/48), 24 - Death mask, LF (4/26/48), 28

Gaito, Constantino, 1878-1945, (Argentina), musician; composer: AM (1/71), 23

Galavis y Hurtado, Eustaquio, (Colombia), Bogotá alcalde, 1779-: PPK, 125

Galdés, Gabriel, (Chile), statesman: AM (1/66), 9

Galicio, Galo, (Ecuador), artist: AM (11/59), 23

Galindo, Alejandro, (Mexico), movie director: NMC, 20-39 pass.

Galindo, Blas, b.1911, (Mexico), musical composer: SM, 249

Galindo, Juan [John Gallagher], b.1802 (Ireland), Maya explorer, 1834: RCH, 27; ART, 132

Galindo, Sergio, b.1926, (Mexico), writer: AM (11/60), 41

Gallegos, Rómulo, 1884-1969, (Venezuela), writer; statesman (President, 1949): MEW, IV, 296; WAP (Ven. vol.), 63; ENB (vol. 22), 960; AM (11/54), 40, (12/64), 4, ((5/66), 8, (6/69), 2-6, (5/73), 24

Galván, Jesús Guerrero, (Mexico), artist: HMM, 113-25 pass.

Gálvez, Bernardo de, 1746-86, (Spain), administrator, New Spain: BBG, 64-65; MEW, VI, 301 - Attacks Pensacola (1781), BCS, 14; AM (June-July, 1976), 7-9; BBG, 64-65 - Birth place, BBG, 64-65 - Father (Martín de Gálvez), BBG, 64-65 - Coat of arms, BBG, 64-65 - Statue in Washington, BBG, 65

Gálvez, Cristina, (Peru), artist: LA (5/31/54), 81

Gálvez, José de, 1730-87, (Spain), official, New Spain: CFT, 304-05, RWP, 90; AHC, 49; SFB, 26; MEW, 302; BBG, 64-65

Gálvez, Juan Manuel, 1887-1955, (Honduras), statesman (President, 1949-54): AM (7/50), 43

Gálvez Suárez, Alfredo, (Guatemala), painter: AM (2/79), 53

Gama, Luis, 1830-82, (Brazil), poet; lawyer: DEL, 246; CDB, 162-63

Gambero, Griselda, b.1928, (Argentina), writer: AM (10/78), 20

Gamarra, José, (Uruguay), artist (no pic.): wk., CLA, 31 (1964)

Gante, Pedro de, 1486-1572, (Spain), missionary, Mexico: NCE, VI, 281

Garáfulic, Lily, b.1914, (Chile), sculptor (no pic.): wk., CHL, 261; LF (5/31/54), 80

Garay, Juan de, 1528-83, (Spain), administrator, La Plata: DAB, 146-47 - Founds Buenos Aires (1580), CEF (vol. 2), 524

Garcés, Francisco, (Spain), missionary, California: CCM, 12

García, Calixto, 1832-98, (Cuba), General, Spanish American war: HNM (vol. 98), 835; TCP, 546-47; AM (June-July, 1972), 6

García, Joaquín Toney, (Uruguay), painter (no pic.): wk., AM (3/65), 24-29

García, Juan, (Cuba), military, 1898: LF (6/13/38), 23 (with Elbert Hubbard)

García, Kjell Eugenio Laugerud, (Guatemala), statesman (President, 1975-): NG (11/74), 667, (6/76), 820; BBY (1975), 334

García, Rosa Idalia, (Dominican Republic), artist: AM (1/69), 36

García Bauer, Carlos, b.1916, (Guatemala), member OAS Council: AM (2/66), 41

García Calderón, Francisco, 1834-1905, (Peru), statesman (President, 1881-84): CLI, 121

García Caturla, Alejandro, 1906-40, (Cuba), musician: AM (2/50), 22

García-Godoy, Héctor, 1921-70, (Dominican Republic), statesman (President, 1965-66): AM (9/65), 41, 43, (7/66), 45

García Márquez, Gabriel, b.1928, (Colombia), writer: AM (Nov.-Dec., 1967), 37, (June-July, 1972), 24-25, (4/78), 3, (3/79), 45; MEW, IV, 315; GSL, 170-71

García Menocal, Mario, 1866-1941, (Cuba), statesman (President, 1913-21): TCP, 546-47; MEW, VII, 362

García Monge, Joaquín, 1881-1958, (Costa Rica), educator; editor: AM (7/50), 6, (1/59), 15; CEF (vol. 12), 152; AM (1/79), 33

García Morales, Luis, (Venezuela), writer: AM (5/66), 8
García Moreno, Gabriel, 1821-75, (Ecuador), statesman (President, 1860-65,
    1869-75): NCE, VI, 285; MEW, IV, 316; AM (8/62), 14; EBRF (4), 413
Garcilaso de la Vega, Inca, 1539-1616, (Peru), historian: AM (10/51), 38,
    (7/65), 24, (9/76), S-8, 18-19 - Activities, AM (4/53), 6-7, 30-31 - Tomb,
    AM (7/65), 27
Gardner, Arthur, (United States), diplomat in Cuba, 1953-57: TCP, 1090-91
Gardner, Erle Stanley, b.1889, (United States), writer; explorer, Baja Cali-
    fornia: LF (7/20/62), 57
Garibaldi, Guiseppe, 1807-82, (Italy), military; Uruguay, Brazil: KWW, 134;
    MEW, IV, 321 - Scenes in his life, AM (5/77), 2-7 - Wife (Anita), AM
    (5/77), 2 (in Brazil)
Garrido, Juan A., (Mexico), musician: GPM, 82-83
Garrido, Pablo, b.1905, (Chile), musician; conductor, composer: SM, 217
Garzón, Julio, (Colombia), journalist: AM (6/50), 13 (family)
Gasca, Pedro de la, c.1496-c.1567, (Spain), administrator, Peru: WNC, II,
    539-40; MEW, IV, 333
Gates, William E., (United States), Maya scholar: BPA, plate 23 (c.1915)
Geisel, Ernesto, (Brazil), statesman (President, 1974-): RBT, 64-65; NG
    (11/77), 691; AAY (1978), 130 - In Japan, BBY (vol. 1977), 117
Gelmán, Juan, b.1930, (Argentina), poet: AM (10/64), 21
Gérard, Paul, (Haiti), artist (no pic.): wk., AM (10/78), 10-11
Geraso, Gunther, (Mexico), artist (no pic.): wk., (1977), AM (2/79), 5
Gestido, Oscar D., 1901-67, (Uruguay), statesman (President, 1967): AM
    (3/74), 40
Gil de Castro, José, c.1790-c.1814 (Venezuela), painter (no pic.): wk., CHL,
    209 (of Bolívar)
Gilbert, Araceli, b.1914, (Ecuador), artist: BAC, 15-19 pass.
Giménez, Roberto, (Paraguay), educator; musician: AM (12/65), 38
Ginastera, Alberto Evaristo, b.1916, (Argentina), musician; composer: SM,
    184; MEW, IV, 400; AM (7/58), 12, (7/64), 24, (10/68), 47, (1/71), 22,
    (10/78), 52 - Wife, AM (4/78), 30
Gionneo, Luis, b.1897, (Argentina), musician; composer, conductor: SM, 184
Giorgi, Bruno, b.1908, (Brazil), sculptor (no pic.): wk., CHL, 264
Girona, Julio, (Cuba), painter: AM (11/56), 28-29
Gironella, Alberto, (Mexico), painter: AM (5/69), 7-13
Gladwin, Harold Sterling, b.1889, (United States), archaeologist: FAB, 18
Godoy y Alvarez de Faria, Manuel de, 1767-1851, (Spain), statesman: KCH,
    113; SSH, 248; MEW, IV, 436
Godoy Cruz, Tomás, (Argentina), associate of San Martín: AM (11/66), 6
Goeritz, Mathías, b.1915, (Mexico), architect; artist (no pic.): wk., HCL, 255
Goethals, George Washington, 1858-1928, (United States), engineer, Panama
    Canal: EPC, 33; MEW, IV, 441 - With colleagues, MPB, 432-33 - With
    President Taft, LF (1/24/64), 27
Goitia, Francisco, 1882-1960, (Mexico), artist: AM (2/53), 9-11, 44-45;
    BOL, 86 (1927); HMM, 154
Goldschmidt, Gego (Gertrude), (Venezuela), artist (no pic.): wk., CLA, no.
    32
Gómez, José Miguel, 1858-1921, (Cuba), statesman (President, 1909-13):
    TCD, 546-47
Gómez, José Valentín, 1774-1839, (Argentina), churchman; politician: NCE,
    VI, 605
Gómez, Juan Vicente, 1857-1935, (Venezuela), statesman; dictator, 1908-35:
    DEL, 253; GHS, 564; BMD, 484; MEW, IV, 458 - On horseback, LF
    (7/14/61), 83 - Tomb, WHV, 79
Gómez, Máximo, 1836-1905, (Cuba), revolutionary, patriot: TCP, 546-47;
    WSA, 17; MEW, IV, 459
Gómez de Avellaneda, Gertrudis, 1814-73, (Cuba), writer: AM (10/73), 3,

Goulart, João Belchoir Marquês, b.1918, (Brazil), statesman (President, 1960-64): AM (6/56), 29, (3/74), 34; LF (11/28/55), 46; MEW, IV, 491; EB, 28 - Wife, LF (4/17/64), 26b - With President Kennedy, BBY (vol. 1963), 220 - Overthrown, LF (2/17/64), 38b

Gourgues, Dominique, c.1530-93, (France), in Florida: LEF, 170

Grace, William Russell, 1832-1904, (United States), business (W. R. Grace and Co.): MEW, IV, 502

Graham, Ian, (Britain), Maya explorer: ART, 246 (c.1970)

Granada Arango, Carlos, (Colombia), artist (no pic.): wk., CLA, no. 36 (1969)

Grant, Ulysses Simpson, 1822-85, (United States), military; statesman (President, 1869-77): TCO, 546-47 - In Texas (1845), NMW, 26-27 - In Mexico, CCS, 14 - Signature, RSD, 92

Grassmann, Marcelo, b.1925, (Brazil), artist; engraver: CLA, no. 37 (1958), AM (8/60), 28-29; BNB, 154

Grau, Enrique, b.1920, (Colombia), artist: AM (10/33), 39

Grau San Martín, Ramón, 1887-1969, (Cuba), statesman (President, 1944-48): MEW, IV, 515; LF (6/26/44), 82-83 - Election, LF (6/26/44), 81-84 - With Batista, TCP, 546-47, 1090-91

Gray, George, 1840-1925, (United States), senator, 1898: HNM (vol. 98), 508

Green, Theodore Francis, (United States), senator: Drinking with Trujillo, HHL, II, 234

Grela, Juan, (Argentina), painter (no pic.): wk., AM (3/73), 23-24

Grijalva, Juan de, 1489-1527, (Spain), conquistador, Mexico: WNC, II, 216

Grilo, Sarah, b.1921, (Argentina), artist: AM (1/63), 27; LF (4/31/54), 79

Grotius, Hugo, 1583-1645, (Holland), churchman; politician: MEW, IV, 560 - Signature, RSD, 95

Gruening, Ernest, 1887-1977, (United States), statesman; scholar: GMB, frontispiece, 38-39

Guachalla, Luis Fernando, (Bolivia), diplomat: AM (4/52), 40

Guarnieri, Camargo, b.1907, (Brazil), musician; composer: SM, 216; AM (7/64), 26

Guautemoc, 1497-1522, (Mexico), Aztec Emperor: AM (2/50), 8-11 (remains)

Guayasamín, Oswaldo, b.1919, (Ecuador), painter: AM (2/57), 11-16, (11/59), 22; CHL, 242; NG (2/58), 268

Guedes, Hermano, José, (Brazil), artist (no pic.): wk., CLA, no. 38

Guedes, Joaquim, b.1932, (Brazil), architect: BNB, 154

Güemes, Martín, 1785-1820, (Argentina), military; in "Gaucho War," 1814-21): MEW, V, 5

Guerra, Dora, (El Salvador), poet: AM (6/64), 28

Guerra, García, (Mexico), missionary (17th century): LBT, xvi

Guerrero, Francisco, 1528-99, (Spain), composer in America: NCE, VI, 833

Guerrero, Vicente, 1783-1831, (Mexico), patriot (President, 1829): GFF, 340; MEW, V, 7

Guerrero Galván, Jesús, b.1912, (Mexico), artist: BOL, 130-32

Guevara, Ernesto ("Che"), 1928-67, (Argentina; Cuba): revolutionary: DEL, 266; KWW, 148; TCP, 1090-91; BBP, 29; AM (3/74), 42; MEW, V, 9; LF (3/15/63), 41; HCP, 32, 36, 41 - Family (children), WCC, 125, 265 - In Peking (Feb., 1965), BBY (vol. 1966), 229

Guggenheim, Meyer, 1828-1905, (United States), businessman: BWS, plate 26 (and 7 sons)

Guido, Alfredo, b.1892, (Argentina), artist (no pic.): wk., CLA, no. 29 (1932)

Guignard, Alberto da Veiga, (Brazil), painter: AM (3/50), 10, (4/75), 3-7 (1961)

Guillén, Asilia, 1887-1964, (Nicaragua), painter: AM (10/62), 17-20; CHL, 218

Guillén Roa, Miguel Angel, b.1926, (Paraguay), poet: AM (6/67), 33
Güiráldez, Ricardo, 1886-1927, (Argentina), writer: MEW, V, 16
Guirior, Manuel de, 1708-1788, (Spain), Viceroy of Peru (1776-80): CMP, 104
Gusmão, Alexandre de, b.1895, (Brazil), statesman: Bust, AM (5/50), 21
Gutiérrez, Bartolomeo, 1580-1632, (Mexico), Augustinian monk: HSA, 177
Gutiérrez, Guillermo, (Bolivia), diplomat: AM (6/50), 9
Gutiérrez, José, (Mexico), artist: AM (6/70), 25-29
Gutiérrez, Juan María, 1809-78, (Argentina), politician; historian: AM (4/52), 23
Gutiérrez, Victor Manuel, (Guatemala), communist leader: LF (6/28/54), 14
Gutiérrez Estrada, José María, (Mexico), politician (1840): CLM, 418-19 (1840)
Gutiérrez Gómez, José, (Colombia), diplomat: AM (8/58), 42
Gutiérrez Najara, Manuel, 1859-95, (Mexico), writer, poet: AM (2/60), 8
Guzmán Blanco, Antonio, 1829-99, (Venezuela), statesman (President, 1870-77, 1879-84): DEL, 268; MEW, V, 29
Guzmán Cruchaga, Juan, b.1895, (Chile), poet: SM (4/50), 47
Guzmán Valencia, Rafael, 1878-1938, (Mexico), churchman, Veracruz: NCE, VI, 859

Hamilton, Alexander, 1755-1804, (United States), statesman: MEW, V, 59; AM (8/76), 5, (Nov.-Dec., 1976), 13
Hanke, Louis, b.1905, (United States), scholar: AM (12/50), 11
Harding, Warren G., 1865-1923, (United States), President, 1920-23: MEW, V, 94-95 - Signature, RSD, 98
Harrison, Benjamin, 1833-1901, (United States), President, 1888-92: MEW, V, 116 - Signature, RSD, 99
Hart, Armando, (Cuba), associate of Castro: MRC, 264
Hasbun, Paul, (Chile), churchman; TV director (Santiago): PCA, 64-65
Hawkins, Hamilton S., (United States), Spanish American war leader: HNM (vol. 98), 847
Hawkins, John, 1532-95, (Britain), military: WNC, III, 61, VIII, 196; LSA, 18; AM (1/74), 36; HNM (vol. III), 167; MEW, V, 139; WWE, 17 - Signature, WNC, III, 61
Hay, John, 1838-1905, (United States), Secretary of State: MPB, 303; MEW, V, 145; EBRF (4), 962 - With Bunau-Varilla, MPB, 303
Haya de la Torre, Victor Raúl, 1895-1979, (Peru), APRISTA leader: ALA, 103; LF (2/14/67), 76; MEW, V, 146
Hays, Jack, (United States), commander "Texas Rangers," Mexican War: NMW, 64
Hearst, William Randolph, 1863-1951, (United States), newspaperman: BWS, plate 25; MEW, V, 160
Hemingway, Ernest, 1898-1961, (United States), writer: MEW, V, 183, 184; LF (9/1/52), 34 - House in Havana, Cuba, CCT, 120-21
Henrique, Gastão Manuel, b.1913, (Brazil), painter: BNB, 155
Henríquez y Carvajal, Federico, 1848-1952, (Dominican Republic), writer: AM (9/71), 24-25
Henríquez Ureña, Max, 1885-1911, (Dominican Republic), writer: CEF (vol. 12), 152
Henríquez Ureña, Pedro, 1884-1946, (Dominican Republic), scholar; historian: AM (4/54), 36
Henry the Navigator, Prince, 1394-1480, (Portugal), promoter of discoveries: MEW, V, 216; WNC, II, 29; NCE, VI, 1042; HM, 424; CMF, 53; LF (8/11/47), 27; NRM, 62; BCC, 32, 37; NG (11/60), 621; HE, 31 - Birthplace (Oporto), NG, (11/60), 624 - Point Sagres, PDS, 98 - Sword, NG (11/60), 627 - Statue (Lisbon), NG (11/60), 627

Heras, Juan Gregorio de las, 1780-1866, (Argentina), military; statesman:
   AM (Nov.-Dec., 1968), 14
Heredia Giralt, José María, 1842-95, (Cuba), writer: AM (7/61), 30; CEF
   (vol. 12), 149a
Hernández, Blas, (Cuba), military: TCP, 1090-91
Hernández, Francisco, (United States), in Pan American Union: AM (5/50),
   34, (8/50), 47, (7/51), 2
Hernández, José, 1834-86, (Argentina), writer: WAP (Arg. vol.), 134; MEW,
   V, 228; AM (4/65), 48, (2/73), 8
Hernández de Córdoba, Francisco, d.1518, (Spain), explorer, conquistador:
   AM (8/76), 16-17
Hernández Martínez, Maximiliano, 1882-1966, (El Salvador), statesman
   (President, 1931-44): WES, 144-45
Hernández-Ortega, Gilberto, (Dominican Republic), painter: AM (5/56), 32-33
Herrera, Bartolomé, 1808-65, (Peru), churchman: NCE, VI, 1083
Herrera, Dionisio, c.1790-1850, (Honduras), statesman; head of Central
   American Federation, 1830-33: AM (8/77), 13
Herrera, Leopoldo, (Argentina), educator, Paraná Normal School, 1893-1906:
   AM (4/73), 13
Herrera, Luis Alberto de, 1873-1959, (Uruguay), politician: AM (1/52), 5
   (c.1950)
Herrera, Tomás, 1800-54, (Colombia), statesman; Foreign Minister: HNM
   (vol. 131), 169; AM (Nov.-Dec., 1970), 4-5
Herrera Guevara, Luis, 1891-1945, (Chile), painter: CHL, 219; AM (2/78),
   21-25
Herrera Lane, Felipe, b.1922, (Chile), president Inter-American Development
   Bank: MEW, V, 235
Herrera y Obes, Julio, 1841-1912, (Uruguay), statesman (President, 1890-94):
   GHS, 511
Herring, Hubert Clinton, 1889-1967, (United States), scholar: GMB, 339
Heurtematte, Roberto, (Panama), diplomat: AM (4/52), 40
Hewett, Edgar Lee, b.1865, (United States), archaeologist, Central America:
   BSM, 54-55
Heyerdahl, Thor, b.1914, (Norway), explorer: LF (6/6/69), 70 (and wife) -
   Voyage of the "Ra" (Africa to America), LF (6/6/69), 69-70
Heyn, Pieter Pieterszoon, 1578-1609, (Holland), in Spanish America: NG
   (12/77), 748-49
Hidalgo y Cisneros, Baltásar, 1755-1829, (Spain), viceroy, La Plata: AM
   (5/71), 39
Hidalgo y Costilla, Miguel, 1753-1811, (Mexico), revolutionary: NCE, VI,
   1096; MNC, VIII, 217; DEL, 277; FCL, 85; FWS, 48; AM (3/49), 41,
   (10/50), 26; RWP, 43; MEW, V, 262; BNL, 424-25; BOL, 75; CLI, 29;
   CCW, 242 (idealized); AHC, 67; SHL, 330 - Life scenes, AM (8/53), 6-8 -
   Home (Dolores Hidalgo), WHM, 144 - Church (Dolores), FWS, 48; MIM,
   37 - Monument (Dolores), MIM, 48-49 - Image on coin, FCL, 87 - Bi-
   centennial medals, FCL, 217
Hilton, Ronald, b.1911, (United States), scholar: AM (8/50), 23, (4/56), 20
Hoadley, David, (United States), with Panama railroad: HNM, XVIII, 154
Hodge, Frederick Webb, b.1861, (United States), anthropologist in Central
   America: BSM, 54-55
Holguín, Carlos, (Colombia), chairman, OAS Council: AM (1/69), 43
Holmes, William Henry, 1846-1933, (United States), anthropologist, Mexico:
   WSH, 57
Homar, Lorenzo, (Puerto Rico), artist (no pic.): wk., CLA, no. 40 (1962)
Hoover, Herbert Clark, 1874-1964, (United States), statesman (President,
   1929-33): AM (7/51), 33; MEW, V, 341; EBRF (5), 124 - In Chile, NG
   (2/29), 225-37 pass. - In Honduras, MAA, 52-53 - In Puerto Rico, LF
   (11/30/36), 13 - Signature, RSD, 108

Horurtz, Abraham, (United States), Director, Pan American Sanitary Bureau: AM (Nov.-Dec., 1970), 29

Hostos, Adolfo de, b.1887, (Puerto Rico), historian: AM (1/52), 2

Hostos Bonilla, Eugenio María de, 1839-1903, (Puerto Rico), educator: NCE, VII, 172; MEW, V, 362; CEF (vol. 12), 149b

Houssay, Bernardo Alberto, 1882-1971, (Argentina), physiologist: AM (1/54), 23, (5/77), 32; MEW, V, 369

Houston, Samuel, 1793-1863, (United States), in Texas: WNC, VIII, 230; FWS, 54; MEW, V, 370 - At Alamo, FWS, 55 - With Santa Anna, AHC, 84 (April 21, 1836)

Huaylas, Inti Cussi Huallpa Yupanqui, (Peru), Inca, successor to Atahualpa: AM (2/76), 17

Huayna, Capac, d.1525, (Peru), Inca ruler, GHS, 55

Hubbard, Elbert, 1856-1915, (United States), journalist, Spanish American war: LF (6/13/38), 23

Huerta, Juan Ambrosio, 1823-97, (Peru), churchman: NCE, VII, 186

Huerta, Victoriano, 1854-1916, (Mexico), statesman (President, 1914): BWS, plates 76, 77, 82; MEW, V, 395 - Exile in New York, BWS, plate 98

Huizar, Candelario, b.1888, (Mexico), musician; composer: SM, 248

Hull, Cordell, 1871-1955, (United States), Secretary of State: MEW, V, 411; AM (8/49), 8-11, (11/53), 4, (5/76), 15-17; LF (5/5/41), 27; LK (4/22/41), 24, (11/16/43), 38 - At Pan American Conference, Lima, Dec. 1938, LF (12/26/38), 11

Humboldt, Alexander von, 1769-1859, (Germany), scientist; explorer: AM (8/55), 40 (young man), (5/59), 5, (8/72), 24-25; WNC, VIII, 272; MRM, 185; WTA, 16; LLA, 84-85; MEW, V, 413; BVP, 40 - Signature, RSD, 111

Humphrey, Hubert Horatio, 1911-78, (United States), statesman (Vice President, 1965-69): AM (11/67), 3

Huntington, Ellsworth, 1876-1947, (United States), geographer; anthropologist: HNM (vol. 128), 759-65 (Yucatán)

Hyppolite, Hector, 1889-1948, (Haiti), painter: CHL, 220; CAH, 96ff; LF (9/1/47), 58, 61

Ibáñez, Jorge, b.1940, (Costa Rica), poet: AM (9/65), 30

Ibáñez del Campo, Carlos, 1877-1960, (Chile), statesman (President, 1927-31, 1952-58): DEL, 290; MEW, V, 446 - With President Hoover, NG (2/29), 237 - With Perón, LF (3/16/53), 47

Ibarbourón, Juana de, b.1895, (Uruguay), poet: AM (10/75), 13

Icaza, Jorge Coronel, b.1906, (Ecuador), AM (5/64), 33

Icazbalceta, Joaquín García, 1825-94, (Mexico), scholar: WNC, I, 163 - Signature, WNC, II, 397

Iguasaú, Countess, b.1830, (Brazil), nobility: HAT, 265

Illia, Arturo, (Argentina), politician (President, 1963-1966): LF (7/19/63), 32a; BBY (vol. 1964), 136

Imbert Barreras, Antonio, (Dominican Republic), military: LF (10/18/63), 50

Indabura, Clemente Yerovi, (Ecuador), statesman (President, 1966): BBY (vol. 1967), 305

Inéz de la Cruz, Juana, 1651-95, (Mexico), poet; Catholic Saint: HHL, I, 356; BMD, 232; LBT, xix; MEW, VI, 74; AM (10/51), 17-19, (5/73), 2-7, (2/78), 13

Infante, Pedro, (Mexico), musician: GPM, 82-83

Ingenieros, José, 1877-1925, (Argentina), scientist, humanist: AM (2/51), 18, (8/71), 24-25

Insfrán, Pablo Max, (Venezuela), scholar: AM (8/51), 2

Irigoyen, Hipólito, 1850-1933, (Argentina), statesman (President, 1916-22, 1928-30): MEW, V, 481; BNL, 425 (1916)
Irving, Washington, 1783-1850, (United States), writer: NCE, I, 427; MEW, V, 482; AM (4/72), 8; HNM (vol. 2), 581, (vol. 66), 651 - Home, HNM (vol. 3), 583
Irwin, John N., (United States), diplomat; Peru, 1969: BHG, 266
Isaac, Alberto, b.1925?, (Mexico), movie director: NMC, 160-69 pass.
Isaacs, Jorge, 1837-95, (Colombia), writer: AM (4/62), 36, (3/79), 45; MEW, V, 486
Isabel, Princess, (Brazil), daughter of Pedro II: WDP, 116; CDB, 162-63
Isabella of Castile, 1451-1504, (Spain), Queen: FFI, 36, 132-33; HIC, fr., 68; QKT, 16; SSH, 109; NCE, VII, 664; BCC, 65; MED, 26; MEW, V, 487; HNM (vol. 125), 129-39 pass.; AM (Nov.-Dec., 1971), 2 - Statue, MFI, ibc. - Crown, FFI, 36; MFI, 34 - Scepter, MFI, 8 - Jewel case, MFI, 67 - Mirror, MFI, 93 - Missal, MFI, 67 - Accepts prayer book, MFI, 130 - At prayer, MFI, 96; SSH, 126-27; MHS, 92 - With Ferdinand, NCE, V, 887 - Enters Granada (1492), SSH, 120 - At Granada, BCC, 68 - Attempted assassination, MFI, 81 - Death, MFI, 141; AM (10/75), 29 - Tomb, FCI, 132-33, 338; MFI, 146 [See Ferdinand V]
Isamael, S. E., (Haiti), artist (no pic.): wk., AM (10/78), 10
Iturbide, Agustín de, 1773-1824, (Mexico), military; statesman (Emperor, 1821-22): NCE, VII, 774; CLM, 283; WNC, VIII, 225; FCL, 130; CCS, 10; CCW, 2-47 pass.; RWP, 139; GFF, 328; CBE, 27; MEW, V, 495; AM (8/77), 11; EBRF (5), 475 - Crowned Emperor (May, 1822), DSW, 106; WHM, 142 - Wife and son, GFF, 338 - Palace, AM (2/74), 25 - His flag, SFT, 149 - Image on coins, FCL, 134, 137 - Image on paper money, FCL, 136
Iturrigaray, José de, 1742-1815, (Spain), Viceroy of New Spain: WNC, VIII, 215; RWP, 90-91 (family)
Izá, Ana María, b.1944, (Ecuador), poet: AM (11/64), 30
Izquierdo, María, 1906-56, (Mexico), artist (no pic.): wk., HMM, 142-44; BOL, 139

Jackson, Andrew, 1767-1845, (United States), statesman (President, 1829-37): NG (1/65), 82 - Wife, NG (1/65), 88
Jackson, Thomas Jonathan ("Stonewall"), 1824-63, (United States), military: NMW, 214
Jacques, Amadeo, (France; Uruguay), educator: AM (7/66), 7
Jacques, Gracia, (Haiti), "hatchet man" for Duvalier: LF (7/26/63), 28b
Jagan, Cheddi, (Guyana), politician: LF (10/19/53), 51 (and wife)
Jáuregui y Aldecoa, Agustín de, 1712-84, (Spain), Viceroy of Peru (1780-84): CMP, 105
Jay, John, 1745-1829, (United States), statesman: MEW, V, 540
Jefferson, Thomas, 1743-1826, (United States), statesman (President, 1801-09): MEW, V, 547; AM (8/51), 22, (5/76), 16-17 - Signature, RSD, 116
Jiménez, Flaco, (Mexico), musician (accordian): GPM, 82-83
Jiménez, Juan Ramón, 1881-1958, (Spain; Puerto Rico), poet: NCE, VII, 988; AM (12/65), 37, (Nov.-Dec., 1970), 20
Jiménez de la Espada, Marcos, 1831-98, (Spain), historian: WNC, I, 274
Jiménez de Quesada, Gonzalo, 1509-79, (Spain), conquistador: WNC, II, 580; GHS, 179; MEW, V, 565; AM (June-July, 1971), 21, (June-July, 1972), 24-25, (4/78), 45, (3/79), 31
Joan of the Cross, (Spain; Mexico), sister of Cortés: SSH, 157
João II, c.1455-95, (Portugal), King, 1481-95: SMF, 53; BCC, 169
João III, 1502-57, (Portugal), King, 1521-57: CMF, 12; FCL, 55 (image on coin)
João V, 1689-1750, (Portugal), King, 1706-50: AM (5/50), 22

João VI, 1769-1826, (Portugal), King, 1816-26: HAT, 16, 56; AM (1/77),
   S-5 - Wife (Carlota Joaquim), HAT, 17
Jobím, Antônio Carlos, (Brazil), musician, composer: RBT, 64-65; NG
   (2/78), 272
Johnson, Lyndon Baines, 1908-73, (United States), statesman (President, 1963-
   69): LF (8/9/63), 30b-30c; EBRF (5), 590 - With President Gustavo Díaz
   Ordaz in Mexico (April, 1966); LF (8/68/66), 150; BBY (vol. 1967), 561
Jolimeau, Serge, (Haiti), artist (no pic.): wk., AM (10/78), 8
Joseph, Antonio, (Haiti), artist: CAH, 96ff.
Joseph, Jasmin, (Haiti), painter, sculptor: CAH, 96ff; AM (11/53), 20-23
Josephine, Empress, 1763-1814 (France), wife of Napoleon: RFW, 282
Juan, Don (Spain), son of Ferdinand and Isabel: FFI, 36-37
Juárez, Benito, 1806-72, (Mexico), statesman (President or Executive, 1858-
   72): NCE, VII, 1139; HNM (vol. 109), 865; DEL, 315; FWS, 58; BNL,
   424-25; BOL, 78; CLI, 154; WHM, 158; SMY, 180-81; AHC, 106; GFF,
   350; MEW, VI, 75; AM (10/50), 27, (6/63), 14, (Nov.-Dec., 1972), 11,
   15 - Home, HNM (vol. 64), 217 (interior); AM (Nov.-Dec., 1972), 12 -
   Wife, AM (Nov.-Dec., 1972), 11 - Monument (Mexico City), LMF, 163;
   HMP, 24; AM (Nov.-Dec., 1972), 9 - Statue (Washington, AM (Nov.-Dec.,
   1972), 19 - Bust (Pan American Union), AM (Nov.-Dec., 1972), 20 - Signa-
   ture, RSD, 121 - Tomb, GFF, 352
Juárez Celmán, Miguel, b.1844, (Argentina), statesman (President, 1886-90):
   CCS, 587; HNM (vol. 75), 903 (c.1885)
Julião, Francisco, (Brazil), revolutionary: LF (6/2/61), 88-90
Jurado, Alicia, b.1922, (Argentina), writer: AM (10/78), 22
Justo, Agustín Pedro, 1876-1943, (Argentina), statesman (President, 1932-38):
   NEW, VI, 95; LF (11/30/36), 57
Justo, Juan B., 1865-1928, (Argentina), Socialist Party leader: AM (4/62), 42

Kahlo, Frida, 1910-54, (Mexico), artist; wife of Diego Rivera: HMM, 168-
   70; BOL, 140 (self-portrait)
Kanter, Harry, b.1911, (United States), scholar: AM (6/62), 39
Kaplan, Joel David, (United States), escapee from Mexican jail (Aug. 18, 1971):
   EHT, 116-17
"Kapo," (Jamaica), artist (no pic.): wk., AM (10/78), 32
Karabtchevsky, Isaac, (Brazil), musician, conductor: AM (3/78), 55
Kearney, Stephen Watts, 1794-1848, (United States), general, Mexican war:
   BTM, 203-04; NMW, 104 - His troops, NMW, 106-07
Keith, Minor Cooper, 1848-1929, (United States), businessman; railroad build-
   er: SB, 273; MAA, 52
Kellog, Frank Billings, 1856-1937, (United States), statesman (Secretary of
   State): BWS, plate 137
Kennedy, John Fitzgerald, 1917-63, (United States), statesman (President,
   1961-63): AM (5/76), 16-17; MEW, VI, 165 - In Colombia (Alliance for
   Progress), SBL, 52 - In Costa Rica with President Orlich (March, 1963),
   ALA, 74 - With Khrushchev, MEW, VI, 166 - In Mexico, LF (7/13/62),
   22-27
Kennedy, Robert Francis, 1925-68, (United States), statesman (Attorney Gen-
   eral): MEW, VI, 170; LF (5/10/63), 80
Kent, Jacob F., (United States), Spanish American war leader: HNM (vol.
   98), 847; WSA, 79
Keppel, Augustus, 1725-86 (Britain), military; capture of Havana (1762): TCP,
   546-47
Khrushchev, Nikita, 1894-1971, (Russia), statesman; premier: With Castro
   (Sept., 1960), BHG, 177 - With President Kennedy, MEW, VI, 166
Kidd, William, c.1650-1701, (Scotland), military; pirate: HNM (vol. 106),
   29; AM (5/57), 16-18; BDP, 100, 109, 116, 124
Kidder, Alfred A., 1885-1963, (United States), scientist; explorer: WAK, 38,

55, 82; BSM, 54-55, 278-79

Kino, Eusebio Francisco, 1645-1711, (Mexico), missionary: NCE, VIII, 201;
   AM (10/69), 14, (Nov.-Dec., 1970), 30-35 - Church he founded (Nuestra
   Señora de la Caborca), SST, 46 - Grave, AM (10/69), 19

Kissinger, Henry A., b.1923, (United States), Secretary of State: AM (1/77),
   3-4

Knibb, William, (Britain), abolitionist, Jamaica: AJ, 34

Knox, Henry, 1750-1806, (United States), military; friend of Miranda: AM
   (8/76), 5; EBRF (5), 860

Knox, Philander Chase, 1853-1921, (United States), statesman: BWS, plate
   19

Kondo, Bin, b.1937, (Japan; Brazil), painter: BNB, 155

Korn, Alejandro, 1860-1936, (Argentina), scholar; philosopher: AM (2/51),
   18, (12/65), 3, (8/71), 24-25, (5/75), 36

Korry, Edward, b.1922, (United States), diplomat in Chile, 1967-71: SOA,
   114

Krajcberg, Frans, b.1921, (Poland; Brazil), painter: BNB, 155

Kubitschek de Oliveira, Juscelino, 1902-76, (Brazil), statesman (President,
   1956-61): AM (3/56), 26, (3/73), 24-25; DEL, 319; BBT, 64-65; NG
   (5/60), 720; LF (11/28/55), 46; MEW, VI, 267; EB, 47; BBY (vol. 1966),
   157 - Dedicates Brasília (July, 1958), LF (7/14/58), 121

Kusuno, Tomashige, (Brazil), artist (no pic.): wk., (1976), AM (2/79), 8

Labarca, Amanda, (Chile), scholar, educator: AM (3/66), 33, 35, (8/75), 12

Labrador Ruiz, Enrique, (Cuba), writer: AM (5/49), 39

Lacerda, Carlos, (Brazil), statesman: LF (4/17/64), 38c

Lacerda, Mauricio, (Brazil), statesman: DAC, 204-05

Laet, Joannes de, c.1593-c.1649, (Holland; Flemish), geographer; naturalist
   (no pic.): Signature, WNC, IV, 417

Lafitte, Jean, c.1780-1826, (France), privateer ("pirate of the Gulf"): ACS,
   387; DSW, 109

Laforest, Jean Richard, b.1940, (Haiti), poet: AM (1/65), 21

Lam, Wifredo, b.1902, (Cuba), painter: FWL, 8-30, 130-31, 221; BNI,
   424-25; FWL, 32-250 pass.; CHL, 239; CLA, no. 41; AM (8/78), 47, ibc.

"Lampião," (Virgulino Ferreira da Silva), 1897-1938, (Brazil), bandit in
   Northeast: CBK, 148-49

Landa, Diego de, c.1524-79, (Spain; Mexico), churchman: HHL, I, 320; ART,
   92; GMR, 80; RGS, 22-23, plate 10 - Handwriting, WNC, I, 198; DSC,
   383 - His Maya alphabet, ART, 215

Landaluce, Víctor Patricio, d.1889, (Cuba), painter: AM (9/75), 16-23

Lange, Francisco Curt, b.1903, (Germany; Uruguay), musicologist: AM
   (4/49), 25

Lansing, Robert, 1864-1928, (United States), statesman; Secretary of State:
   MEW, VI, 331

Lanusse, Alejandro, (Argentina), statesman (President, 1971-73): AM (3/74),
   47; BBY (vol. 1972), 92

"La Pola," (Colombia), Independence heroine: AM (2/53), 21-22, 28

Lara, Augustín, (Mexico), musician: GFF, 82-83, 512

La Ratte, Georges, (Jamaica), artist (no pic.): wk., AM (10/78), 8

Lares, Arturo, (Venezuela), editor of El Diario (New York): AM (6/50), 14

Larrañaga, Dámaso Antonio, 1771-1845, (Uruguay), naturalist: AM (Nov.-
   Dec., 1970), 24-25

Lars, Claudio, b.1899, (El Salvador), poet: AM (6/64), 28

La Salle, René Robert Cavelier, Sieur de, 1643-87, (France): JCH, 153;
   NRM, 114; MEW, VI, 338 - At Matagorda Bay (c.1680), LNW, 101

Lasansky, Mauricio, b.1914, (Argentina), artist (no pic.): wk., CLA, no.

42 (1938), no. 43 (1957)

Las Casas, Bartolomé de, 1475-1566, (Spain), churchman: WNC, II, 332;
DEL, 323; AM (10/66), 23, (4/79), 31-32 - With Indians, SBL, 49 - Pro-
tecting Indians, HNM (vol. 64), 411 - Handwritten memorial, NCE, VIII,
448 - Signature, WNC, II, 333; RSD, 131

Lastarria, José Victoriano, 1817-88, (Chile), writer: AM (5/75), 14

Lasuén, Fermín, (Spain), missionary, California (1785-): Statue, CCM, 24

Latham, Ricardo, (Chile), writer: AM (12/54), 38

Laudonnière, René Goulaine de, (France), in Florida: LTV, frontispiece,
71 - Signature, LTV, 278

Lavalle, Juan Bautista de, b.1887, (Peru), OAS council member: AM (2/66),
41

Lavalleja, Juan Antonio, 1778-1853, (Uruguay), Independence leader: CLI,
128; MEW, VI, 359

Lawton, Henry Ware, 1843-99, (United States), military; Spanish American
war: WSA, 79

Lazo, Agustín, b.1900, (Mexico), artist: HMM, 172

Lea, Henry Charles, 1825-1909, (United States), scholar: NCE, VIII, 585;
MEW, VI, 383

Leal, Fernando, b.1900, (Mexico), artist (no pic.): wk., HMM, 34

Leclerc, Charles Victor Emanuel, 1772-1802, (France), General in Haiti:
RFW, 214; AM (11/53), 6, (Aug.-Sept., 1973), 9 (wife)

Lee, Doris, (United States; Cuba; Mexico), painter (no pic.): wk., LF
(5/12/47), 72-78

Lee, Fitzhugh, 1835-1905, (United States), diplomat (1898): HNM (vol. 98),
458; WSA, 7

Lee, Robert Edward, 1807-70, (United States), military; Mexican War: NMW,
143

Léger, Jacques Nicolas, b.1859, (Haiti), scholar: AM (7/54), 40

Leguía, Augusto Bernardino, 1863-1932, (Peru), statesman (President, 1908-
12, 1919-30): MEW, VI, 406

Leloir, Luis F., (Argentina), chemist: NG (3/75), 319

Lemos, Fernando, b.1926, (Brazil), artist; designer: BNB, 155

Le Moyne d'Iberville, Pierre, 1661-1706, (France), in Caribbean: NCE,
VII, 312

Lemus, José María, b.1911, (El Salvador), statesman (President, 1956-60):
AM (7/59), 26 (and family)

León, Argeliero, (Cuba), musician: AM (2/50), 22

León, Luis Agustín, (Argentina), statesman: AM (10/65), 44

León de la Barra, Francisco, 1863-1929, (Mexico), statesman (President,
1911): HNM (vol. 135), 525

León Valencia, Guillermo, (Colombia), conservationist: LF (5/20/57), 45

Leonardi, Eduardo, (Argentina), military; statesman (President, 1955): LF
(10/10/55), 47 (family), (10/17/55), 147, (11/28/55), 45

Leoni, Raul, b.1905, (Venezuela), statesman (President, 1964-69): AM
(6/69), 5; BBY (vol. 1965), 853; LF (10/13/63), 43 - Election disturbances
(Dec., 1963), LF (10/13/63), 42-43 - Receives presidential sash, WHV,
146 - With Rómulo Betancourt, BVP, 36

Leopoldina, (Austria; Brazil), wife of Pedro I: HAT, 76

Le Parc, Julio, (Argentina), artist: AM (8/66), 19-22; CLA, no. 44 (1966)

Lepervanche, René, (Venezuela), diplomat; in OAS: (3/52), 40 - Family,
AM (11/52), 29

Lerdo de Tejada, Miguel, 1812-61, (Mexico), politician: NCE, VIII, 673;
GPM, 82

Lerner, Jaime, (Brazil), mayor of Curitiba: NG (2/78), 265

Lerreynaga, Miguel, (Nicaragua), statesman: Bust, AM (3/65), 22

Lescot, Elie, b.1883, (Haiti), statesman (President, 1941-46): NG (9/44),

308 - With President Roosevelt, LF (11/1/43), 31

Levingston, Robert Marcelo, b.1920, (Argentina), statesman (President, 1970-71): BBY, (vol. 1971), 104

Lewis, Meriwether, 1774-1809, (United States), explorer: MNC, VII, 556; MEW, VI, 471

Leyes de Chávez, María Concepción, (Paraguay), chairman Inter-American Commission of Women, AM (3/54), 40

Lezama Lima, José, b.1910, (Cuba), writer: AM (4/78), 8

Lezana, Francisco Javier, (Spain; Mexico), churchman; viceroy in revolutionary period: WNC, VII, 216

Liautaud, Georges, (Haiti), sculptor: CAH, 96ff; AM (5/56), 32-33

Liberti, Juan Carlos, (Argentina), painter (no pic.): wk., AM (3/33), 21-22

Libster, Myrtha, (Paraguay), poet: AM (6/67), 33

Lihn, Enrique, b.1929, (Chile), poet: AM (5/64), 19

Lima, Alceu Amoroso, (Brazil), writer: AM (5/52), 40, (9/52), 2, (3/55), 43

Lima, Joaquim Manoel Rodrigues, (Brazil), statesman (President, 1892-96): PBF, 112-13

Lima, Jorge de, 1893-1953, (Brazil), poet: NCE, VIII, 758: AM (6/51), 37, (10/52), 39

Lima, Manoel de Oliveira, 1867-1928, (Brazil), scholar: AM (5/73), 30, 32 (1902), 34 (1925)

Limantour, José Ives, (Mexico), Secretary of Finance under Díaz: BWS, plates 3, 28, 63; CLI, 156

Limón, José, (Mexico), dancer: AM (4/53), 13-16

Linares, Antonio, (Mexico), military; with Iturbide: Image on coin (1811), ·FCL, 90-92

Lindbergh, Charles A., 1902-1974, (United States), aviator: NG (5/28), 543, 601 - Trips to Latin America, NG (5/28), 530-601 - In Cuba (decorated by President Machado), NG, 601 - In Mexico, NG, 533-34 - In Costa Rica, NG, 561-64 - In Panama, NG, 566-74 - In Colombia, NG, 574-77 - In Puerto Rico, NG, 588-91 - In Haiti, NG, 594-97 - In Dominican Republic, NG, 591-93

Lindo, Hugo, 1917, (El Salvador), poet: AM (6/64), 29

Lindo, Juan, 1790-1857, (Honduras), statesman: AM (7/57), 32

Link, Edwin, (United States), undersea explorer in Caribbean: LF (5/9/55), 127 (wife)

Linowitz, Sol M., b.1913, (United States), diplomat: AM (12/66), 4

Liz, Domingo, (Dominican Republic), sculptor: AM (1/69), 33

Lizaso, Félix, b.1891, (Cuba), historian: AM (12/50), 2

Lleras Camargo, Alberto, b.1906, (Colombia), statesman; diplomat (President, 1945-46, 1958-62): AM (4/49), 48, (7/50), 43, (3/52), 4, (1/59), 9, (1/71), 24-25; DEL, 341; MEW, VI, 536; LF (5/20/57), 45 - Director General, Pan American Union (1948-54): AM (4/65), 22

Lleras Restrepo, Carlos, b.1908, (Colombia), statesman (President, 1966-70): AM (3/74), 41; SCP, 33; BBY (vol. 1967), 214

Lleras Restrepo, Cecilia de la Fuente de, (Colombia), wife of president: AM (10/69), 38

Llop Bru, Roser, (Chile), artist (no pic.): wk., CLA, no. 11 (1966)

Loaysa, Jerónimo de, 1498-1575, (Spain; Peru), first archbishop: NCE, VIII, 946

Lobato, José Bento Monteiro, (Brazil), childrens' writer: AM (6/50), 30

Lobo, Fernando, (Brazil), diplomat: AM (10/53), 40 (family), (1/55), 27

Locke, John, 1632-1704, (Britain), philosopher: MEW, VI, 545

Lodge, Henry Cabot, 1850-1924, (United States), statesman; Committee on Foreign Relations, 1898: HNM (vol. 98), 508; WSA, 24

Macaya, Margarite O. de, (Costa Rica), chairman, Inter-American Commission of Women: AM (3/66), 45, (11/66), 45, (8/75), 13
Macentyre, Eduardo, b.1929, (Argentina), artist: NG (3/75), 301; CLA, no. 46 (1973)
Maceo, Antonio, 1845-96, (Cuba), patriot; revolutionary: TCP, 546-47; WSA, 17; CCT, 120; MEW, VII, 60
MacEoin, Gary, (United States), writer; Latin Americanist: AM (10/52), 2
Machado, Anesia Pinheiro, (Brazil), woman pilot: AM (4/51), 32
Machado, Jorge Moreira, b.1904, (France; Brazil), architect: BNB, 156
Machado de Assis, Joaquím María, 1839-1908, (Brazil), writer: AM (12/49), 32, (10/52), 20, (6/54), 39; MEW, VII, 63; NCE, VIII, 516, IX, 27; DEL, 350 - Image on coin, EB, 36 - Death mask, AM (9/52), 37 - Signature, RSD, 143
Machado y Morales, Gerardo, 1871-1939, (Cuba), statesman (President, 1923-33): MEW, VII, 62; LF (4/28/61), 20; TCP, 546-47 (and wife, 1928); EBRF (6), 446
MacVeagh, Wayne, 1833-1917, (United States), statesman; Panama Canal negotiations: HNM (vol. 131), 172
Madariaga, Salvador, b.1886, (Spain), writer: AM (1/52), 37 (c.1950)
Madero, Francisco Indalecio, 1873-1913, (Mexico), statesman; military (President, 1911-13): MFG, 4; DEL, 352; BHG, 28 (1911); MEW, VII, 83; HNM (vol. 135), 523 (c.1916) - Father, BWS, plate 46 - His three sons, BWS, plate 65 (1910) - His friends, PZB, 75, 77; BWS, plate 77 - With revolutionary leaders, BWS, plate 75 (1911); BHG, 64-65 - Welcomed in his camp, HNM (vol. 135), 709 (1911) - Enters Mexico City, (June 7, 1911), BWS, plate 72 - After being elected president, WHM, 159 - Peace meeting, Chapultepec palace, MFG, 45 - His flag, SFT, 159 - His horse, BWS, plate 47; HMI, 118-19
Madison, James, 1751-1836, (United States), statesman (President, 1809-17): AM (8/51), 22; MEW, VII, 83
Maeck, Philippe, b.1928, (Brazil), artist (no pic.): wk., (5/31), 54 (1954)
Magalhães, Juracy Montenegro, (Brazil), statesman (President, 1931-37): PBF, 112-13
Magellan, Ferdinand, c.1480-1521, (Portugal; Spain), explorer: WNC, II, 593-94; MED, 314; LNW, 10; NCE, IX, 59; HNM (vol. 81), 357, (vol. 149), 467, 580; NRM, 89; NG (11/60), 614; RMP, 128; CMF, 27 (young man); CMF, 132 (c.1520), 193; MEW, 88; HE, 118 - Ships, HNM (vol. 81), 358 - "Vitoria," PFV, 32; HNM (vol. 149), 477; HE, 136-45 pass. - His adventures, NG (6/76), 723-35 - Leaves Brazil natives, CMF, 94 - "Giants" in Patagonia, CMF, 114, 117 - Killing penguins, Patagonia, CMF, 111 - In Strait, CMF, 211-13; MED, 390-95, 607 - Enters Pacific, HNM (vol. 149), 577 - Lands seen in Pacific, MED, 411, 418 - Meets Ladrones, HNM (vol. 149), 483 - Meets native king, HNM (vol. 149), 785 - Killed (Mactán), MED, 426, 431; CMF, 189; NG (6/76), 745 - Signature, RSD, 144; WNC, II, 592; LNW, 39; HNW (vol. 149), 474; RMP, 128
Magloire, Paul, b.1907, (Haiti), statesman (President, 1950-56): AM (4/52), 20, (3/55), 41
Mahan, Alfred Thayer, 1840-1914, (United States), military: WSA, 26
Maldonado, Estuardo, b.1930, (Ecuador), artist: BAC, 38-40
Mallea, Eduardo, b.1903, (Argentina), writer: AM (3/55), 29
Mama Huaca, (Peru), Inca princess: MAC, 339 (with handmaidens)
Mañach, Jorge, 1898-1961, (Cuba), scholar: AM (11/61), 26-27, (3/73), 36
Mancera, Marques, (Spain), viceroy, New Spain (17th century): AM (2/78), 15
Manco Capac, c.1500-45, (Peru), Inca: WNC, I, 228; MEW, VII, 132 - Image on coin (1915), WNC, I, 228
Manger, William, b.1899, (United States), with Pan American Union: AM (6/50), 40, (5/58), 8-10 (and family)

Mann, Horace, 1796-1859, (United States), educator (friend of Sarmiento): AM (8/64), 28 (and Mrs. Mann)
Manoel I, 1469-1521, (Portugal), King, 1495-1515: HE, 189
Manzur, David, b.1929, (Colombia), artist: AM (5/61), 20-21, (1/62), 29
Mar, José de la, (Ecuador), patriot: AM (Nov.-Dec., 1974), 16
Marchena, Enrique de, b.1908, (Dominican Republic), musician; composer: SM, 281
Marcier, Emeric, (Brazil), painter (no pic.): wk., LF (5/31/54), 83
Marcy, William Leonard, 1786-1857, (United States), politician; Secretary of War, 1845-49: BTM, 203-04
Margil de Jesús, Antonio, 1657-1726, (Mexico), Franciscan missionary: NCE, IX, 203 - Preaching to Indians, ELA, 96
María Luisa de Parma, 1754-1819, (Austria; Spain), wife of Charles IV: AHS, 220-21; DG, 33, 213; SSH, 248; RW, 96
Mariano, José, (Brazil), politician; editor: CDB, 162-63
Mariátegui, José Carlos, 1895-1930, (Peru), writer: MEW, VII, 188
Maris, Mona, (Argentina), movie star: LA (2/3/41), 51
Mariscal, Ignacio, (Mexico), diplomat (c.1880): GFF, 361
Markham, Clements R., 1830-1916, (Britain), scholar: WNC, I, 272
Mármol, José, 1817-87, (Argentina), writer: WAP (Arg. vol.), 131
Márquez, Francisco, b.1833, (Mexico), boy hero, Chapultepec (Sept., 1847): DSW, 217
Márquez, Leonardo, (Mexico), military ("Tiger of Tacubaya"): SMT, 180-81
Márquez Sterling, Manuel, b.1899, (Cuba), diplomat; scholar: BWS, plate 81
Martí y Pérez, José Julián, 1853-95, (Cuba), patriot; scholar: DEL, 358; TCP, 546-47; CCT, 120; HCP, 25; EC, VIII, 300; MEW, VII, 216; WAP (Carib. vol.), 26; AM (12/50), 18-19, 26, (6/63), 13, (12/65), 2, (1/67), 30-35, (June-July, 1973), 24-25; CEF (vol. 12), 149b; EBRF (6), 652 - His teacher, AM (June-July, 1975), 24-25 - In New York City, AM (1/73), 7-12 - Revolutionary Committee, New York City (1892), HCP, 25 - Funeral urn, Santiago, Cuba, AM (June-July, 1975), 24-25 - Monument, Plaza of the Revolution, WIT, 71 - Statue, Matanzas, AM (1/47), 18 - Bust commemorated (Jan. 23, 1953), AM (3/53), 40
Martín, Edgardo, b.1910, (Cuba), musician: AM (2/50), 22
Martín, Vicente, (Uruguay), painter: AM (8/78), 10
Martínez, Estéban José, (Spain), Nootka Sound area: AM (6/70), 5
Martínez, José de Jesús, b.1929, (Panama), poet: AM (7/64), 15
Martínez, Luis, (Mexico), churchman (archbishop, 1937): BWS, plate 160
Martínez, Ramos, (Mexico), muralist: AM (4/77), 19-22
Martínez, Ricardo, (Mexico), artist (no pic.): wk., LF (6/3/46), 60
Martínez Benito, Teodoro, (Mexico), ceramic artist: WM, 112 (and wife)
Martínez de Campos, Arsenio, 1831-1900, (Spain), Captain-General in Cuba: TCP, 546-47; WSA, 19
Martínez Fernández y Martínez de la Sierra, Estéban José, d.1742, (Spain), explorer, Northwest coast of United States: CFT, 304-05
Martínez Mendoza, Herón, (Mexico), ceramic artist: WM, 114-17
Martínez Treuba, Andrés, 1884-1959, (Uruguay), statesman (President, 1951-52): AM (1/52), 5
Martínez Vargas, Ricardo, (Bolivia), diplomat: AM (12/50), 41
Martínez, Carlos, (Brazil), diplomat: LF (12/8/41), 155 (and wife)
Martins, María, b.1906, (Brazil), sculptor (no pic.): wk., CHL, 265
Martyr d'Anghiera, Peter, 1457-1526, (Italy; Spain), historian: NCE, XI, 223
Marx, Roberto Burle, b.1909, (Brazil), landscape artist: AM (6/54), 10-12; HCL, 254; BNB, 152
Masferrer, Alberto, 1868-1932, (El Salvador), writer: AM (2/73), 24-25
Masferrer, Rolando, (Cuba), politician: TCP, 1090-91 (1947)
Masias, John, 1585-1645, (Peru), Dominican churchman (Lima 1622-45): HSA, 239

Mason, John Alden, (United States), archaeologist: AM (9/62), 33
Mason, John Young, 1799-1859, (United States), statesman; Secretary of Navy:
    BTM, 203-04
Mata, Santiago, (Mexico), sculptor in wood: BPS, 461
Matamoros, Mariano, 1770-1814, (Mexico), Independence leader: MEW, VII,
    251
Mateo Sagasta, Praxedes, (Spain), Prime Minister, 1898: WSA, 21
Matías Mella, Ramón, 1816-1864, (Dominican Republic), military: AM (9/71),
    24-25
Matta Echaurrén, Roberto, b.1912, (Chile), artist (no pic.): wk., CHL, 246
Matta Echaurrén, Sebastián Antonio, (Chile), artist (no pic.): wk., CLA, no.
    48 (1947), no. 49 (1965)
Mauck, Willfred, (United States), scholar: AM (10/49), 46
Maudslay, Alfred Percival, (United States), Maya explorer: RCH, 29; ART,
    203; GMR, 81-82 - Headquarters, Chichén Itzá (1889), BPA, plates 5, 6;
    BLM, 23
Mauritz, Jan (Nassau-Siegen), 1604-79, (Holland), in Brazil: WNC, VIII, 352;
    MEW, VI, 20
Mavignier, Almir, (Brazil), artist (no pic.): CLA, no. 50 (1961)
Maximilian, 1832-67, (Austria; Mexico), Emperor, 1863-67: HNM (vol. 109),
    866 (1885); FCL, 168; FWS, 61; WHM, 152; MEW, VII, 274; AMT, 189-91
    (young man); EBRF (6), 713 - The Empress (Carlotta), AMT, 180-81
    (young girl); PCL, 167; FWS, 61; WHM, 152; SMT, 180-81 (1925); AM
    (Nov.-Dec., 1972), 24-25 - Before going to Mexico, AHC, 98 - Offered
    Mexican crown at Miramar, SMT, 180-81 - Leaves Miramar, SMT, 180-
    81 - Enters Mexico City, SMT, 180-81 - French-Mexican troops fight,
    SMT, 180-81 - Prepares for death, SMY, 180-81 - Firing Squad, LF
    (2/15/54), 46 - Execution (June 19, 1867), ALA, 46; SBL, 26; AM (10/50),
    27; AHC, 103; MEW, VII, 275; SMT, 180-81 - Shrine at site of death
    dedicated (1901), SMT, 180-81 - Casket leaves Mexico, SMT, 180-81 -
    Casket arrives in Vienna, SMT, 180-81 - Monument, Querétaro, GFF,
    147 - His father and mother, SMT, 180-81 - His bedroom, HMP, 17 -
    His flag, SFT, 149 - His coinage, FCL, 172-74 - Signature, RSD, 152
May, Charles, (United States), military; Mexican war: NMW, 33
Maytorena, José María, (Mexico), revolutionary; politician: MFG, 4, 200
    (1925)
Maza, Fernando, (Argentina), artist: AM (1/63), 31
M'Boy, Cássio, (Brazil), artist: AM (2/60), 12-17
McClellan, George Brinton, 1826-85, (United States), military; Mexican war:
    NMW, 143
McCullum, Shelby, (United States), politician, 1989: HNM (vol. 98), 508
McKinley, William, 1843-1901, (United States), statesman (President, 1897-
    1901): MEW, VII, 307; TCP, 546-47; WSA, 21; NG (5/65), 708; EBRF
    (6), 455 - War cabinet (1898), WSA, 26 - At Pan American Exposition,
    (Buffalo, Sept. 5, 1901): MEW, VII, 307
Mederos de González, Elena, (Cuba), educator; feminist; stateswoman: AM
    (5/79), 31
Medici, Emilio Garrastazú, b.1906, (Brazil), statesman (President, 1969-73):
    RBT, 64-65; AM (3/74), 75; BBY (vol. 1971), 172, (vol. 1972), 157
Medina, José Toribio, 1852-1930, (Chile), scholar; historian; bibliographer:
    AM (10/52), 22-23, 44 (and friends), (10/72), 42 (1917); CEF (vol. 12),
    149b
Medina Vidal, Jorge, b.1930, (Uruguay), poet: AM (9/64), 20
Meggers, Betty J., (United States), anthropologist: AM (5/54), 46
Meiggs, Henry, 1811-77, (United States), businessman; engineer: CCS, 402
Mejía, Tomás, (Mexico), military: SMT, 180-81
Mejía, Toribio, (Peru), archaeologist: AM (10/78), 40
Mejía Sánchez, Ernesto, b.1923, (Nicaragua), poet: AM (10/65), 37

Mejía Valera, Manuel, (Mexico), artist: AM (6/60), 43
Meléndez, Concha, b.1904, (Puerto Rico), writer: AM (June-July, 1976), 14
Melgar, Agustín, b.1829, (Mexico), young hero, Chapultepec (Sept., 1847):
    DSW, 217
Melgarejo, Mariano, 1818-71, (Bolivia), statesman (President, 1865-70):
    CRH, 120 - Image on coin (1865), FCL, 50
Mello, Domitila de Castro Canto e, (Brazil), friend of Pedro I: HAT, 116 -
    Her sedan chair, HAT, 117 - Her horse, HAT, 117
Melo e Souza, João Baptista de, (Brazil), writer: AM (1/52), 2
Mendaña de Neyra, Alvaro, 1541-95, (Spain), Pacific explorer: MEW, VII,
    345
Mendes, Murilo, b.1901, (Brazil), poet: AM (9/54), 19
Méndez, Leopoldo, b.1902, (Mexico), artist (no pic.): wk., CLA, nos. 51,
    52 (1944); AM (9/49), 12; HMM, 32, 192
Méndez, Ramón Ignacio, 1775-1839, (Venezuela; Colombia), churchman: NCE,
    IX, 647
Méndez Montenegro, Julio César, b.1915, (Guatemala), statesman (President,
    1966-70): KHG, 59
Méndez Montenegro, María, b.1911, (Guatemala), politician: LF (2/3/58), 22
Mendoca, Hernando de, (Peru), 17th century bishop of Cuzco: NCE, IV, 756
Mendoza, Antonio de, 1490-1552, (Spain), first viceroy, New Spain (1535-50):
    CCH, frontispiece; MEW, VII, 356 - Signature, WNC, II, 254
Mendoza, García Hurtado de, 1535-1609, (Peru), colonial administrator; Chile:
    WNC, 550
Mendoza, Jaime, 1874-1939, (Bolivia), intellectual; writer: AM (9/76), 21-
    26 - Birthplace, AM (9/76), 22 - Wife, AM (9/76), 24
Mendoza, María Luisa, b.1931, (Mexico), writer: AM (10/78), 23
Mendoza, Quirino, (Mexico), musician: GPM, 82-83
Menéndez de Avilés, Pedro, 1519-74, (Spain), in Florida: JCH, 64; AM
    (10/74), 26, (9/76), 10 - At St. Augustine (Sept. 8, 1565), LEF, frontis-
    piece; MEW, VII, 357 - Home in Avilés, Spain, LEF, 70 - Church where
    buried, LED, 70-71 - Monument, Avilés, LEF, 70-71
Menezes, José Ferreira de, d.1881, (Brazil), journalist: CDB, 162-63
Menezes de Oliva, María Augusta, (Brazil), musician; pianist: AM (3/50), 46
Mera de Jimón, Gregoria, (Mexico), ceramic artist: WM, 111
Mercado, Melchor María, 1841-68, (Bolivia), painter (no pic.): wk., CHL,
    211
Mercator, Gerhardus (Gerhard Kremer), 1512-94, (Belgium), geographer;
    cartographer: NCE, III, 170; WNC, IV, 371; EW, VII, 367 - His map of
    world (1538), NCE, III, 171 - Signature, RSD, 154
Mérida, Carlos, b.1893, (Guatemala), artist: AM (3/50), 8, (6/50), 24-27,
    (5/56), 34-35; BOL, 121; CHL, 238; HMM, 160-62
Meyer, Augusto, b.1902, (Brazil), poet: AM (9/54), 19
Meza, Guillermo, b.1917, (Mexico), artist: HMM, 112, 176-79
Michel, Alfonso, (Mexico), artist (no pic.): wk., LF (6/3/46), 60
Mignone, Francisco, b.1897, (Brazil), musician; composer: SM, 216
Miles, Nelson Appleton, 1839-1925, (United States), military; in Cuba 1898:
    TCP, 546-47; WSA, 42, 115
Miller, Edward G., (United States), diplomat: AM (2/51), 25
Miller, Joaquin, 1841-1913, (United States), journalist: HNP, 22 (in Mana-
    gua); FLC, 159 (1900)
Miller, Luiza, b.1922, (Brazil), sculptor: BNB, 156
Miller, William, c.1796-1861, (Britain), military; Latin American Indepen-
    dence revolution (1817-24): AM (Nov.-Dec., 1974), 16; MES, 215; WNC,
    VIII, 336
Mills, Roger Quarles, 1832-1911, (United States), statesman (1898): HNM
    (vol. 98), 508
Mina, Francisco Javier, 1789-1817, (Spain; Mexico), revolutionary; patriot:

WNC, VIII, 223

Mindlin, Vera, (Brazil), artist (no pic.): wk., CLA, no. 53

Miramón, Miguel, 1831-67, (Mexico), statesman (President, 1859-60): NCE, IX, 895; SMT, 180-81

Miranda, Carmen, (Portugal; Brazil), singer; movie star: AM (8/53), 11; LF (2/3/41), 50; WLI, 52-53

Miranda, Francisco, 1750-1816, (Venezuela), Independence leader: WNC, VIII, 325; RLM, I, 36, 38 (1781), 103, 132, 216, 308 (1806), fr. (1788); CLI, 66; AM (3/67), 20-27, (8/76), 2; MEW, VII, 433; WAP (Ven. vol.), 55 - Sebastián de Miranda house; Caracas, RLM, I, 4 - House in London, CAB, 80-81 - Passport from Louis XVI, AM (4/50), 16 - Field Marshal appointment (France), 1792, AM (4/50), 16 - Letter of introduction to Washington, AM (4/50), 14 - In prison, DEL, 328; RLM, II, 209; AM (4/50), 13, (3/67), 34 - Tomb, Caracas, AM (3/67), 31

Miró Cardona, José, (Cuba), Batista opponent: LF (1/19/59), 31

Misheau, Rodolfo, (Guatemala), artist: AM (1/63), 30

Mistral, Gabriela (Lucilia Godoy y Alcayega), 1889-1957, (Chile), poet: NCE, IX, 979; BNL, 424 (1946); GGM, 72-73 (various ages); MEW, VII, 437; WAP (Arg. vol.), 210; AM (10/49), 29 (3/51), 37, (3/71), 24-25, (5/72), 15; GGT, 72-73; CEF (vol. 12), 152

Mitchell, Eleanor, (United States), librarian: AM (9/54), 28

Mitchell-Hodges, Frederick A., (Britain), Maya explorer: BPA, plate 16 (c.1955)

Mitre, Bartolomé, 1823-1906, (Argentina), military; statesman (President, 1962-68): NCE, I, 78; DEL, 380; MEW, VII, 441; AM (10/52), 36, (8/71), 32 (1846), (9/72), 18, 19 - In his library, AM (9/72), 19 - Later life, AM (9/72), 23

Mogrovejo y Robles, Toribio Alfonso de, 1538-1606, (Peru), churchman; archbishop, Lima (1581-1606): NCE, IX, 1000; HSA, 209

Molina, Arturo Armando, b.1927, (El Salvador), statesman (President, 1972-): WES, 144-45

Molina, Juan Ignacio, c.1740-1829, (Chile), patriot: WNC, VIII, 345

Molina Enríquez, Andrés, (Mexico), politician: BWS, plate 4

Molinari, Luis, b.1929, (Ecuador), artist: BAC, 32-35

Monagas, José Tadeo, 1784-1868, (Venezuela), statesman (President, 1846-50, 1855-59): CLI, 104; HNM (vol. 17), 195 (residence)

Moncado, José María, 1871-1945, (Nicaragua), statesman (President, 1928-32): NG (5/32), 611

Moncayo, José Pablo, b.1912, (Mexico), musician; pianist: SM, 249

Mondragón, Manuel, (Mexico), politician; military: BWS, plate 76

Monge, Carlos, 1884, (Peru), biologist: AM (1/51), 13

Monroe, James, 1758-1831, (United States), statesman (President, 1816-24): WNC, VII, 344; MEW, VII, 476; AM (5/76), 16-17 - Signature, RSD, 159

Montalbán, Ricardo, b.1911, (Mexico), movie star: LA (11/21/49), fc.

Mont'Alverne, Francisco de, (Brazil), churchman: AM (8/71), 24-25

Montalvo, Juan María, 1832-89, (Ecuador), writer: MEW, VII, 482; AM (6/57), 28, (8/62), 13 (c.1880), (6/64), 12, (12/65), 2, (9/72), 24-25, (8/74), 27

Monte, Domingo del, 1804-53, (Cuba), writer: WAP (Carib. vol.), 33

Montenegro, Ernesto, b.1885, (Chile), writer: AM (3/49), 48

Montenegro Nervo, Roberto, b.1887, (Mexico), artist (no pic.): wk., BOL, 138; HMM, 30, 164

Monterroso, Augusto, (Mexico), writer: AM (6/60), 42

Montes, Ismael, 1861-1933, (Bolivia), statesman (President, 1905-09): GHS, 484; CLI, 126

Montes de Oca, Fernando, b.1830, (Mexico), young cadet martyr, Chapultepec (Sept., 1847): DSW, 217

Móntez, María, (Dominican Republic), movie star: LA (2/3/41), 51; LK

414, 448, 680; Wife, MED, 262
Morisseay, Roland, b.1933, (Haiti), poet: AM (1/65), 21
Morley, Sylvanus G., 1883-1948, (United States), Maya explorer, 1915-32:
    BSM, 54-279 pass.; BPA, plates 12, 13 (c.1930); WAK, 55 - His wife,
    BPA, plate 13 (c.1930); BSM, 55 (1923) - His sister, BSM, 150-51 (1923) -
    With President Cárdenas, BSM, 278-79
Morones, Luis, (Mexico), Minister of Labor under Calles: BWS, plate 127
Morrow, Dwight Whitney, 1873-1931, (United States), ambassador to Mexico:
    BWS, plates 137, 144; MEW, VII, 534
Moscoso, Teodoro, Jr., b.1910, (Puerto Rico), businessman: AM (6/50), 3,
    (1/64), 2; NFP, 92-93; WPR, 64-65
Moscoso Cárdenas, Alfonso, b.1911, (Ecuador), diplomat: AM (3/52), 32
Mosquera, Tomás Cipriano de, 1798-1878, (Colombia), statesman (President,
    1845-49, 1861-64, 1865-67): DEL, 394; CLI, 206; MEW, VII, 543
Motolinía, Toribio de, c.1520-69, (Spain; Mexico), missionary: Signature,
    WNC, II, 343
Moto e Silva, Djanira da, (Brazil), artist (no pic.): wk., AM (3/78), 41
Mourelle, Francisco Antonio, (Spain), explorer, northwest coast of America
    (18th century): CFT, 304-05
Muñoz, Morella, (Venezuela), singer: AM (2/65), 42
Muñoz, Oscar, (Colombia), artist (no pic.): wk., AM (4/77), 27, (2/79), 7
Muñoz Marín, Luis, b.1898, (Puerto Rico), statesman; governor, 1949-64:
    NFP, 92-93; WHP, 108; AM (6/62), 43; NG (4/51), 421; LF (3/15/54), 19,
    (3/11/57), 80-84 - Family, LF (3/11/57), 84 - Inaugurates Commonwealth,
    WPR, 64-65
Muñoz Rivera, Luis, 1859-1916, (Puerto Rico), statesman: NFP, 92-93;
    MEW, VIII, 16; WPR, 64-65; EBRF (7), 102
Murillo, Gerardo, b.1925, (Mexico), painter ("Dr. Atl"): AM (8/65), 23-27
Murillo, Pedro Domingo, d.1810, (Bolivia), patriot: AM (10/73), 24-25
    (1809) - Plaza Murillo, (La Paz), dedicated (Mar., 1943), EA, IV, 171
Mussfeldt, Peter, (Ecuador), artist (no pic.): wk., CLA, no. 54
Mutís, José Celestino, 1732-1808, (Spain; Colombia), naturalist: CE, XIV,
    204; NCE, X, 146; MEW, VIII, 41; AM (2/69), 30, (8/72), 24-25

Nabuco de Araujo, Joaquím Aurêlio Barreto, 1849-1910, (Brazil), statesman;
    writer: HAT, 281; DEL, 403; AM (10/49), 19-21, (10/50), 37, (3/73),
    32; COB, 162-63; MEW, VIII, 49; NAB, 138 - Birthplace, AM (10/49), 20
    (Recife) - Father, AM (10/49), 21 - Sister, AM (10/49), 21
Nacho, Tata (Ignacio Fernández Esperón), (Mexico), musician; conductor:
    GPM, 82-83
Nandiño, Elías, b.1903, (Mexico), writer: AM (11/60), 39
Nannetti, Guillermo, (Colombia), diplomat; educator; writer: AM (8/49), 46,
    (3/50), 47
Napoleon I (see Bonaparte)
Napoleon III, 1808-73, (France), Emperor: NCE, X, 214; SMT, 180-; MEW,
    VIII, 67 - Wife, Eugenie, SMT, 180-81 - Signature, RSD, 164
Nariño, Antonio, 1765-1823, (Colombia), statesman: MEW, VIII, 71; AM
    (June-July, 1971), 23
Narváez, Pánfilo, c.1478-1528, (Spain), explorer: WNC, II, 286; MEW, VIII,
    72 - Signature, ENC, II, 286
Navo, Pedro, (Brazil), poet: AM (9/54), 20
Necochea, Matiano, 1791-1849, (Argentina), military: AM (9/75), 35
Nedo, M. F., (Venezuela), artist (no pic.): wk., CLA, no. 55
Negret, Edgar, b.1920, (Colombia), painter: CHL, 257; AM (6/50), 14, (8/57),
    14-19, (1/63), 28
Negrete, Jorge, 1911-53, (Mexico), musician: GPM, 82-83
Nehemkis, Peter, (United States), businessman: AM (3/65), 39

Nelzahuacóyotl, (Mexico), Aztec king in Texcoco: RSG, 5

Neri, María Francesca Josepha de San Philipe, (Mexico), religious; nun:
NCE, XII, 328 (Puebla, 1769)

Neruda, Pablo, 1904-1973, (Chile), poet; diplomat: AM (3/71), 24-25, (1/72),
11, (5/72), 14-15, (June-July, 1975), 37, (4/78), 3; WAP (Arg. vol.), 211;
GSL, 170-71; DPP, 16-175 pass. (activities; friends)

Nervo, Amado, 1870-1919, (Mexico), poet: AM (6/64), 13, (10/70), 10; WAP
(Mex. vol.), 197

Niemeyer Soares Filho, Oscar, b.1907, (Brazil), architect: AM (9/59), 9-15;
CHL, 288-90 pass.; MEW, VIII, 130; BNB, 156

Nieto del Río, Félix, 1888-1953, (Chile), diplomat: AM (3/50), 46, (10/51),
40, (2/53), 40

Niño, Carmelo, b.1951, (Venezuela), artist (no pic.): wk., AM (10/76), 27

Nixon, Richard Milhaus, 1913-, (United States), statesman (President, 1969-
73): MEW, VIII, 137 - Wife, LF (5/19/58), 24 - Latin American tour
(1958), PLA, 47; LF (5/19/58), 20-25 - In Caracas, LF (5/26/58), 32-38,
(2/14/67), 68 - In Lima, AM (3/74), 29; LF (2/14/67), 68 - With Castro
(April, 1959), BHG, 176-77

Nobiling, Elizabeth, b.1902, (Brazil), engraver: BNB, 156

Núñez, Enrique, (Argentina), guitarist: AM (4/79), 39

Núñez, Rafael, 1823-94, (Colombia), politician; writer: HNM (vol. 71), 52
(1885); CCS, 256

Núñez Cabeza de Vaca, Alvar, c.1490-c.1557, (Spain), conquistador: WNC,
II, 287; MEW, II, 301 - Signature, WNC, II, 287

Núñez del Prado, Carrasco, (Bolivia), artist (no pic.): wk., LF (5/31/54), 81

Núñez del Prado, Marina, b.1910, (Bolivia), sculptor: CHL, 259; AM (6/50),
16

Obando, José María, 1795-1861, (Colombia), politician; military: DEL, 421

Obin, Philomé, b.1891, (Haiti), artist: CAH, 96ff; NG (1/76), 85; LF (9/1/47),
61

Obregón, Alejandro, b.1920, (Colombia), painter: CHL, 241; AM (5/56), 32-33

Obregón, Alvaro, 1880-1928, (Mexico), military; statesman (President, 1920-
24): HMI, 118-19; DEL, 422; BNL, 424-25; GMB, 119; BWS, plates 109-
18 pass.; MEW, VIII, 171; EBRF, (7), 464 - As soldier, BWS, plate 85 -
Cabinet, BWS, plate 122 - With Villa (1914), LF (1/12/48), 15; FWS, 64 -
With Pershing (1914), LF (1/12/48), 15 - At banquet where he was assassinated, BWS, 139; AHC, 161

Ocampo, Miguel, (Argentina), artist (no pic.): wk., AM (2/79), 8

Ocampo, Victoria, 1891-1979, (Argentina), writer; editor: AM (12/65), 18,
(9/71), 13, 14 (c.1930), (5/76), 2-4, (5/79), 3-8; MVO, 195-96 (family;
different ages)

Ocaranza, Manuel, (Mexico), guerrilla (1866), AHC, 118

Odnoposoff, Ricardo, (Argentina), musician (violin): AM (10/53), 9

O'Donnell, Leopoldo, 1808-67, (Spain), Captain-General, Cuba: TCP, 546-47

Oduber Guirós, Daniel, b.1921, (Costa Rica), statesman (President, 1974-78):
AM (10/75), 18

O'Gorman, Juan, b.1905, (Mexico), architect; artist (murals): BLA, 64-65;
BOL, 100-01; BMD, 284; HMP, 46; CHL, 271 (University of Mexico) -
Home, KML, 125

O'Higgins, Ambrosio, c.1720-1801, (Ireland; Spain; Chile; Peru), Viceroy:
WNC, VIII, 322; AM (3/53), 10, (9/58), 17-21 - Birthplace, Ireland, AM
(3/53), 10

O'Higgins, Bernardo, 1778-1843, (Chile), statesman; Independence leader:
WNC, VIII, 330; DEL, 424; MES, 265; MEW, VIII, 190; WAP (Arg. vol.),
199; AM (3/53), 11, (6/58), 18-21, (8/65), 16, (9/65), 14, (4/67), 21,
(Nov.-Dec., 1970), 24-25, (4/72), 36, (June-July, 1976), 16-17; SHL, 331 -

With San Martín (Maipú), AM (9/65), 14 - Abduction (1822), AM (6/58), 22 - Resigns as Supreme Director of Chile (1823), BLP, 71 - At Battle of Chacabuco, AM (6/58), 20 - Monument, Santiago, HNM (vol. 75), 563; CCS, 474 - Image on coin, FCL, 40

Ohtake, Tomie, b. 1913, (Japan; Brazil), painter: BNB, 157

Ojeda, Alonso de, c. 1465-1515, (Spain), explorer: MED, 186, 188

Ojeda, Fabricio, (Venezuela), revolutionary (pro-Castro): LF (6/2/61), 86-87

Olaya Herrera, Enrique, 1880-1937, (Colombia), writer: AM (12/61), 22; BCB, 178

O'Leary, Daniel Florencio, 1800-52, (Britain), revolutionary with Bolívar: MBW, 172; AM (3/53), 12, (11/62), 39

Olhovich, Sergio, (Mexico), movie director: NMC, 138, 145 pass.

Oliveira, Geraldo Teles de ("G. T. O. "), (Brazil), AM (3/70), 46

Oliveira, Marley de, (Brazil), poet: AM (2/64), 33

Oliver, Covey T., b. 1913, (United States), government official: AM (8/68), 48

Oller, Francisco, b. 1833, (Puerto Rico), painter: AM (9/67), 3, 5, 24-27

Olmedo, Alex., b. 1936, (Peru), tennis player: LF (4/5/59), 131-36

Olmedo, José Joaquín, 1780-1847, (Ecuador), writer: CEF (vol. 12), 149a

Olmos, Andrés de, c. 1491-1570, (Spain; Mexico), Franciscan missionary: NCE, X, 683

Omar, Payo, (Colombia), artist (no pic.): wk., CLA, 75

Oña, Pedro de, 1570-c. 1643, (Spain; Peru), viceroy: NCE, X, 695

Oñate, Juan de, c. 1549-c. 1624, (Mexico), explorer; His inscription on rock (1606), Southwest United States: AM (10/76), 13

O'Neill, Carlota, (Spain; Mexico), writer: AM (10/78), 24

Onganía, Juan Carlos, b. 1914, (Argentina), statesman (President, 1966-70): AM (4/67), 2, (10/69), 40 (and wife); LF (2/14/67), 80; BBY (vol. 1967), 108

Onís, Federico de, 1885-1966, (United States), scholar: AM (2/78), 41, 45

Orbón, Julián, b. 1926, (Cuba), musician; composer: AM (2/50), 22, (7/64), 27

Oreamuno, J. Rafael, (Costa Rica), diplomat: AM (2/52), 28, (12/52), 40

Orellano, Francisco de, c. 1511-46, (Spain; Peru), explored Amazon: AM (9/72), 24-25

Orfila, Alejandro, (Argentina), Secretary-General, OAS: AM (June-July, 1975), 2

Oribe, Manual Caferino, 1792-1857, (Uruguay), Independence leader: DEL, 431

Orlandi, Alicia, (Argentina), artist (no pic.): wk., CLA, no. 56 (1962)

Orlando, Felipe, (Cuba), painter: AM (2/58), 16-17

Orlando Rodríguez, Luis, (Cuba), Castro friend: LF (1/19/59), 31

Orlich Bolmarcich, Francisco José, 1907-69, (Costa Rica), statesman (President, 1962-66): NG (7/65), 131 - With President Kennedy (San José, 1963), ALA, 74

Orozco, José Clemente, 1883-1949, (Mexico), painter: HHM, 62-83 pass. ; AM (11/49), 24-27, (June-July, 1977), 43-44; AHC, 126, 150; BOL, 31-117 pass. ; MEW, VIII, 217; LF (11/22/48), 69; BLA, 148-49; CLA, no. 57 (1928), no. 58 (1930); EBR (13), 741

Orozco, Pascual, d. 1916, (Mexico), military: HNM (vol. 135), 523

Orozco y Berra, Manuel, 1816-81, (Mexico), scholar: WAP (Mex. vol.), 196

Orozco Romero, Carlos, b.1898, (Mexico), painter (no pic.): wk., HMM, 119, 174

Orrego Salas, Juan, b.1918, (Chile), musician; composer: AM (7/64), 25

Ortiz, Adalberto, b.1914, (Ecuador), artist: AM (3/78), 50-51

Ortiz, Emilio, (Mexico), artist (no pic.): wk., CLA, no. 59 (1969)

Ortiz, Fernando, 1881-1969, (Cuba), scholar: AM (6/59), 7

Ortiz, Josefa, (Mexico), Independence era: AM (4/74), 24-25

Ortiz, Roberto Mario, 1886-1942, (Argentina), statesman (President, 1928-40): LF (11/13/39), 66
Ortiz de Domínguez, Josefa, d.1820, (Mexico), patriot wife of governor of Querétaro: FCL, 88 - Image on coin, FCL, 89
Orton, James, 1830-77, (United States), South American explorer (1867-77): AM (3/60), 27-30
O'Shaughnessy, Mrs. Nelson, (United States), acting diplomat (1911): HNM (vol. 135), 707
Osório, Manuel Luiz, (Brazil), military (mid-1870s): KPA, 35
Osorio, Oscar, b.1910, (El Salvador), statesman (President, 1950-56): AM (4/52), 4
Ospina Pérez, Mariano, 1891-1976, (Colombia), statesman (President, 1946-50): BCB, 178-79
Ostrower, Fayga, 1920, (Poland; Brazil), engraver: BNB, 157
Osuna, Rafael, b.1940, (Mexico), tennis champion: LA (9/20/63), 95
Otero, Alejandro, b.1921, (Venezuela), painter: CHL, 240; AM (5/56), 32-33, (8/77), bc.
Othón, Manuel José, 1858-1906, (Mexico), poet: WAP (Mex. vol.), 197
Ovando, Nicolás, 1460-1518, (Spain), conquistador: AM (10/76), 18-19
Oyarzún, María Eugenio, (Chile), diplomat: AM (Nov.-Dec., 1976), 26

Pachacutec Yupanqui, died c.1490, (Peru), Inca ruler: GHS, 51
Pacheco, José Emilio, b.1939, (Mexico), poet: AM (10/63), 11
Pacheco, María Luisa, b.1919, (Bolivia), painter: AM (1/63), 28; CHL, 245
Pacheco Areco, Jorge, (Uruguay), statesman; President, 1967-72: BBY (vol. 1972), 721
Padilla, Ezequiel, (Mexico), statesman: LF (2/9/42), 28; LK (6/30/42), 16-19 - Family, LK (6/30/42), 19
Padilla Nervo, Luis, b.1896, (Mexico), diplomat: AM (3/52), 3, 42
Páez, José Antonio, 1790-1873, (Venezuela), statesman (President, 1831-35, 1838-42): MEW, VIII, 254; DEL, 428; MBW, 172-73; CLI, 61; GJA, fr., 98, 178; EBRF (7), 672; AM (5/69), 5 - Birthplace site, GJA, 18 - His horse "Caballero," GJA, 34 - Image on coin, FCL, 48 - Signature, GJA, 162
Páez Vilaro, Carlos, b.1923, (Uruguay), artist: AM (Aug.-Sept., 1973), 42-47, (Nov.-Dec., 1977), 59
Paine, Thomas, 1737-1809, (Britain), philosopher; revolutionary: AM (8/76), 5; MEW, VIII, 259 - Signature, RSD, 171
Palacio, Luis, (Argentina), artist: AM (2/60), 23
Palacios y Sojo, Feliciano, (Venezuela), grand uncle of Bolívar: AM (8/75), 26
Palau, Francisco de, died c.1648, (Mexico), California missionary: CE, III, 179
Palma, Clemente, 1872-1946, (Peru), writer: CLI, 258
Palma, Ricardo, 1833-1919, (Peru), writer; historian: NCE, 935; CLI, 258; AM (5/71), 24-25, (June-July, 1971), 31; MEW, VIII, 268; WAP (Br. vol.), 182; CEF (vol. 12), 149a
Pani, Mario, b.1911, (Mexico), architect: CHL, 269; LF (2/24/47), 99
Pardo, Manuel, 1834-78, (Peru), statesman (President, 1872-76): CLI, 118
Pardo García, Germán, b.1902, (Mexico), writer: AM (6/60), 41
Paredes y Arrillaga, Mariano, (Mexico), military (1840s): CLM, 418-19; NMW, 59
Pareja Diezcanseco, Alfredo, b.1908, (Ecuador), writer: AM (11/59), 22, (5/64), 32
Parisot, Aldo, (Brazil), musician: AM (8/58), 27

Parkman, Francis, 1823-93, (United States), writer; historian: WNC, IV, 257; MEW, VIII, 289; EBR (13), 1019 - Signature, WNC, IV, 157
Paroissién, Diego, 1783-1827, (Chile), Surgeon, Army of Andes: AM (Nov.-Dec., 1968), 15
Parra, Nicanor, b.1914, (Chile), poet: AM (5/64), 16, (4/78), 4
Pastene, Juan Bautista, (Panama; Chile), with Valdivia: WNC, II, 531
Pastor, Celso, (Peru), diplomat: AM (4/66), 41 (with family)
Patiño, Simón Iturri, 1862-1947, (Bolivia), industrialist: MEW, VIII, 308
Patrocinio, José do, (Brazil), journalist; politician: CDB, 162-63
Patterson, Richard C., Jr., (United States), diplomat (Guatemala, 1948-51): BHG, 65
Paul VI, 1897-1978, (Italian), Pope: MEW, VIII, 319 - At Eucharistic Congress (Bogotá), LF (9/6/68), 64-67; BBY (vol. 1969), 209
Paz, Enrique, (Argentina), editor, La Prensa: LF (3/12/51), 34
Paz, José Clemente, (Argentina), editor, La Prensa (1869-): LF (3/12/51), 34
Paz, Juan Carlos, b.1897, (Argentina), musician; composer: SM, 185
Paz, Octavio, b.1914, (Mexico), writer: AM (7/63), 31, 33, (10/63), 10, (9/77), 44, (4/28), 4
Paz Estenssoro, Víctor, b.1907, (Bolivia), statesman (President, 1952-56, 1960-64): MEW, 331; ALA, 102; BHG, 628-29; DEL, 458 (with carriage); BBY (vol. 1965), 190 - Wife, AM (9/53), 28, (6/62), 43 - With President Kennedy (Oct., 1963), BHG, 129
Pazo, Rodolfo O., (Chile), artist: AM (6/63), 31
Peçanha, Nilo Procópio, 1867-1924, (Brazil), statesman (President, 1909-10): PBF, 112-13
Pedrell, Carlos, 1878-1941, (Uruguay), musician; composer: SM, 153
Pedro I, 1798-1834, (Portugal), Emperor of Brazil, 1822-31: CEL, 460; AM (7/49), 16-19, 34; HAT, 57 (child); GHS, 408; WDP, 10; MEW, VIII, 342 - Parents (João VI and Carlota Joaquina), AM (7/49), 17 - First wife (Leopoldina), HAT, 76; WDP, 10 - Second wife (Amélia Leuchtenberg), HAT, 198 - Mistress (Marquesa de Santos) and palace, HAT, 188 - "I will remain" declaration (Jan. 9, 1822), AM (7/49), 18 - "Cry of Ypiranga" (Sept. 7, 1822), BHB, 601; AM (8/51), 4 - Acclaimed Emperor (1822), BRJ, 77 - Statue (Rio de Janeiro), CCS, 692; AM (1/74), 34 - Image on coin, FCL, 58
Pedro II, 1825-91, (Brazil), Emperor, 1831-89: DEL, 461; CCS, 682; HAT, 249, 265; CRH, 310; BNL, 424-25; GHS, 523; BMD, 298; RBT, 64-65; CDB, 162-63; WDP, fr., 364; EA, IV, 472; MEW, VIII, 343 - As boy, WDP, 40 (age one); HAT, 232 (age four) - Middle age, WDP, 116, 120 (1865) - With sisters, WDP, 40 - Wedding, AM (7/49), 18 - Daughter Isabel, HAT, 258 - Empress (Theresa Christina), CCS, 685; HAT, 258 - His family (c.1888), WDP, 324; HAT, 258 - Coronation, WDP, 58; HAT, 233; AM (7/49), 18, (1/74), 31, (Nov.-Dec., 1975), 16-17 - His crown, NG (1/67), 108 - Coach, AM (1/74), 32 - Palace (Petropolis), CCS, 687 - Palace (São Cristovão), AM (8/51), 5 - At Niagara Falls (1876), WDP, 202 - Masonic regalia, AM (7/49), 19 - Image on coin, CCW, illus., 817 - Signature, RSD, 174
Peixoto, Floriano, 1839-95, (Brazil), statesman (President, 1891-94): MEW, VIII, 349
Peláez, Amelia, b.1897, (Cuba), artist: AM (3/50), 10, (12/54), 12-17
Pelé (Edson Arantes de Nascimento), b.1941, (Brazil), soccer player: KP, 65-71, BPSH, fr., 1-63 pass.; RBT, 64-65; AM (10/77), 47 - Wife, AM (10/77), 47 - Signature, RSD, 174
Pellecer, Carlos Manuel, (Guatemala), communist leader: LF (10/12/53), 170, (6/28/54), 15
Pena, Afonso Augusto Moreira, 1847-1909, (Brazil), statesman (President, 1906-09): PBF, 112

Peña, Feliciano, (Mexico), artist (no pic.): wk., LF (6/3/46), 58
Peña y Peña, Manuel de la, 1789-1850, (Mexico), jurist (1840): CLM, 473
Peñaherrera, Luis Antonio, (Ecuador), diplomat: AM (2/52), 40
Peñalba, Alicia, b.1918, (Chile), sculptor (no pic.): wk., CHL, 263
Peñalba, Rodrigo, (Nicaragua), artist (no pic.): AM (3/50), 9
Penna, Carlos Víctor, (Argentina), scholar; librarian: AM (2/52), 5
Pereira, Astrogildo, (Brazil), communist organizer: DAC, 204-05
Pereira, Manoel Vitorino, (Brazil), statesman (Vice President, 1889-90): PBF,
    112-13
Pereira, Rafael, (Guatemala), painter (no pic.): wk., KHG, 86
Pereyra, Juana, (Uruguay), civil engineer: AM (10/49), 31
Pérez, Carlos Andrés, b.1922, (Venezuela), statesman (President, 1974-78):
    Visit with Shah of Iran, AM (1/38), 74 - Before Mexican Congress (Mar.,
    1976), AAY (1976), 585 - In Italy (1977), AAY (1977), 543
Pérez, Faustino, (Cuba), Castro associate: LF (1/19/59), 31
Pérez, Guillo, (Dominican Republic), artist: AM (1/69), 34
Pérez, Santiago, (Venezuela), politician: AM (3/52), 40
Pérez Fernández, Joaquín, (Argentina), dancer: AM (10/52), 12-15
Pérez Holguín, Melchor, b.1660, (Colombia), painter: NCE, VI, 50
Pérez Jiménez, Marcos, b.1914, (Venezuela), statesman (President, 1950-
    58): AM (2/57), 27; LF (12/15/62), 34-35, (2/3/58), 16; ENB (vol. 22),
    906 - Cabinet, LF (1/20/58), 31 - Riots against, WHV, 141; LF (1/20/58),
    31, (2/3/58), 16-21 - Overthrown, LF (2/3/58), 16-21 - Refugee in Miami
    (1958), WHV, 142 - Trial (Caracas) April, 1965, BBY (vol. 1966), 796
Perón, Eva Duarte, 1919-1952, (Argentina), wife of President Perón: Mother
    and sisters, BEF, 40-41 - At various ages, BEF, 40-41 - Actress, BEF,
    40-41 - Before and after marriage, BEF, 72-73 - Social life, BEF, 104-
    05 - In Madrid, BED, 72-73 - In Paris, Geneva, Rome, BEF, 104 -
    Death, funeral, burial, GEF, 168-69 - Death mask, BEF, 169
Perón, Juan Domingo, 1895-1975, (Argentina), statesman; military (President,
    1946-55, 1973-75): DEL, 467; MEW, VIII, 367; EA, II, 275; AM (3/74),
    23 - In Chile, LF (3/16/53), 47-50, (4/11/49), 22 - Jockey Club burned,
    LF (5/25/53), 39 - Anti-Perón revolt (June, 1955), LF (7/4/55), 14-15
    (9/12/55), 35-43 - Escapes to Paraguay, LF (10/17/55), 147-52, (11/28/55),
    45-47 - Returns (1973), AAY (vol. 1973), 100; BBY (vol. 1974), 97-98 -
    Signature, RSD, 175
Perón, María Estela Martínez de, (Argentina), stateswoman (President, 1974-
    76): NG, (3/75), 332; AAY (1975), 100, (1976), 94
Perry, Mathew Calbraith, 1794-1858, (United States), military (Mexican war):
    BTM, 203-04
Pershing, John J., 1860-1948, (United States), military: EBRF (7), 890 -
    With Villa and Obregón (1914), LF (1/12/48), 15 - Searching for Villa,
    BWS, plates 111, 112 - Signature, RSD, 175
Pessoa, Epitácio da Silva, 1865-1942, (Brazil), statesman (President, 1919-
    22): DAC, 204-05; LPB, 103; PBF, 112-13
Pétion, Alexandre Sabès, 1770-1818, (Haiti), statesman (President, 1807-18):
    WH, 20; WAP (Carib. vol.), 49; AM (11/52), 27
Pettoruti, Emilio, b.1892, (Argentina), painter (cubist): CHL, 249; AM
    (3/50), 11, (4/72), 25-30
Peurifoy, John E., (United States), diplomat (Guatemala): BGH, 176
Phelps, Anthony, b.1928, (Haiti), poet: AM (1/65), 21
Philip II, 1527-98, (Spain), King, 1556-98: GKT, 24 (Prince); NCE, XI,
    272 (1551); BMM, II, 997 (1555); GKT, 30 (1553), 71, 77 (1555), 148
    (1580), 210; AHS, 156-57; MA, 140-44; SSH, 164-65; CS, 88; LSA, fr.;
    MEW, VIII, 441 - Wife, Mary Tudor, GKT, 39 (1554), 57 - Wife, María
    of Portugal, GKT, 22 - Wife, Elizabeth of Valois, GKT, 100 - Wife, Anne
    of Austria, GKT, 142 - Son, Don Carlos, GKT, 103 - Daughter (Isabela
    Clara Eugenia), GKT, 176 - Sister, GKT, 33 - Apartment (Escorial), GKT,

206 - Coat of arms, KCH, 88 - Armor, GKT, 29, 59 - Saddle, GKT, 60 -
Medal of Honor (1548), GKT, 26 - At prayer, SSH, 192-93 - Handwriting,
LSA, 88 - Signature, RSD, 176 - Fleet seizes Azores (1582), SSH, 191 -
Image on coins (1588), GKT, 188 - Image on cameo, GKT, 165 - Medallion,
GKT, 45 - Statue, KCH, 84; GKT, 41
Philip III, 1578-1621, (Spain), King, 1598-1621: SSH, 197; SKT, 218; MEW,
VIII, 413 - His chair, SKT, 229
Philip IV, 1605-65, (Spain), King, 1621-65: AHS, 156-57; CS, 88; KCH, 86;
LHS, 175; SSH, 200; MEW, VIII, 415 - Wife (Mariana of Austria), KCH,
79; SSH, 201 - With family, SSH, 209 - Signature, RSD, 177
Philip V, 1683-1746, (France; Spain), King, 1700-46: SSH, 219; MEW, VIII,
417
Philip, John Woodward, 1840-1900, (United States), military (Spanish Ameri-
can war): HNM (vol. 98), 853
Philoctète, René, b.1922, (Haiti), poet: AM (1/65), 21
Piazzolla, Astor, (Argentina), musician: AM (1/78), 21
Pichón Riviere, Marcelo, (Argentina), poet: AM (10/64), 21
Pico, Andrés, (Mexico), military; Mexican war: NMW, 119
Pico, Pío, (Mexico), governor of California (1846); NMW, 118
Picón-Salas, Mariano, b.1901, (Venezuela), writer; historian: AM (12/50),
2, (8/51), 2, (5/65), 6-7 (wife), (3/72), 32
Pierce, Franklin, 1804-69, (United States), statesman (President, 1852-56):
MEW, VIII, 437; NMW, 175
Piérola, Nicolás de, 1839-1913, (Peru), statesman (President, 1879-84, 1895-
99): CLI, 190
Pigafetta, Francisco Antonio, c.1480-1534, (Italian), navigator: NG (6/76),
730; HE, 152 (age 40) - Statue, PFV, fr.
Pike, Zebulon, 1779-1813, (United States), explorer; military: MEW, VIII,
442 - At Santa Fe, New Mexico, DSW, 137
Pineda, Duque Roberto, (Colombia), musician; composer: AM (7/64), 27
Pinheiro Machado, José Gomes de, (Brazil), military: KPA, 63
Pinho, João Ferreira de Araújo, (Brazil), statesman (President, 1908-11):
PBF, 112-13
Pinochet Ugarte, Augusto, b.1915, (Chile), statesman (President, 1973-): AM
(8/76), 1; SDA, 270; AAY (1976), 166, (1977), 155, 156 - With Secretary
Kissinger (1977), AAY (1977), 289
Pinto, Aníbal, 1825-84, (Chile), statesman (President, 1876-81): GHS, 428
Pinzón, Martín Alonso, c.1440-1493, (Spain), navigator; explorer: BCC, 97
Pinzón, Vicente Yáñez, c.1460-c.1524, (Spain), navigator; explorer: HE, 68
Piwonka Ovalle, Alberto, b.1917, (Chile), architect (no pic.): wk., CHL, 282
Piza, Arthur Luis, (Brazil), artist (no pic.): wk., CLA, no. 60
Pizarnik, Alejandra, b.1936, (Argentina), poet: AM (10/64), 19
Pizarro, Francisco, 1470-1541, (Spain; Peru), conquistador: WNC, II, 532-
33; DEL, 482; LNW, 20; CCH, 46; MEW, VIII, 478 - Before Emperor
Charles V, AHS, 76-77 - With Almagro and De Luque, ELA, 63 - Builds
ship on Gallo Island, AM (5/71), 24-25 - Landing place, Ecuador, CCS,
325 - Meets Atahualpa, ELA, 66 - Battles Indians under Atahualpa (1532),
HHL, I, 86 - Captures Atahualpa, NCE, IV, 185; AM (3/49), 22, (1/72),
4 - Enters Cuzco (1533), GKT, 182 - Assassinated by Almagro the Young-
er, AM (5/71), 24-25, (2/74), 20 - Mummy, NG (6/30), 753, (2/38), 526;
FLC, 80 - Statue (Trujillo, Spain), AM (10/77), fc. - Signature, LNW, 20;
RSD, 181
Pizarro, Gonzalo, c.1505-48, (Spain; Peru), conquistador: Captive, GKT, 10 -
Led to execution, AM (2/74), 21
Plate, Juan, b.1911, (Paraguay), diplomat: AM (2/66), 41
Plattner, Karl, b.1919, (Brazil), artist (no pic.): wk., LF (5/31/54), 82
Plaza, Juan Bautista, b.1898, (Venezuela), musician; composer: AM (2/65),
42
Plaza, Luis Guillermo, (Argentina), lawyer: AM (1/52), 2

Prescott, William Hickling, 1796-1859, (United States), scholar: WNP, II,
    426; NCE, I, 411 - Bust, HNM, I, 138 - Library, WNC, II, 577
Prester John, (Egypt), explorer to East (12th century): CE, XII, 401; BCC,
    41; HE, 34
Prestes, Luís Carlos, 1898, (Brazil), politician; communist leader: LF
    (11/22), 37; MEW, IX, 11 - Military cadet (1919), DFC, 204-05 - Prison-
    er, DFC, 204-05
Preston, Andrew W., (United States), "Father" of United Fruit Company:
    MAA, 52
Prieto, Guillermo, 1818-97, (Mexico), writer: GFF, 390; HMM (vol. 71),
    267 (c. 1885)
Prío Socorrás, Carlos, b.1903, (Cuba), statesman (President, 1948-52):
    TCP, 1090-91 (and wife); LF (3/24/52), 21
Proctor, Redfield, 1831-1908, (United States), military, 1898: HNM (vol. 98),
    506
Pucciarelli, Mario, (Argentina), artist: AM (12/60), 18-20
Pueyrredón, Carmen, (Argentina), debutante: LF (5/5/41), 122-25
Pueyrredón, Juan Martín de, 1777-1850, (Argentina), statesman (Supreme
    Director, United Provinces), 1816-19: AM (11/66), 6, (Nov.-Dec., 1968),
    15 - Home, AM (9/66), 2-7
Pueyrredón, Prilidiano, 1823-70, (Argentina), painter (no pic.): wk., CHL,
    213
Puig, Manuel, b.1932, (Argentina), writer: AM (4/74), 7
Putnam, Samuel, 1892-1950, (United States; Brazil), writer: AM (5/49), 49

Quadros, Jânio, b.1917, (Brazil), statesman (President, 1961): RBT, 64-65
Queiroz, Raquel de, b.1910, (Brazil), writer: WAP (Br. vol.), 99
Quinqueta Martín, Benito, (Argentina), artist: AM (5/78), 30-34
Quintana, Manuel, 1834-1906, (Argentina), statesman (President, 1904-06):
    AM (4/70), 11
Quintana Roo, Andrés, 1787-1851, (Mexico), politician; writer: CLM, 418-19
Quintanilla, Luis, 1900-1980, (Mexico), diplomat: AM (9/49), 34, (1/50), 31,
    (5/50), 41, (9/51), 43, (5/52), 31, (8/52), 40
Quintero, José, (Panama), theater director: AM (9/55), 32
Quiroga, Juan Facundo, c.1788-1835, (Argentina), caudillo: MEW, IX, 65
Quiroga, Vasco de, c.1470-1565, (Mexico), churchman: NCE, XII, 32; WHM,
    133; AM (12/58), 11-12 (activities)
Quirós, Rodrigo, b.1944, (Costa Rica), poet: AM (9/65), 33
Quitman, John Anthony, 1798-1858, (United States), military; Mexican war:
    BTM, 234-35

Rackam, John, (Britain), pirate, Caribbean, 1720: BDP, 11
Raleigh, Walter, 1552-1618, (Britain), military; explorer: LNW, 23; JCH,
    72; NCE, V, 396; MEW, IX, 86; AM (8/67), 16 - Coat of arms, JCH,
    77 - Company emblem, LNW, 147 - Relations with Indians, ADN, 170-77 -
    Signature, RSD, 187; WNC, III, 105; LNW, 23
Ramalho, João, c.1490-1580, (Brazil), "Father of São Paulo": FCL, 56
    (image on coin)
Rameau, Cameau, (Haiti), artist (no pic.): AM (10/78), 12
Ramírez, José Agustín, (Mexico), guitarist: GPM, 82-83
Ramírez Vázquez, Pedro, (Mexico), architect (Archaeological Museum): NG
    (10/68), 507
Ramírez Villamizar, Eduardo, b.1923, (Colombia), painter (no pic.): wk.,
    CHL, 242
Ramos, Graciliano, 1892-1953, (Brazil), novelist; journalist: NCE, XII, 74
Ramos Arizpe, Miguel, 1775-1843, (Mexico), churchman; politician: CLM,

Ripstein, Arturo, (Mexico), movie director: NMC, 148-57 pass.
Riva Agüero, José de la, 1783-58, (Peru), statesman (President, 1823): AM
    (10/73), 18
Riva Palacio, Vicente, 1832-96, (Mexico), writer: GFF, 380
Rivadavia, Bernardino, 1780-1845, (Argentina), statesman (President, 1826-
    27): CLI, 138; MEW, IX, 208
Rivadeneira, Jorge, (Ecuador), sculptor: AM (10/70), 47
Rivas, Pedro Geoffray, b.1908, (El Salvador), poet: AM (6/64), 30
Rivera, Diego, 1886-1957, (Mexico), painter: NCE, XII, 526 (1918); BOL,
    104; CLA, no. 76; FWS, 127; BNL, 424-25; HMM, 37; EBRF (8), 601 -
    At work, BWS, plate 119 - Paintings, NCE, XII, 526 (1932); HPC, 174-75
    (Tenochtitlán); BOL, 42-108 pass.; CHL, 226; ELA, 147, 149; HNM, 26-
    55 pass.; AHC, 6-192 pass.; JTG, 43; AM (Nov.-Dec., 1972), 30-37,
    (June-July, 1977), 39-40; LF (3/3/41), 53-56, (11/3/47), 104-06 (Del Prado
    mural) - Wife (Frida Kahlo), BOL, 140 (self-portrait); LF (2/22/37), 12,
    (3/14/38), 28 - Funeral, LF (12/9/57), 52 - Signature, RSD, 192
Rivera, José Eustacio, 1888-1928, (Colombia), writer: MEW, IX, 203
Rivera, José Fructuosa, 1785-1854, (Uruguay), statesman (President, 1830-
    34, 1838-40): DEL, 534; AM (6/51), 26; MEW, IX, 212
Rivero Castillo, Jacinto, (Paraguay), artist (no pic.): CLA, no. 78 (1966)
Roberts, Bartholomew, 1682-1722, (Britain), pirate: AM (3/57), 16-18
Robertson, William, 1721-93, (Scotland), historian: WNC, I, 269
Robles, Marco Aurelio, b.1906, (Panama), statesman (President, 1964-68):
    AM (3/66), 42
Roca, Julio Argentino, 1843-1914, (Argentina), statesman (President, 1880-
    86): GHS, 502; AM (4/75), 10 - Statue, LF (8/11/52), 19
Roca Rey, Joaquín, b.1923, (Peru), painter (no pic.): wk., CHL, 259
Rocafuerte, José Vicente, 1783-1847, (Ecuador), statesman (President, 1834-
    39): Image on coin (1928), FCL, 44
Rocca, Antonio, (Argentina), wrestler: AM (10/56), 25-27
Rockefeller, David, b.1915, (United States), banker: AM (11/67), 3
Rockefeller, Laurance, b.1910, (United States), businessman: LF (1/5/59),
    35 - His Puerto Rico hotel, LF (1/5/59), 33-35
Rockefeller, Nelson, 1908-1979, (United States), businessman; philanthropist;
    statesman: LF (4/27/42), 80-89; LK (7/27/43), 14 - Venezuela farm, LF
    (12/8/58), 53-58
Rodel, José Ramón, (Spain), naval commander (Callao, 1821): AM (10/60),
    30
Rodó, José Enrique, 1872-1917, (Uruguay), writer: CLI, 274; AM (6/57),
    29, (3/61), 72, (12/65), 3, (3/68), 11, (4/71), 23, (8/74), 27; MEW, IX,
    245; CEF (vol. 12), 151 - Monument (Montevideo), WAP (Ven. vol.), 205
Rodrigues, Sergio, b.1927, (Brazil), architect: BNB, 158
Rodríguez, Alirio, (Venezuela), artist (no pic.): wk., (1976), AM (2/79), 6
Rodríguez, Alonso, b.1598, (Brazil), Jesuit missionary (Blessed): HSA,
    253
Rodríguez, Ismael, (Mexico), movie director: NMC, 44
Rodríguez, José Ramón, (Dominican Republic), diplomat: AM (9/53), 40
Rodríguez, Juan Carlos, (Argentina), artist (no pic.): wk., CLA, no. 79
Rodríguez, Manuel, 1917-47, (Spain; Mexico), bull fighter ("Manolete"): LF
    (4/29/46), 105-10
Rodríguez, Simón, 1771-1854, (Venezuela), Tutor of Bolívar: AM (12/61),
    21, (9/74), 24-25; WAP (Ven. vol.), 61
Rodríguez Cabrillo, Juan, d.1543, (Portugal), navigator: AM (9/76), 15
Rodríguez Lozano, Manuel, b.1895, (Mexico), painter (no pic.): wk., CHL,
    234; HMM, 132-33
Rogers, William, b.1913, (United States), Secretary of State: AM (5/73),
    14; LF (1/24/69), 16 b-25
Rogers, Woodes, born c.1678, (Britain), explorer; politician; pirate: RCV,

160 (1729, with family); ASB, 134; BDP, 156-57 - His ships (around the world, 1708-11), RCV, iv - Lands in California (1709), RCV, 208 - Captures Acapulco, RCV, 240 - Searching ladies at Guayaquil, RCV, 128

Rojas, Carlos, (Bolivia), artist: AM (10/73), 43

Rojas, Cristóbal, 1858-90, (Venezuela), painter: BVP, 40

Rojas, Ezequiel, (Colombia), philosopher: NCE, VIII, 488

Rojas, Gabriel, (Spain), conquistador; with Pizarro at Cuzco: WNC, II, 523

Rojas, Ricardo, 1882-1957, (Argentina), scholar; writer: AM (9/50), 47; CLI, 268

Rojas Pinilla, Gustavo, 1900-74, (Colombia), statesman (President, 1953-57): AM (3/74), 24; BCB, 178-79; LF (5/20/57), 43; MEW, IX, 254 - Overthrow, LF (5/20/57), 43-45

Rolón, José, 1883-1945, (Mexico), musician; composer: SM, 248

Rolz Bennett, José, (Guatemala), scholar: AM (4/52), 37

Romano, Arturo, (Mexico), Director, Archaeological Museum: NG (10/68), 498

Romero, Francisco, 1891-1962, (Argentina), philosopher: AM (11/62), 7, (12/65), 3, (8/71), 24-25

Romero, José, 1888-1961, (Mexico), publisher; painter: NCE, III, 308

Romero, María Manuela, (Mexico), painter: NCE, II, 123

Romero, Matías, 1837-98, (Mexico), diplomat: GFF, 366

Romero, Silvio, 1851-1914, (Brazil), writer: AM (1/52), 9-31 pass., (10/52), 20, (8/71), 24-25, (2/72), 24-25 - Birthplace, AM (1/52), 11

Rondón, Cândido Mariano da Silva, 1865-1958, (Brazil), engineer; explorer: MEW, IX, 262 - Bust, AM (2/77), 6

Roosevelt, Franklin D., 1882-1945, (United States), statesman (President, 1933-45): AM (11/49), 3, (5/76), 16-17 - At Buenos Aires Conference (1936), ALA, 7; LF (12/14/36), 9-12; AM (5/50), 3 - Caribbean visit, LF (11/30/36), 12 - Monument, Managua, CEF (vol. 15), 783 - Signature, RSD, 195

Roosevelt, Theodore, 1858-1919, (United States), statesman (President, 1901-09): MEW, IX, 271; HNM (vol. 98), 841; TCP, 546-47; NG (10/58), 573-90 pass. - With Rough Riders, TCP, 546-47; EA, VIII, 302; WSA, 42, 85 - At Panama Canal (Nov., 1906), MPB, 430; WBE (vol. 15), 103 - Explores "River of Doubt" (1913), AM (10/70), 15-23 - Activities, LF (11/23/48), 92-100

Root, Elihu, 1845-1937, (United States), statesman; Secretary of State: MEW, IX, 276

Rosa, Gustavo, (Brazil), artist: AM (June-July, 1976), 17-19

Rosa, J. Guimarães, b.1908, (Brazil), writer: WAP (Br. vol.), 102; AM (4/78), 4

Rosa e Silva, Francisco da, (Brazil), Pernambuco politician (1896-1911): LPB, 103

Rosado del Valle, Julio, (Puerto Rico), painter: NFP, 92-93

Rosario Sánchez, Francisco del, 1817-1861, (Dominican Republic), statesman: AM (9/71), 24-25

Rosas, Juan Manuel José Domingo Ortiz de, 1793-1877, (Argentina), dictator, 1829-52: DEL, 541; CCS, 573; GHS, 494; CLI, 142; AM (8/61), 15, (8/71), 31, (9/72), 20; MEW, IX, 278; WAP (Arg. vol.), 114 - His country house, CCS, 575 - His palace, HNM (vol. 75), 897

Rosas, Juventino, (Mexico), musician: GPM, 82

Ross, Donald, 1837-1922, (Britain), health expert: HMH, 36, 52 (wife) - In Panama with Gorgas, HMH, 158

Rossell, Carmelina, (Cuba), singer: AM (10/52), 40

Rosszanet, Guillermo, b.1930, (Panama), poet: AM (7/64), 17

Rowan, Andrew Summers, 1857-1943, (United States), military (carried "message to García"): WSA, 40

Rowe, Leo Stanton, 1871-1946, (United States), scholar; Director-General,

Pan American Union: AM (3/50), 3, (8/56), 27, (4/65), 22, (3/71), 41
Rubio, Alberto, b.1926, (Chile), poet: AM (5/64), 19
Rubio Orbe, Gonzalo, (Mexico), Director, Indian Institute: AM (5/72), 44
Rugendas, Johann Moritz, 1802-58, (Bavaria; Chile), painter (no pic.): wk.,
    CHL, 207
Ruiz, Antonio M., b.1897, (Mexico), artist (no pic.): wk., HMM, 148, 150
Ruiz, Francisco Amighette, (Costa Rica), engraver: AM (2/69), 10-15
Ruiz, Hipólito, (Colombia), scientist: AM (8/72), 24-25
Ruiz, Macedonio Oscar, b.1906, (Argentina), architect (no pic.): wk., CHL,
    287
Ruiz de Alarcón y Mendoza, Juan, c.1581-1639, (Spain; Mexico), dramatist:
    NCE, I, 241
Ruiz Cortinas, Adolfo, b.1892, (Mexico), statesman (President, 1952-58):
    HMI, 118-19 - Inauguration, (12/15/52), 24-25
Ruiz-Guiñazú, Enrique, (Argentina), statesman: Visit to United States, LF
    (6/2/41), 22-23
Ruiz Matute, Miguel Angel, (Honduras), artist: AM (9/70), 47
Rulfo, Juan, b.1918, (Mexico), writer: AM (4/78), 4
Rush, Richard, 1780-1859, (United States), statesman; diplomat: HNM (vol.
    109), 863
Rusk, Dean, b.1909, (United States), Secretary of State: LF (1/17/69), 56-
    62a - At Montevideo (Nov. 16, 1965), BBY (1966), 695

Sá, Mem de, 1504-72, (Portugal), governor in Brazil: MEW, IX, 343
Saavedra, Cornelio de, 1761-1829, (Argentina), Independence leader: AM
    (4/60), 36, (5/71), 38
Saavedra Lamas, Carlos, 1878-1959, (Argentina), statesman: AM (3/74), 30;
    MEW, IX, 347
Sabáto, Ernesto, b.1911, (Argentina), writer: MEW, IX, 349; AM (4/78), 8
Sabogal, José, 1888-1856, (Peru), artist (no pic.): wk., CLA, no. 80 (1949)
Sadler, Frank H., (United States), naval commander, Canal Zone (1939): LF
    (11/6/39), 92
Sáenz, Guido, (Costa Rica), musician; pianist: AM (2/73), 7
Sáenz, Manuela, 1796-1859, (Peru), Bolivar's mistress: AM (11/62), 38;
    (12/65), 22, (4/74), 24-25
Sáenz, Moisés, (Mexico), writer: CLA, no. 86
Sagasta, Praxedes Mateo, 1825-1903, (Spain), Prime Minister, 1898: HNW
    (vol. 98), 461
Sahagún, Bernardino, 1499-1590, (Spain), Missionary; historian: WNC, I,
    156; NCE, XII, 849; GFF, 375; RSG, 5
Saint Brendan, (Ireland), sailed to America (565?): LNW, 5; BCC, 46 -
    Ship, NG (12/77), 770-97 pass., fc.
Saint Francis Blanco, b.1571, (Mexico), missionary: HSA, 136
Saint Francis de San Miguel, b.1543, (Mexico), missionary (1581-83): HSA,
    137
Saint Francis Solano, 1549-1610, (Argentina), missionary: HSA, 217
Saint Louis Bertrand, 1526-81, (Colombia), missionary (1562-69): HSA, 181
Saint Mariana of Jesus (Paredes y Flores), 1618-45, (Ecuador), missionary
    nurse: HSA, 199-204
Saint Martín de Aguirre, b.1567, (Mexico), missionary: HSA, 136
Saint Martín de Porres, 1579-1639, (Peru), "Black Saint of Lima": HSA,
    225
Saint Peter Baptist Blásquez, b.1546, (Mexico), missionary, 1581-83: HSA,
    133
Saint Philip of Jesus, 1572-97, (Mexico), first native saint of America: On
    Cross, HSA, 125
Saint Rose of Lima, 1586-1617, (Peru), HSA, 232; BMD, 143 - Statue (Quito),
    NCE, V, 95

"Salarrué" (Salvador Salazar Anué), b. 1899, (El Salvador), writer: AM (7/52), 41

Salas, Marco, (Colombia), painter: AM (1/50), 31

Salatino, Carlos Alberto, (Argentina), artist: AM (6/69), 44

Salaverry, Arabella, b. 1940, (Costa Rica), poet: AM (9/65), 34

Salazar, Enrique, (Mexico), priest; missionary: LF (7/14/52), 97-103

Salcedo, José Joaquín, b. 1922, (Colombia), churchman: NCE, IX, 566

Salóm, Bartolomé, 1780-1830, (Venezuela), military (Callao battle, 1821): AM (10/60), 30

Salt, Titus, (Britain; Peru), businessman: Monument, PWL, 68

Salvatierra, Juan María, 1644-1717, (Mexico), missionary: NCE, XII, 994; CE, III, 178

Samico, Gilván José Maria Luis, b. 1928, (Brazil), engraver: CLA, no. 81; BNB, 158

Sampson, William Thomas, 1840-1902, (United States), military, Spanish American War: HNM (vol. 98), 853; WSA, 61

Sánchez, Celia, (Cuba), Castro secretary: LF (6/2/61), 87; LUR, 104

Sánchez, Edgar, (Venezuela), artist (no pic.): wk., (1976), AM (2/79), 6

Sánchez, Emilio, (Cuba), artist (no pic.): wk., CLA, no. 82 (1973 and 1975), AM (2/79), 4

Sánchez, Pedro, (Mexico), Director, Pan American Institute of Geography and History, 1930-55: AM (June-July, 1978), 27

Sánchez de Bustamante, Antonio, 1865-1951, (Cuba), scholar; internationalist: AM (11/51), 32, (3/75), 22

Sánchez Cerro, Luis, 1889-1933, (Peru), statesman (President, 1930-31): AM (3/78), 10

Sánchez Hernández, Fidel, b. 1927, (El Salvador), statesman (President, 1967-72): AM (3/74), 42

Sánchez Macgregor, Joaquín, b. 1928, (Mexico), poet: AM (10/63), 10

Sánchez Navarro, Juan, 1765-1867, (Mexico), scholar: AM (3/66), 13 - His estate (Zacatecas), AM (4/72), 12-17

Sánchez Parodi, Ramón, (Cuba), Chief "Interest Section," Washington: AAY (vol. 1978), 166

Sánchez de Tagle, Francisco Manuel, 1782-1847, (Mexico), writer: CLM, 418-19

Sánchez Villela, Roberto, b. 1913, (Puerto Rico), statesman (Governor, 1964-68): PCI, 942

Sanders, William, (United States), official Pan American Union: AM (1/58), 34 - Family, AM (7/58), 30-31

Sandi, Luis, b. 1905, (Mexico), musician; composer; conductor: SM, 249

Sandino, César Augusto, 1893-1934, (Nicaragua), revolutionary: With his generals, CRH, 270 - Flag, NG (5/32), 611

Sandoval, Gonzalo de, d. 1528, (Spain), conquistador: WNC, 388 - Signature, WNC, 387

Sandoval Cabrera, Miguel Angel, b. 1903, (Guatemala; United States), composer: AM (4/79), 21-23 - Wife, AM (4/79), 24

Sandrini, Luis, (Argentina), comedian: AM (3/58), 11-14 (and family)

Sanín Cano, Baldomero, 1861-1957, (Colombia), writer: CEF (vol. 12), 150

San Martín, José Francisco de, 1778-1850, (Argentina), military; Independence leader: NCE, XII, 1035; DEL, 550; CCW, 257; GHS, 334; CLI, 68; WAP (Arg. vol.), 199; AM (9/50), 6, (6/51), fc., (9/65), 16, (4/67), 20, (10/70), 35, (Nov.-Dec., 1970), 24-25, (4/72), 35, (3/75), 24-25; SHL, 331; EBR (16), 225 - Middle age and old age, AM (2/78), 2 - Crosses Andes, AM (9/50), 8, (9/65), 19 - Meets O'Higgins (Maipú), AM (9/65), 14, (Nov.-Dec., 1968), 17 - With Bolívar (Guayaquil, July, 1822), AM (9/50), 7; SBL, 28 - His cavalry commission signed, FCL, 269 - Independence declared (Lima, July 28, 1821): AM (10/73), 17, (4/74), 23 - Received by

Argentina congress, AM (Nov.-Dec., 1968), 18 - Statue, WNC, VIII, 335,
339; HNM (vol. 75), 901; ELA, 154 - Image on Argentine coin (1950), FCL,
34 - Centennial celebration, Pan American Union, AM (10/50), 40 - Signature, RSD, 200
Sans de Santa María, Carlos, (Colombia), statesman; diplomat: AM (6/58),
33, (1/67), 43, (5/67), 45 - Receives honorary degree, AM (Nov.-Dec.,
1970), 7
Santa Anna, Antonio López de, 1794-1876, (Mexico), military; statesman
(President, 1833-35, 1841-42, 1844-45, 1846-47, 1853-55): WNC, VIII,
227-28; CLM, 66, 418-19; DEL, 552; FWS, 52; WHM, 147; CMS, 221
(late in life); GFF, 348 (late in life); BTM, 234; MEW, IX, 395 - Wife,
DSW, 115 - His hacienda, GFF, 346 - At Tampico (1929), DSW, 111 -
With Sam Houston (April 21, 1836), AHC, 84 - Drilling troops, NMW,
54-55 - Uniform, NMW, 150-51 - Medals, CLM, 528 - Signature, CLM,
188; RSD, 200
Santa Cruz, Andrés, 1792-1865, (Bolivia), statesman (President, 1826-27,
1829-39): DEL, 553; CLI, 114; MEW, IX, 396; AM (10/73), 24-25, (9/75),
22
Santa Cruz Wilson, Domingo, b.1899, (Chile), musician; composer: AM (7/64), 25;
SM, 217
Santa Cruz y Espejo, Eugenio de, 1747-95, (Ecuador), Independence leader:
AM (Nov.-Dec., 1970), 24-25, (9/72), 24-25
Santa María de Oro, Justo, (Argentina), churchman, Independence period:
AM (11/66), 7
Santamaría, Juan, 1821-56, (Costa Rica), boy hero: CR, 20 - Monument
(Alajuela), SCR, 25
Santana, Pedro, 1801-64, (Dominican Republic), statesman (President, 1844-
48, 1853-56, 1858-61): MEW, IX, 398
Santander, Francisco de Paula, 1792-1840, (Colombia), statesman (Vice President and President, 1821-27): DEL, 555; MBW, 172-73; MEW, IX, 400;
AM (12/65), 30, (4/67), 21, (12/70), 24-25 - Image on coin, FCL, 41
Santo, João Oliveira, (Brazil), economist: AM (2/69), 16
Santos, Agnaldo dos, b.1926, (Brazil), sculptor: BNB, 158
Santos, Marquesa, (Brazil), mistress of Pedro I: HAT, 116, 189 (age 60) -
Her second husband (Rafael Tobías de Aguiar), HAT, 189
Santos, Máximo, 1847-99, (Uruguay), statesman (President, 1882-86): CCS,
595; HNM (vol. 75), 905 (c.1885)
Santos Chocano, José, 1875-1934, (Peru), poet: AM (5/61), 40; WAP (Br.
vol.), 183
Santos-Dumont, Alberto, 1873-1932, (Brazil), aviator; balloonist: AM (11/49),
9-11, (9/66), 17-22; RBT, 64-65 - Image on coin, EB, 36
Sarmiento, Domingo Faustino, 1811-88, (Argentina), writer; educator; statesman (President, 1868-74): NCE, III, 589; PSU, fr.; DEL, 558; HHL, II,
56; WAP (Arg. vol.), 135; MEW, IX, 411; EBRF (8), 904; AM (11/52),
18, 30-31, (5/53), 39 (1852), (1/59), 22, (8/61), 14, (8/64), 27, (8/71),
32, (2/72), 24-25 - Mother, PSU, 19 - Birthplace, AM (2/72), 24-25;
PSU, 23-24 - With Argentina embassy staff, Washington (1865), PSU, 158 -
Home, Asunción, Paraguay, where he died, PSU, 36 - Sarmiento Historical
Museum, Buenos Aires, AM (2/72), 24-25
Sarmiento de Gamboa, Pedro, c.1532-c.1589, (Spain), explorer, Pacific:
MEO, 694-97
Sas, André, b.1900, (Peru), musician; composer: SM, 280
Sasson, Mayer, (Colombia), engineer: AM (4/79), 45
Saville, Marshall Howard, 1867-1935, (United States), archaeologist, Central
America: BSM, 150
Sayão, Bidú, b.1906, (Brazil), singer: AM (6/50), 14, (5/51), 11
Schaerer, Eduardo, 1873-1941, (Paraguay), statesman (President, 1912-16):

GHS, 518
Schendel, Mira, b.1919, (Switzerland; Brazil), painter: BNB, 158
Schettini, Eugenio F., (Argentina), Buenos Aires mayor: NG (11/66), 664
Schick Gutiérrez, René, 1910-67, (Nicaragua), statesman (President, 1963-67): HNP, 3
Schinca, Milton, b.1926, (Uruguay), poet: AM (9/64), 20
Schley, Winfield Scott, 1830-1909, (United States), Naval officer, Spanish American War: HNM (vol. 98), 853; WSA, 61-62
Schmidel, Ulrich, c.1510-c.1579, (Germany; Argentina), explorer, La Plata: LNW, 24; MED, 564 (vignette)
Schrender, Jan, (Ecuador), artist: AM (2/61), 17-20
Schubrick, W. Branford, (United States), officer, Mexican war: BTM, 234-35
Scott, Hugh Lenox, 1853-1934, (United States), officer in Mexico (1914): MFG, 150
Scott, Irving Murray, 1837-1903, (United States), engineer (builder of "Oregon"): HNM (vol. 98), 703
Scott, James Brown, 1866-1943, (United States), jurist: AM (3/76), 16-17
Scott, Winfield, 1786-1866, (United States), General, Mexican war: WNC, VII, 389; BTM, 203-04; MEW, IX, 489; NMW, 128, 200 - Enters Mexico City, BTM, 2345; NMW, 217 (1848)
Scully, Michael, (United States), writer: AM (2/55), 48
Seabra, José Joaquín, 1855-1942, (Brazil), statesman; President, 1920-24: PBF, 112-13
Seeger, Charles, 1886-1979, (United States), musicologist (at Pan American Union): AM (3/52), 40
Seegers, Scott, (United States), journalist; founded Americas, Pan American Union: AM (10/51), 2, (11/54), 48
Segall, Lázaro, 1890-1958, (Brazil), artist: AM (10/51), 24-27 (1928); CLA, nos. 83, 84
Segura, Francisco "Pancho," b.1922, (Ecuador), tennis player: LF (1/13/61), 95-102
Senior, Clarence, 1903-75, (United States), writer; sociologist: AM (6/49), 46, (8/61), 36
Sepúlveda, Juan Ginés de, 1490-1573, (Spain), churchman: AM (10/66), 26, (4/79), 35
Serna, José de la, 1769-1833, (Spain): viceroy, Peru: AM (9/75), 34
Serra, Junípero, 1713-84, (Mexico), missionary; churchman: NCE, XIII, 124; WNC, VIII, 214; CCM, 20; MEW, IX, 518; AM (11/56), 29 (1773) - First mission, Baja California, HOB, 71 - Library (Carmel mission), NCE, II, 1070 - Letter (December 19, 1779), NCE, XIII, 124 - Last communion, DSW, 77 - Room where he died, NCE, XIII, 125 - Statue, CE, 180
Severino, José, (Dominican Republic), artist: AM (1/69), 35-36
Sevilla Sacasa, Guillermo, (Nicaragua), diplomat: HNP, 34; AM (2/66), 41; AM (8/51), 40, (7/59), 29
Seward, William Henry, 1801-72, (United States), statesman (Secretary of State, 1861-69): MEW, IX, 529
Shafter, William Rufus, 1835-1906, (United States), general, Spanish American war: HNM (vol. 98), 839; WSA, 42
Shelley, Jaime Augusto, 1937, (Mexico), poet: AM (10/63), 12
Siccardi, Honorio, b.1897, (Argentina), musician; composer: SM, 184
Sicre, Juan José, b.1898, (Cuba), sculptor: AM (10/68), 29-34, (Nov.-Dec., 1974), 30-35
Sierra Méndez, Justo, 1848-1912, (Mexico), historian: AM (12/49), 33; MEW, X, 59
Sigsbee, Charles Dwight, 1845-1923, (United States), commander of "Maine": HNM (vol. 98), 643; WSA, 6
Sigüenza y Góngora, Carlos, 1645-1700, (Mexico), scholar: LBT, xx

Silva, Djanira de Mota e, (Brazil), painter: RBT, 64-65
Silva, Fernando, (Nicaragua), poet: AM (10/67), 39
Silva, José Antonio de, (Brazil), artist: RBT, 64-65; AM (3/78), 41-44
Silva, José Gonçalves da, (Brazil), statesman (President, 1890-91): PBF, 112-13
Silva, Julio Martins da, (Brazil), artist: AM (3/78), 47-48
Silva, Luis Alves de Lima e, (Duque de Caxias), 1803-80, (Brazil), military: KPA, 35 (c.1870); MEW, II, 41
Silveira, Elisa Martins da, (Brazil), painter (no pic.): wk., LF (5/31/54), 83
Silveira, Regina Scalizilli, b.1939, (Brazil), architect: BNB, 159
Siqueiros, David Alfaro, b.1898, (Mexico), painter: HNM, 22, 88, 90; NG (8/68), 192; HMN, 91-106 pass.; AHC, 155; MEW, X, 76; LF (6/3/46), 60; BOL, 119-24; CHL, 270 (University of Mexico); CLA, nos. 85 (1930), 86-87 (1931); AM (8/49), 24-25 (and wife), (10/72), 12-19, (June-July, 1977), 40-42
Slidell, John, c.1793-1871, (United States), diplomat: BTM, 203-04; NMW, 23
Sloane, Luis, (Argentina), engraver (no pic.): wk., AM (9/74), 14-16
Smith, Carleton Sprague, b.1905, (United States), scholar; musician: AM (10/50), 1
Smith, Earl, (United States), diplomat in Cuba (1957-59): TCP, 1090-91
Smith, Persifor F., (United States), general, Mexican war: BTM, 234-35
Smith, William, (United States), military; friend of Miranda: AM (8/51), 22
Soares, Vital Henriques Batista, (Brazil), statesman: PBF, 112-13
Sobrinho, Francisco Matarrazo, (Brazil), architect: AM (4/64), 2-4
Sojo, Vicente Emilio, b.1887, (Venezuela), musician; composer: SM, 153
Solari, Luis A., (Uruguay), artist (no pic.): wk., (1976), AM (2/79), 6
Solarte, Tristán, b.1924, (Panama), poet: AM (7/64), 13
Solórzano Pereyra, Juan de, 1575-1655, (Spain), jurist; historian: WNC, VIII, 247
Somoza, Anastasio García, 1896-1956, (Nicaragua), statesman (President, 1937-47): MEW, X, 130; AM (7/50), 43; NG (7/44), 179; LF (1/24/55), 40-41, (10/8/56), 30-35; DEL, 569; HNP, 26, 30 - Assassinated (Sept., 1956), LF (10/8/56), 30-35 - Tomb, LF (10/8/56), 34
Somoza, Guillermo Sevilla, (Nicaragua), diplomat: AM (5/50), 41
Somoza DeBayle, Anastasio, b.1925, (Nicaragua), statesman (President, 1967-79): HNP, 27 (1971), 32; AM (3/74), 42; LF (10/8/56), 33-34; BBY (vol. 1968), 577
Somoza DeBayle, Luis, 1922-67, (Nicaragua), statesman (President, 1957-63): LF (10/8/56), 21-24
Soper, Fred L., b.1893, (United States), health expert: AM (10/75), 30, 37; HMH, 221
Soriano, Juan, b.1920, (Mexico), artist: LF (6/3/36), 60
Sosa, Francisco, (Mexico), writer: GFF, 383
Sotelo, Luis, d.1624, (Mexico), churchman: HSA, 171 - Burned at stake, Japan, HSA, 167
Soteno, Pedro, (Mexico), artist: NG (5/78), 662-63
Soto, Hernando de, 1500-42, (Spain), explorer: WNC, 252; LNW, 21; JCH, 63; AM (9/76), 11 - Buried in Mississippi River, HNM (vol. 12), 26; AM (2/74), 23 - Signature, WNC, 253; LNW, 21
Soto, Jesús Rafael, b.1923, (Venezuela), painter (no pic.): wk., CLA, no. 88
Soto Alfaro, Bernardo de, 1854-1931, (Costa Rica), statesman (President, 1885-89): HNM (vol. 75), 681; CCS, 222
Sotomayor, Antonio, (Bolivia), artist (no pic.): wk., AM (2/79), 52

Suro, Pieda de, (Ecuador), chairman Inter-American Commission of Women:
    AM (10/69), 39
Szpigel, Samuel, b.1936, (Brazil), architect: BNB, 159
Szyszlo, Fernando de, b.1925, (Peru), painter (no pic.): wk., CHL, 434, no.
    90

Tabara, Enrique, b.1930, (Ecuador), artist: BAC, 21-25
Tacón, Miguel, 1775-1855, (Spain), captain-general in Cuba: TCP, 546-47
Taft, William Howard, 1857-1930, (United States), statesman (President,
    1909-13): MEW, X, 327; MPB, 520; NG (5/30), 527 (and wife); EBRF
    (9), 764 - With General Goethals, Panama, LF (1/24/64), 27 - With Colo-
    nel Gaillard, Panama, MPB, 520 - Signature, RSD, 218
Tagle y Portocarrero, José Bernardo de, 1779-1825, (Peru), statesman
    (President, 1823-24): AM (10/73), 19
Tamayo, Franz, 1879-1956, (Bolivia), writer: AM (June-July, 1978), 7 (4
    ages)
Tamayo, Rufino, b.1899, (Mexico), painter: GRT, plate 133 (1934), plate
    14 (1942), plate 135 (1945), plate 136 (1950 with wife), plate 138 (1957),
    plate 139 (1959), plates 140-46 (1960), plate 141 (1962), plate 142 (1969),
    plate 143 (1971), plates 144-46 (1974) - Paintings, AM (3/50), 9, (12/53),
    9-12, 30-31, (10/63), 23-29, (8/74), 33, 26-27; GRT, 14-25 pass., plates
    6-132 pass.; LF (6/3/46), 59, (3/16/53), 98-102, (5/31/54), 78; BOL,
    133-35; CHL, 235; CLA, fr. (1964), no. 91; HMM, 118, 138-40 - Wife
    (Olga Flores Rivas), AM (3/79), 42
Tannenbaum, Frank, 1893-1969, (United States), scholar: AM (11/49), 46,
    (4/70), 28
Tavares de Sá, Hernane, b.1911, (Brazil), writer; diplomat: AM (3/49), 48,
    (3/50), 47
Taylor, Henry Clay, 1845-1904, (United States), leader, Spanish American
    war: HNM (vol. 98), 853
Taylor, Maxwell, b.1901, (United States), military: LF (5/10/63), 81
Taylor, Zachary, 1784-1850, (United States), military; statesman (President,
    1849-50): KWW, 314; BTM, 2-3-4; MEW, X, 373; NG (1/65), 106; NMW,
    83 (cartoon) - His staff, NMW, 88-89 - "Army of Occupation" (1845),
    NMW, 20-21 - Receives surrender of Monterrey, NMW, 76 - At Battle of
    Buena Vista, MEW, X, 374 - Signature, RSD, 219
Teach, Edward ("Blackbeard"), (Britain), pirate: AM (3/57), 16-18; BDP,
    136, 142
Tello, Julio, 1880-1947, (Peru), archaeologist: AM (10/78), 39-40
Tello, Manuel, b.1899, (Mexico), statesman: AM (2/54), 40 (and family),
    (3/55), 41
Terra, Gabriel, 1873-1942, (Uruguay), statesman (President, 1933-36): AM
    (3/73), 24-25; MEW, X, 389
Terragas, Luis, (Mexico), Governor Chihuahua: HNM (vol. 94), 373
Theresa Christina, b.1821, (Brazil), wife of Pedro II: CCS, 885; HAT, 248;
    WDP, 116 (middle age), 364 (old age)
Thoby-Marcelin, Philippe, b.1904, (Haiti), writer: AM (6/49), 38, (11/53),
    14
Thomen, Luis Francisco, (Dominican Republic), diplomat: AM (2/52), 28,
    (3/52), 40 (family), (9/52), 40
Thompson, Edward Herbert, 1860-1935, (United States), explorer; diplomat:
    GMR, 128-29 - Excavating at Labna, WSH, 69
Thompson, Howard, (United States), correspondent Spanish American war:
    HNM (vol. 98), 941
Thompson, J. Eric S., b.1898, (England), explorer: BSM, 214-15;
    BPA, plate 13 (with wife)
Thompson, Katherine Louise Rawls, (United States), swimmer in Montevideo:

Tufino, Rafael, (Puerto Rico), artist (no pic.): wk., CLA, no. 94 (1955)
Tupac Amarú, José Gabriel Condorcanqui, 1742-81, (Peru), Indian martyr:
    MEW, XI, 19 - Enters Cuzco, HMI, 158 - Executed, HMI, 163
Tupac Yupanqui, (Peru), Inca ruler: GHS, 53 - With wife (coya) in litter,
    MAC, 339
Turple, David (United States), statesman (1898): HNM (vol. 98), 508
Twiggs, David Samuel, 1790-1862, (United States), military, Mexican war:
    BTM, 203-04
Tyler, John, 1790-1862, (United States), statesman (President, 1841-45):
    MEW, XI, 41 - Signature, RSD, 226

Ugarte, Manuel, 1878-1951, (Argentina), writer: CLI, 266
Uhle, Frederick Max, b.1856, (Peru), archaeologist: WSH, 74
Ulate Blanco, Otilio, 1892, (Costa Rica), statesman (President, 1949-53): AM
    (1/53), 23
Unánue Pavón, José Hipólito, 1755-1833, (Peru), scholar: AM (12/61), 21,
    (Nov.-Dec., 1970), 24-25; MEW, XI, 55 - Statue, San Marcos University,
    PER, 21
Urdaneta, Francisco, (Colombia), revolutionary: AM (9/62), 23 (c.1862);
    WAP (Ven. vol.), 105
Uribe, Blanca, (Colombia), musician; pianist: AM (2/68), 44
Uribe, Raúl, (Mexico), artist (no pic.): wk., HMM, 146
Uribe-Holguín, Guillermo, b.1880, (Colombia), musician; composer: SM, 280
Urquina, Miguel Rafael, (El Salvador), diplomat: AM (3/68), 45
Urquiza, Justo José de, 1800-70, (Argentina), statesman (President, Argentina
    Confederation, 1854-60): MEW, XI, 64; AM (8/71), 31 - Statue (Paraná),
    RPS, 168-69
Urruchúa, Demetrio, b.1902, (Argentina), artist (no pic.): wk., CLA, no.
    95
Urrútia Lleó, Manuel, b.1901, (Cuba), politician (Provisional President,
    1959): LF (1/12/59), 18, (1/19/59), 30, (7/27/59), 28-29; LUR, 171
Urtecho, José Coronel, b.1906, (Nicaragua), poet: AM (10/67), 34
Uslar-Pietri, Arturo, b.1906, (Venezuela), writer; scholar: AM (6/50), 47

Vaca de Castro, Cristóbal, 1492-1562, (Spain), governor of Peru (1542): WNC,
    II, 535
Valcárcel, Luis Eduardo, b.1891, (Peru), scholar: AM (10/49), 46
Valcárcel, Teodoro, 1900-42, (Peru), musician; composer: SM, 280
Valdés, Cayetano, (Spain), explorer northwest coast of North America (18th
    century): CFT, 304-05
Valdez Subercaseaux, Gabriel, (Chile), statesman: AM (11/65), 45
Valdivia, Pedro de, c.1497-1553, (Spain), conquistador, Chile: WNC, II,
    529-30; AM (3/71), 24-25; MEW, XI, 67
Valencia, Gabriel, (Mexico), military (1840): CLM, 418-19
Valencia, Guillermo León, 1908-1971, (Colombia), statesman (President, 1962-
    66): SCP, 33; AM (3/49), bc. (home); BBY (vol. 1963), 282
Valencia Tovar, Alvaro, (Colombia), military: BCB, 178-79
Valenzuela, Luisa, b.1938, (Argentina), writer: AM (10/78), 21
Valle, José Cecilio del, 1777-1834, (Honduras), statesman; Independence
    leader: AM (Nov.-Dec., 1976), 16, (8/77), 7-13 - Statue, AM (8/77), 8 -
    Bust, AM (8/77), ifc.
Valle, Rafael Heliodoro, 1891-1959, (Honduras), diplomat; scholar: AM
    (6/49), 46, (5/50), 41, (11/51), 40, (2/52), 40, (6/53), 21, (7/53), 24 -
    Awarded Colombian Cross of Bogotá, AM (6/55), 31
Vallejo, César Abraham, 1895-1938, (Peru), writer: AM (Nov.-Dec., 1968),
    42; MEW, XI, 74; WAP (Br. vol.), 183

Vallejo, José Joaquín, 1811-58, (Chile), writer: AM (5/75), 12
Van Buren, Martin, 1782-1862, (United States), statesman (President, 1837-41): MEW, XI, 78 - Signature, RSD, 227
Vancouver, George, c.1758-98, (Britain), explorer: HHG, 286
Vanderbilt, Cornelius, 1794-1877, (United States), businessman; friend of William Walker: HNP, 23
Vane, Charles, (Britain), pirate, 18th century Caribbean: BDP, 10
Varela y Morales, Félix, 1788-1855, (Cuba), educator; priest; patriot: AM (4/27), 9
Vargas, Diego de, (Spain), colonial administrator, Mexico: DSW, 63 (c.1690)
Vargas, Pedro, (Mexico), singer: GPM, 82-83 (young man)
Vargas, Getulio Dornelles, 1883-1954, (Brazil), statesman (President, 1930-45, 1951-54): DAC, 204-05; DEL, 611; BNL, 424-25; EA, IV, 474; LF (5/22/39), 62, (11/23/36), 40, (12/14/36), 11; MEW, XI, 95; NG (10/42), 505; RBT, 64-65; LPB, 104 - As gaucho, HHL, II, 404; WBE (vol. 2), 474 - With President Roosevelt, NG (1/44), 42 - Bust (by Jo Davidson), LF (7/21/41), 19 - Body lies in state (Aug., 1954), LF (11/28/55), 44
Vargas de Icaya, Adela, (Nicaragua), artist (no pic.): wk., HNP, 48
Vargas Llosa, Mario, b.1936, (Peru), novelist: AM (4/74), 3, (4/78), 4, AM (3/79), 3, (10/77), 3-5
Varnhagen, Francisco Adolfo de, 1816-78, (Brazil), writer; historian: MEW, XI, 96
Varona, Enrique José, 1849-1933, (Cuba), scholar; writer: AM (2/51), 18, (11/62), 9, (12/65), 2, (12/67), 12, (8/71), 24-25
Vasconcellos, Salomão, 1877-1925, (Brazil), physician; writer; scholar: AM (5/78), 18
Vasconcelos, José, 1882-1959, (Mexico), educator; scholar: AM (2/51), 18, (6/62), 40, (11/62), 8, (8/71), 24-25; MEW, XI, 100; CEF (vol. 12), 151
Vásquez, Carlos, (Chile), artist: AM (9/69), 46
Vásquez, Horacio, 1860-1936, (Dominican Republic), military; statesman (President, 1902-03, 1924-30), MEW, XI, 105
Vásquez Castañeda, Dagoberto, b.1922, (Guatemala), muralist (no pic.): wk., CHL, 276
Vaz Ferreira, Carlos, 1872-1958, (Uruguay), educator: AM (Nov.-Dec., 1973), 25
Vázquez, Francisco, (Mexico), painter: HMM, 189
Vázquez de Arce y Caballos, Gregorio, 1638-1711, (Colombia), painter: NCE, XIV, 582
Vaughan, John, b.1650, (Britain), governor Jamaica: PBK, 172-73
Vega, Juan de la, (Mexico), sports writer: AM (3/50), 47
Vega, Jorge Luis de la, (Argentina), artist (no pic.): wk., CLA, no. 96 (1966)
Velarde, Héctor, (Peru), architect: AM (9/53), 2
Velasco, José María, 1840-1912, (Mexico), painter (taught Rivera): MEW, XI, 107; WHM, 179; CHL, 208; AM (1/79), 5 (1894), 4-11 (works) - Early home, AM (1/79), 7
Velasco, Juan de, 1727-1819, (Ecuador), historian: AM (2/67), 20
Velasco, Luis de, 1511-64, (Spain), viceroy, New Spain, 1590-95: MEW, XI, 108; PMC, 132
Velasco Alvarado, (Peru), statesman (President, 1968-75): BHG, 266 (1969); AM (3/74), 46
Velasco Ibarra, José María, 1893-1979, (Ecuador), statesman (President, dictator, 1934-35, 1944-47, 1952-56, 1960-61, 1968-72): DEL, 615; MEW, XI, 109; AM (10/69), 40, (3/74), 48; BBY (vol. 1967), 307, (vol. 1971), 296
Velásquez, José Antonio, b.1906, (Honduras), painter: CHL, 119; AM (9/72), 46 (and wife)
Velásquez de Cuellar, Diego de, c.1465-1523, (Spain), conquistador: WNC, II, 350; MEW, XI, 115; WAP (Carib. vol.), 27 - Founds Cuban town (1514),

AM (2/77), 6

Vélez, Lupe, (Mexico), actress: LK (1/2/40), 34-36

Vengoechea, Julio, (Venezuela), artist (no pic.): wk., AM (10/76), 27

Venier, Bruno, (Argentina), artist: AM (4/71), 46

Verissimo, Erico Lopes, b.1905, (Brazil), writer; scholar: AM (6/52), 2, (1/54), 48, (2/63), 34

Vernon, Edward, 1684-1757, (Britain), admiral in Caribbean: WNC, VIII, 292

Verrazzano, Giovanni da, c.1484-c.1528, (Italy), explorer: JCH, 30; MGE, 133; NCE, XIV, 626; MEW, XI, 128 - Statue, ACS, 35 - Bust, MGE, 130

Vespucci, Amerigo, 1454-1512, (Italy), explorer: WNC, II, 139-41; JCH, 13; ACS, 19; CE, XV, 385 (3 pics.); NCE, XIV, 632; MED, 279; BCC, 257; MEW, XI, 136; LF (10/11/54), 106 (4 pics.); HE, 120 - Landing in New World: LNW, 78, 158; PDS, 232 (allegory) - Indians encountered, JCH, 14; MED, 295 - His cousin (Simonetta), MED, 277 - Birth celebration (Florence), LF (10/11/54), 114 - Handwriting, WNC, II, 130, 138 - Signature, RSD, 230

Viana, Aurelio Rodrigues, (Brazil), statesman: PBF, 112-13

Viana, Fernando Mendes, b.1933, (Brazil), poet: AM (2/64), 31

Viana, Luis, (Brazil), statesman: PBF, 112-13

Victoria, Guadalupe, 1786-1843, (Mexico), military: GFF, 343; CLM, 258-59

Vidal, Francisco de, 1801-63, (Peru), military (Battle of Junín): AM (9/75), 35

Vidal, Miguel Angel, (Argentina), artist: AM (1/68), 43, (3/77), ibc.

Vidal Zuglio, Luis, (Uruguay), statesman: AM (11/65), 45

Videla, Jorge Rafael, (Argentina), statesman (President, 1976-): BBY (1977), 142; AAY (vol. 1978), 93

Vieira, Antônio, 1608-97, (Brazil), churchman: NCE, XIV, 653; HHL, I, 214; MEW, XI, 151

Vieira, Severino dos Santos, (Brazil), statesman: PBF, 112-13

Vilches, Eduardo, (Chile), artist (no pic.): wk., CLA, no. 97 (1967)

Villa, Carlos, (Colombia), musician; violin prodigy: AM (6/52), 22-23

Villa, Francisco ("Pancho"), (Doroteo Arango), 1877-1923, (Mexico), military; politician: HMI, 118-19; AHC, 135; MEW, XI, 155 - With wife (Luz Carrol de Villas), NG (8/68), 154 - With soldiers, PZB, 74, 78 - With followers, AHC, 138-142 - Home (Chihuahua), SST, 71 (interior) - With friends, PZB, 75; BWS, plates 70, 108, 120 - On horse, PZB, 78; BWS, plate 86 - With Obregón, BWS, plate 90; FWS, 64 - With Obregón and Pershing, WHM, 165 - With Zapata, AHC, 138; ALA, 123 - Blows up railroad, HAC, 242 - Signature, RSD, 230

Villa, Ignacio, (Cuba), singer: AM (9/56), 27-29

Villa, Lucha, (Mexico), musician: GPM, 82-83

Villacis, Aníbal, b.1927, (Cuba), artist: BAC, 27-31

Villa-Lobos, Heitor, 1887-1959, (Brazil), composer: MEW, XI, 156; LEM, 480; NCE, XIV, 669; SM, 216; DEL, 622; BNL, 424-25; AM (10/50), 14-15, (12/53), 19, (3/55), fc., (4/72), 19-20, (Nov.-Dec., 1973), 18-23, (10/78), 55 - Father, AM (4/72), 19 - His choir, AM (4/72), 22

Villanueva, Carlos Raúl, b.1900, (Venezuela), architect (no pic.): wk., CHL, 279 (Olympic pool), 281 (library)

Villarroel, Gualberto, 1908-46, (Bolivia), statesman (President, 1943-46): BHG, 64-65; LF (8/12/46), 29 - Revolt against, LF (8/12/46), 28-29 - Hanged, LF (8/12/46), 29

Villeda Morales, Ramón, (Honduras), statesman (President, 1957-63): BBY (vol. 1964), 409

Vinadé Román, Elena, (Cuba), writer: AM (1/52), 2

Violich, Francis, (United States), architect: AM (9/49), 46

Vital, Pauléus, (Haiti), artist (no pic.): wk., AM (10/78), 10-11

02: HNM (vol. 98), 847; TCP, 546; WSA, 42

Woodford, Stewart Lydon, 1833-1913, (United States), military; diplomat in Spain (1898): HNM (vol. 98), 459

Worth, William Jenkins, 1794-1849, (United States), military; Mexican war: NMW, 72; BTM, 203-04 - Troops, NMW, 70-71

Wyld, Federico Lenhoff, (Guatemala), physician: AM (2/75), 26

Wythe, George, b.1893, (United States), scholar: AM (5/50), 34

Ydígoras Fuentes, Miguel, b.1895, (Guatemala), statesman (President, 1958-63): LF (2/3/58), 23

Yllanes, A. Mário, (Bolivia), artist (no pic.): wk., CLA, no. 98

Yriart, Juan Felipe, (Uruguay), diplomat: AM (1/52), 29 (c.1950)

Yupanque, (Peru), Inca: WNC, I, 228

Zabala Ruiz, Manuel, b.1930, (Ecuador), poet: AM (11/64), 32

Zachrisson, Julio, (Panama), artist (no pic.): wk., CLA, no. 99 (1963)

Zalce, Alfredo, b.1908, (Mexico), artist (no pic.): wk., CLA, no. 100 (1946)

Zaldumbide, Gonzalo, 1884-1965, (Ecuador), writer: AM (11/59), 21

Zañartú, Enrique, b.1921, (Chile), artist (no pic.): wk., CLA, no. 101; CHL, 246

Zapata, Emiliano, 1879-1919, (Mexico), statesman; revolutionary: FWS, 79; BOL, 80, 87; PZB, fr.; BWS, plates 72, 115; BMD, 528; MEW, XI, 514; AM (9/68), 4 - Rivera portrait (1932), CLA, no. 77; HNM, 16-17; AM (4/55), 4 - Siqueiros portrait, CLA, no. 85 (1930) - His curandera (Apolinaria Flores), HHL, 452 - His soldiers, BNL, 424-25; SBL, 31-32; AM (9/68), 5; PZB, 73; BWS, plates 87-88, 103-05 - His followers, AM (11/49), 4, (9/68), 7; AHC, 131; RM, 48 - With Villa, AHC, 118-19, 138 - Monument, Cuautla, NG (12/34), 751

Zapata de Cárdenas, Luis, c.1515-90, (Colombia), archbishop, Bogotá: NCE, XIV, 1112; DEL, 641

Zapata Olivella, Manuel, b.1920, (Colombia), writer: AM (8/72), 20

Zaragoza, Ignacio, 1829-62, (Mexico), military: Statue, Monterrey, SST, 122

Zavala, Lorenzo de, 1788-1837, (Mexico), politician (Vice President, Republic of Texas, 1836): DSW, 113

Zavala Ortiz, Miguel Angel, (Argentina), statesman: AM (11/65), 45

Zavala Vallado, Silvio, b.1909, (Mexico), scholar: AM (2/50), 42

Zea, Francisco Antonio, 1766-1822, (Colombia), writer; scholar: AM (5/69), 5

Zelaya, Daniel, (Argentina), artist (no pic.): wk., CLA, no. 102

Zelaya, José Santos, 1853-1919, (Nicaragua), statesman (President, 1893-1909): MEW, XI, 518

Zelaya Coronado, Jorge Luis, (Guatemala), diplomat: AM (8/75), 41

Zemurray, Samuel, (United States), businessman, Central America: MAA, 52-53

Zéndegui, Guillermo de, (Cuba), editor in chief of Americas: AM (8/77), 48

Zorrilla de San Martín, Jean, 1855-1931, (Uruguay), poet: AM (10/70), 12, (2/76), 33; MEW, XI, 535; CEF (vol. 12), 150

Zudánez, Jaime, b.1772, (Bolivia), statesman (no pic.): Signature, AM (10/71), 9

Zuleta-Angel, Eduardo, b.1899, (Colombia), diplomat: AM (1/50), 31, (3/50), 46, (6/50), 40, (10/54), 40 (family)

Zuloaga de Tovar, María Luisa, (Venezuela), artist (pottery): AM (6/53), 17-19

Zumárraga, Juan de, c.1468-1548, (Spain; Mexico), churchman: NCE, XIV, 1138; CLM, 122; MEW, XI, 537

Zúñiga, Alvaro Manrique de, (Spain), viceroy, Mexico (1585-90): PMC, 108

REFERENCE-KEY INDEX

In order to make this Guide helpful and easy to use, I have selected picture references from books, periodicals, and encyclopedias published or reprinted chiefly in the past 40 years. Many earlier publications in English are out of print or difficult to find, and often do not contain pictures. In a few instances I have listed 19th century publications with pictures in order to show by contrast or comparison conditions then and now.*

There are of course many collections and archives of illustrations, some about Latin America, but these are not available in book or periodical form and hence are not listed here. The best known collection is the Bettmann Archive in New York City which has recently issued The Bettmann Archive Pictorial History of the World. An indication of the picture collections in New York City, for example, may be found in the Yellow Pages of the Manhattan Telephone Directory where some 70 are listed. Unpublished collections of pictures about Latin America may be found in the Columbus Memorial Library of the Pan American Union and in the Library of Congress in Washington. Scholarly and scientific organizations, such as the American Geographical Society, the National Geographic Society, etc., have good collections as do college and university libraries, business corporation libraries and, of course, newspapers, especially the New York Times. However, these may or may not be available to the public, although in some cases pictures may be purchased or rented.

---

*A note should be made here about illustrations in daily newspapers and weekly news magazines such as Time, Newsweek, U.S. News, People, Money, Sports Illustrated, Us and others where pictures are endlessly repeated and duplicated. Many of these deal with immediate, currently newsworthy or transient events and persons and they often stress sensational, unusual, spectacular, romantic and sex-oriented subjects. Most of these pictures can be located through tables of contents, indexes, the Readers' Guide, or by examining the publication nearest the date of the event. To have listed illustrations from these publications would have needlessly multiplied references to the same events and persons, and this does not seem to me logical, practical or defensible. Besides, the total size of the Guide would have been almost doubled without adding much new information. These periodicals are of course available in most libraries which more and more are transferring them to microfilm, often making the material unsatisfactory for the observations of details.

BAC   Bernitz, Jacqueline: Abstract Currents in Ecuadorean Art (New York, Center for Inter-American Relations, 1977)

BAP   Berdecio, Robert; Applebaum, Stanley: Posada's Popular Mexican Prints (New York, Dover Publications, 1972)

BAR   Butland, Gilbert J.: Latin America; A Regional Geography (New York, John Wiley and Sons, 1973)

BBG   Boeta, José Rodulfo: Bernardo de Gálvez (Madrid, Publicaciones Españoles, 1977)

BBP   Bailey, Bernadine: Bolivia in Pictures (New York, Sterling Publishing Co., 1974)

BBY   Britannica Book of the Year (Chicago, Encyclopaedia Britannica, Inc., 1964-1978)

BCA   Buttrey, Theodore V.: Coinage of the Americas (New York, The American Numismatic Society, 1973)

BCB   Broderick, Walter J.: Camilo Torres. A Biography of the Priest-Guerrilla (Garden City, Doubleday and Co., 1975)

BCC   Bradford, Ernie: Christopher Columbus (New York, The Viking Press, 1973)

BCI   Blume, Helmut: The Caribbean Islands (New York, Longman, 1977)

BCP   Bianchi, Lois: Chile in Pictures (New York, Sterling Publishing Co., 1977)

BCR   Bauer, Arnold J.: Chilean Rural Society from the Spanish Conquest to 1930 (Cambridge, Cambridge University Press, 1975)

BCS   Brinckerhoff, Sidney B.; Chamberlain, Pierce A.: Spanish Military Weapons in Colonial America, 1700-1821 (Harrisburg: Stackpole, 1972)

BCT   Beals, Ralph L.: Cherán; A Sierra Tarascan Village (New York, Cooper Square Publishing Co., 1973)

BDA   Benson, Elizabeth (editor): Death and the Afterlife in Pre-Columbian America (Washington, Dumbarton Oaks, 1975)

BDP   Botting, Douglas: The Pirates (Alexandria, Va., Time-Life Books, 1978)

BEF   Barbes, John: Evita First Lady; A Biography of Eva Perón (New York, Grove Press, 1978)

BEW   Beals, Ralph L.: Ethnology of the Western Mixe (New York, Cooper Square Publishers, 1973)

BFF   Burland, C. A.; Forman, Werner: Feathered Serpent and Smoking Mirror (New York, G. P. Putnam's Sons, 1975)

BGK   Bailey, James: The God-Kings and the Titans; The New World Ascendancy in Ancient Times (New York, St. Martin's Press, 1973)

BGL   Brigham, William T.: Guatemala: The Land of the Quetzal; A Sketch (Gainesville, University of Florida Press, 1965)

BHB   Bowen, David: Hello, Brazil (New York, Grosset and Dunlap, 1967)

BHG   Blasier, Cole: The Hovering Giant; United States Responses to Revolutionary Change in Latin America (Pittsburgh, University of Pittsburgh Press, 1976)

BHS   Bowen, David: Hello, South America (New York, W. W. Norton and Co., 1964)

BIG   Beezley, William H.: Insurgent Governor; Abraham González and the Mexican Revolution in Chihuahua (Lincoln, University of Nebraska Press, 1973)

BIM   Benítez, Fernando: In the Magic Land of Peyote (New York, Warner Books, 1975) (see BML)

BJB   Boot, Adrian; Thomas, Michael: Jamaica; Babylon on a Thin Wire (New York, Schocken Books, 1977)

BLA   Burns, E. Bradford: Latin America; A Concise Interpretative History (Englewood Cliffs, Prentice-Hall, 1972)

BLM   Bolles, John S.: Las Monjas; A Major Pre-Mexican Complex at Chichén Itzá (Norman, University of Oklahoma Press, 1977)

tor, Legislator, Statesman (Reading, Maine, Allen and Unwin, 1977)

CAH Christensen, Eleanor Ingalls: The Art of Haiti (New York, A. S. Barnes and Co., 1975)

CBE Carpenter, Allen; Balow, Tom: The Enchantment of Central America; Honduras (Chicago, Children's Press, 1971)

CBK Chandler, Billy Jaynes: The Bandit King; Lampião of Brazil (College Station, Texas A. and M. University Press, 1978)

CCC Craven, Roy C., Jr.; Bullard, William R., Jr.; Kampen, Michael E.: Ceremonial Centers of the Maya (Gainesville, University of Florida Press, 1974)

CCH Chapman, Charles Edward: Colonial Hispanic America; A History (New York, Hafner Publishing Co., 1971)

CCM Crump, Spencer: California's Spanish Missions; Their Yesterdays and Todays (Corona del Mar, Trans-Anglo Books, 1973)

CCP Crosley, Harry: The Cave Paintings of Baja California; The Great Murals of an Unknown People (San Diego, Copley Books, 1975)

CCS Curtis, William Elery: The Capitals of Spanish America (New York, Frederick A. Praeger, 1969)

CCT Chadwick, Lee: Cuba Today (Westport, Lawrence Hill and Co., 1975)

CCW Carson, R. A. G.: Coins of the World (New York: Harper and Brothers, 1962)

CDB Conrad, Robert: The Destruction of Brazilian Slavery, 1850-1888 (Berkeley, University of California Press, 1972)

CE The Catholic Encyclopedia (New York, The Encyclopedia Press. 15 volumes, Index, 1907-1914; Supplement I, 1922)

CEF Compton's Encyclopedia and Fact-Index (Chicago, F. E. Compton Co., 22 vols., 1973)

CEN Cowles Encyclopedia of Nations (New York, Cowles Education Corporation, 1968)

CFE Collier, George A.: Fields of the Tzotzil; The Ecological Bases of Tradition in Highland Chiapas (Austin, University of Texas Press, 1975)

CFG Chickering, Carol Rogers: Flowers of Guatemala (Norman, University of Oklahoma Press, 1973)

CFI (1 and 2) Chiappelli, Fredi: First Images of America. The Impact of the New World on the Old (Berkeley, University of California Press, 2 vols., 1976)

CFT Cook, Warren L.: Flood Tide of Empire; Spain and the Pacific Northwest, 1543-1819 (New Haven, Yale University Press, 1973)

CGB Cohodas, Marvin: The Great Ball Court at Chichén Itzá, Yucátan, Mexico (New York, Garland Publishing, Inc., 1978)

CGS Couffer, Jack and Mike: Galapagos Summer (New York, G. P. Putnam's Sons, 1975)

CHI Chile (Washington, Pan American Union, 1969)

CHL Castedo, Leopoldo: A History of Latin American Art and Architecture (New York, Frederick A. Praeger, 1969)

CHM Charroux, Robert: The Mysteries of the Andes (New York, Avon, 1977)

CHS Courlander, Harold: Haiti Singing (New York, Cooper Square Publishing Co., 1973)

CIZ Chiñas, Beverly: The Isthmus Zapotecs; Women's Role in Cultural Context (New York, Holt, Rinehart and Winston, 1973)

CL Cassel, Jonathon F.: Lacandon Adventure (Last of the Mayas) (San Antonio, The Naylor Co., 1974)

CLA Castleman, Riva: Latin American Prints from the Museum of Modern Art (New York, Center of Inter-American Relations, 1974)

CLC Comins, Jeremy: Latin American Crafts and Their Cultural Backgrounds (New York, Lothrup, Lee and Shepard Co., 1974)

CLI Calderón, F. García: Latin America; Its Rise and Progress (New York,

Charles Scribner's Sons, 1913)

CLM Calderón de la Barca, Fanny: Life in Mexico; The Letters of Fanny Calderón de la Barca (Garden City, Doubleday and Co., 1843)

CLP Caraman, Philip: The Lost Paradise; The Jesuit Republic in South America (New York, The Seabury Press, 1976)

CM Collaer, Paul: Music of the Americas; An Illustrated Music Ethnology of the Eskimo and American Indian Peoples (New York, Frederick A. Praeger, 1973)

CMA Corson, Christopher: Maya Anthropomorphic Figurines from Jaina Island, Campeche (Ramona, Calif., Ballena Press, 1976)

CMC Carroll, Richard: The Motor Camper's Guide to Mexico and Baja California (San Francisco, Chronicle Books, 1975)

CMF Cameron, Ian: Magellan and the First Circumnavigation of the World (New York, Saturday Review Press, 1973)

CMP Campbell, Leon G.: The Military and Society in Colonial Peru, 1750-1810 (Philadelphia, American Philosophical Society, 1978)

CMS Covarrubias, Miguel: Mexico South; The Isthumus of Tehuantepec (New York, Alfred A. Knopf, 1967)

COE Collier's Encyclopedia (New York, Macmillian Educational Corp., 23 vols., 1976)

COL Colombia (Washington, Pan American Union, 1968)

CPM Cornelius, Wayne A.: Politics and the Migrant Poor in Mexico City (Stanford, Stanford University Press, 1975)

CR Costa Rica (Washington, Pan American Union, 1967)

CRH Chapman, Charles Edward: Republican Hispanic America; A History (New York, Hafner Publishing Co., 1971)

CS Clissold, Stephen: Spain (New York, Walker and Co., 1969)

CSI Craton, Michael: Searching for the Invisible Man; Slaves and Plantation Life in Jamaica (Cambridge, Harvard University Press, 1978)

CSM Capa, Cornell; Stycos, J. Mayone: Margin of Life; Population and Poverty in the Americas (New York, Grossman Publishers, 1974)

CSP Cisneros, Florencia García: Santos of Puerto Rico and the Americas (Detroit, Blaine Ethridge Books, 1979)

CTA Cousteau, Jacques-Yves; Diolé, Philippe: Three Adventures: Galapagos, Titicaca, the Blue Holes (Garden City, Doubleday and Co., 1973)

CTC Clark, Odis H.: The Token Coinage of Guatemala (San Antonio, Almanzar, 1974)

DAA Davis, Emily C.: Ancient Americans; The Archaeological Story of Two Continents (New York, Cooper Square Publishers, 1975)

DAB Douglass, William A.; Bilbao, Jon: Amerikanuok Basques in the New World (Reno, University of Nevada Press, 1975)

DAC Dulles, John W. F.: Anarchists and Communists in Brazil, 1900-1935 (Austin, University of Texas Press, 1973)

DAH Davies, Nigel: The Aztecs; A History (New York, G. P. Putnam's Sons, 1974)

DCB Dulles, John W. F.: Castello Branco; The Making of a Brazilian President (College Station, Texas A. and M. University Press, 1978)

DCS Deuel, Leo (editor): Conquistadors Without Swords; Archaeologists in the Americas (New York, Schocken Books, 1974)

DEL Delpar, Helen (editor): Encyclopedia of Latin America (New York, McGraw-Hill Book Co., 1974)

DFG Davis, L. Irby: A Field Guide to the Birds of Mexico and Central America (Austin, University of Texas Press, 1972)

DFM Dorner, Gerd: Folk Art of Mexico (New York, A. S. Barnes and Co., 1962)

DG D'Auvergne, Edmund B.: Godoy; The Queen's Favorite (Boston, The

Gorham Press, 1917?)
DHA Denhardt, Robert M.: The Horse of the Americas (Norman, University of Oklahoma Press, 1975)
DIA Dockstader, Frederick, J.: Indian Art of the Americas (New York, Museum of the American Indian, Heye Foundation, 1973)
DIS Dockstader, Frederick J.: Indian Art in South America (Greenwich, New York Graphic Society Publishers, 1967)
DLC Dempewolff, Richard F.: Lost Cities and Forgotten Tribes (New York, Pocket Books, 1974)
DMH Drown, Frank and Marie: Mission to the Headhunters (Grand Rapids, Zondervan Publishing House, 1973)
DPP de Costa, René: The Poetry of Pablo Neruda (Cambridge, Harvard University Press, 1979)
DPT Dunning, John S.: Portraits of Tropical Birds (Wynnewood, Pa., Livingston Publishing Co., 1970)
DSN Dillon, Brian D.: Salinas de los Nueve Cerros (Socorro, N.M., Ballena Press, 1978)
DSW Daniels, George G. (editor): The Spanish West (New York, Time-Life Books, 1976)
DT Daley, Robert: Treasure (New York, Ballantine Books, 1977)
DTA D'Harcourt, Raoul: Textiles of Ancient Peru and Their Techniques (Seattle, University of Washington Press, 1974)

EA Encyclopedia Americana (New York, Americana Corporation, 30 vols., 1977)
EAW Engel, Frederic André: An Ancient World Preserved; Relics and Records of Prehistory in the Andes (New York, Crown Publishers, 1976)
EB Egan, E. W.: Brazil in Pictures (New York, Sterling Publishing Co., 1974)
EBP Epstein, David G.: Brasilia, Plan and Reality; A Study of Planned and Spontaneous Urban Development (Berkeley, University of California Press, 1973)
EBR The New Encyclopaedia Britannica. Macropedia--Knowledge in Depth (Chicago, Encyclopaedia Britannica Inc., 30 vols., 1974), 19 vols.
EBRF The New Encyclopaedia Britannica. Micropedia--Ready Reference (Chicago, Encyclopaedia Britannica Inc., 30 vols., 1974), 10 vols. and Guide
ECC Erasmus, Charles J.; Miller, Solomon; Faron, Louis C.: Contemporary Change in Traditional Communities of Mexico and Peru (Urbana, University of Illinois Press, 1978)
ECP Evans, Lancelot O.: The Caribbean in Pictures (The English-Speaking Islands) (New York, Sterling Publishing Co., 1968)
ECU Ecuador (Washington, Pan American Union, 1968)
EDG El Dorado; The Gold of Ancient Colombia from El Museo del Oro, Banco de la República, Bogotá, Colombia (New York, Center for Inter-American Relations, 1974)
EFG Edwards, Ernest P.: A Field Guide to the Birds of Mexico (Sweet Briar, The Author, 1972)
EFW Evans, I. O.: Flags of the World (New York, Grosset and Dunlap, 1970)
EGM Evans, Tom and Mary Ann: Guitars; Music, History, Construction and Players from Renaissance to Rock (New York: Paddington Press, 1977)
EI Encyclopedia International (New York, Grolier Corp., 20 vols., 1972)
ELA Ellis, Joseph E.: Latin America; Its Peoples and Institutions (Beverly Hills, Glencoe Press, 1975)
ELS El Salvador (Washington, Pan American Union, 1968)
ENB Encyclopaedia Britannica (Chicago, Encyclopaedia Britannica, Inc., 19

vols., 1969)
ENI   Edlin, Herbert and Maurice Nimmo: The Illustrated Encyclopedia of Trees, Timbers and Forests of the World (New York, Harmony Books, 1978)
EPC   English, Peter: Panama and the Canal Zone (New York, Sterling Publishing Co., 1973)
ESA   Engel, Lyle Kenyon: South America (New York, Simon and Schuster, 1973)
ESB   Easby, Elizabeth Kennedy; Scott, John F.: Before Cortés; Sculpture of Middle America.... (New York, The Metropolitan Museum, 1970)
ESL   Eggleston, Hazel: St. Lucia Diary; A Caribbean Memoir (Greenwich, Devon-Adair, 1978)
ESS   Engel, Lyle Kenyon: Travel Guide to Mexico (New York, Simon and Schuster, 1973)
EST   Emmerich, André: Sweat of the Sun and Tears of the Moon (New York, Hacker Art Books, 1977)
ETB   Evenson, Norma: Two Brazilian Capitals. Architecture and Urbanism in Rio de Janeiro and Brasília (New Haven, Yale University Press, 1973)

FAB   Fell, Barry: America B.C. (New York, Pocket Books, 1978)
FAR   Friedrich, Paul: Agrarian Revolt in a Mexican Village (Chicago, University of Chicago Press, 1977)
FBM   Fodor, Eugene; Birnbaum, Stephen: Fodor's Mexico 1974 (New York, David McKay Co., 1973)
FCH   Foreign Policy Association (editor): A Cartoon History of United States Foreign Policy 1776-1976 (New York, William Morrow Co., 1975)
FCL   Furber, E. A. (editor): The Coinages of Latin America and the Caribbean (Lawrence, Quarterman Publications Inc., 1971)
FCV   Furst, Jill Leslie: Codex Vindobonensis Mexicanas I: A Commentary (Albany, State University of New York, 1978)
FDT   Fry, Maxwell; Drew, Jane: Tropical Architecture in the Humid Zone (New York, Reinhold Publishing Corporation, 1956)
FEW   Fairbridge, Rhodes W. (editor): The Encyclopedia of World Regional Geology. Part I, Western Hemisphere.... (Stroudsburg, Dowden, Hutchinson and Ross Inc., 1975)
FFI   Fernández-Armesto, Felipe: Ferdinand and Isabella (New York, Taplinger Publishing Co., 1975)
FFS   Fodor, Eugene; Fisher, Robert C.: Fodor's South America 1976 (New York, David McKay Co., 1976)
FFW   Ferdinand, Charles: The Fascinating World of Butterflies (Garden City, Hanover House, 1958)
FLC   Fiske, Turbesé Lummis and Keith Lummis: Charles F. Lummis; The Man and His West (Norman, University of Oklahoma Press, 1975)
FM   Fieger, Erwin, etc.: Mexico (New York, Universe Books, 1973)
FPH   Field, Frederick V.: Pre-Hispanic Mexican Stamp Designs (New York, Dover Publications Inc., 1974)
FRM   Ferguson, William M.; Royce, John Q.: Maya Ruins of Mexico in Color (Norman, University of Oklahoma Press, 1977)
FWL   Fouchet, Max-Pol: Wifredo Lam (New York, Rizzoli, 1977)
FWS   Fox, James J.; Wilgus, A. Curtis: The Story of Mexico (Cincinnati: McCormick-Mathers Publishing Co., 1975)

GC   Gay, Carlo T. E.: Chalcancingo (Portland, Ore.: International Scholarly Book Service, Inc., 1972)
GCM   Graham, Ian: Corpus of Maya Hieroglyphic Inscriptions (Cambridge, Peabody Museum of Archaeology and Ethnology, Vol. II, part 2, 1978)

GCR   Goldman, Albert: Carnival in Rio (New York, Hawthorn Books Inc., 1978)

GCW   Graig, William D.: Coins of the World 1750-1850 (Racine, Western Publishing Co., Inc., 1971)

GEC   Graham, Ian; Von Euw, Eric: Corpus of Maya Hieroglyphic Inscriptions; Naranjo (Cambridge, Peabody Museum of Archaeology and Ethnology, Vol. II, part 1, 1975)

GEM   Goodman, Frances S.: The Embroidery of Mexico and Guatemala (New York, Charles Scribner's Sons, 1976)

GFF   Gooch, Fanny Chambers: Face to Face with the Mexicans (New York, Fords, Howard and Hulbert, 1887)

GGM   (and GGT) Gazarian-Gautier, Merie-Lisa: Gabriela Mistral; The Teacher from the Valley of Elqui (Chicago, Franciscan Herald Press, 1978)

GGP   Gritzner, Charles F.: Guyana in Pictures (New York, Sterling Publishing Co., 1975)

GGW   Grunfeld, Frederic V.: Games of the World (New York, Ballantine Books, 1977)

GHS   Griewe, W. F.: History of South America; From the First Human Experience to the Present Time (Cleveland, Central Publishing Co., 1913)

GJA   Graham, R. B. Cunningham: José Antonio Páez (New York, Cooper Square Publishers Inc., 1970)

GJR   Graham, Maria Dundas (Lady Maria Calcott): Journal of a Residence in Chile During the Year 1822 and a Voyage from Chile to Brazil in 1823 (New York, Frederick Praeger, 1969)

GJV   Graham, Maria Dundas (Lady Maria Calcott): Journal of a Voyage to Brazil and a Residence There, During Part of the Years 1821, 1822, 1823 (New York, Frederick Praeger, 1969)

GKT   Grierson, Edward: King of Two Worlds; Philip II of Spain (New York, G. P. Putnam's Sons, 1974)

GLG   Glover, Michael: Legacy of Glory; The Bonaparte Kingdom of Spain 1808-1813 (New York, Charles Scribner's Sons, 1971)

GLM   Gutiérrez Ceballos, Luis: Luis Montiel and His Guajiro Tapestries (New York, Center for Inter-American Relations, 1975)

GLT   Gauld, Charles A.: The Last Titan; Perceval Farquhar: American Entrepreneur in Latin America (Stanford, Institute of Hispanic American and Luso-Brasilian Studies, 1964)

GMB   Gruening, Ernest: Many Battles; The Autobiography of Ernest Gruening (New York, Liveright Publishing Corporation, 1973)

GMF   Giffords, Gloria Kay: Mexican Folk Retablos; Masterpieces in Tin (Tucson, University of Arizona Press, 1974)

GMR   Gallenkamp, Charles: Maya; The Riddle and Rediscovery of a Lost Civilization (New York, David McKay Co., Inc., 1976)

GMV   Golding, Morton J.: The Mystery of the Vikings in America (Philadelphia, J. B. Lippincott, 1973)

GPE   Gorham, J. Richard (editor): Paraguay: Ecological Essays (Miami, Academy of Arts and Sciences of the Americas, 1973)

GPM   Geijerstam, Claes af: Popular Music in Mexico (Albuquerque, University of New Mexico Press, 1976)

GPW   Glover, Michael: The Peninsular War, 1807-1814. A Concise Military History (Hamden, Archon Books, 1974)

GR   Gibson, Hugh: Rio (Garden City, Doubleday, Doran and Co., 1937)

GRH   Gordon, Cyrus H.: Riddles in History (New York, Crown Publishers, 1974)

GRT   Genauer, Emily: Rufino Tamayo (New York, Harry N. Abrams, Inc., 1974)

GSA   González-Wippler, Migene: Santería; African Magic in Latin America (New York, The Julian Press, 1973)

GSL   Guibert, Rita: Seven Voices: seven Latin American Writers Talk to

Rita Guibert (New York, Alfred A. Knopf, 1973)
GUA   Guatemala (Washington, Pan American Union, 1967)
GXB   Gay, Carlo T. E.: Xochipala; The Beginnings of Olmec Art (Princeton, The Art Museum, Princeton University, 1972)

HAC   Helms, Mary W.: Middle America; A Cultural History of Heartland and Frontiers (Englewood Cliffs, Prentice-Hall, Inc., 1975)
HAE   Hales, John R.: Age of Exploration (New York, Time Inc., 1974)
HAS   Hester, Thomas R. (editor): Archaeological Studies of Mesoamerican Obsidian (Socorro, N. M. Ballena Press, 1978)
HAT   Harding, Bertita: Amazon Throne; The Story of the Braganzas of Brazil (Indianapolis, Bobbs-Merrill Co., 1941)
HC   Henle, Fritz: Casals (New York, American Photographic Book Publishing Co., 1975)
HCM   Harvey, Marian: Crafts of Mexico (New York, Macmillian Publishing Co., Inc., 1973)
HCP   Haverstock, Nathan A.; Hoover, John P.: Cuba in Pictures (New York, Sterling Publishing Co., 1974)
HCR   Hannau, Hans W.: In the Coral Reefs of the Caribbean, Bahamas, Florida, Bermuda (Garden City, Doubleday and Co., 1974)
HDA   Howard, Joseph H.: Drums in the Americas (New York, Oak Publications, 1967)
HE   Humble, Richard: The Explorers (Alexandria, Time-Life Books, 1978)
HGA   Hunter, C. Bruce: A Guide to Ancient Maya Ruins (Norman, University of Oklahoma Press, 1974)
HGD   Healy, David: Gunboat Diplomacy in the Wilson Era; The United States Navy in Haiti, 1915-1916 (Madison, University of Wisconsin Press, 1976)
HGM   Hunter, C. Bruce: A Guide to Ancient Mexican Ruins (Norman, University of Oklahoma Press, 1977)
HHD   Haverstock, Nathan A.; Hoover, John P.: Dominican Republic in Pictures (New York, Sterling Publishing Co., 1976)
HHE   Haverstock, Nathan A.; Hoover, John P.: El Salvador in Pictures (New York, Sterling Publishing Co., 1976)
HHG   Heawood, Edward: A History of Geographical Discovery in the Seventeenth and Eighteenth Centuries (New York, Octagon Books, 1969)
HHL   Hanke, Lewis (editor): A History of Latin American Civilization; Sources and Interpretations (Boston, Little, Brown and Co., 2 vols., 1973)
HIC   Howard, D. O.: Isabella of Castile (New York, Funk and Wagnalls Co., 1894)
HJ   Hunte, George: Jamaica (New York, Hippocrene Books Inc., 1976)
HLA   Hague, Eleanor: Latin American Music Past and Present (Santa Ana, The Fine Arts Press, 1934)
HLV   Halsell, Grace: Los Viejos; Secrets of Long Life from the Sacred Valley (Emmaus, Rodale Press, 1976)
HM   Herrmann, Paul: Conquest by Man (New York, Harper and Brothers Publishers, 1954)
HMA   Hughes, James B.: Mexican Military Arms; The Cartridge Period 1866-1967 (Houston, Deep River Armory Inc., 1968)
HMC   Helfritz, Hans: Mexican Cities of the Gods; An Archaeological Guide (New York, Frederick A. Praeger, 1970)
HMH   Harrison, Gordon: Mosquitoes, Malaria and Man; A History of the Hostilities Since 1880 (New York, E. P. Dutton and Co., Inc., 1978)
HMI   Hellman, Judith Adler: Mexico in Crisis (New York, Holmes and Meier Publishers, 1978)
HMM   Helm, MacKinley: Modern Mexican Painters (New York, Dover Publications, 1974)
HMN   Hay, Clarence L., et al. (editors): The Maya and Their Neighbors....

(New York, Dover Publications, 1977)
HMP Hall, Barbara J.: Mexico in Pictures (New York, Sterling Publishing Co., 1977)
HNA Hannau, Hans W.: The Netherlands Antilles (New York, Hastings House Publishers, 1970?)
HND Holand, Hjalmar R.: Norse Discoveries and Explorations in America, 982-1362 (New York, Dover Publications, 1968)
HNM Harper's New Monthly Magazine (Harper's Monthly Magazine): (New York, Harper and Brothers, 1850-date)
HNP Haverstock, Nathan A.; Hoover, John P.: Nicaragua in Pictures (New York, Sterling Publishing Co., 1974)
HOB Hunter, Jim: Offbeat Baja (San Francisco, Chronicle Books, 1977)
HON Honduras (Washington, Pan American Union, 1967)
HPC Hardoy, Jorge E.: Pre-Columbian Cities (New York, Walker and Co., 1973)
HPG Hinshaw, Robert E.: Panajachel; A Guatemalan Town in Thirty-Year Perspective (Pittsburgh, University of Pittsburgh Press, 1975)
HPP Haverstock, Nathan A.; Hoover, John P.: Paraguay in Pictures (New York, Sterling Publishing Co., 1975)
HQS Hanbury-Tenison, Robin: A Question of Survival for the Indians of Brazil (New York, Charles Scribner's Sons, 1973)
HRD Halperin, Maurice: The Rise and Decline of Fidel Castro (Berkeley, University of California Press, 1974)
HSA Habig, M. A.: Saints of the Americas (Huntington, Ind., Our Sunday Visitor, 1974)
HSC Henfrey, Colin; Sori, Bernardo: Chilean Voices; Activists Describe Their Experiences of the Popular Unity Period (New York, Humanities Press, 1977)
HTT Hargreaves, Dorothy and Bob: Tropical Trees Found in the Caribbean, South America, Central America and Mexico (Portland, Ore., Hargreaves Industrial, 1965)
HUP Haverstock, Nathan A.; Hoover, John P.: Uruguay in Pictures (New York, Sterling Publishing Co., 1975)
HWI Hunte, George: The West Indian Islands (New York, Viking Press, 1972)

IDO Isbell, Billie Jean: To Defend Ourselves; Ecology and Ritual in an Andean Village (Austin, University of Texas Press, 1979)
IDS Ivanova, Anna: The Dance in Spain (New York, Praeger Publishers, 1970)
IMC Ivanoff, Pierre: Monuments of Civilization: Maya (New York, Grosset and Dunlap, 1970)

JAA Jordan, E. L.: Animal Atlas of the World (Maplewood, N.J.: Hammond Inc., 1969)
JAC Jones, Edward H., Jr. and Margaret S.: Arts and Crafts of the Mexican People (Pasadena, Ward Ritchie Press, 1971)
JCA Joyce, Thomas A.: Central America and West Indian Archaeology (New York, Hacker Art Books, 1973)
JCH Johnson, Adrian: A Cartographical History of the Exploration of North America (New York, Viking Press, 1974)
JIV Jones, Tristan: The Incredible Voyage; A Personal Odyssey (Kansas City, Sheed Andrews and McMeel, 1977)
JSA Jacobs, Charles and Babette: South America Travel Digest (Los Angeles, Paul Richmond and Co., 1970)
JSM Jackson, Donald Dale; Wood, Peter: The Sierra Madre (New York,

Time-Life Books, 1975)
JTG Jones, Susanne; Tobis, David (editors): Guatemala (Berkeley, North
American Congress on Latin America, 1974)

KAA Kubler, George: The Art and Architecture of Ancient America. The
Mexican, Maya and Andean Peoples (Baltimore, Penguin Books, 1962)
KAF Kapp, Kit S.: Mola Art from the San Blas Indians (North Bend, Ohio,
K. S. Kapp Publications, 1972)
KCF Kepler, Angela Kay: Common Ferns of Loquillo Forest, Puerto Rico
(San Juan, Inter-American University Press, 1975)
KCH Kamen, Henry: A Concise History of Spain (New York, Charles Scrib-
ner's Sons, 1973)
KDM Kelley, David Hamiston: Deciphering the Maya Script (Austin, Univer-
sity of Texas Press, 1976)
KEL Karst, Kenneth L.; Schwartz, Murray L.; Schwartz, Audrey J.: The
Evolution of Law in the Barrios of Caracas (Los Angeles, Latin American
Center, University of California, 1973)
KHG Karen, Ruth: Hello, Guatemala (New York, Grosset and Dunlap Inc.,
1970)
KMA Kelemen, Pál: Medieval American Art; Masterpieces of the New World
Before Columbus (New York, The Macmillan Co., 1956)
KML Kirby, Rosina Greene: Mexican Landscape Architecture from the Street
and from Within (Tucson, University of Arizona Press, 1972)
KMT Kemper, Robert V.: Migration and Adaptation; Tzintzuntzan Peasants
in Mexico City (Beverly Hills, Sage Publications, 1977)
KP Kowet, Don: Pelé (New York, Atheneum, 1976)
KPA Keith, Henry; Hayes, Robert A.: Perspectives on Armed Politics in
Brazil (Tempe, Center for Latin American Studies, Arizona State Univer-
sity, 1976)
KV Kristos, Kyle: Voodoo (Philadelphia, J. B. Lippincott Co., 1976)
KWW Keegan, John; Wheatcroft, Andrew: Who's Who in Military History
(New York, William Morrow and Co., 1976)

LAE Lathrop, Donald W.: Ancient Ecuador; Culture, Clay and Creativity
(Chicago, Field Museum of Natural History, 1976)
LAO Lehmann, Walter; Doering, Heinrich: The Art of Old Peru (New York,
Hacker Art Books, 1975)
LAP Lands and People; North America (vol. 5); South America and Central
America (vol. 6): (New York, Grolier Inc., 1972)
LAT Latin American Travel Guide (New York, Compsco Publishing Co.,
1973)
LBI Lowe, Arbon Jack: Barbados; Island in the Sun (Washington, Pan Amer-
ican Union, 1975)
LBT Leonard, Irving A.: Baroque Times in Old Mexico; Seventeenth-Century
Persons, Places and Practices (Ann Arbor, University of Michigan Press,
1971)
LEF Lyon, Eugene: The Enterprise of Florida; Pedro Menéndez de Avilés
and the Spanish Conquest of 1565-1568 (Gainesville, University Presses of
Florida, 1976)
LEL Larden, Walter: Estancia Life; Agricultural, Economic and Cultural
Aspects of Argentine Farming (Detroit, Blaine Ethridge Books, 1974)
LEM Larousse Encyclopedia of Music (Secaucus, Chartwell Books Inc.,
1971)
LF Life Magazine (Chicago, Time Inc., 1936-1972)
LHS Lavin, James D.: A History of Spanish Firearms (New York, Arco
Publishing Co., 1965)

LIW   Linsenmaier, Walter: Insects of the World (New York, McGraw-Hill Book Co., 1972)

LK   Look (Des Moines; New York, Cowles Education Corporation, 1937-1971)

LLA   Lurie, Edward: Louis Agassiz; A Life in Science (Chicago, University of Chicago Press, 1960)

LMJ   Lerner, Ira T.: Mexican Jewry in the Land of the Aztecs; A Guide (Mexico City, B. Costa-Amic, 1973)

LNW   Lehner, Ernst and Johanna: How They Saw the New World (New York, Tudor Publishing Co., 1966)

LOR   Lukert, Karl W.: Olmec Religion; A Key to Middle America and Beyond (Norman, University of Oklahoma Press, 1976)

LP   Lothrop, Samuel Kirkland: Pre-Columbian Designs from Panama (New York, Dover Publications, Inc., 1976)

LPB   Levine, Robert M.: Pernambuco in the Brazilian Federation, 1889-1937 (Stanford, Stanford University Press, 1978)

LPC   Lapiner, Alan: Pre-Columbian Art of South America (New York, Harry N. Abrams Inc., 1976)

LSA   Lewis, Michael: The Spanish Armada (New York, Thomas Y. Crowell Co., 1968)

LSH   Lynch, John: Spain Under the Hapsburgs; Vol. II, Spain and America, 1598-1700 (New York, Oxford University Press, 1969)

LTA   Lothrop, S. K.: Treasures of Ancient America; The Arts of Pre-Columbian Civilizations from Mexico to Peru (Geneva, Skira, 1964)

LTT   Lowe, Arbon Jack (editor): Trinidad and Tobago; Aspiring and Achieving Together (Washington, Pan American Union, 1974)

LTV   Laudonnière, René: Three Voyages (Gainesville, University of Florida Press, 1975)

LUL   Lindop, Edmund: Understanding Latin America (Boston, Ginn and Co., 1966)

LUR   Llerena, Mario: The Unsuspected Revolution; The Birth and Rise of Castroism (Ithaca, Cornell University Press, 1978)

MA   Mattingly, Garrett: The Armada (Boston, Houghton Mifflin Co., 1959)

MAA   McCann, Thomas P.: An American Company; The Tragedy of United Fruit (New York, Crown Publishers, 1976)

MAC   Means, Philip Ainsworth: Ancient Civilizations of the Andes (New York, Gordian Press Inc., 1964)

MAM   Morley, Sylvanus Griswold: The Ancient Maya (Stanford, Stanford University Press, 1956)

MBB   Martínez, Oscar J.: Border Boom Town; Ciudad Juárez Since 1848 (Austin, University of Texas Press, 1978)

MBW   McNerney, Robert F., Jr.: Bolívar and the War of Independence (Memoirs of General Daniel Florencio O'Leary) (Austin, University of Texas Press, 1970)

MC   Markham, Clements R.: Cuzco... and Lima... (Millwood, Kraus Reprint Co., 1973)

MCA   Moser, Don: Central American Jungle (New York, Time-Life Books, 1975)

MCJ   Marshall, Woodville K. (editor): The Colthurst Journal (Millwood, K.T.O. Press, 1977)

MCL   McBride, George McCutchen: Chile; Land and Society (Port Washington, Kennikat Press, 1971)

MCP   Monaghan, Jay: Chile, Peru and the California Gold Rush of 1849 (Berkeley, University of California Press, 1973)

MCR   Meyer, Jean A.: The Cristero Rebellion. The Mexican People Between Church and State 1926-1929 (New York, Cambridge University Press, 1976)

MCS Mata, Leonardo J.: The Children of Santa María Cauqué; A Prospective Field Study of Health and Growth (Cambridge, M.I.T. Press, 1978)

MDS Mackay, James A.: The Dictionary of Stamps in Color (New York, The Macmillan Co., 1973)

MED Morison, Samuel Eliot: The European Discovery of America; The Southern Voyages A.D. 1492-1616 (New York, Oxford University Press, 1974)

MEI Mann, Peggy: Easter Island, Land of Mysteries (New York, Holt, Rinehart and Winston, 1976)

MES Mulhall, Michael G.: The English in South America (New York, Arno Press, 1977)

MEW The McGraw-Hill Encyclopedia of World Biography (New York, McGraw-Hill Book Co., 12 vols., 1973)

MEX Mexico (Washington, Pan American Union, 1968)

MFA Muser, Curt: Facts and Artifacts of Ancient Middle America... (New York, E. P. Dutton, 1978)

MFE Means, Philip Aimsworth: Fall of the Inca Empire and the Spanish Rule in Peru 1530-1780 (New York, Gordian Press, 1964)

MFG McCreary, Guy Weddington: From Glory to Oblivion; The Real Truth About the Mexican Revolution (New York, Vantage Press, 1974)

MFI McKendrick, Melveena: Ferdinand and Isabella (New York, Harper and Row, 1968)

MGA McInerny, Derek; Gerard, Geoffrey: All About Tropical Fish (New York, The Macmillan Co., 1958)

MGB Meyer de Schauensee, Rodolphe: A Guide to the Birds of South America (Wynnewood, Livingston Publishing Co., 1970)

MGE Morison, Samuel Eliot: The European Discovery of America; The Great Explorers (New York, Oxford University Press, 1978)

MHC Mercer, Henry C.: The Hill-Caves of Yucatán. A Search for Evidence of Man's Antiquity in the Caverns of Central America (Norman, University of Oklahoma Press, 1975)

MHI Métreux, Alfred: The History of the Incas (New York, Schocken Books, 1970)

MHP Morrison, Tony and Hawkins, Gerald S.: Pathways to the Gods (New York, Harper and Row, 1978)

MHS McKendrick, Melveena: The Horizon Concise History of Spain (New York, Heritage Publishing Co., 1972)

MIM McGready, Robert N. (editor): Illustrated Mexico Vacation Guide (Maplewood, Hammond Inc., 1974)

MIS Morley, Sylvanus Griswold: An Introduction to the Study of the Maya Hieroglyphics (New York, Dover Publications Inc., 1975)

MKF Mankiewicz, Frank; Jones, Kirby: With Fidel; A Portrait of Castro and Cuba (New York, Ballantine Books, 1975)

MMP Miller, Arthur G.: The Mural Painting of Teotihuacán (Washington, Dumbarton Oaks, 1973)

MNS Mellafe, Rolando: Negro Slavery in Latin America (Berkeley, University of California Press, 1975)

MOC Mead, Charles W.: Old Civilizations in Inca Land (New York, Cooper Square Publishers, Inc., 1972)

MP Masters, Robert V.: Peru in Pictures (New York, Sterling Publishing Co., 1972)

MPA Mann, Graciela and Hans: The Twelve Prophets of Aleijadinho (Austin, University of Texas Press, 1967)

MPB McCullough, David: The Path Between the Seas; The Creating of the Panama Canal 1870-1914 (New York, Simon and Schuster, 1977)

MPF Markgraf, Vera; d'Antoni, Hector: Pollen Flora of Argentina (Tucson, University of Arizona Press, 1978)

MPP Meyer, Karl E.: The Plundered Past (New York, Atheneum, 1977)

MPS Menzel, Dorothy: Pottery Style and Society in Ancient Peru (Berkeley, University of California Press, 1976)

MRC Matthews, Herbert L.: Revolution in Cuba (New York, Charles Scrib-
     ner's Sons, 1975)
MSM Morley, Sylvanus G.: In Search of Maya Glyphs (Santa Fe, Museum
     of New Mexico Press, 1970)
MT   Meyer, Karl E.: Teotihuacán (New York, Newsweek, 1973)
MTT Marshall, Anthony D.: Trinidad-Tobago (New York, Franklin Watts
     Inc., 1975)
MVO Meyer, Doris: Victoria Ocampo; Against the Wind and Tide (New York,
     George Braziller, 1979)
MVT Mexico's Vacation Travel Guide (New York, Simon and Schuster, 1978)
MWD Maxwell, Nicole: Witch Doctor's Apprentice (New York, Collier Books,
     1975)

NAB Nabuco, Joaquim: Abolitionism; The Brazilian Antislavery Struggle
     (Urbana, University of Illinois Press, 1977)
NBK The New Book of Knowledge (New York, Grolier, 21 vols., 1972)
NCE New Catholic Encyclopedia (New York, McGraw-Hill Book Co., 15 vols.,
     1967)
NCF Nesmith, Robert J.: The Coinage of the First Mint of the Americas at
     Mexico City 1536-1572 (Lawrence, Quarterman Publications Inc., 1977)
NCN Nuttall, Zelia (editor): The Codex Nuttall. A Picture Manuscript from
     Ancient Mexico (New York, Dover Publications, 1975)
NDI Nunis, Doyce B., Jr.: The Drawings of Ignacio Tirsch; A Jesuit Mis-
     sionary in Baja California (Los Angeles, Dawson's Book Shop, 1972)
NFM Newcomb, Rexford: The Franciscan Mission Architecture in Alta Cal-
     ifornia (New York, Dover Publications, 1973)
NFP Newlon, Clarke: Famous Puerto Ricans (New York, Dodd, Mead and
     Co., 1975)
NG   National Geographic (Washington, National Geographic Society, 1888-date)
NIC Nicaragua (Washington, Pan American Union, 1964)
NIL Nott, David: Into the Lost World (Englewood Cliffs, Prentice-Hall Inc.,
     1975)
NKC Núñez del Prado, Oscar; Whyte, William Foote: Kuyo Chico; Applied
     Anthropology in an Indian Community (Chicago, University of Chicago Press,
     1973)
NMC Nevares, Beatriz Reyes: The Mexican Cinema; Interviews with Thirteen
     Directors (Albuquerque, University of New Mexico Press, 1976)
NMP Nolen, Barbara (editor): Mexico is People; Land of Three Cultures
     (New York, Charles Scribner's Sons, 1973)
NMW Nevin, David: The Mexican War (Alexandria, Time-Life Books, 1978)
NPH Nadaillac, Marqués de: Pre-Historic America (New York, Humanities
     Press, 1970)
NRM Newby, Eric: The Rand McNally World Atlas of Explorations (New
     York, Rand McNally and Co., 1975)
NRQ Niemeyer, E. V., Jr.: Revolution in Querétaro; The Mexican Consti-
     tutional Convention of 1916-17 (Austin, University of Texas Press, 1974)

OAS Orlove, Benjamin S.: Alpacas, Sheep and Men; The Wool Export
     Economy and Regional Society in Southern Peru (New York, Academic
     Press, 1977)
OIA Osborne, Harold: Indians of the Andes; Aymaras and Quechuas (New
     York, Cooper Square Publishing Co., Inc., 1973)
OIC Osborne, Lilly de Jongh: Indian Crafts of Guatemala and El Salvador
     (Norman, University of Oklahoma Press, 1975)
OLA Olien, Michael D.: Latin Americans; Contemporary Peoples and Their
     Cultural Traditions (New York, Holt, Rinehart and Winston, Inc., 1973)

OTM Ober, Frederick A.: Travels in Mexico and Life Among the Mexicans
(Boston, Estes and Lauriat, 1887)

PAN Panama (Washington, Pan American Union, 1964)
PAR Paraguay (Washington, Pan American Union, 1967)
PBC Pepper, Choral: Baja California; Vanished Missions, Lost Treasures,
Strange Stories Tall and True (Los Angeles, The Ward Ritchie Press, 1973)
PBF Pang, Eul-Soo: Bahia in the First Brazilian Republic (Gainesville,
University Presses of Florida, 1979)
PBK Pope, Dudley: The Buccaneer King; The Biography of Sir Henry Mor-
gan 1635-1688 (New York, Dodd, Mead and Co., 1977)
PBP Perkins, Clifford Alan: Border Patrol; With the United States Immi-
gration Service on the Mexican Boundary, 1910-1954 (El Paso, Texas West-
ern Press, 1978)
PCA Protopapas, George: Chile; Allende and After (Huntington, Ind., Our
Sunday Visitor, 1975)
PCF Peterson, Roger Tory; Chalif, Edward L.: A Field Guide to Mexican
Birds (Boston, Houghton Mifflin Co., 1973)
PCI Personalities Caribbean: The International Guide to Who's Who in the
West Indies, Bermuda, Bahamas (Detroit, Blaine Ethridge Books, 1973)
PDA Peterson, Harold F.: Diplomat of the Americas; A Biography of
William I. Buchanan (1852-1909) (Albany, State University of New York
Press, 1977)
PDS Parry, J. H.: The Discovery of the Sea (New York, Dial Press, 1974)
PEC Parsons, Francis B.: Early Seventeenth Century Missions of the South-
west (Tucson, Dale Stuart King Publisher, 1975)
PER Peru (Washington, Pan American Union, 1969)
PFT Pertchik, Bernard and Harriet: Flowering Trees of the Caribbean (New
York, Rinehart and Co., 1951)
PFV Pigafetta, Antonio: First Voyage Around the World (Manila, Filipiniana
Book Guild, 1969)
PLA Plaza, Galo: Latin America Today and Tomorrow (Washington, Acropolis
Books Ltd., 1971)
PMA Perl, Lila: Mexico, Crucible of the Americas (New York, William
Morrow and Co., 1978)
PMC Powell, Philip Wayne: Mexico's Miguel Caldera; The Taming of Amer-
ica's First Frontier (1548-1597) (Tucson, University of Arizona Press,
1977)
PMF Parker, Ann; Neal, Avon: Molas; Folk Art of the Cuna Indians (New
York, Crown Publishers Inc., 1977)
PMG Patterson, Carmen L.: The Maya of Guatemala; Their Life and Dress
(Seattle, University of Washington Press, 1976)
PMM Poniatowska, Elena: Massacre in Mexico (New York, Viking Press,
1971)
PMN Prieto, Carlos: Mining in the New World (New York, McGraw-Hill Co.,
1973)
PMT Pettit, Florence M. and Robert M.: Mexican Folk Toys, Festival Dec-
oratives and Ritual Objects (New York, Hasting House Publishers, 1978)
POE Peoples of the Earth (New York, Danbury Press, 20 vols., 1973)
PPK Phelan, John Leddy: The People and the King; The Comunero Revolu-
tion in Colombia 1781 (Madison, University of Wisconsin Press, 1978)
PPR Perl, Lila: Puerto Rico; Island Between Two Worlds (New York, Mor-
row, 1979)
PSU Patton, Edda Clayton: Sarmiento and the United States (Evansville,
University of Evansville Press, 1977)
PTU Price, John A.: Tijuana; Urbanization in a Border Culture (Notre
Dame, University of Notre Dame Press, 1973)
PWL Perry, Roger: Wonders of the Llamas (New York, Dodd, Mead and

Co., 1977)

PZB Parkinson, Roger: Zapata, a Biography (New York, Stein and Day Publishers, 1975)

QLV Quinn, David Beers (editor): The Last Voyage of Thomas Cavendish 1591-92 (Chicago, University of Chicago Press, 1975)

RAC Reichel-Dolmatoff, Gerardo: Amazon Cosmos; The Sexual and Religious Symbolism of the Tukano Indians (Chicago, University of Chicago Press, 1971)

RBT Rodman, Selden: The Brazil Traveler; History, Culture, Literature and the Arts (Old Greenwich, Devin-Adair Co., 1975)

RCH Robicsek, Francis: Copán, Home of the Maya Gods (New York, Museum of the American Indian, Heye Foundation, 1972)

RCS Rouse, John E.: The Criollo; Spanish Cattle in the Americas (Norman, University of Oklahoma Press, 1977)

RCV Rogers, Woodes: A Cruising Voyage Round the World (New York, Dover Publications, 1970)

RFW Roberts, W. Adolphe: The French in the West Indies (New York, Cooper Square Publishers, 1971)

RJL Rodríguez Monegal, Emir: Jorge Luis Borges; A Literary Biography (New York, Dutton, 1978)

RLM Robertson, William Spence: The Life of Miranda (New York, Cooper Square Publishers, 2 vols., 1969)

RM Ross, Patricia Fent: Mexico (Grand Rapids, The Fideler Co., 1975)

RMP Roditi, Eduard: Magellan of the Pacific (New York, McGraw-Hill Book Co., 1972)

RPC Ryan, Paul B.: The Panama Canal Controversy; United States Diplomacy and Defense Interests (Stanford, Hoover Institution Press, 1977)

RPG Rue, Leonard Lee: Pictorial Guide to the Mammals of North America (New York, Thomas Y. Crowell Co., 1967)

RPS Reina, Ruben E.: Paraná; Social Boundaries in an Argentine City (Austin, University of Texas Press, 1974)

RSC Ricard, Robert: The Spiritual Conquest of Mexico (Berkeley, University of California Press, 1974)

RSD Rawlins, Ray: The Stein and Day Book of World Signatures (New York, Stein and Day, 1978)

RSG Robicsek, Francis, The Smoking Gods; Tobacco in Maya Art, History and Religion (Norman, University of Oklahoma Press, 1978)

RSJ Reichel-Dolmatoff, Gerardo: The Shaman and the Jaguar; A Study of Narcotic Drugs Among the Indians of Colombia (Philadelphia, Temple University Press, 1975)

RSM Ranney, Edward: Stone Work of the Maya (Albuquerque, University of New Mexico Press, 1974)

RST Reck, Gregory G.: In the Shadow of Tlaloc; Life in a Mexican Village (New York, Penguin Books, 1978)

RTA Roth, Hal: Two Against Cape Horn (New York, W. W. Norton, 1978)

RW Read, Jan: War in the Peninsula (Salem, N.H., Faber and Faber, 1977)

RWP Rink, Paul: Warrior Priests and Tyrant Kings; The Beginnings of Mexican Independence (Garden City, Doubleday and Co., 1976)

SAC Stickney, Brian; Almanzar, Alcedo: The Coins and Paper Money of Nicaragua (San Antonio, Almanzar, 1974)

SAI Shao, Paul: Asiatic Influences in Pre-Columbian American Art (Ames, Iowa State University Press, 1976)

Books, 1978)

SSH Smith, Bradley: Spain: A History in Art (New York, Simon and Schuster, 1966)

SSM Spinden, Herbert J.: A Study of Maya Art: Its Subject Matter and Historical Development (New York, Dover Publications, 1975)

SSS Sharp, William Frederick: Slavery on the Spanish Frontier; The Colombian Chocó 1680-1810 (Norman, University of Oklahoma Press, 1976)

SST Shotwell, Robyn E. (editor): The Sunset Travel Book: Mexico (Menlo Park, Lane Books, 1974)

SSW Stidworthy, John: Snakes of the World (New York, Grosset and Dunlap, 1971)

STB Severin, Tim: The Brendan Voyage (New York, McGraw-Hill Books Co., 1978)

STC Sertima, Ivan Van: They Came Before Columbus (New York, Random House, 1976)

SWA Singer, Julia: We All Come from Puerto Rico (New York, Atheneum, 1977)

SWC Singer, Julia: We All Come from Someplace; Children of Puerto Rico (New York, Atheneum, 1976)

TAE Heyerdahl, Thor: The Art of Easter Island (Garden City, Doubleday and Co., 1975)

TCA Tax, Sol (editor): The Civilizations of Ancient America (New York, Cooper Square Publishers, Inc., 1967)

TCP Thomas, Hugh: Cuba; The Pursuit of Freedom (New York, Harper and Row Publishers, 1971)

TFS Taylor, Alice (editor): Focus on South America (New York, Praeger Publishers, 1973)

THA Tinker, Edward Laroque: The Horsemen of the Americas (Austin, University of Texas Press, 1968)

TMP Toor, Frances: Mexican Popular Arts (Detroit, Blaine Ethridge Books, 1973)

TMW Tinker, Ben: Mexican Wilderness and Wildlife (Austin, University of Texas Press, 1978)

TND Thompson, A. Landsborough: A New Dictionary of Birds (New York, McGraw-Hill Book Co., 1964)

TPM Toneyama, Kojin: The Popular Arts of Mexico (New York, Weatherhill, 1974)

TSL Trento, Salvatore Michael: The Search for Lost America; The Mysteries of the Stone Ruins (Chicago, Contemporary Books, Inc., 1978)

TTG Thompson, J. Eric S.: Thomas Gage's Travels in the New World (Norman, University of Oklahoma Press, 1969)

UHA Urbanski, Edmund Stephen: Hispanic America and Its Civilizations (Norman, University of Oklahoma Press, 1979)

URU Uruguay (Washington, Pan American Union, 1968)

VAC Vaillant, George C.: Artists and Craftsmen in Ancient Central America (Detroit, Blaine Ethridge Books, 1973)

VAM Von Hagen, Victor Wolfgang: The Aztec and Maya Papermakers (New York, Hacker Art Books, 1977)

VEH Verney, Peter: The Earthquake Handbook (New York, Paddington Press, 1979)

VEN Venezuela (Washington, Pan American Union, 1968)

VFC Von Hagen, Victor Wolfgang: F. Catherwood (Barre, Mass., Barre Publishers, 1968)

VIP Vanden Berghe, Pierre L.; Primov, George P.: Inequality in the Peruvian Andes: Class and Ethnicity in Cuzco (Columbia, University of Missouri Press, 1977)
VSC Vogt, George W.: Standard Catalog of Mexican Coins, Paper Money and Medals (Iola, Wis., Krause Publications, 1978)
VSL Voss, Gilbert L.: Seashore Life of Florida and the Caribbean.... (Miami, E. A. Seemann Publishing Co., 1976)
VWS Von Winning, Hasso: The Shaft Tomb Figures of West Mexico (Los Angeles, Southwest Museum, 1974)

WAA Webb, Kempton; Lyons, Marion; Decker, David: Anglo-America; Latin America (New York, Sadlier, 1967)
WAC Warmke, Germaine L.; Abbott, R. Tucker: Caribbean Sea Shells (New York, Dover Publications, 1975)
WAD Wallis, Ethel Emily: Aucas Downriver; Dayuma's Story Today (New York, Harper and Row, 1973)
WAK Woodbury, Richard B.: Alfred V. Kidder (New York, Columbia University Press, 1973)
WAM West, Robert C.; Augelli, John P.: Middle America: Its Lands and Peoples (Englewood Cliffs, Prentice-Hall, Inc., 1976)
WAP The World and Its People (New York, Greystone Press, 5 vols. on Latin America, 1964-1966)
WB Worcester, Donald E.: Brazil: From Colony to World Power (New York, Charles Scribner's Sons, 1973)
WBE The World Book Encyclopedia (Chicago, World Book-Childcraft International, 22 vols., 1978)
WBP Wyden, Peter, Bay of Pigs; The Untold Story (New York, Simon and Schuster, 1979)
WCB Wellman, Frederick L.: Coffee: Botany, Cultivation and Utilization (New York, Interscience Publishers, Inc., 1961)
WCC Wald, Karen: Children of Che; Child Care and Education in Cuba (Palo Alto, Ramparts Press, 1978)
WCF Webb, Kempton E.: The Changing Face of Northeast Brazil (New York, Columbia University Press, 1974)
WCK Wetherington, Ronald K.: The Ceramics of Kaminaljuyu, Guatemala (University Park, Pennsylvania State University Press, 1978)
WDP Williams, Mary Wilhelmine: Dom Pedro, the Magnanimous, Second Emperor of Brazil (Chapel Hill, University of North Carolina Press, 1937)
WES White, Alastair: El Salvador (New York, Praeger Publishers, 1973)
WH Weddle, Ken: Haiti in Pictures (New York, Sterling Publishing Co., 1974)
WHM Weeks, Morris, Jr.: Hello, Mexico (New York, W. W. Norton and Co., 1970)
WHP Weeks, Morris, Jr.: Hello, Puerto Rico (New York, Grosset and Dunlap, Inc., 1972)
WHV Weeks, Morris, Jr.: Hello, Venezuela (New York, W. W. Norton and Co., 1968)
WIA Willey, Gordon R.: An Introduction to American Archaeology (Englewood Cliffs, Prentice-Hall, Inc., 2 vols., 1966-1971)
WID Wolff, Werner: Island of Death; A New Key to Easter Island's Culture Through an Ethno-Psychological Society (New York, Hacker Art Books, 1973)
WIT Ward, Fred: Inside Cuba Today (New York, Crown Publishers, 1978)
WLI Woll, Allen: The Latin Image in American Films (Los Angeles, Latin American Center, U.C.L.A., 1977)
WM Whitaker, Irwin and Emily: A Potter's Mexico (Albuquerque, University of New Mexico Press, 1978)
WNC Winsor, Justin (editor): Narrative and Critical History of America

(Boston, Houghton Mifflin and Co., 8 vols., 1889)

WOE   Wicke, Charles R.: Olmec, an Early Art Style of Pre-Columbian Mexico (Tucson, University of Arizona Press, 1971)

WP   Weddle, Ken: Honduras in Pictures (New York, Sterling Publishing Co., 1976)

WPC   Winning, Hasso von: Pre-Columbian Art of Mexico and Central America (New York, Harry N. Abrams Inc., 1968)

WPM   Westheim, Paul and others: Prehispanic Mexican Art (New York, G. P. Putnam's Sons, 1972)

WPR   Wagenheim, Kal: Puerto Rico: A Profile (New York, Praeger Publishers, 1970)

WSA   Werstein, Irving: 1898: The Spanish-American War (New York, Cooper Square Publishers, Inc., 1966)

WSH   Willey, Gordon R.; Sabloff, Jeremy A.: A History of American Archaeology (London, Thames and Hudson, 1974)

WTA   Whymper, Edward: Travels Amongst the Great Andes of the Equator (London, Charles Knight and Co., Ltd., 1972)

WTL   Wilbert, Johannes: The Thread of Life: Symbolism of Miniature Art from Ecuador (Washington, Dumbarton Oaks, 1974)

WWE   Wilson, Derek: The World Encompassed; Francis Drake and his Great Voyage (New York, Harper and Row, 1977)

WYF   Wilbert, Johannes: Yupo Folktales (Los Angeles, University of California Press, 1974)

WZP   Whitecotton, Joseph W.: The Zapotecs: Princes, Priests and Peasants (Norman, University of Oklahoma Press, 1977)

ZCV   Zellers, Margaret: Caribbean Vacation Travel Guide, Including Bahamas-Bermuda (New York, Simon and Schuster, 1978)

ZSA   Zink, David: The Stones of Atlantis (Englewood Cliffs, Prentice-Hall, 1978)